lonely planet

Dublin

"All you've got to do is decide to go
and the hardest part is over.

So go!"

TONY WHEELER, COFOUNDER – LONELY PLANET

Contents

Left: Trinity College (p52)

Above: Guinness Storehouse (p102)

Right: Statue of Oscar Wilde, Merrion Square (p83)

North of the Liffey
p120

Temple Bar
p92

Kilmainham & the Liberties
p100

Grafton Street & Around
p50

Merrion Square & Around
p78

Docklands & the Grand Canal
p142

Welcome to Dublin

Dublin's key ingredients: a thousand-year history, marinated until rich in heritage and sprinkled with hedonism. Visit and enjoy.

A Handsome History

Dublin has been making waves since the 9th century, and while you may have to dig deep to find traces of its Viking past, the city's rich history since then is in evidence all around you, from its medieval castle and cathedrals to the splendour of the 18th century, when Dublin was the most handsome Georgian city in the Empire and its magnificent public and private buildings reflected the elevated status of its most privileged burghers. How power was wrested from their hands is another story, and one you'll learn in its museums and walking tours.

Personality Goes a Long Way

Georgian elegance aside, Dublin mightn't seem as sexy or as sultry as other European capitals, but Dubliners will tell you that pretty things are as easy to like as they are to forget. Their beloved capital, about which they can be brutally unsentimental, has personality, which is much more important and lasts far longer. Garrulous, amiable and witty, Dubliners at their ease are the greatest hosts of all, a charismatic bunch whose soul and sociability are so compelling and infectious that you mightn't ever want to leave.

Hold Your Hour & Have Another

To experience Dubliners at their most comfortable and convivial, you'll have to spend some time in a pub. Dublin's relationship with alcohol is complex and conflicted, but at its very best, a night out in the pub remains the city's favourite social lubricant and one of the most memorable experiences of a visit to Ireland. Everyone has their favourite pub: for some it's a never-changing traditional haunt; for others, it's wherever the beautiful people are currently at. Either way, you'll have over 1000 to choose from.

All the World is Dublin

As you stroll through the city, you might come across a group of young Koreans hawking phonecards from their shop hatches. Or Nigerian teenagers rustling through beaded curtains into African salons for hair extensions, while upstairs their parents belt out gospel hymns in makeshift churches. Next door, Russians leave the supermarket laden with tinned caviar. This is the new, confidently multicultural Dublin, where locals queue up to try a new sushi joint or pop around the corner to buy sumac from their local halal grocer, who'll break away from a conversation in Arabic to say 'howarye' in a thick, Dublin accent.

Why I Love Dublin

By Fionn Davenport, Author

As a Dubliner what I love most about my city is that it's big enough to always keep me entertained and amused, but small enough that I can get from its head to its heel in virtually no time at all. It's a big capital village, really, and its inhabitants live accordingly – if you walk around town enough you'll always run into people you know. I love that the city wears everything on its sleeve, from its fascinating history to its brilliant personality, and that it understands that quality of life trumps all other things.

For more about our authors, see p256.

Above: Ha'Penny Bridge, River Liffey

Dublin's
Top 10

A Dublin Pub *(p34)*

1 'A good puzzle would be to cross Dublin without passing a pub', mused Leopold Bloom in James Joyce's *Ulysses*. An impossible conundrum, given there's at least one on every street, but the answer is simple: go into each one you find. One hundred years later, the alpha and omega of all social life in Dublin remains the bar, and you have more than 1000 to choose from, from traditional boozers to trendy bars. It's where you'll meet Dubliners at their convivial, easy-going best and get a proper sense of what makes this city tick. TEMPLE BAR (P97)

🍷 *Drinking & Nightlife*

Trinity College *(p52)*

2 Since its foundation in 1592, Trinity College has become one of the world's most famous universities; the alma mater of Swift, Wilde and Beckett, and the home of the world's most famous illuminated manuscript, the *Book of Kells*. Its 16 hectares are an oasis of aesthetic elegance, its cobbled quadrangles lined with handsome neoclassical buildings that lend an air of magisterial calm to the campus, evident as soon as you walk through Front Arch.

👁 *Grafton Street & Around*

Dublin City Gallery – The Hugh Lane

(p122)

3 Hanging on the walls of a magnificent Georgian pile is arguably the city's finest collection of modern and contemporary art, which runs the gamut from impressionist masterpieces (by Degas, Monet, Manet et al) to such Irish artists as Dorothy Cross and Sean Scully. The gallery's extra-special treat is Dublin-born Francis Bacon's actual London studio, brought over piece by piece and painstakingly reassembled in all its glorious mess.

👁 *North of the Liffey*

Grafton Street *(p50)*

4 A stroll up pedestrianised Grafton St is always warranted, if only to observe the perambulations of Dubliners of every distinction, from distracted lovers to bag-laden shoppers. Along its length an assortment of street performers set the mood, providing the soundtrack for a memorable stroll. On any given day you can listen to a guitarist knock out some electrifying bluegrass, applaud young conservatory students putting Mozart through his paces, or stare down a silver-skinned mime artist and see who moves first. You will.

🛍 *Grafton Street & Around*

National Gallery *(p82)*

5 The National Gallery's art collection is an impressive one, a history of art spread across six centuries and 54 separate galleries, including a beautiful new wing with a terrific cafe. The marquee names include Goya, Caravaggio and Van Gogh, but no less impressive are the paintings by luminaries such as Orpen, Reynolds and Van Dongen. Don't miss the Jack B Yeats room; as you find your way there, you'll pass the odd Rembrandt, Velazquez and Vermeer.

👁 *Merrion Square & Around*

Kilmainham Gaol *(p111)*

6 Ireland's struggle for independence was a bloody and tempestuous journey, and this forbidding prison played a role in it for nearly 150 years. Unoccupied since 1924, it is now a museum with an enthralling exhibit on the history of Irish nationalism. The guided tour of its grim cells and corridors is highly memorable, and it finishes in the yard where the leaders of the failed 1916 Easter Rising were executed.

◉ *Kilmainham & the Liberties*

St Stephen's Green *(p61)*

7 Dublin is blessed with green spaces, but none is so popular or so beloved by its citizens as St Stephen's Green, the main entrance to which is through an arch at the southern end of Grafton St. When the sun burns through the cloud cover, virtually every blade of grass is occupied: by students, lovers and workers on a break. Many a business meeting is conducted along its pathways, which run past flower gardens, playgrounds and old Victorian bandstands.

◉ *Grafton Street & Around*

Chester Beatty Library *(p60)*

8 Alfred Chester Beatty was a mining magnate with exceedingly good taste, and the fruit of his aesthetic sensibility is gathered in this remarkable museum. Books, manuscripts and scrolls were his particular love, and his collection includes one of the world's best gathering of Qu'rans, the finest collection of Chinese jade books in existence, and some of the earliest biblical parchments ever found. The remainder of the collection is fleshed out with tablets, paintings, furniture and other beautiful objets d'art.

⊙ *Grafton Street & Around*

National Museum of Ireland
(p80, p126)

9 The artefacts of a nation are found in this eminent institution, which opened in 1890 with a collection of coins, medals and 'significant Irish antiquities', including the museum's most famous pieces – the Tara Brooch and the Ardagh Chalice, both dating from around the 8th century. The collection now numbers more than four million objects split across three separate museum buildings, including prehistoric archaeological finds and Celtic and medieval treasures; an extensive folklore collection; and the stuffed beasts and skeletons of the natural history section. TARA BROOCH

⊙ *Merrion Square & Around; North of the Liffey*

Guinness Storehouse *(p102)*

10 One of the world's most famous beer brands, Guinness is as inextricably linked with Dublin as James Joyce and...no, we can't think of anything else. An old fermentation plant in the St James Gate Brewery has been converted into a seven-storey museum devoted to the beer; you can learn about the company's history, how the beer is made and how it became the brand it is today. The top floor has an atrium bar where you put the theory to the test and drink a pint. Is this why the Guinness Storehouse is the most popular attraction in town?

⊙ *Kilmainham & the Liberties*

What's New

Restaurant Revolution

Hardened and tempered by the economic crisis, restaurateurs have learnt (some to their enormous cost) what works and what doesn't. The result is a battery of new eateries that combine culinary ambition with a commitment to providing value for money. You'll find evidence of this in all price categories, from the budget cafes that take greater care in the breads and fillings they use in their sandwiches to the top-end restaurants that work extra hard to provide a more accessible cuisine without sacrificing the brilliance that brought them to the top of the pile.

Tea Culture

New cafes such as Clement & Pekoe and Wall & Keogh have raised the caffeine bar by offering a range of loose-leaf teas and specialist coffees served in wonderful settings. (p69)

The Marker

The Marker, the only new hotel to have opened in Dublin since 2011, is a five-star luxury experience in the Grand Canal Dock, housed in an eye-catching building designed by Portuguese architect Manuel Aires Mateus. (p177)

The Dolls Store

Antique dolls and teddy bears from the last century are attraction enough, but what kid with a damaged teddy or doll won't need to visit the hospital section of the Dolls Store in the Powerscourt Townhouse Shopping Centre, where their stricken toy will get the repairs and TLC it so desperately needs? (p25)

Vintage Cocktail Club

A discreet knock on the plain metal door will transport you upstairs into the Vintage Cocktail Club, where the cocktails are big and lethal, the food excellent and the atmosphere a mix between '60s Vegas lounge and Depression-era speakeasy. (p96)

Segway Tours

The most distinctive way to tour the city's historical and architectural sites is aboard your own personal Segway, available from Glide Tours. (p213)

Croke Park Skyline

The newest part of the Croke Park Experience is the Skyline, a guided tour around the stadium's roof that ends on a platform that extends right over the pitch. (p140)

Forbidden Fruit

Boutique festivals are the new megagig, and Forbidden Fruit, with its bespoke line-up of cool old bands and today's hipster favourites, is one of the best. (p22)

Imaginosity

A learning wonderland for the kids, Imaginosity is the ideal place for the little 'uns to get inspired while the big 'uns do a little retail therapy at the ginormous Dundrum Town Centre next door. (p24)

For more recommendations and reviews, see **lonelyplanet. com/dublin**

Need to Know

For more information, see Survival Guide (p207)

Currency
Euro (€)

Language
English

Visas
Not required for most citizens of Europe, Australia, New Zealand, USA and Canada.

Money
ATMs are widespread. Credit cards (with PIN) accepted at most restaurants, hotels and shops.

Mobile Phones
All European and Australasian phones work in Dublin; some North American (non-GSM) phones don't. Check with provider. Prepaid SIM cards cost from €10.

Time
Western European time (UTC/GMT November to March; plus one hour April to October).

Tourist Information
Dublin Tourism has two offices in the city centre and branches in both airport terminals.

Your Daily Costs

Budget: less than €80
➡ Dorm bed: €14–20
➡ Cheap meal in cafe or pub: €10–15
➡ Bus ticket: up to €2.20
➡ Sightseeing in museums with free admission
➡ Pint: €4.50–5

Midrange: €80–200
➡ Budget hotel double: €60–100
➡ Midrange hotel or townhouse double: €100–150
➡ Lunch and/or dinner in decent restaurant: €25
➡ Guided tours and admission to paid attractions: €20

Top End: over €200
➡ Double in top-end hotel: from €180
➡ Dinner in top-end restaurant: €50

Advance Planning
One month before Book accommodation, especially in summer. Book tickets for bigger live gigs, especially touring musicians and comedians.

Two weeks before Secure accommodation in off-season. Book weekend performances for main theatres, and Friday or Saturday night reservations at top-end restaurants.

Three days before Book weekend tables at the trendiest or most popular restaurants.

Useful Websites
Discover Ireland (www.discover ireland.ie) Official website of Discover Ireland.

Dublin Tourism (www.visit dublin.com) Official website of Dublin Tourism.

Dublintown (www.dublintown. ie) Comprehensive list of events.

Journal.ie (www.journal.ie) Excellent online newspaper.

Nialler9 (http://nialler9.com) Best website for music in the city, with reviews and listings.

Overheard in Dublin (www. overheardindublin.com) Proof that the general public are better than any scriptwriter.

Lonely Planet (www.lonely planet.com/dublin) Destination information, hotel bookings, travel forum and more.

WHEN TO GO

Weather is at its best from June to August. November to February is cold but dry(ish); September can be warm; May sees rain and sun.

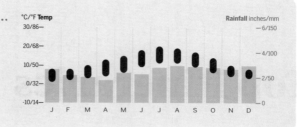

Arriving in Dublin

Dublin Airport Buses to the city centre run every 10 to 15 minutes between 6am and midnight; taxis (€25) take around 45 minutes.

Dun Laoghaire ferry terminal DART (one way €2.80) to Pearse Station (for south Dublin) or Connolly Station (for north Dublin); bus 46A to St Stephen's Green, or bus 7, 7A or 8 to Burgh Quay.

Dublin Port terminal Busáras buses (adult/child €2.50/1.25) are timed to coincide with arrivals and departures.

For much more on **arrival** see p208

Getting Around

➡ **Bus** Useful for getting to the west side of the city and the suburbs.

➡ **Cycling** The city's rent-and-ride Dublinbikes scheme is the ideal way to cover ground quickly.

➡ **DART** Suburban rail network that runs along the eastern edge of the city along Dublin Bay.

➡ **Luas** A two-line light-rail transport system that links the city centre with southern suburbs.

➡ **Taxi** Easily recognised by light green-and-blue 'Taxi' sign on door; can be hailed or picked up at ranks in the city centre.

➡ **Walking** Dublin's city centre is compact, flat and eminently walkable – less than 2km from one end of the city centre to the other.

For much more on **getting around** see p209

Sleeping

Like most cities, the closer to the city centre you want to stay, the more you'll pay – and the room sizes get smaller accordingly. Budget travellers will largely be confined to the handful of good hostels in the city. Although there are some good midrange options north of the Liffey, the biggest spread of accommodation is south of the river, ranging from elegant Georgian townhouses in the midrange bracket to the city's top hotels. There's also a range of excellent options in the circular belt of suburbs immediately south of the city centre. Prices go up dramatically at peak times, such as during summer and festivals.

Useful Websites

Dublin City Centre Hotels (http://dublin.city-centre-hotels.com) Hotel bookings with a range of budget options.

Go Ireland (www.goireland. com) Hotels, B&Bs and self-catering accommodation.

Daft.ie (www.daft.ie) If you're looking to rent in Dublin, this is the place to look.

For much more on **sleeping** see p167

Top Itineraries

Day One

Grafton Street & Around (p50)

 Start with a stroll through the grounds of **Trinity College**, visiting the **Book of Kells** and the **Long Room** before ambling up **Grafton St** to **St Stephen's Green**. For more beautiful books and artefacts, drop into the **Chester Beatty Library**. On your way, you can do a spot of retailing in **Powerscourt Townhouse Shopping Centre** or the many boutiques west of Grafton St.

> ✕ **Lunch** The two-course lunch special at Coppinger Row (p66) is a steal.

Merrion Square & Around (p78)

Pick your heavyweight institution, or visit all three: the **National Museum of Ireland – Archaeology** (if only for the Ardagh Chalice and Tara Brooch), the **National Gallery** (be sure to check out the Jack B Yeats room) and the **National Museum of Ireland – Natural History**, which the kids will surely enjoy.

> ✕ **Dinner** Fade Street Social (p66) serves up gourmet tapas.

Temple Bar (p92)

 Dublin's one-time party zone still likes to have a good time, and is definitely at its most animated in the evenings, where you have the choice of a **traditional music session**, some decent clubbing at **Mother** (Saturdays only) or just straight up drinking at any of the district's many **pubs**.

Day Two

Kilmainham & the Liberties (p100)

 Begin with a little penance at either (or both) of Dublin's medieval cathedrals, **St Patrick's** and **Christ Church**, before pursuing pleasure at Dublin's most popular tourist attraction, the **Guinness Storehouse**; make sure to sample the almost perfect Guinness you get at the end of the visit.

> ✕ **Lunch** Fumbally Cafe (p118) has great soups, sandwiches and coffee.

Kilmainham & the Liberties (p100)

 Go further west to Kilmainham, visiting first the fine collection at the **Irish Museum of Modern Art** (don't forget to visit the gardens too) before going out the back entrance and stepping into **Kilmainham Gaol**, the tour of which offers one of the most illuminating and interesting insights into Ireland's struggle for independence you'll get on your travels. If the weather is good, a stroll in the **War Memorial Gardens** is also recommended.

> ✕ **Dinner** Organic grub at L Mulligan Grocer (p136), in Stoneybatter.

North of the Liffey (p120)

Walshe's of Stoneybatter is a superb traditional bar, full of interesting locals and hipster blow-ins looking for a 'real' Dublin experience. Alternatively, you could take in a play at either the **Gate** or Ireland's national theatre, the **Abbey**. Use the Luas to get you from Stoneybatter (get on at the Museum stop) and alight at Abbey St.

Guinness Storehouse (p102)

Day Three

North of the Liffey (p120)

 After walking the length of **O'Connell St**, pausing to admire the bullet holes in the **General Post Office**, explore the collection of the **Dublin City Museum – The Hugh Lane** including Francis Bacon's reconstructed studio. The **Old Jameson Distillery**, to the west in Smithfield, is the place to learn about (and taste) Irish whiskey.

> ✖ **Lunch** Get great sandwiches, wraps and baps at Third Space (p134).

North of the Liffey (p120)

The collection of the **National Museum of Ireland – Decorative Arts & History** is excellent, but you'll be distracted by the stunning 18th-century barracks that is its home. The nearby cemetery at **Arbour Hill** is where the executed leaders of the Easter Rising are buried, while further west again is the broad expanse of the **Phoenix Park**, the largest city park in Europe.

> ✖ **Dinner** Chapter One (p136) is ideal for a special occasion. Book ahead.

Grafton Street & Around (p50)

 The biggest choice of nightlife is in the streets around Grafton St. There are traditional **pubs**, trendy new **bars** and **music venues**. You can drink, talk and dance the night away, or go see a show at the **Gaiety Theatre**. Whatever you choose, everything is easily reached in what is a pretty compact district.

Day Four

North of the Liffey (p120)

 You'll get a particularly interesting insight into the vagaries of Irish history with a visit to **Glasnevin Cemetery**, the final resting place of so many Irish notables – but be sure to take the brilliant tour. The **National Botanic Gardens** are just around the corner, and well worth an amble. Sporting fans will enjoy the tour of **Croke Park**, Ireland's biggest stadium and HQ of the Gaelic Athletic Association.

> ✖ **Lunch** Wuff (p135) in Stoneybatter has a great range of lunch options.

Howth (p158)

 Hop on a DART and head northwards to the suburb of Howth, a nice fishing village at the foot of a bulbous headland overlooking Dublin Bay. There are great walks around the headland itself, but if you prefer something a little more sedate, there's a fine selection of **pubs** in the village and some excellent seafood **restaurants** along the pier. There's also a terrific **farmers market** at weekends.

> ✖ **Dinner** The Winding Stair (p136) serves beautiful Irish cuisine.

Merrion Square & Around (p78)

By now you've probably discovered a favourite pub. A return visit is always recommended, but if you have the time, a visit to **O'Donoghue's** on Merrion Row is guaranteed to be memorable: a beautiful traditional bar that is always full of revellers and there's a good chance there'll be a trad music session on.

If You Like...

Great Pubs

Kehoe's Beautiful traditional pub with elegant Victorian bar beloved of locals and visitors alike. (p71)

Fallon's Great neighbourhood bar at the edge of the Liberties frequented by locals and hipsters in the know. (p118)

John Kavanagh's It's worth the trek to the north Dublin suburb of Glasnevin for this traditional classic. (p137)

Stag's Head The most picturesque of Dublin's traditional bars hasn't changed a jot since it was remodelled in 1895. (p69)

James Toner's Flagstone floors and an old-style bar make this a favourite boozer for the local business crowd, who come here to unwind. (p91)

Ryan's On the doorstep of the Phoenix Park is a Victorian gem that also does excellent food. (p137)

Walshe's Wonderful local pub frequented by old men in flat caps and young arty types in...flat caps. (p136)

Traditional Music

Cobblestone The best pub in Dublin to hear good trad, both old-style and contemporary. (p139)

O'Donoghue's Folk music's unofficial HQ during the 1960s, it still holds regular sessions of traditional music throughout the week. (p91)

Ha'Penny Bridge Inn A regular session of ballads, folk and traditional music takes place on Sunday nights in the upstairs room of this Temple Bar pub. (p98)

DAVID SOANES PHOTOGRAPHY / GETTY IMAGES ©

Four Courts (p130)

Devitt's From Thursday to Saturday there are open sessions, which are open to everyone – so long as you're really, really good at playing traditional music. (p72)

Oliver St John Gogarty The sessions here may be strictly for tourists, but they're lots of fun and, more importantly, performed by some really excellent musicians. (p96)

Irish History

Kilmainham Gaol Ireland's troubled and bloody struggle for independence is revealed in a visit to this historic jail, where rebels were incarcerated and the leaders of the 1916 Easter Rising executed. (p111)

Glasnevin Cemetery Almost everyone who was anyone in the last two centuries of Irish history is interred at this cemetery, and their stories are brought to life (ahem) by the excellent tours. (p140)

1916 Rebellion Walking Tour A detailed and informative walking tour of all the sites and stories associated with the Easter Rising make this one of the best ways to get to grips with this particular episode in history. (p213)

Pat Liddy Walking Tour A wide variety of themed historical walks led by Dublin's best-known local historian and tour guide. (p213)

Jeanie Johnston An exact replica of a 19th-century Famine ship that gives a first-hand impression of what it was like to sail across the Atlantic. (p144)

Admiring Art

Irish Museum of Modern Art The 20th- and 21st-century art hangs on its walls but you'll soon be distracted by the elegant surroundings and beautiful gardens. (p112)

Dublin City Gallery – The Hugh Lane Impressionist masterpieces and Francis Bacon's actual studio, reconstructed piece by exacting piece, are the highlights of this wonderful gallery. (p122)

National Gallery Home of the Irish State's art collection, including a Caravaggio and a whole room dedicated to Jack B Yeats. (p82)

Royal Hibernian Academy (RHA) Gallagher Gallery Privately run gallery where installations, sound pieces and other treats complement the contemporary paintings. (p87)

Museum Meanders

National Museum of Ireland – Archaeology The country's most important cultural institution is the repository of its most valuable and sacred historical treasures. (p80)

Chester Beatty Library Best small museum in Ireland, with breathtaking collection of sacred books and objets d'art from the Middle East and Asia. (p60)

Little Museum of Dublin This museum tells the story of Dublin in the 20th century through items, photographs and objects donated by Dubliners themselves. (p63)

Natural History Museum The Dead Zoo's collection of two million stuffed beasts has hardly changed since Scottish explorer

For more top Dublin spots, see the following:

➡ Eating (p29)

➡ Drinking & Nightlife (p33)

➡ Entertainment (p38)

➡ Shopping (p41)

➡ Sports & Activities (p43)

Dr David Livingstone cut the ribbon in 1857. (p86)

Live Gigs

Workman's Club A great spot for left-of-centre stuff, from electronica to alt rock and beardy folk music. (p97)

Whelan's The spiritual home of the singer-songwriter, you can get up close and personal at this terrifically intimate venue. (p72)

Twisted Pepper The place to see cutting-edge performers from hip-hop artists to composers of electronica. (p139)

Vicar Street A mid-sized venue that generally hosts soul, folk and foreign music. (p119)

O2 The place to see your favourite touring international superstar, along with 23,000 others. (p147)

Markets & Shopping

Powerscourt Townhouse Shopping Centre The city's most elegant shopping centre, replete with stores selling everything from hand-crafted leather bags to hats by Irish designers. (p77)

George's St Arcade Beneath the arches of this Victorian arcade you'll find everything from secondhand LPs to patchouli oil. (p77)

Cow's Lane Designer Mart New Irish designers sell their wares – stuff you can wear as well as decorations for your home – at this popular weekend market. (p98)

Cathach Books Rare books, maps and first editions are found in this beautiful bookshop that specialises in Irish titles. (p75)

Barry Doyle Design Jewellers Fancy a bespoke bit of Celtic jewellery? This lovely shop in the George's St Arcade is the place to go. (p77)

Eating Out

Chapter One Michelin-starred and beloved by its regulars, this is one of the best restaurants in town. (p136)

Musashi Noodles & Sushi Bar Japanese food and presentation never seen before in Dublin. Excellent sushi but also a wide range of other specialities. (p135)

Fade Street Social Gourmet tapas and delicious mains courtesy of renowned chef Dylan McGrath. (p66)

L Mulligan Grocer Organic Irish grub and delicious craft beers in a traditional pub setting. (p136)

Restaurant Patrick Guilbaud For the ultimate splash-out meal, this is arguably the best restaurant in Ireland. (p88)

Literary Locations

Marsh's Library Founded in 1701, Ireland's oldest library is home to more than 25,000 books and manuscripts dating back to the 1400s. (p113)

The Old Library, Trinity College The world's most famous illuminated gospels (the *Book of Kells*) and the Long Room, a magnificent cathedral of books, scrolls and ancient manuscripts. (p53)

Dublin Writers Museum Dublin's literary heritage explored through writers' personal possessions, scribblings and memorabilia. (p131)

Bloomsday Edwardian gear is de rigueur on June 16 if you want to celebrate Dublin's unique tribute to James Joyce. (p21)

Green Spaces

St Stephen's Green The city's favourite sun trap, with every blade of its manicured lawns occupied by lounge lizards and lunchers. (p61)

Merrion Square Perfectly raked paths meander by beautifully maintained lawns and flower beds. (p83)

Phoenix Park Dublin's biggest park, home to deer, the zoo, the president and the US ambassador. (p123)

Iveagh Gardens Delightful, slightly dishevelled gardens hidden behind St Stephen's Green. (p63)

War Memorial Gardens The best-kept open secret in town are these magnificent gardens by the Liffey. (p118)

Georgian Buildings

Leinster House Richard Cassels built this home for the Duke of Leinster; it's now the home of the Irish parliament. (p86)

Charlemont House Lord Charlemont's city dwelling, now home to the Dublin City Gallery – the Hugh Lane, was one of the city's finest Georgian homes. (p122)

Powerscourt Townhouse Shopping Centre Once home to the third Viscount Powerscourt, Robert Mack's beautiful building is now a popular shopping centre. (p77)

Four Courts The home of the highest courts in the land is the joint effort of Thomas Cooley and James Gandon. (p130)

Custom House James Gandon announced his arrival in Dublin with this architectural stunner. (p144)

Bank of Ireland Now a bank, it was designed by Edward Lovett Pearce for the Irish parliament. (p63)

Month by Month

January

🎆 New Year's Celebrations

Experience the birth of another year with a cheer among thousands of revellers at Dublin's iconic Christ Church Cathedral.

February

☆ Jameson Dublin International Film Festival

Most of Dublin's cinemas participate in the city's film festival, a two-week showcase for new films by Irish and international directors, that features local flicks, arty international films and advance releases of mainstream movies.

🏃 Six Nations Rugby

Ireland, winners of the 2009 Grand Slam, play their three home matches at the Aviva Stadium in the southern suburb of Ballsbridge. The season runs from February to April.

March

🍷 St Patrick's Festival

The mother of all Irish festivals, where hundreds of thousands gather to 'honour' St Patrick on city streets and in venues throughout the centre over four days around 17 March. Events include the three-day Guinness Fleadh music festival in Temple Bar.

May

🎆 Dublin Writers Festival

Four-day literature festival in mid-May attracting Irish and international writers to its readings, performances and talks.

🎆 Bloom in the Park

Ireland's largest gardening expo with over 90,000 visitors coming to the Phoenix Park over one weekend mid-month to eat food, listen to music and yes, test their green thumbs.

☆ International Dublin Gay Theatre Festival

A fortnight at the beginning of May devoted exclusively to gay theatre – plays by gay writers past and present that have a gay or gay-related theme.

June

🎆 Bloomsday

On 16 June folk wander around the city dressed in Edwardian gear, talking nonsense in dramatic tones. They're not mad; they're only Bloomsdayers commemorating James Joyce's epic *Ulysses* through readings, performances and re-created meals.

🍴 Taste of Dublin

Since 2005 the city's best restaurateurs have shared their secrets and their dishes with each other and the public at the wonderful

Taste of Dublin in the Iveagh Gardens, which takes place over a long weekend in June and features talks, demonstrations and lessons as well as the chance to eat some extraordinary grub.

☆ Forbidden Fruit

An alternative music festival in the grounds of the Irish Museum of Modern Art over the first weekend in June. (www.forbidden fruit.ie)

🏃 Women's Mini-Marathon

A 10km charity run on the second Sunday of the month that attracts up to 40,000 participants (including some poorly disguised men).

July

☆ Oxegen

Music festival over the 12 July weekend; manages to pack a few dozen heavyweight acts into its four-day line-up. Strictly for the young or the young-at-heart.

☆ Longitude

A three-day alt music festival (www.longitude.ie) in mid-July featuring old and new acts, art installations and food stalls at Marlay Park.

☆ Street Performance World Championships

The world's best street performers test their skills over two July weekends in Merrion Square – from jugglers to sword-swallowers. www.spwc.ie

August

🏃 Dublin Horse Show

The first week of August is when Ireland's horsey set trot down to the Royal Dublin Society (RDS) for the social highlight of the year. Particularly popular is the Aga Khan Cup, an international-class competition packed with often heart-stopping excitement in which eight nations participate.

🏃 Liffey Swim

Five hundred lunatics swim 2.5km from Rory O'More Bridge to the Custom House in late August – one can't but admire their steel wills.

September

🏃 All-Ireland Finals

The climax of the year for fans of Gaelic games as the season's most successful county teams battle it out for the All-Ireland championships in hurling and football, on the second and fourth Sundays in September respectively.

☆ Culture Night

For one night in September, there is free entry to museums, churches, galleries and historic homes throughout the city, which host performances, workshops and talks.

☆ Dublin Fringe Festival

This excellent theatre showcase precedes the main theatre festival with 700 performers and 100 events – ranging from cutting edge to crap – and takes place over three weeks. It's held in the Famous Spiegeltent, which has been erected in different positions in recent years.

🍺 Arthur's Day

A beer-and-music fuelled celebration of the anniversary of the founding of the Guinness factory takes place throughout the city on 26 September.

☆ Bulmers Comedy Festival

Big laughs over three weeks from an ever-widening choice of comic talents, both known and unknown. It takes place at more than 20 venues throughout the city.

October

☆ Dublin Theatre Festival

This two-week festival at the beginning of the month is Europe's oldest theatre festival and showcases the best of Irish and international productions at various locations around town.

🏃 Dublin City Marathon

If you fancy a 42km (and a bit) running tour through the streets of the city on the last Monday of October, you'll have to register at least three weeks in advance. Otherwise, you can have a lie-in and watch the winner cross the finishing line on O'Connell St at around 10.30am.

Top: Celebrating St Patrick's Festival

Bottom: Bloomsday, James Joyce Cultural Centre (p131)

CONLETH MC KERNAN / GETTY IMAGES ©

☆ Hard Working Class Heroes

The only showcase in town for unsigned Irish acts, this three-day music festival features 100 bands and musicians playing at venues on and around Camden St on the south side of the city.

🎆 Samhain/ Hallowe'en

Tens of thousands take to the city streets on 31 October for a night-time parade, fireworks, street theatre, drinking and music in this traditional pagan festival celebrating the dead, end of the harvest and Celtic new year.

December

🏃 Christmas Dip at the 40 Foot

At 11am on Christmas Day, a group of very brave swimmers jump into the icy waters at the 40 Foot, just below the Martello Tower in the southern suburb of Sandycove, for a 20m swim to the rocks and back.

🏃 Leopardstown Races

Blow your dough and your post-Christmas crankiness at this historic and hugely popular racing festival at one of Europe's loveliest courses. Races run from 26 to 30 December.

WAYNE WALTON / GETTY IMAGES ©

With Kids

Kid-friendly? You bet. Dublin loves the little 'uns, and will enthusiastically ooh and aah at the cuteness of your progeny. But alas such admiration hasn't fully translated into services that include widespread and accessible baby-changing facilities.

Meerkats, Dublin Zoo (p123)

Hands-on Museums

If your kids are between three and 14, spend an afternoon at Ark Children's Cultural Centre (p94), which runs activities aimed at stimulating participants' interest in science, the environment and the arts – but be sure to book well in advance.

Only five-minutes' walk from the Stillorgan stop on the Luas is **Imaginosity** (www.imaginosity.ie; The Plaza, Beacon South Quarter, Sandyford; adults/child €8/7; ⊙9.30am-5.30pm Tue-Fri, 10am-6pm Sat & Sun, 1.30-5.30pm Mon), the country's only designated interactive museum for kids. Over the course of two hours they can learn, have fun and get distracted by the museum's exhibits and activities.

Viking Adventures

There are loads of ways to discover Dublin's Viking past, but Dvblinia (p113), the city's Viking and medieval museum, has interactive exhibits that are specifically designed to appeal to younger visitors.

Kids of all ages will love a **Viking Splash Tour** (Map p238; ☑01-707 6000; www.viking splash.com; adult/child/family €20/12/65), where you board an amphibious vehicle, put on a plastic Viking hat and roar at passersby as you do a tour of the city before landing in the water at the Grand Canal basin.

Dublin Zoo

A recommended mobile option is a hop-on hop-off open-top bus tour (p212), which helps you get your bearings and lets the kids enjoy a bit of Dublin from the top deck. You can use the bus to get to Dublin Zoo (p123), where you can hop aboard the zoo train and visit the animals. There's roughly 400 animals from 100 different species across eight different habitats that range from an Asian jungle to a family farm, where kids get to meet the inhabitants up close.

NEED TO KNOW

➡ **Accommodation** Larger chain hotels (where a flat room rate usually applies), a serviced apartment, or a hostel where you can house the whole family in one room (usually with a private bathroom) are the best bet for young families. Most hotels provide cots at no extra charge.

➡ **Dining Out** Most restaurants have high chairs. Some high-end or trendy eateries actively discourage children after 6pm when they're busier.

➡ **Public Transport** Children under five years of age travel free on all public transport.

➡ **Pubs** Unaccompanied minors are not allowed in pubs; accompanied children can remain until 9pm (10pm May to September).

➡ **Admission** Family tickets are available to most attractions.

➡ **Breastfeeding** Although breastfeeding in Dublin is not a common sight, you can do so pretty much everywhere without getting so much as a stare.

➡ **Nappy Changing** There are virtually no nappy-changing facilities in Dublin, so you'll have to make do with a public toilet.

➡ **Babysitting** Agencies such as **Belgrave Agency** (☑01-280 9341; www.nanny.ie; 55 Mulgrave St, Dun Laoghaire; per hr €10-12 plus 21% VAT) and **Executive Nannies** (☑01-873 1273; www.executivenannies.com; 43 Lower Dominick St; per hr €18-21) provide professional nannies. The average charge is €15 per hour, plus taxi fare. The agency will fax a form to your hotel that must be signed beforehand.

➡ **Resources** Parents with young children should check out www.eumom.com; an excellent site about family-friendly accommodation is www.babygoes2.com.

➡ **For more information** Check out Lonely Planet's *Travel with Children* for information and inspiration on how to make travelling with children as hassle-free as possible.

Only in Ireland

Across the river from Dvblinia is the National Leprechaun Museum (p130), which despite it's high-sounding name is really just a romper room for kids with a little bit of Irish folklore thrown in for good measure. The optical illusion tunnel (which makes you appear smaller to those at the other end), the room full of oversized furniture, the wishing wells and, invariably, the pot of gold, are especially appealing for little ones.

Doll & Teddy-Bear Hospital

On the 2nd floor of the Powerscourt Townhouse Shopping Centre is the **Dolls Store** (Map p240; Powerscourt Townhouse Shopping Centre; ⏰10am-6pm Mon-Sat), which sells all kinds of dolls and doll houses, but should your little one's doll or teddy get 'ill', this is also the home of Ireland's only doll and teddy-bear hospital.

Wide, Open Spaces

While it's always good to have a specific activity in mind, don't forget Dublin's parks – from St Stephen's Green (p61) to Merrion Square (p83) to the Phoenix Park (p123), the city has plenty of green spaces for the kids to run wild in.

Like a Local

Dublin is, depending on your perspective, a small city or a very large village, which makes it at once easy to navigate but difficult to understand. Spend enough time here and you'll realise exactly what we mean.

Ha'Penny Bridge, River Liffey

Dubliners

Dubliners are, for the most part, an informal and easygoing lot who don't stand on excessive ceremony and generally prefer not making too much of a fuss. Which doesn't mean that they don't abide by certain rules, or that there isn't a preferred way of doing things in the city. But the transgressions of the unknowing are both forgiven and often enjoyed – the accidental faux pas are a great source of entertainment in a city that has made 'slagging', or teasing, a veritable art form. Indeed, slagging is a far more reliable indicator of the strength of friendship than virtually any kind of compliment: a fast, self-deprecating wit and an ability to take a joke in good spirits will win you plenty of friends.

A Local's Guide to Dublin's Neighbourhoods

Although relatively small for a capital city, Dublin's neighbourhoods all have distinctive identities that are determined by those who live and socialise there.

Grafton Street & Around

The city centre is lived in by the relatively few who can afford its exorbitant rents but socialised in by virtually everybody. Full of hipster bars, trendy watering holes and some of the city's most popular traditional pubs, you'll find students, 20-somethings, the bohemian crowd and plenty more besides enjoying a night out. This area is also full of great restaurants, so older folk out for a good meal and a less raucous drink will also make their way here.

Merrion Square & Around

Many of the professions – from law to medicine to accountancy – have offices in the fine Georgian buildings that line the streets and squares of this elegant neighbourhood. The bars and restaurants here – including some of the city's best eateries – generally cater to a more affluent crowd. If there's talk of sport here, it's usually about rugby – soccer and Gaelic sports are very much in the minority.

Temple Bar

This cobbled neighbourhood used to be where tourist went to cause mayhem, and while it's quietened down somewhat in recent years, it's still the unofficial 'party zone' of Dublin. Weekend nights see every pub full – usually of visitors, but also of Dubliners out for a knees-up and a hook-up with the aforementioned visitors. Temple Bar's reputation meant that the cool crowd would never be seen here, but in the last couple of years it has become something of a hipster hangout...in an ironic way, y'know?

Kilmainham & the Liberties

This is strictly daytime territory for outsiders – the lack of restaurants and bars means that only locals are to be found here when the sun goes down. But it is precisely that lack of night time traffic that makes the couple of worthwhile bars in these neighbourhoods so damn good.

North of the Liffey

The traditionally working-class neighbourhoods of the north inner city have long been blighted by poverty and its resultant social ills, which has made the area around O'Connell St – especially the northern end and the streets immediately east of it – a hot spot for potential trouble late at night, when the pubs close. By then, though, those attending a play at the Gate or Abbey theatres will have long left the area. To the west, the Smithfield area never took off the way it was planned, but it's still full of apartments occupied by young professionals on the rise. Immediately west again is Stoneybatter, Dublin's version of Brooklyn – lots of young, bohemian hipsters and immigrants that have brought new life to a traditional neighbourhood. The bars and eateries draw in the trendy crowd from all over.

The Rounds System

The rounds system – the simple custom where someone buys you a drink and you buy one back – is the bedrock of Irish pub culture. It's summed up in the Irish saying: 'It's impossible for two men to go to a pub for one drink'. Nothing will hasten your fall from social grace here like the failure to uphold this pub law. The Irish are extremely generous and one thing they can't abide is tight-fistedness.

Another golden rule about the system is that the next round starts when the first person has finished (or preferably just about to finish) their drink. It doesn't matter if you're only halfway through your pint, if it's your round, get them in.

Your greatest challenge will probably be trying to keep up with your fellow drinkers, who may keep buying you drinks in every round even when you've still got a clatter of unfinished pints in front of you and you're sliding face first down the bar.

For Free

Dublin has a reputation for being expensive and there's no doubt you can haemorrhage cash without too much effort. But the good news is you can see and experience much of what's great about Dublin without having to spend a cent.

Museums

The nation's cultural and historic patrimony is yours to enjoy at no cost.

National Museum of Ireland All three Dublin branches of the National Museum – Archaeology (p80), Decorative Arts & History (p126) and Natural History (p86) – are free of charge, and you're welcome to wander in and explore its myriad treasures and fascinating exhibits at your leisure.

National Gallery (p82) The state's proud collection of art, from the Middle Ages up to the modern age, is well represented on the walls of the National Gallery.

Chester Beatty Library (p60) The city's foremost small museum is a treasure trove of ancient books, illuminated manuscripts, precious scrolls and other gorgeous objets d'art.

Green Spaces

Dublin is blessed with green spaces, all but one of which is open to the public.

St Stephen's Green (p61) The city's most popular park is always packed with folks looking to take advantage of the good weather.

Merrion Square (p83) The most elegant of Dublin's free parks has beautiful lawns, delicate flower beds and a statue of Oscar Wilde (among others).

Iveagh Gardens (p63) A little wilder and not as well known as the city's other parks is this bit of countryside smack in the middle of the city.

Phoenix Park (p123) The largest non-wildlife enclosed park in Europe is huge – big enough to house the President, the American ambassador, the zoo, a herd of fallow deer and more green space than you could ever need.

Personalised Tours

Exploring the city under your own steam is free, but you can also get some guided help at no cost.

iWalks (www.visitdublin.com/iwalks) Download your own walking tour from the tourist office website and explore the city with an expert's voice leading the way.

Glasnevin Cemetery Tours (p140) Excellent free guided tours of the country's most famous resting place.

Salmon dish, Restaurant Patrick Guilbaud (p88)

 # Eating

Most Dubliners will tell you that the foodie scene has never been better than it is right now – austerity notwithstanding. The last couple of years has seen a bunch of brilliant new eateries open their doors, offering more inventive menus and more competitive pricing. Leaner times have led restaurateurs and chefs to roll up their sleeves and re-imagine virtually everything they do, and the result has been remarkable.

Local Specialities

It's a wonder the Irish retain their good humour amid the perpetual potato-baiting they endure. But, despite the stereotyping, potatoes are still paramount here and you'll see lots of them on Dublin menus. The mashed potato dishes colcannon and champ (with cabbage and spring onion respectively) are two of the tastiest recipes you'll find.

Most meals are usually meat based, with beef, lamb and pork common options. The most Dublin of dishes is coddle, a working-class concoction of rashers, sausages, onions, potato and plenty of black pepper. More easily available is the national edible icon, Irish stew, the slow-simmered one-pot wonder of lamb, potatoes, onions, parsley and thyme (note, no carrots).

The most famous Irish bread, and one of the signature tastes of Ireland, is soda bread. Irish flour is soft and doesn't take well to yeast as a raising agent, so Irish bakers of the 19th century leavened their

NEED TO KNOW

Price Ranges

€   €15 or less for a main course

€€   €15 to €25 for a main course

€€€   More than €25 for a main course

Opening Hours

➡ **Cafes** 8am to 5pm Monday to Saturday

➡ **Restaurants** Noon–10pm (or midnight); food service generally ends around 9pm. Top-end restaurants often close between 3pm and 6pm; restaurants serving brunch open around 10am.

Booking Tables

Reserving a table has become just about compulsory for most of the city's restaurants from Thursday to Saturday, and for the hippest ones all week. Many of the latter have also gone for the multiple-sittings system, which means 'yes, we have a table for you at 7pm but could you please vacate by 9pm?' In response, some places have snubbed the reservations system in favour of the get-on-the-list, get-in-line policy that usually encourages a pre-dinner drink in a nearby pub.

Tipping

It's industry standard these days to tip between 10% and 12% of the bill, unless the waiter has dumped the dinner in your lap and given you the finger, while the gratuity for exceptional service is only limited by your generosity and/or level of inebriation. If you're really unhappy don't be afraid to leave absolutely nothing, though it will very rarely come to that.

Decent Deals

Online voucher sites such as **Groupon** (www.groupon.ie) and **Living Social** (www.livingsocial.com) offer heavily discounted vouchers for some restaurants, including some really good eateries. Lunch and early-bird specials are also great for discounted dining.

bread with bicarbonate of soda. Combined with buttermilk, it makes a superbly light-textured and tasty bread, and is often on the breakfast menus at B&Bs. Scones, tarts and biscuits are specialities too.

Vegie Bites

Vegetarians are having it increasingly easier in Dublin as the capital has veered away from the belief that food isn't food until your incisors have had to rip flesh from bone, and towards an understanding that healthy eating leads to, well, longer lives. There's a selection of general restaurants that cater to vegetarians beyond the token dish of mixed greens and pulses, including **Nude** (Map p240; ☑01-675 5577; 21 Suffolk St; wraps €5-6; ☺Mon-Sat; ▣all city centre), Yamamori (p67) and Chameleon (p96).

Solidly vegetarian places include **Blazing Salads** (Map p240; 42 Drury St; mains €4-9; ☺10am-6pm Mon-Sat, to 8pm Thu), with organic breads, Californian-style salads and pizza; **Cornucopia** (Map p240; www.cornucopia.ie; 19 Wicklow St; mains €10-13; ☺8.30am-9pm Mon & Tue, 8.30am-10.15pm Wed-Sat, noon-9pm Sun; ☑), Dublin's best-known vegetarian restaurant, serving wholesome salads, sandwiches and a selection of hot main courses; **Fresh** (Map p240; top fl, Powerscourt Townhouse Shopping Centre, 59 South William St; lunch €6-12; ☺9.30am-6pm Mon-Sat, 10am-5pm Sun), a long-standing restaurant serving a variety of salads, dairy and gluten-free dishes, and filling, hot daily specials; and **Govinda's** (www.govindas.ie; mains €7-11), an authentic beans-and-pulses place run by the Hare Krishna with restaurants on Aungier St, Merrion Row and Middle Abbey St.

Organic & Farmers Markets

For more info on local markets, check out www.irishfarmersmarkets.ie, www.irishvillagemarkets.com or local county council sites such as www.dlrcoco.ie/markets.

Dublin Food Co-op (p119) Everything in this market hall is organic and/or ecofriendly. Saturday is when it's all on display – Dubliners from all over drop in for their responsible weekly shop.

Coppinger Row Market (Map p240; Coppinger Row; ☺9am-7pm Thu) It's small but packs a proper organic punch, with freshly baked breads, delicious hummus and other goodies.

DINING IN DUBLIN

Aingeala Flannery, a food critic with *Day & Night* magazine – available every Friday in the *Irish Independent* (www.irishindependent.ie) – gives us the rundown on Dublin dining.

Best thing about eating out in Dublin? The southside city centre is so small you can walk from place to place in a matter of minutes and check out menus and atmosphere, and decide where you want to eat. And you don't always need a reservation, even on the weekends.

Favourite restaurant for...a special occasion? In spite of L'Gueuleton's (p68) frustrating no-reservations policy, once you're in the door you'll be seduced by the rustic French cooking – using local and seasonal ingredients, of course. There's an ever-changing wine list and waiters who know their stuff. For a more formal occasion, check out The Hot Stove (p136). It's new and smart and close to the city's main theatres.

...a quick bite? The sandwiches in Honest to Goodness (p64) are excellent. They roast their own meats and bake their own breads. And if you happen to hit it on a Friday, the do the sloppiest Sloppy Joe around – only to be eaten alone with your sleeves rolled up to the elbow. Love it.

...a cheap meal? Musashi Noodles & Sushi Bar (p135) serves the best sushi and sashimi in Dublin. The fish is always spanking fresh. Cheap and sushi aren't words that go together in Dublin, but this place is a gem and deservedly popular.

...a romantic night out? For hot, dirty romance I'd hit 777 (p66), which is sultry and fun. In Chez Max (p68) the lighting is very kind, the music is seductive, the staff are good-looking and charming, there's a smoking area...and the wine flows freely.

Harcourt St Food Market (Map p238; www.irishfarmersmarkets.ie; Park Pl, Station Bldgs, Upper Hatch St; ☺10am-4pm Thu) Organic vegies, cheeses, olives and meats made into dishes from all over the world.

People's Park Market (☑087 957 3647; People's Park, Dun Laoghaire; ☺11am-4pm Sun) Organic meat and veg, local seafood, Irish fruit and farm cheeses.

When to Eat

Breakfast Usually eaten before 9am, although hotels and B&Bs will serve until 11am Monday to Friday, and to noon at weekends. Many cafes serve an all-day breakfast.

Lunch Usually a sandwich or a light meal between 12.30pm and 2pm. On weekends Dubliners have a big meal (called dinner) between 2pm and 4pm.

Tea No, not the drink, but the evening meal – also confusingly called dinner. A Dubliner's main daily meal, usually eaten around 6.30pm.

Eating by Neighbourhood

➡ **Grafton Street & Around** The best choice of restaurants and cafes in all price brackets. (p64)

➡ **Merrion Square & Around** Sandwich bars and Michelin-starred gourmet experiences, but little in between. (p88)

➡ **Temple Bar** A fine selection of food-as-fuel eateries, ethnic cuisine and the best fast-food joint in town. (p94)

➡ **Kilmainham & the Liberties** Limited to a couple of great cafes and Dublin's most famous chipper. (p118)

➡ **North of the Liffey** The most transformed of the city's neighbourhoods, with a fine selection of cafes, midrange restaurants and ethnic cuisine. (p134)

➡ **Docklands & the Grand Canal** A handful of vaguely trendy restaurants. (p145)

Lonely Planet's Top Choices

Chapter One (p136) Sublime cuisine, fabulous service and a wonderfully relaxed atmosphere.

Coppinger Row (p66) Buzzy spot serving Mediterranean cuisine allegedly favoured by members of a certain Dublin supergroup.

Fade Street Social (p66) Gourmet tapas and traditional mains by Dublin superchef Dylan McGrath.

Fumbally Cafe (p118) Beautiful warehouse cafe beloved of Dublin's hipster crowd.

Musashi Noodles & Sushi Bar (p135) Authentic Japanese cuisine – including the city's best sushi.

Paulie's Pizza (p145) Delicious Neapolitan pizza in a New York–style diner atmosphere.

Best by Budget

€

Fumbally Cafe (p118) Great warehouse space with filling sandwiches and good coffee.

Honest to Goodness (p64) Compact eatery that is always full.

Zaytoon (p94) Middle Eastern joint with the best fast food in town.

Third Space (p134) Wonderful place to eat tarts and linger.

Crackbird (p94) All kinds of deep-fried chicken with tasty sides.

€€

Fade Street Social (p66) Gourmet tapas in a gorgeous room.

Damson Diner (p66) Great grub with Southeast Asian flavour.

Musashi Noodles & Sushi Bar (p135) The best Japanese food in town.

Wuff (p135) Lovely room, great brunch and welcoming atmosphere.

€€€

Chapter One (p136) The food is sublime, the atmosphere is wonderfully relaxed.

L'Ecrivain (p90) Excellent cuisine *a la* Francaise.

Restaurant Patrick Guilbaud (p88) Perhaps the best restaurant in Ireland, where everything is just right.

Thornton's (p68) Modern cuisine by one of the best chefs in the country.

Best Irish Cuisine

Chapter One (p136) Nobody knew Irish cuisine could taste this good!

Winding Stair (p136) Classic Irish dishes given an elegant twist.

Pig's Ear (p68) Hearty, filling food prepared like your ancestors never could.

Avoca (p67) Wonderful 2nd-floor cafe serving Irish treats.

Hot Stove (p136) New spot making a splash with its fish and meat dishes.

Best Quick Bites

Honest to Goodness (p64) Tasty sandwiches and hot stuff to go.

Soup Dragon (p134) Get in line for the city's best liquid lunches.

Lemon (p65) Crêpes both savoury and sweet like you'd get in France.

Best Italian

Bottega Toffoli (p65) Tiny, tucked-away cafe serving mouth-watering food from the chef's family recipe book.

Paulie's Pizza (p145) The best, most authentic pizza in town.

La Dolce Vita (p95) Excellent antipasti dishes to be washed down with lashings of good wine.

Best Asian

Yamamori (p67) Tasty Japanese classics north and south of the Liffey.

Musashi Noodles & Sushi Bar (p135) For the best sushi in town.

Saba (p67) Thai and Vietnamese classics in a handsome dark-wood room.

Best to Linger

Simon's Place (p65) Grab a sandwich and stare out at the world through the windows.

Third Space (p134) Perpetual refills, great music...is that the time?

L Mulligan Grocer (p136) When you're done eating, stay for the beer.

Temple Bar (p97)

Drinking & Nightlife

If there's one constant about life in Dublin, it's that Dubliners will always take a drink. Come hell or high water, the city's pubs will never be short of customers, and we suspect that exploring a variety of Dublin's legendary pubs and bars ranks pretty high on the list of reasons why you're here.

NEED TO KNOW

Opening Hours

Last orders are at 11.30pm Monday to Thursday, 12.30am Friday and Saturday and 11pm Sunday, with 30 minutes drinking-up time each night. However, many central pubs have secured late licences to serve until 1.30am or even 2.30am (usually pubs that double up as dance clubs).

Tipping

The American-style gratuity is not customary in bars. If there's table service, it's polite to give your server the coins in your change (up to €1).

Made to Measure

➡ When drinking stout, beer or ale, the usual measure is a 'pint' (568mL).

➡ Half a pint is called a 'glass'.

➡ If you come to Ireland via Britain and drink spirits (or 'shorts' as they're called here), watch out: the English measure is a measly 25mL, while in Dublin you get a whopping 35mL, nearly 50% more.

Nonsmoking

Smoking is illegal indoors in all locales; many have converted the unused yard into a 'beer garden' so that smokers can get their fix without having to leave.

Pubs

The pub – or indeed anywhere people gather to have a drink and a chat – remains the heart of the city's social existence and the broadest window through which you can experience the very essence of the city's culture, in all its myriad forms. There are pubs for every taste and sensibility, although the traditional haunts populated by flat-capped pensioners bursting with insightful anecdotes are about as rare as hen's teeth and most Dubliners opt for their favourite among a wide selection of trendy bars, designer boozers and hipster locales. But despair not, for it is not the spit or sawdust that makes a great Dublin pub but the patrons themselves, who provide a reassuring guarantee that Dublin's reputation as the pub capital of the world remains in perfectly safe (if occasionally unsteady!) hands.

Stag's Head (p69)

Bars & Clubs

Dubliners like to throw down some dance-floor moves, but for the most part they do it in bars equipped with a late license, a decent sound system and a space on the floor. It's all changed from even a decade ago, when clubbing was all the rage: these days fewer people pay to simply go dancing, preferring instead the option of dancing in a bar they've been in most of the evening. DJs are an increasingly rare breed, but the ones that thrive usually play it pretty safe; the handful of more creative DJs (including occasional international guests) play in an increasingly restricted number of venues.

The busiest nights are Thursday to Saturday, and most clubs are free if you arrive before 11pm. After that, you'll pay between €5 to €10.

Cafes

Dublin's coffee junkies are everywhere, looking for that perfect barista fix that will kill the hunger until the next one. You can top up at any of the chains – including that one from Seattle – but we reckon your caffeine craving will get the best fix at individual locales such as Clement & Pekoe (p69), Brother Hubbard (p134), Wall & Keogh (p69), and Brioche (p65).

LGBT Dublin

Una Mullally, a features writer for the Irish Times, *helped us compile some tips and recommendations for LGBT visitors to Dublin.*

Drinking & Nightlife

North King St

Parnell St

Lower O'Connell St

Capel St

River Liffey

North of the Liffey
More traditional bars;
one excellent nightclub.
(p136)

Lower Ormond Quay

Temple Bar
Cheesy, fun touristy-type bars.
(p96)

High St

Nassau St

Dawson St

Grafton Street & Around
The best choice of
bars and clubs.
(p69)

Patrick St

Merrion Square & Around
Classic pubs for
after-work crowd.
(p90)

Kilmainham & the Liberties
Strictly traditional local haunts.
(p118)

Wexford St

Lower Leeson St

Grand Canal

Dublin is a pretty gay city and a magnet for LGBT people around the country. The best thing about Dublin's gay scene is that it's very mixed across gender, age and nationality. Unlike bigger cities, bars and clubs generally have a good mix of men and women, unless you're heading to a specific event. Look beyond the mainstream venues and nights and you'll find a more alternative and queer undercurrent.

The Front Lounge (p96) is a beautiful, chilled-out bar and the perfect place to start your night or wind down after work. Pantibar (p137), with its alternative drag shows, make-and-do nights and basement pool room is always fun. Mother (p97) is a small Saturday-night club on Copper Alley that plays the best music in town if you're looking for a sweaty and fun disco where Sister Sledge and LCD Soundsystem rule.

Where to Drink

With over 1000 pubs spread across the city, you'll have your choice of where to wet your beak. The plethora of pubs in Temple Bar is a favourite place to start – here you'll find a selection of contemporary bars (some with gaudy themes) and 'traditional' boozers (strangely devoid of locals but full of Spanish tourists). We urge you to explore further afield: the pubs around Grafton St are a great mix of old-style pubs and stylish modern spots. Camden St, southwest of St Stephen's Green, is very popular, as is Dawson St and Merrion Row – the latter has a couple of long-established favourites.

North of the Liffey has a selection of fine old pubs and genuine locals (read: visitors will be given the once-over) but there are a handful of popular bars, including the city's best gay bar, on Capel St.

Above: Whelan's (p72).
Left: Cobblestone (p139)

Lonely Planet's Top Choices

Anseo (p70) Unpretentious, unaffected and incredibly popular.

Grogan's Castle Lounge (p70) Favourite haunt of Dublin's writers and painters.

James Toner's (p91) Closest thing you'll get to a country pub in the heart of the city.

Kehoe's (p71) Atmospheric pub in the city centre.

Long Hall (p70) One of the city's most beautiful and best-loved pubs.

No Name Bar (p69) Great bar in a restored Victorian townhouse.

Best Pint of Guinness

Kehoe's (p71) Stalwart popular with locals and tourists.

John Mulligan's (p147) Perfect setting for a perfect pint.

Grogan's Castle Lounge (p70) Great because the locals demand it!

Fallon's (p118) Centuries of experience.

Best Choice of Beer

L Mulligan Grocer (p136) A wide range of cask ales.

Porterhouse (p96) Serves its own delicious brews.

Best Terraces

Bruxelles (p71) Drink next to Phil Lynott.

Cafe en Seine (p72) Elegance and heaters.

Beggar's Bush (p147) With convenient bench seating.

Grogan's Castle Lounge (p70) On-street overspill.

Best Traditional Pubs

John Mulligan's (p147) Traditional's gold standard.

Long Hall (p70) Stylishly old-fashioned.

Hartigan's (p91) The bare essentials.

Stag's Head (p69) Popular with journalists and students.

Best DJ Bars

Whelan's (p72) Classic and contemporary rock.

Dice Bar (p137) Dive bar with an eclectic range, from rock to lounge and dance.

Bernard Shaw (p71) Great DJs playing a mix of tunes.

Globe (p70) Soul, funk, disco and alt rock.

Best Club Nights

Hep Cat Club, Twisted Pepper (p139) (Monday) Swing, jive and jump jive...and they do dance classes!

Notorious, Button Factory (p97) (Thursday) Hip-hop by a local crew with occasional international guests.

Mud, Twisted Pepper (p139) (Friday) Drum 'n' bass, grime, dubstep and the odd bit of reggae.

Mother, Mother (p97) (Saturday) Disco, electro and pop...not for the faint-hearted.

Propaganda, Academy (p139) (Saturday) Indie rock and disco.

Best New Bars

Bernard Shaw (p71) Old-style new hipster hangout.

No Name Bar (p69) Genteel, elegant and crowded.

37 Dawson St (p69) The 'in' bar of 2013.

A Solitary Pint

Kehoe's (p71) Best in the early afternoon.

John Mulligan's (p147) Just a ticking clock for noise.

Grogan's Castle Lounge (p70) Artistic contemplation.

Best Local Haunts

Fallon's (p118) The Liberties' favourite bar.

Old Royal Oak (p119) Shh. Strictly for insiders.

John Kavanagh's (p137) A poorly kept secret.

Best Musical Pubs

O'Donoghue's (p91) The unofficial HQ of folk music.

Cobblestone (p139) Best sessions in town.

Auld Dubliner (p97) Traditional sessions for tourists.

Entertainment

Believe it or not, there is life beyond the pub or, more accurately, around it. There are comedy clubs and classical concerts, recitals and readings, marionettes and music – lots and lots of music. The other great Dublin treat is the theatre, where you can enjoy a light-hearted musical alongside the more serious stuff by Beckett, Yeats and O'Casey – not to mention a host of new talents.

Theatre

Despite Dublin's rich theatrical heritage, times are tough for the city's thespians. Once upon a time, everybody went to the theatre to see the latest offering by Synge, Yeats or O'Casey. Nowadays, a night at the theatre is the preserve of the passionate few, which has resulted in the city's bigger theatres taking a conservative approach to their programming and many fringe companies having to make do with non-theatrical spaces to showcase their skills – and that's if they manage to stay afloat at all: 24 companies went to the wall between 2009 and 2013 due to the recession.

Nevertheless, a Dublin performance of, say, *Plough and the Stars* or *The Playboy of the Western World* remains a special experience. The Abbey and the Gate are the city's most important theatres, but you'll also find shows in pubs, offices and other spaces appropriated for the purpose.

Theatre bookings can usually be made by quoting a credit-card number over the phone, then you can collect your tickets just before the performance. Expect to pay anything between €12 and €25 for most shows, with some costing as much as €30. Most plays begin between 8pm and 8.30pm. Check www. irishtheatreonline.com to see what's playing.

THEATRE FESTIVALS

For two weeks in October most of the city's theatres participate in the **Dublin Theatre Festival** (www.dublintheatrefestival.com), originally founded in 1957 and today a glittering parade of quality productions and elaborate shows.

Initially a festival for those shows too 'out-there' or insignificant to be considered for the main festival, **Dublin Fringe Festival** (www. fringefest.com) is now a three-week extravaganza with more than 100 events and over 700 performances. The established critics may keep their ink for the bigger do, but we strongly recommend the Fringe for its daring and diversity.

Comedy

The Irish have a reputation for hilarity – mostly off-the-cuff, iconoclastic humour – but the funniest of them generally find their way out of Ireland and onto bigger stages – such as Dara O'Briain, Dylan Moran and Chris O'Dowd, who's a bona fide star thanks to films such as *Bridesmaids* (2011).

The highlight of the comedy year is the annual **Bulmers International Comedy Festival** (www.bulmerscomedy.ie), which takes place at 20-odd venues over three weeks, usually in September, and features a barrel-load of local and international talent. Big laughs.

Film

Of the five cinemas in the city centre, three (Screen, Irish Film Institute and Lighthouse) offer a more offbeat list of foreign releases and art-house films. Save yourself the hassle of queuing and book your tickets online, especially for Sunday-evening screenings of popular first-run films. Out on the piss Friday and Saturday nights, most Dubliners have neither the energy nor the cash for more of the same, so it's a trip to the cinema at the end of the weekend. Admission prices are generally around €6 for afternoon shows, rising to €10 after 5pm. If you have a student card, you pay only €6 for all shows.

Live Music

POPULAR

Dubliners love their live music and support local acts as enthusiastically as they do touring international stars – even if the latter command the bigger crowds and ticket prices. You can sometimes buy tickets at the venue itself, but you're better off using an agent. Prices for gigs range dramatically, from as low as €5 for a tiny local act to anywhere up to €110 for the really big international stars. The listings sections of both paper and online resources will have all the gigs.

TRADITIONAL & FOLK

The best place to hear traditional music is in the pub, where the 'session' – improvised or scheduled – is still best attended by foreign visitors who appreciate the form far more than most Dubs and will relish any opportunity to drink and toe-tap to some extraordinary virtuoso performances.

Also worth checking out is the **Temple Bar Trad Festival** (http://templebartrad.com), which takes place in the pubs of Temple Bar over the last weekend in January. For online info on sessions, check out www.dublinsessions.ie.

Entertainment by Neighbourhood

➡ **Grafton Street & Around** The entertainment heartland of Dublin has something for everyone. (p72)

➡ **Merrion Square & Around** Quiet at nighttime except for the pubs, some of which have live music. (p90)

➡ **Temple Bar** From clubbing to live traditional music, you'll find a version of it in Temple Bar. (p97)

➡ **Kilmainham & the Liberties** The Irish Museum of Modern Art hosts the occasional concert. (p119)

➡ **North of the Liffey** Live gigs, traditional music and the city's two most historic theatres dominate the entertainment skyline. (p137)

NEED TO KNOW

Bookings

Theatre, comedy and classical concerts are usually booked directly through the venue. Tickets for touring international bands and big-name local talent are either sold at the venue or through a booking agency such as **Ticketmaster** (Map p240; ☑0818 719 300; www.ticketmaster.ie), which sells tickets to every genre of big- and medium-sized show – but be aware that it charges between 9% and 12.5% service charge per ticket.

Pre-Theatre Deals

Look out for good-value pre-theatre menus in some restaurants, which will serve dinner before opening curtain and coffee and drinks after the final act.

Business Hours

➡ Doors for most gigs open at 7pm.

➡ By law, gigs in bigger venues and arenas finish by 11pm.

Newspaper Listings

The Herald (www.herald.ie; €1.30) Thursday edition has good listings page.

Hot Press (www.hotpress.com) Fortnightly music mag; Ireland's answer to *NME* or *Rolling Stone*.

Irish Times (www.irishtimes.com; €2) Friday listings pullout called *The Ticket*.

Irish Independent (www.independent.ie; €1.90) *Night/Day* listings pullout on Friday.

Online Listings

Entertainment.ie (www.entertainment.ie) For all events.

MCD (www.mcd.ie) Biggest promoter in Ireland.

Nialler9 (www.nialler9.com) Excellent indie blog with listings.

Sweebe (www.sweebe.com) Over 200 venues listed.

What's On In (www.whatsonin.ie) From markets to gigs and club nights.

➡ **Docklands & the Grand** Canal Dublin's biggest theatre is the only reason to make your way eastward along the Liffey. (p147)

Lonely Planet's Top Choices

Cobblestone (p139) Best traditional sessions in town.

Dublin Fringe Festival (p38) Exciting new theatre.

Gate Theatre (p139) Masterfully presented classics.

Twisted Pepper (p139) Top-class club venue.

Whelan's (p72) For the intimate gig.

Workman's Club (p97) To see the best new bands.

Best Live Music Venues

Cobblestone (p139) For traditional music.

O2 (p147) Big-name acts only.

Whelan's (p72) Singer-songwriter HQ.

Workman's Club (p97) Who's cool, right now.

Best Theatres

Gate Theatre (p139) Wonderful old classic.

Peacock Theatre (p139) For interesting fringe plays.

Bord Gais Energy Theatre (p147) The best indoor venue in town.

Best Busking Spots

Grafton St From hard rock to Japanese Noh.

Temple Bar Comedy, poetry and earnest guitars.

Henry St Dublin's wannabe hip-hop artists.

Best Festivals

Dublin Fringe Festival (p38) Best of contemporary theatre.

St Patrick's Festival (p21) A city goes wild.

Taste of Dublin (p21) A weekend of gourmet goodness.

Forbidden Fruit (p22) Excellent alternative music fest.

Best for High Culture

Abbey Theatre (p137) Top names in Irish theatre.

Bloomsday (p21) Making sense of *Ulysses*.

Culture Night (p22) Art, architecture and heritage.

Best for Comedy

Ha'Penny Bridge Inn (p98) Local humour hits and misses.

International Bar (p71) Rising crop of Irish talent.

Laughter Lounge (p139) Established names and visiting stars.

Shopping

If it's made in Ireland – or pretty much anywhere else – you can find it in Dublin. Grafton St is home to a range of largely British-owned high-street chain stores, but you'll find the best local boutiques in the surrounding streets. On the north side, pedestrianised Henry St has international chain stores, as well as Dublin's best department store, Arnott's.

Traditional Irish Products

Traditional Irish products such as crystal and knitwear remain popular choices, and you can increasingly find innovative modern takes on the classics. But steer clear of the mass-produced junk whose joke value isn't worth the hassle of carting it home on the plane: trust us, there's no such thing as a genuine *shillelagh* (Irish fighting stick) for sale anywhere in town.

Fashion

Men's bespoke tailoring is rather thin on the ground. Designers have tried to instil a sense of classical style in the Dublin male, but the species doesn't seem too interested – any pressed shirt and leather shoe seems to suffice.

Streetwear is very trendy and the most obvious buyers are the city's younger consumers. They spend their Saturdays, off-days and lunch hours ambling about Grafton St and its side streets on the south side, or Henry St and its surrounds on the far side of the Liffey.

At the other end of the fashion spectrum, you'll find all the knit and tweed you want at Avoca Handweavers (p74) or Blarney Woollen Mills (p76).

Markets

In recent years Dublin has gone gaga for markets. Which is kind of ironic, considering the city's traditional markets, such as Moore St, were ignored by those same folks who now can't get enough of the homemade hummus on sale at the new gourmet spots. It's all so...Continental.

Shopping By Neighbourhood

➡ **Grafton Street & Around** Grafton St has traditionally been *the* shopping street, but the preponderance of British-owned chain stores means you'll find the same kind of stuff you can get almost anywhere. To really get the most of the area's retail allure, get off Grafton St and head into the grid of streets surrounding it, especially to the west, where you'll find some of Dublin's most interesting outlets. (p74)

➡ **Temple Bar** Dublin's most touristy neighbourhood has a pretty diverse mix of shops, from tourist-only tat retailers to the weird and (sometimes) wonderful; it's a place where you can get everything from a Celtic-design wall-hanging to a handcrafted bong. A couple of Dublin's best markets take place in this area on Saturday. (p98)

➡ **North of the Liffey** Northside shopping is all about the high-street chain store and the easy-access shopping centre, which is mighty convenient for Dubliners looking for everyday wear at decent prices. (p126)

NEED TO KNOW

Opening Hours
➡ 9.30am to 6pm Monday to Wednesday, Friday and Saturday

➡ 9.30am to 8pm Thursday

➡ noon to 6pm Sunday

Duty Free
Non-EU residents are entitled to claim VAT (Value Added Tax) on goods (except books, children's clothing or educational items) purchased in stores operating the Cashback or Taxback return program. The voucher you get with goods must be filled in and stamped at last point of exit from the EU; you can then post it back for a refund of duty paid.

Online Resources
The Savvy Shopper (www.thesavvyshopper. ie) Shopping tips and designer sales.

Lonely Planet's Top Choices

Avoca Handweavers (p74) Irish knits and handicrafts.

Barry Doyle Design Jewellers (p77) Beautiful bespoke creations.

Cathach Books (p75) For that rare first edition.

Claddagh Records (p99) Traditional and folk music.

Costume (p75) High-end women's fashion.

Sheridan's Cheesemongers (p76) A proper cheese shop.

Best Markets

Book Fair (p98) Rummage through secondhand books.

Cow's Lane Designer Mart (p98) A real market for hipsters bringing together over 60 of the best clothing, accessory and craft stalls.

Meeting House Square Market (p98) The city's best open-air food market.

Moore Street Market (p141) Open-air, steadfastly 'Old Dublin' market, with fruit, fish and flowers.

Best for Fashion

Louis Copeland (p76) Fabulous suits made to measure, as well as ready-to-wear suits by international designers.

Alias Tom (p75) Dublin's best designer menswear store.

Costume (p75) Exclusive contracts with some of Europe's most innovative designers.

Bow Boutique (p74) Beautiful boutique showcasing original designs and made-to-measure clothing.

Flip (p99) Hip Irish label offering retro men's fashion.

Best Guaranteed Irish

Avoca Handweavers (p74) Our favourite department store in the city has myriad homemade gift ideas.

Barry Doyle Design Jewellers (p77) Exquisite handcrafted jewellery with unique contemporary designs.

Cathach Books (p75) For that priceless first edition or a beautiful, leather-bound copy of Joyce's *Dubliners*.

Louis Copeland (p76) Dublin's very own top tailor with his made-to-measure suits.

Best for Homewares

O'Sullivan Antiques (p119) Fine furniture and furnishings from the Georgian, Victorian and Edwardian eras.

Article (p74) Beautiful tableware and decorative home accessories made by Irish designers.

Avoca Handweavers (p74) Stylish but homey brand of modern Irish life.

Best Museum Shops

Chester Beatty Library (p60) A wonderful little gift shop with postcards, books, posters and other memorabilia of this extraordinary museum.

Dublin City Gallery – The Hugh Lane Shop (p122) A cultural playground for adults, where you can dig out masterpiece colour-by-number prints, cloth puppets, unusual wooden toys and beautiful art and pop-culture hardbacks.

Irish Museum of Modern Art (p112) Offers a comprehensive selection of coffee-table books on Irish contemporary art.

Best for Jewellery

Angles (p76) Handmade contemporary Irish jewellery.

Appleby (p76) High-quality silver and gold jewellery.

Barry Doyle Design Jewellers (p77) Handmade jewellery exceptional in its beauty and simplicity.

Rhinestones (p77) Fine antique and quirky costume jewellery from the 1920s to 1970s.

Hurling team, Croke Park (p44)

Sports & Activities

To many Dubliners, sport is a religion. For an ever-increasing number, it's all about faith through good works such as jogging, amateur football, cycling and yoga; for everyone else, observance is enough, especially from the living-room chair or the pub stool.

Activities

Public sporting facilities are limited – there is only a handful of public tennis courts, for instance – so most visitors have to make do with their hotel gym or a run in the park.

GOLF

A round of golf is a highlight of many an Irish visit. Dublin's suburban courses are almost all private clubs, but many of them allow visitors on a pay-to-play basis. Tough times means reduced green fees, especially if you book online beforehand. You'll generally need your own transport if you wish to head to any of the major courses.

The best courses within easy reach of the city are **Killeen Castle** (www.killeencastle.com; Dunsany, Co Meath; green fee €30-50) in Dunsany, Co Meath; **Carton House** (☑505 2000; www.cartonhouse.com; Co Kildare; green fees Mon-Thu €60, Fri-Sun €70), just outside Maynooth in County Kildare; **Portmarnock** (☑01-846 2968; www.portmarnockgolfclub.ie; Golf Links Rd, Portmarnock; green fee €175), by the sea in north

NEED TO KNOW

Sporting Seasons

➡ **Football** April to October

➡ **Gaelic Sports** April to September

➡ **Rugby Internationals** February to April

Planning Ahead

➡ **Two months** Tickets for rugby internationals or the latter stages of the Gaelic championship

➡ **One month** Leinster rugby matches in Heineken Cup

➡ **One week** Local football matches and Gaelic league games

Online Resources

Gaelic Athletic Association (www.gaa.ie)

Football Association of Ireland (www.fai.ie)

Irish Rugby Football Union (www.irfu.ie)

Horse Racing Ireland (www.goracing.ie)

Golf Union of Ireland (www.gui.ie)

county Dublin; and **Druid's Glen** (☎287 3600; www.druidsglen.ie; green fee €180), 45km south of the city in County Wicklow.

Spectator Sport

Sport has a special place in the Irish psyche, probably because it's one of the few occasions when an overwhelming expression of emotion won't cause those around you to wince or shuffle in discomfort. Sit in a pub while a match is on and watch the punters foam at the mouth as they yell pleasantries at the players on the screen, such as 'they should pay me for watching you!'

GAELIC FOOTBALL & HURLING

Gaelic games are at the core of Irishness; they are enmeshed in the fabric of Irish life and hold a unique place in the heart of its culture. Of the two main games, football is by far the most popular – and Dublin (www.hill16.ie) is the second-most successful county, after its great rival Kerry. Hurling has traditionally never been as popular, but in recent years the Dublin team has done very well.

The big event in both sports is the All-Ireland championship, a knockout contest that begins in April and ends on the first (for hurling) and third (for football) Sunday in September with the All-Ireland Final, played at a jam-packed **Croke Park** (Clonliffe Rd; ☐3, 11, 11A, 16, 16A or 123 from O'Connell St), which is also where the Dubs play all of their championship matches. The All-Ireland's poorer cousin is the National Football League (there's also a National Hurling League), which runs from February to mid-April. Dublin plays its league matches at **Parnell Park** (Clantarkey Rd, Donnycarney; adult/child €10/7; ☐20A, 20B, 27, 27A, 42, 42B, 43 or 103 from Lower Abbey St or Beresford Pl), which is smaller and infinitely less impressive than Croke Park but a great place to see these games up close. Tickets for league games can be easily bought at the ground; tickets for All-Ireland matches get tougher to find the further on the competition is, but those that are available can be bought at the **GAA Ticket Office** (☎01-865 8657; 53A Dorset St).

FOOTBALL

Although Dubliners are football-mad, the five Dublin teams that play in the **League of Ireland** (www.leagueofireland.com) are semi-pro, as the best players are all drawn to the glamour of the English Premier League. The season runs from April to November; tickets are available at all grounds.

The national side plays its home games at the world-class **Aviva Stadium** (Map p254; ☎01-647 3800; www.avivastadium.ie; 11-12 Lansdowne Rd); a relatively high pricing structure and the general mediocrity of the team means that home matches don't usually sell out and you can buy tickets (€30 to €60) from the **Football Association of Ireland** (FAI; ☎01-676 6864; www.fai.ie).

RUGBY

Rugby is a big deal in certain parts of Dublin – generally the more affluent neighbourhoods of south Dublin – but the successes of both provincial side Leinster and the national team have catapulted rugby to the forefront of sporting obsessions.

Three-time European champions Leinster play home games at the **Royal Dublin Society Showgrounds** (RDS Showground; Map p254; ☎01-668 9878; Merrion Rd, Ballsbridge). Tickets for both competitions are available at **Elvery's** (Map p240; ☎01-679 4142; Suffolk St) and at its branch on **Dawson St** (Map p240; ☎01-679 1141; Dawson St); at the Spar opposite the Donnybrook Rugby Ground; or online from the **Irish**

Rugby Football Union (IRFU; Map p254; ☎01-660 0779; www.irishrugby.ie; 62 Lansdowne Rd) or **Leinster Rugby** (www.leinsterrugby.ie).

The premier competition is the yearly Six Nations championship, played between February and April by Ireland, England, France, Italy, Scotland and Wales. Home matches are played at the Aviva Stadium; tickets are available from the IRFU.

HORSE & GREYHOUND RACING

Horse racing is a big deal in Dublin, especially when you consider that Irish trainers are amongst the best in the world and Irish jockeys dominate the field in British racing. There are several racecourses within driving distance of the city centre that host good quality meetings throughout the year. These include the **Curragh** (☎04-544 1205; www.curragh.ie; County Kildare), which hosts five classic flat races between May and September; **Fairyhouse** (☎01-825 6167; www.fairyhouse.ie; County Meath; admission €14-22;

🚌special from Busáras), home of the Grand National on Easter Monday; and **Leopardstown** (☎01-289 3607; www.leopardstown.com; 🚌special from Eden Quay), where the big event is February's Hennessy Gold Cup. The flat racing season runs from March to November, while the National Hunt season – when horses jump over things – is October to April. There are also events in summer.

Traditionally the poor-man's punt, greyhound racing (the dogs) has been smartened up in recent years and partly turned into a corporate outing. It offers a cheaper alternative to horse racing. Dublin's two dog tracks are **Harold's Cross Park** (☎01-497 1081; www.igb.ie; 151 Harold's Cross Rd; adult/child €10/6; ⏱6.30-10.30pm Mon, Tue & Fri; 🚌16 or 16A from city centre) and **Shelbourne Park** (Map p254; ☎01-668 3502, on race nights 01-202 6601; www.igb.ie; Bridge Town Rd, Ringsend; adult/child €10/6; ⏱7-10.30pm Wed, Thu & Sat; 🚌3, 7, 7A, 8, 45 or 84 from city centre).

Explore Dublin

DUBLIN'S
TOP SIGHTS

Neighbourhoods at a Glance

❶ Grafton Street & Around p50

The bustling heart of the city centre revolves around pedestrianised Grafton St and the warren of streets around it. Within its easily walkable confines, this neighbourhood is where most of the action takes place, where you'll find the biggest range of pubs and restaurants, and where most Dubliners come

to blow off some retail steam. Many of the city's most important sights and museums are here, as is Dublin's best-loved city park, St Stephen's Green.

❷ Merrion Square & Around p78

Genteel, sophisticated and elegant, the exquisite Georgian architecture spread around

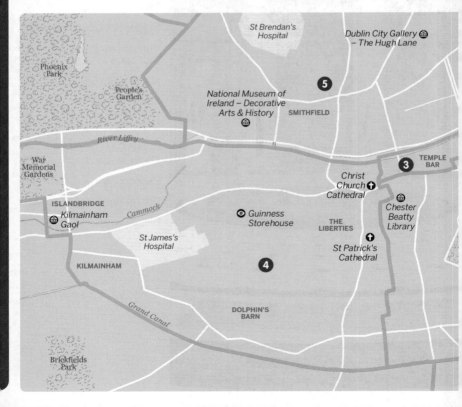

handsome Merrion Sq is a near-perfect mix of imposing public buildings, museums, and private offices and residences. It is round these parts that much of moneyed Dublin works and plays, amid the neoclassical beauties thrown up during Dublin's 18th-century prime. Beauties such as the home of the Irish parliament at Leinster House and, immediately surrounding it, the National Gallery, the main branch of the National Museum of Ireland and the Natural History Museum.

❸ Temple Bar p92

Many weekend visitors will barely venture beyond the cobbled borders of Dublin's so-called 'cultural quarter,' such is the nature of the distractions on offer. Temple Bar is all about fun – mostly in the pubs – and on summer evenings the party spills out onto the street, lending the whole place something of a carnival atmosphere. There are plenty of restaurants here too as well as some interesting art galleries and shops that do provide a change of pace.

❹ Kilmainham & the Liberties p100

Dublin's oldest and most traditional neighbourhoods would scarcely attract any visitors were it not for the presence of the Guinness Brewery, which dominates the city centre's western edge and is home to its most visited museum. Dublin's two medieval cathedrals are here too, while further west are the country's premier modern-art museum and a historic site that is worth every effort to visit.

❺ North of the Liffey p120

Grittier than its more genteel southside counterpart, the neighbourhoods immediately north of the River Liffey offer a fascinating mix of 18th-century grandeur, traditional city life and the multicultural melting pot that is contemporary Dublin. Beyond its widest, most elegant boulevard you'll find art museums and whiskey museums, bustling markets and some of the best ethnic eateries in town. Oh, and Europe's largest enclosed park – home to the president, the US Ambassador and the zoo.

❻ Docklands & the Grand Canal p142

If it was built in the last 15 years, chances are it's in the docklands (jokingly called 'Canary Dwarf' in reference to London's own dockland development), east of the city centre towards Dublin Bay. The most interesting area is around Grand Canal Dock, just south of the Liffey, which is home to affluent apartment dwellers, a handful of nice eateries and the city's biggest theatre, designed by Daniel Libeskind.

NEIGHBOURHOODS AT A GLANCE

Grafton Street & Around

Neighbourhood Top Five

❶ Basking quietly in the aesthetic glow of the magnificent collection at the **Chester Beatty Library** (p60), one of the finest museums in Ireland.

❷ Staring in wonderment at the colourful pages of the *Book of Kells*, the world's most famous illuminated gospel, before visiting the majestic Long Room of the **Old Library** (p53) at **Trinity College** (p52).

❸ Enjoying a sunny, summer afternoon on the grass in **St Stephen's Green** (p61), where Dubliners come to rest, romance and remind themselves of what makes life worth living.

❹ Exploring the marvellous collection of donated historical objects in the **Little Museum of Dublin** (p63).

❺ Indulging in a night out: dinner in one of the area's fabulous **restaurants** (p64) followed by a pint or more in a **pub** (p69), such as **Kehoe's** (p71).

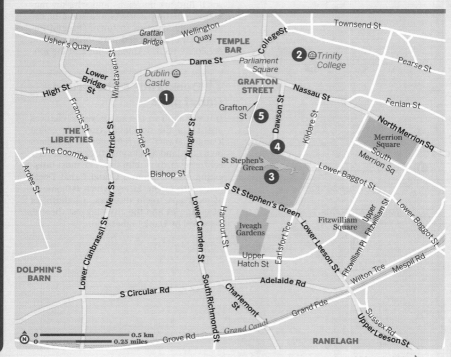

For more detail of this area see Map p238 and p240 ➡

Explore Grafton Street & Around

Grafton St and its surrounding precinct are something of a flexible feast of activities and sights, but it'll take you two days to even begin to do them justice – and much longer if you really want to get to the heart of what this part of the city is all about. The main attraction is Trinity College, whose pleasures and treasures can be explored in no more than a couple of hours; right on its doorstep is Grafton St itself, always worth an amble for a little retail experience or just to take in the sound of one of its many buskers. Just south of Grafton St is the centrepiece of Georgian Dublin, St Stephen's Green, beautifully landscaped and dotted with statuary that provides a veritable who's who of Irish history. But to really get the most out of the neighbourhood, you'll need to get off Grafton St and into the warren of narrow lanes and streets to the west of it – here you'll find a great mix of funky shops and boutiques, some of our favourite eateries, and a handful of the best bars in the city. Further west again is Dublin Castle and the Chester Beatty Library, both of which can be explored in half a day. Thankfully, Dublin's compact size means you don't have to stay here to have it all at your doorstep, but if you do, be aware that most of the lodgings are among the priciest in town.

Local Life

→ **Hangouts** Grogan's Castle Lounge (p70) is the artiest of the city's bohemian pubs; the Stag's Head (p69) is a Victorian classic; sit at the window in hip Clement & Pekoe (p69) and watch the fashion parade outside.

→ **Retail** Costume (p75) is the place for high-end women's fashions; wander the boutiques of the Powerscourt Townhouse (p77) for quirky one-offs and local fashions.

→ **Sustenance** Damson Diner (p66) is home to the best cheeseburger in town; buzzy Coppinger Row (p66) has a terrific Mediterranean menu.

→ **Markets** Every Thursday you can load up on goodies at the small Coppinger Row Market (p30).

Getting There & Away

→ **Bus** All cross-city buses make their way to – or through, at least – this part of the city.

→ **Tram** The Luas Green Line has its terminus at the south end of Grafton St, on the west side of St Stephen's Green.

Lonely Planet's Top Tip

The most interesting shops in town are in the warren of streets between Grafton St and South Great George's St; here you'll also find some of the best lunch deals.

Best Places to Eat

→ Damson Diner (p66)
→ Honest to Goodness/ Push 88 (p64)
→ Fade Street Social (p66)
→ Thornton's (p68)

For reviews, see p64

Best Places to Drink

→ Stag's Head (p69)
→ Hogan's (p70)
→ No Name Bar (p69)
→ Long Hall (p70)

For reviews, see p69

Best Places to Shop

→ Sheridan's Cheesemongers (p76)
→ Costume (p75)
→ George's St Arcade (p77)
→ Powerscourt Townhouse Shopping Centre (p77)

For reviews, see p74

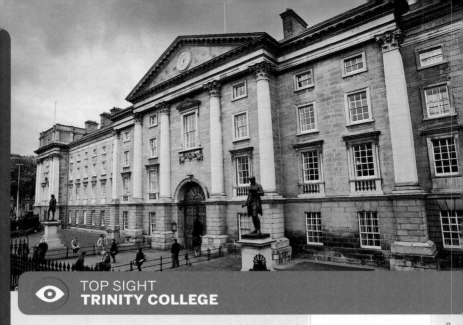

DAVID SOANES PHOTOGRAPHY/GETTY IMAGES ©

TOP SIGHT
TRINITY COLLEGE

This calm and cordial retreat from the bustle of contemporary Dublin is not just Ireland's most prestigious university, but a throwback to those far-off days when a university education was the preserve of a very small elite who spoke passionately of the importance of philosophy and the need for empire.

Today's alumni are an altogether different bunch, but Trinity still looks the part, and on a summer's evening, when the crowds thin and the chatter subsides, there are few more delightful places to be.

A great way to see the grounds is on a **walking tour** (Map p240; ☑01-896 1827; admission €5, incl Book of Kells €10; ⊘every 40min 10.15am-3.40pm Mon-Sat, 10.15am-3pm Sun mid-May–Sep), which depart from the College Green entrance.

DON'T MISS...
- ⇒ Long Room
- ⇒ *Book of Kells*
- ⇒ Science Gallery
- ⇒ Walking Tour

PRACTICALITIES
- ⇒ Map p240
- ⇒ ☑01-896 1000
- ⇒ www.tcd.ie
- ⇒ ⊘8am-10pm
- ⇒ ▣all city centre

History
The college was established by Elizabeth I in 1592 on land confiscated from an Augustinian priory in an effort to stop the brain drain of young Protestant Dubliners, who were skipping across to Continental Europe for an education and were becoming 'infected with popery'. Trinity went on to become one of Europe's most outstanding universities, producing a host of notable graduates – how about Jonathan Swift, Oscar Wilde and Samuel Beckett at the same alumni dinner?

It remained completely Protestant until 1793, but even when the university relented and began to admit Catholics, the Church forbade it; until 1970, any Catholic who enrolled here could consider themselves excommunicated.

Front Square & Parliament Square
The elegant **Regent House entrance** on College Green is guarded by statues of the writer Oliver Goldsmith (1730-74) and the orator Edmund Burke (1729-97). The railings outside are a popular meeting spot.

Through the entrance, past the Students Union, are Front Sq and Parliament Sq, the latter dominated by the 30m-high **Campanile**, designed by Edward Lanyon and erected from 1852 to 1853 on what was believed to be the centre of the monastery that preceded the college. According to superstition, students who pass beneath it when the bells toll will fail their exams. To the north of the Campanile is a **statue of George Salmon**, the college provost from 1886 to 1904, who fought bitterly to keep women out of the college. He carried out his threat to permit them in 'over his dead body' by dropping dead when the worst happened. To the south of the Campanile is a **statue of historian WEH Lecky** (1838–1903).

Chapel & Dining Hall

North of Parliament Sq is the 1799 **Chapel** (Map p240; ☏896 1260), designed by William Chambers and featuring fine plasterwork by Michael Stapleton, Ionic columns and painted-glass windows. It has been open to all denominations since 1972 and is only accessible by organised tour. Next is the **Dining Hall** (Map p240; Parliament Sq; ⊘closed to public), originally built by Richard Cassels in the mid-18th century. The great architect must have had an off day because the vault collapsed twice and the entire structure was dismantled 15 years later. The replacement was completed in 1761, but extensively restored after a fire in 1984.

Library Square & the Old Library

On the far east of Library Sq, the red-brick **Rubrics Building** (Map p240) dates from around 1690, making it the oldest building in the college. Extensively altered in an 1894 restoration, it underwent serious structural modification in the 1970s.

If you are following the less studious-looking throng, you'll find yourself drawn south of Library Sq to the **Old Library** (Map p240; Library Sq), home to Trinity's prize possession and biggest crowd-puller, the astonishingly beautiful *Book of Kells*.

Upstairs is the highlight of Thomas Burgh's building, the magnificent 65m **Long Room** (Map p240; East Pavilion, Library Colonnades; adult/student/child €9/8/free; ⊙9.30am-5pm Mon-Sat year-round, noon-4.30pm Sun Oct-Apr, 9.30am-4.30pm Sun May-Sep) with its barrel-vaulted ceiling. It's lined with shelves containing 200,000 of the library's oldest manuscripts, busts of scholars, a 14th-century harp and an original copy of the Proclamation of the Irish Republic.

BOOK OF KELLS

The world-famous *Book of Kells*, dating from around AD 800 and thus one of the oldest books in the world, was probably produced by monks at St Colmcille's Monastery on the remote island of Iona. It contains the four gospels of the New Testament, written in Latin, as well as prefaces, summaries and other text. If it were merely words, the *Book of Kells* would simply be a very old book – it's the extensive and amazingly complex illustrations (the illuminations) that make it so wonderful. The superbly decorated opening initials are only part of the story, for the book has smaller illustrations between the lines. For more information on this incredible manuscript's history, see p62.

The Long Room's unlikeliest film appearance was in *Star Wars Episode II: Attack of the Clones*, as the Jedi Archive, complete with barrel-vaulted ceiling and similar statuary.

STEP INTO THE PAST

Ireland's most prestigious university, founded on the order of Queen Elizabeth I in 1592, is an architectural masterpiece, a cordial retreat from the bustle of modern life in the middle of the city. Step through its main entrance and you step back in time, the cobbled stones transporting you to another era, when the elite discussed philosophy and argued passionately in favour of empire.

Standing in Front Square, the 30m-high **Campanile 1** is directly in front of you with the **Dining Hall 2** to your left. On the far side of the square is the Old Library building, the centrepiece of which is the magnificent **Long Room 3**, which was the inspiration for the computer-generated imagery of the Jedi Archive in *Star Wars Episode II: Attack of the Clones*. Here you'll find the university's greatest treasure, the **Book of Kells 4**. You'll probably have to queue to see this masterpiece, and then only for a brief visit, but it's very much worth it.

Just beyond the Old Library is the very modern **Berkeley Library 5**, which nevertheless fits perfectly into the campus' overall aesthetic: directly in front of it is the distinctive **Sphere Within a Sphere 6**, the most elegant of the university's sculptures.

DON'T MISS

➡ Douglas Hyde Gallery, the campus' designated modern art museum

➡ Cricket match on pitch, the most elegant of pastimes

➡ Pint in the Pavilion Bar, preferably while watching the cricket

➡ Visit to the Science Gallery, where science is made completely relevant

Campanile
Trinity College's most iconic bit of masonry was designed in the mid-19th century by Sir Charles Lanyon; the attached sculptures were created by Thomas Kirk.

Chapel

Main Entrance

Dining Hall
Richard Cassels' original building was designed to mirror the Examination Hall directly opposite on Front Square: the hall collapsed twice and was rebuilt from scratch in 1761.

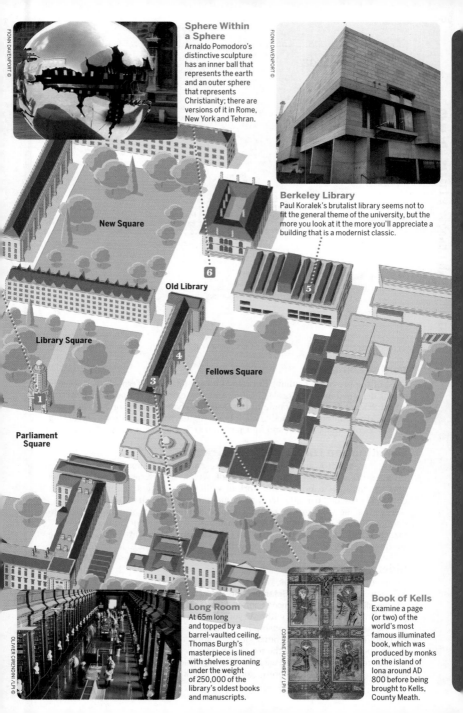

Sphere Within a Sphere
Arnaldo Pomodoro's distinctive sculpture has an inner ball that represents the earth and an outer sphere that represents Christianity; there are versions of it in Rome, New York and Tehran.

Berkeley Library
Paul Koralek's brutalist library seems not to fit the general theme of the university, but the more you look at it the more you'll appreciate a building that is a modernist classic.

New Square

Old Library

Library Square

Fellows Square

Parliament Square

Long Room
At 65m long and topped by a barrel-vaulted ceiling, Thomas Burgh's masterpiece is lined with shelves groaning under the weight of 250,000 of the library's oldest books and manuscripts.

Book of Kells
Examine a page (or two) of the world's most famous illuminated book, which was produced by monks on the island of Iona around AD 800 before being brought to Kells, County Meath.

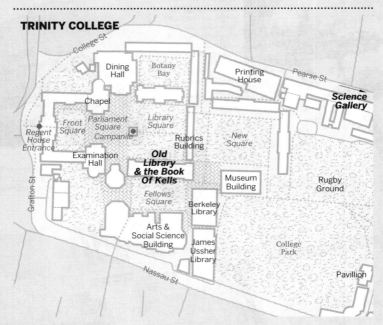

Fellows' Square

West of the brutalist, brilliant **Berkeley Library** (Map p240; Fellows' Sq; ☻closed to public), designed by Paul Koralek in 1967 and now closed to the public, the Arts & Social Science Building is home to the **Douglas Hyde Gallery**, one of the country's leading contemporary galleries. It hosts regularly rotating shows presenting the works of top-class Irish and international artists across a range of media.

Examination Hall & College Park

On the way back towards the main entrance, past the Reading Room, is the late-18th-century Palladian **Examination Hall**, which closely resembles the chapel opposite because it too was the work of William Chambers. It contains an oak chandelier rescued from the Irish parliament (now the Bank of Ireland).

Towards the eastern end of the complex, **College Park** is a lovely place to lounge around on a sunny day and occasionally you'll catch a game of cricket, a bizarre sight in Ireland. Keep in mind that **Lincoln Place Gate** is located in the southeast corner of the grounds, providing a handy shortcut to Merrion Sq.

Science Gallery

Although part of the campus, you'll have to walk along Pearse St to get into Trinity's newest attraction, the **Science Gallery** (www.sciencegallery.ie; Pearse St; ☻exhibitions usually noon-8pm Tue-Fri, noon-6pm Sat & Sun) `FREE`. Since opening in 2008, it has proven immensely popular with everyone for its refreshingly lively and informative exploration of the relationship between science, art and the world we live in. Exhibits have touched on a range of fascinating topics including the science of desire and an exploration of the relationship between music and the human body. The ground-floor **Flux Café** (Pearse St; ☻8am-8pm Tue-Fri, noon-6pm Sat & Sun), bathed in floor-to-ceiling light, is a pretty good spot to take a load off.

STEFAN DAMM/HUBER/4CORNERS ©

TOP SIGHT
DUBLIN CASTLE

If you're looking for a medieval castle straight out of central casting you'll be disappointed; the stronghold of British power here for 700 years is principally an 18th-century creation that is more hotch-potch palace than turreted castle.

History

Only the Record Tower survives from the original Anglo-Norman fortress, which was built in the early 13th century and served as the centre of English colonial administration until 1922.

When Henry VIII's firm-handed representative in Ireland, Lord Deputy Henry Sidney, took charge in 1565, he declared the castle to be 'ruinous, foul, filthy and great decayed' – and he wasn't far wrong. Until then most of the king's deputies in Ireland had been Anglo-Irish lords who preferred living in their own castles than taking up residence at Dublin Castle, and so it fell into disrepair. Sidney oversaw a 13-year building program that saw the construction of a 'a verie faire house for the Lord Deputie or Chief Governor to reside in' as well as a new chapel and the Clock Tower.

Sidney's new castle became the permanent residence of the monarch's chief representative – known at different times as the Justiciar, Chief Lieutenant, Lord Lieutenant or Viceroy – until the construction of the vice-regal lodge in the Phoenix Park in 1781 (now Áras an Uachtaráin, the residence of the President).

The new castle reflected the changing status of English power in Ireland – Henry's conquest of the whole island ('beyond the Pale') and his demolition of the old Anglo-Irish hegemony resulted in the castle no longer being a colonial outpost but the seat of English power and the administrative centre for all of Ireland – a new role that brought with it a huge civil service.

DON'T MISS...

➡ Chapel Royal
➡ State Apartments
➡ View from Bedford Tower

PRACTICALITIES

➡ Map p238
➡ ☏01-677 7129
➡ www.dublincastle.ie
➡ Dame St
➡ adult/child €4.50/2
➡ ⏱10am-4.45pm Mon-Sat, noon-4.45pm Sun
➡ 🚌50, 54, 56A, 77, 77A

JUSTICE FOR ALL?

The Figure of Justice that faces Dublin Castle's Upper Yard from the Cork Hill entrance has a controversial history. The statue was seen as a snub by many Dubliners, who felt Justice was symbolically turning her back on the city. If that wasn't enough, when it rained the scales would fill with water and tilt, rather than remaining perfectly balanced. Eventually a hole was drilled in the bottom of each pan, restoring balance, sort of.

During British rule, the castle's social calendar was busiest for the six weeks leading up to St Patrick's Day with a series of lavish dinners, levées and balls for the city's aristocratic residents – even during the Famine years.

The Irish parliament met in the Great Hall, which burnt down (along with most of the rest of the castle) in the great fire of 1684 – the parliament eventually moved in 1731 to what is now the Bank of Ireland building in College Green.

Below ground, the castle dungeons were home to the state's most notorious prisoners, including – most famously – 'Silken' Thomas Fitzgerald, whose defeated challenge to Henry VIII in 1534 kicked off Henry's invasion of Ireland in the first place. Needless to say, the native Irish came to view the castle as the most menacing symbol of their oppressed state.

When it was officially handed over to Michael Collins on behalf of the Irish Free State in 1922, the British viceroy is reported to have rebuked Collins for being seven minutes late. Collins replied, 'We've been waiting 700 years, you can wait seven minutes.' The castle is now used by the Irish government for meetings and functions, and can only be visited on a guided tour.

Chapel Royal

As you walk in to the grounds from the main Dame St entrance, there's a good example of the evolution of Irish architecture: on your left is the **Victorian Chapel Royal** (occasionally part of the Dublin Castle tours), decorated with more than 90 heads of various Irish personages and saints carved out of Tullamore limestone. The interior is wildly exuberant, with fan vaulting alongside quadripartite vaulting, wooden galleries, stained glass and lots of lively looking sculpted angels.

Record Tower

Beside the Victorian Chapel Royal is the **Norman Record Tower**, which has 5m-thick walls and now houses the **Garda Museum**, which follows the history of the Irish police force. It doesn't have all that much worth protecting, but the views are fab (ring the bell for entry). On your right is the **Georgian Treasury Building**, the oldest office block in Dublin, and behind you, yikes, is the uglier-than-sin **Revenue Commissioners Building** of 1960.

Upper Yard

Heading away from the eyesore that is the Revenue Commissioners Building, you ascend to the Upper Yard. On your right is a **Figure of Justice** with her back turned to the city, reckoned by Dubliners to be an appropriate symbol for British justice. Next to it is the 18th-century **Bedford Tower**, from which the Irish Crown Jewels were stolen in 1907 and never recovered. Opposite is the entrance to the tours.

DUBLIN CASTLE

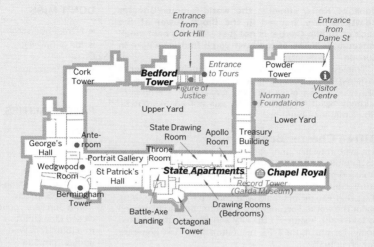

Guided Tours

The 45-minute **guided tours** (departing every 20 to 30 minutes, depending on numbers) are pretty dry, seemingly pitched at tourists more likely to ooh and aah over period furniture than historical anecdotes, but they're included in the entry fee. You get to visit the **State Apartments**, many of which are decorated in dubious taste. There are beautiful chandeliers (ooh!), plush Irish carpets (aah!), splendid rococo ceilings, a Van Dyck portrait and the throne of King George V. You also get to see **St Patrick's Hall**, where Irish presidents are inaugurated and foreign dignitaries toasted, and the room in which the wounded James Connolly was tied to a chair while convalescing after the 1916 Easter Rising – brought back to health to be executed by firing squad.

The highlight is a visit to the **subterranean excavations** of the old castle, discovered by accident in 1986. They include foundations built by the Vikings (whose long-lasting mortar was made of ox blood, eggshells and horse hair), the hand-polished exterior of the castle walls that prevented attackers from climbing them, the steps leading down to the moat and the trickle of the historic River Poddle, which once filled the moat on its way to join the Liffey.

⊙ TOP SIGHT
CHESTER BEATTY LIBRARY

Book of Kells, shmells...the world-famous Chester Beatty Library, housed in the Clock Tower at the back of Dublin Castle, is not just Ireland's best small museum, but one of the best you'll find anywhere in Europe.

This extraordinary collection, so lovingly and expertly gathered by New York mining magnate Alfred Chester Beatty – a man of exceedingly good taste – is breathtakingly beautiful and virtually guaranteed to impress. How's that for a build-up?

Alfred Chester Beatty

An avid traveller and collector, Alfred Chester Beatty (1875–1968) was fascinated by different cultures and amassed more than 20,000 manuscripts, rare books, miniature paintings, clay tablets, costumes and any other objets d'art that caught his fancy and could tell him something about the world. Fortunately for Dublin, he also happened to take quite a shine to the city and made it his adopted home. In return, the Irish made him their first honorary citizen in 1957.

Art of the Book

The collection is spread over two levels. On the ground floor you'll find the Art of the Book, a compact but stunning collection of artworks from the Western, Islamic and East Asian worlds. Highlights include the finest collection of Chinese jade books in the world and illuminated European texts featuring exquisite calligraphy that stand up in comparison with the *Book of Kells*. Audiovisual displays explain the process of bookbinding, paper-making and printing.

Sacred Traditions

The 2nd floor is home to Sacred Traditions, a wonderful exploration of the world's major religions through decorative and religious art, enlightening text and a cool cultural-pastiche video at the entrance. The collection of Qu'rans dating from the 9th to the 19th centuries (the library has more than 270 of them) is considered by experts to be the best example of illuminated Islamic texts in the world. There are also outstanding examples of ancient papyri, including renowned Egyptian love poems from the 12th century, and some of the earliest illuminated gospels in the world, dating from around AD 200. The collection is rounded off with some exquisite scrolls and artwork from China, Japan, Tibet and Southeast Asia, including the two-volume Japanese *Chogonka Scroll*, painted in the 17th century by Kano Sansetu.

The Building

As if all of this wasn't enough for one visit, the library also hosts temporary exhibits that are usually too good to be missed. Not only are the contents of the museum outstanding, but the layout, design and location are also unparalleled, from the marvellous Silk Road Café (p66) and gift shop, to the Zen rooftop terrace and the beautiful landscaped garden out the front. These features alone would make this an absolute Dublin must-do.

DON'T MISS...

➡ Nara e-hon scrolls
➡ Ibn al-Bawwab Qu'ran
➡ New Testament papyri

PRACTICALITIES

➡ Map p238
➡ ☏01-407 0750
➡ www.cbl.ie
➡ Dublin Castle
➡ ⊙10am-5pm Mon-Fri, 11am-5pm Sat, 1-5pm Sun year-round, closed Mon Oct-Apr, free tours 1pm Wed, 3pm & 4pm Sun
➡ ⊒50, 51B, 77, 78A or 123

 SIGHTS

TRINITY COLLEGE   HISTORIC BUILDING
See p52.

DUBLIN CASTLE   HISTORIC BUILDING
See p57.

CHESTER BEATTY LIBRARY   MUSEUM
See p60.

ST STEPHEN'S GREEN   PARK
Map p238 (☺dawn-dusk) As you watch the assorted groups of friends, lovers and individuals splaying themselves across the nine elegantly landscaped hectares of St Stephen's Green, consider that those same hectares once formed a common for public whippings, burnings and hangings. These days, the harshest treatment you'll get is the warden chucking you off the green for playing football or Frisbee.

The buildings around the square date mainly from the mid-18th century, when the green was landscaped and became the centrepiece of Georgian Dublin. The northern side was known as the Beaux Walk and it's still one of Dublin's most esteemed stretches, home to Dublin's original society hotel, the **Shelbourne**. Nearby is the tiny **Huguenot Cemetery**, established in 1693 by French Protestant refugees.

Railings and locked gates were erected in 1814, when an annual fee of one guinea was charged to use the green. This private use continued until 1877 when Sir Arthur Edward Guinness pushed an act through parliament opening the green to the public once again. He also financed the central park's gardens and ponds, which date from 1880.

The main entrance to the green today is beneath **Fusiliers' Arch** (Map p240), at the top of Grafton St. Modelled to look like a smaller version of the Arch of Titus in Rome, the arch commemorates the 212 soldiers of the Royal Dublin Fusiliers who were killed fighting for the British in the Boer War (1899–1902).

Across the road from the western side of the green is the 1863 **Unitarian Church** (Map p238; ☺worship 7am-5pm) and the early-19th-century **Royal College of Surgeons** (Map p238), which has one of the finest facades on St Stephen's Green. During the 1916 Easter Rising, the building was occupied by rebel forces led by Countess Markievicz (1868–1927). The columns are scarred from the bullet holes.

Spread across its bucolic lawns and walkways are some notable artworks, beginning with one of the **Countess** (Map p238) in the southeast corner. Guinness money built the park, so Sir Arthur has also been immortalised, with an 1892 statue on the park's western side. Just north of here, outside the railings, is a statue of Irish patriot Robert Emmet (1778–1803), who was born across the road where numbers 124 and 125 stand; his actual birthplace has been demolished. The statue was placed here in 1966 and is a replica of an Emmet statue in Washington, DC. There is also a bust of poet James Clarence Mangan (1803–49) and a curious 1967 **statue of WB Yeats** (Map p238) by Henry Moore. The centre of the park has a **garden for the blind** (Map p238; St Stephen's Green, Southside), complete with signs in Braille and plants that can be handled. There is also a **statue of the Three Fates** (Map p238), presented to Dublin in 1956 by West Germany in gratitude for Irish aid after WWII. In the corner closest to the Shelbourne Hotel is a **monument to Wolfe Tone** (Map p238), the leader of the abortive 1798 invasion; the vertical slabs serving as a backdrop to Wolfe Tone's statue have been dubbed 'Tonehenge'. At this entrance is a **memorial** (Map p238) to all those who died in the Famine.

On the eastern side of the green is a **children's playground** (Map p238) and to the south there's a fine old **bandstand**, erected to celebrate Queen Victoria's jubilee in 1887. Musical performances often take place here in summer. Near the bandstand is a **bust of James Joyce** (Map p238), facing Newman House (p62), part of University College Dublin (UCD), where Joyce was once a student. On the same side as Newman House is **Iveagh House**. Originally designed by Richard Cassels in 1730 as two separate houses, they were bought by Benjamin Guinness in 1862 and combined to create the family's city residence. After independence the house was donated to the Irish State and is now home to the Department of Foreign Affairs.

Of the many illustrious streets fanning from the green, the elegant Georgian Harcourt St has the most notable addresses. Edward Carson was born at No 4 in 1854. As the architect of Northern Irish unionism, he was never going to be the most popular figure in Dublin, but he did himself no

THE PAGE OF KELLS

The history of the *Book of Kells* (p53) is almost as fascinating as its illuminations. It is thought to have been created around AD 800 by the monks at St Colmcille's Monastery on Iona, a remote island off the coast of Scotland. Repeated looting by marauding Vikings forced the monks to flee to Kells, County Meath, along with their masterpiece. It was stolen in 1007, then rediscovered three months later buried underground. The *Book of Kells* was brought to Trinity College for safekeeping in 1654, and is now housed in the Old Library (p53), with half a million visitors queueing up to see it annually. The 680-page (340-folio) book was rebound in four calf-skin volumes in 1953.

And here the problems begin. Of the 680 pages, only two are on display – one showing an illumination, the other showing text – hence the 'page of Kells' moniker. No getting around that one, though: you can hardly expect the right to thumb through a priceless treasure at random. No, the real problem is its immense popularity, which makes viewing it a rather unsatisfactory pleasure. Punters are herded through the specially constructed viewing room at near lightning pace, making for a quick-look-and-move-along kind of experience.

To really appreciate the book, you can get your own reproduction copy for a mere €22,000. Failing that, the Old Library bookshop stocks a plethora of souvenirs and other memorabilia, including Otto Simm's excellent *Exploring the Book of Kells* (€12.95), a thorough guide with attractive colour plates, and a popular DVD showing all 680 pages for €31.95.

favours acting as the prosecuting attorney during Oscar Wilde's trial for homosexuality. George Bernard Shaw lived at No 61.

NEWMAN HOUSE   NOTABLE BUILDING
Map p238 (85-86 St Stephen's Green South; adult €5; ☺tours noon, 2pm, 3pm & 4pm Tue-Fri Jun-Aug; ◻10, 11, 13, 14 or 15A, ◻St Stephen's Green) One of the finest examples of Georgian architecture open to the public are these two townhouses, founded by Cardinal Newman as the Catholic University of Ireland in 1865. The alma mater of James Joyce, Pádraig Pearse and Éamon de Valera can be visited by **guided tour**.

The college was founded as an alternative to the Protestant hegemony of Trinity College, which was the only option available to those seeking third-level education in Ireland. Newman House is still part of the college, which later decamped to the suburb of Belfield and changed its name to University College Dublin.

The house comprises two exquisitely restored townhouses; No 85, the granite-faced original, was designed by Richard Cassels in 1738 for parliamentarian Hugh Montgomery, who sold it to Richard Chapel Whaley, MP, in 1765. Whaley wanted a grander home, so he commissioned another house next door at No 86.

Aside from Cassels' wonderful design, the highlight of the building is the plasterwork, perhaps the finest in the city. For No 85, the artists were the Italian stuccodores Paolo and Filipo LaFranchini, whose work is best appreciated in the wonderfully detailed Apollo Room on the ground floor. The plasterwork in No 86 was done by Robert West, but it is not quite up to the high standard of next door.

When the newly founded, Jesuit-run Catholic University of Ireland took possession of the house in 1865, alterations were made to some of the more graphic plasterwork, supplying the nude figures with 'modesty vests'.

During Whaley's residency, the house developed certain notoriety, largely due to the activities of his son, Buck, a notorious gambler and hell-raiser who once walked all the way to Jerusalem for a bet and somehow connived to have himself elected to parliament at the tender age of 17. During the university's tenure, however, the residents were a far more temperate lot. The Jesuit priest and wonderful poet Gerard Manley Hopkins lived here during his time as professor of classics, from 1884 until his death in 1889. Hopkins' bedroom is preserved as it would have been during his residence, as is the classroom where the young James

Joyce studied while obtaining his Bachelor of Arts degree between 1899 and 1902.

NEWMAN UNIVERSITY CHURCH CHURCH

Map p238 (☎01-478 0616; www.university church.ie; 83 St Stephen's Green South; ◷8am-6pm; ◻10, 11, 13, 14 or 15A, ◻St Stephen's Green) Cardinal Newman didn't care too much for the Gothic style of his day, so the 1856 church attached to his Catholic University of Ireland at Newman House is a neo-Byzantine charmer. Its richly decorated interior was mocked at first but has since become the preferred surroundings for Dublin's most fashionable weddings.

LITTLE MUSEUM OF DUBLIN MUSEUM

Map p240 (☎01-661 1000; www.littlemuseum. ie; 15 St Stephen's Green North; adult/student/child €6/5/4; ◷10am-5pm Mon-Fri) The idea is ingeniously simple: a museum, spread across two rooms of an elegant Georgian building, devoted to the history of Dublin in the 20th century, made up of memorabilia contributed by the general public. You don't need to know anything about Irish history or Dublin to appreciate it: visits are by guided tour and everyone is presented with a handsome booklet on the history of the city.

Since opening in 2011, the contributions have been impressive – amid the nostalgic posters, time-worn bric-a-brac and wonderful photographs of personages and cityscapes of yesteryear are some extraordinary finds, including a lectern used by JFK on his 1963 visit to Ireland and an original copy of the fateful letter given to the Irish envoys to the treaty negotiations of 1921, whose contradictory instructions were at the heart of the split that resulted in the Civil War. There's also a new cafe on the premises.

IVEAGH GARDENS GARDENS

Map p238 (◷dawn-dusk year-round; ◻all city centre, ◻St Stephen's Green) These beautiful gardens may not have the sculpted elegance of the other city parks, but they never get too crowded and the warden won't bark at you if you walk on the grass. They were designed by Ninian Niven in 1863 as the private grounds of **Iveagh House**, and include a rustic grotto, cascade, fountain, maze and rosarium. Enter the gardens from Clonmel St, off Harcourt St.

MANSION HOUSE NOTABLE BUILDING

Map p240 (Dawson St; ◻all city centre, ◻St Stephen's Green) Built in 1710 by Joshua Dawson – after whom the street is named – this has been the official residence of Dublin's mayor since 1715, and was the site of the 1919 Declaration of Independence and the meeting of the first parliament. The building's original brick Queen Anne style has all but disappeared behind a stucco facade added in the Victorian era.

ROYAL IRISH ACADEMY LIBRARY

Map p240 (☎01-676 2570; www.ria.ie; 19 Dawson St; ◷10am-5.30pm Mon-Thu, 10am-5pm Fri; ◻all city centre, ◻St Stephen's Green) **FREE** Ireland's pre-eminent society of letters has an 18th-century library that is home to several important documents, including a collection of ancient manuscripts such as the *Book of Dun Cow;* the *Cathach of St Columba;* and the entire collection of 19th-century poet Thomas Moore (1779–1852).

BANK OF IRELAND NOTABLE BUILDING

Map p240 (☎01-671 1488; College Green; ◷10am-4pm Mon-Fri, 10am-5pm Thu; ◻all city centre) A sweeping Palladian pile occupying one side of College Green, this magnificent building was the Irish Parliament House until 1801 and is the first purpose-built parliament building in the world. The original building, the central colonnaded section that distinguishes the present-day structure, was designed by Sir Edward Lovett Pearce in 1729 and completed by James Gandon in 1733.

When the parliament voted itself out of existence through the 1801 Act of Union, the building was sold under the condition that the interior would be altered to prevent it ever again being used as a debating chamber. It was a spiteful strike at Irish parliamentary aspirations, but while the central House of Commons was remodelled and offers little hint of its former role, the smaller **House of Lords** (admission free) chamber survived and is much more interesting. It has Irish oak woodwork, a mahogany longcase parliament clock and a late-18th-century Dublin crystal chandelier. Its design was copied for the construction of the original House of Representatives in Washington, DC, now the National Statuary Hall. There are tours of the House of Lords (10.30am, 11.30am and 1.45pm Tuesday), by Dublin historian and author Éamon MacThomás, which

COLLEGE GREEN STATUARY

The imposing grey sculptures adorning **College Green** (Map p240) are monuments to two of Ireland's most notable patriots. In front of the bank is Henry Grattan (1746–1820), a distinguished parliamentary orator, while nearby is a modern memorial to the patriot Thomas Davis (1814–45). Where College St meets Pearse St, another traffic island is topped by a 1986 sculpted copy of the *Steyne* (the Viking word for 'stone'), which was erected on the riverbank in the 9th century to stop ships from grounding and removed in 1720.

include a talk as much about Ireland and life in general as the building itself, whose exterior was the inspiration for the British Museum in London.

WHITEFRIARS STREET
CARMELITE CHURCH   CHURCH

Map p240 (☎01-475 8821; 56 Aungier St; ⏰8am-6.30pm Mon & Wed-Fri, 8am-9.30pm Tue, 8am-7pm Sat, 8am-7.30pm Sun; 🚌16, 19, 19A, 83 or 122 from Trinity College) If you find yourself mulling over the timing of a certain proposal – or know someone who needs some prompting – walk through the automated glass doors of this church and head for the remains of none other than St Valentine, donated by Pope Gregory XVI in 1836.

The Carmelites returned to this site in 1827, when they re-established their former church, which had been seized by Henry VIII in the 16th century. In the northeastern corner is a 16th-century Flemish oak statue of the Virgin and Child, believed to be the only wooden statue in Ireland to have escaped the Reformation unscathed.

CITY HALL   MUSEUM

Map p238 (www.dublincity.ie; Castle St; adult/student/child €4/2/1.50; ⏰10am-5.15pm Mon-Sat; 🚌all city centre) One of the architectural triumphs of the Dublin boom was the magnificent restoration of City Hall, originally built by Thomas Cooley as the Royal Exchange between 1769 and 1779, and botched in the mid-19th century when it became the offices of the local government. Thankfully, the more recent restoration has restored it to its gleaming Georgian best.

The rotunda and its ambulatory form a breathtaking interior, bathed in natural light from enormous windows to the east. A vast marble statue of former mayor and Catholic emancipator Daniel O'Connell stands here as a reminder of the building's links with Irish nationalism (the funerals of both Charles Stewart Parnell and Michael Collins were held here). Dublin City Council still meets here on the first Monday of the month, gathering to discuss the city's business in the Council Chamber, which was the original building's coffee room.

There was a sordid precursor to City Hall in the shape of the Lucas Coffee House and the adjoining Eagle Tavern, in which the notorious Hellfire Club was founded by Richard Parsons, Earl of Rosse, in 1735. Although the city abounded with gentlemen's clubs, this particular one gained a reputation for messing about in the arenas of sex and Satan, two topics that were guaranteed to fire the lurid imaginings of the city's gossipmongers.

The striking vaulted basement hosts a multimedia exhibition **The Story of the Capital**, which traces the history of the city from its earliest beginnings to its hoped-for future – with ne'er a mention of sex, Satan or sex with Satan. More's the pity, as the info is quite overwhelming and the exhibits are a little text-heavy. Still, it's a pretty slick museum with informative audiovisual displays.

IRISH-JEWISH MUSEUM   MUSEUM

Map p238 (☎01-453 1797; www.jewishmuseum.ie; 3 Walworth Rd; ⏰11am-3.30pm Sun-Thu May-Sep, 10.30am-2.30pm Sun, 11am-3pm Mon Oct-Apr) Housed in an old synagogue, this museum recounts the history and cultural heritage of Ireland's small but prolific Jewish community. It was opened in 1985 by the Belfast-born, then-Israeli president, Chaim Herzog. The various memorabilia includes photographs, paintings, certificates, books and other artefacts.

 **EATING**

HONEST TO
GOODNESS/PUSH 88   RESTAURANT €

Map p240 (www.honesttogoodness.ie; 12 Dame Court; mains €6-12) Downstairs, Honest to Goodness serves wholesome sandwiches, tasty soups and a near-legendary Sloppy

Joe. Upstairs, Push 88 is Honest after dark, specialising in meatballs dished a whole variety of ways – with salad, sweet potato mash or between two slices of homemade bread. Great food and great fun in a terrific atmosphere (helped along by the upstairs bar).

FALLON & BYRNE
DELI €

Map p240 (www.fallonandbyrne.com; Exchequer St; mains €5-10; ⊙8am-9pm Mon-Wed, 8am-10pm Thu & Fri, 9am-9pm Sat, 11am-7pm Sun) Dublin's answer to the American Dean and Deluca chain is this upmarket food hall and wine cellar, which is where discerning Dubliners come to buy their favourite cheeses and imported delicacies, as well as get a superb lunch-to-go from the deli counter. Sandwiches and a range of excellent dishes from lamb cous cous to vegetarian lasagne have transformed desktop dining forever. Upstairs is an elegant **brasserie** (Map p240; ☑01-472 1000; ⊙lunch & dinner) that serves Irish-influenced Mediterranean cuisine.

BRIOCHE
FRENCH €

Map p240 (www.brioche.ie; 65 Aungier St; dishes €4.50-8; ⊙8am-5pm Mon-Sat & 5.30-10pm Tue-Sat) By day, this is a regular cafe that serves excellent sandwiches and coffee. By night it is Brioche Ce Soir, where classically trained chef Gavin McDonagh engages the full range of his skills with a series of French tasting plates, all made with locally sourced ingredients and served in a wonderful brasserie atmosphere. A hidden treat.

CRAVE
SANDWICHES €

Map p240 (79 South Great George's St; sandwiches €4.95-6.95; ⊙9am-5pm Mon-Wed, 10am-8pm Thu-Sat; ☎) A new arrival on the scene, this lovely cafe opted for a 'downtown baroque' decor and a menu that specialises in gourmet pitta sandwiches. Our favourite is the pittalicious (Parma ham and gorgonzola) served with a rocket-and-cous-cous salad. Linger a while and take advantage of the free wi-fi.

BOTTEGA TOFFOLI
ITALIAN €

Map p238 (34 Castle St; sandwiches & salads €9-12; ⊙8am-4pm Tue & Wed, to 9pm Thu & Fri, 11am-8pm Sat, 1-8pm Sun) Tucked away on a side street that runs alongside Dublin Castle is this superb Italian cafe, the loving creation of its Irish-Italian owners. Terrific

sandwiches (beautifully cut prosciutto, baby tomatoes and rocket salad drizzled with imported olive oil on homemade *piadina* bread) and its pizzas are as good as any you'd get out of a Neapolitan oven.

NEON
ASIAN €

Map p238 (☑01-405 2222; www.neon17.ie; 17 Camden St; mains €10-12; ⊙noon-11pm, delivery from 5pm) A brilliant new spot that specialises in authentic Asian street food from Thailand and Vietnam, served in takeaway boxes, which you can eat at home or in the canteen-style dining room. Hardened palates can jump right into the super-spicy *pad ki mow* noodles; more delicate tastebuds can live with a delicious massaman curry. They also deliver.

LEMON
PANCAKES €

Map p240 (66 South William St; pancakes from €4.50; ⊙9am-7pm Mon-Sat, 10am-6pm Sun) Dublin's best pancake joint has branches on both sides of Grafton St, one on South William and the other on **Dawson St** (Map p240; 61 Dawson St). Each serves up a wide range of sweet and savoury crêpes – those paper-thin ones stuffed with a variety of goodies and smothered in toppings – along with super coffee in a buzzy atmosphere that is popular with literally everyone.

BEWLEY'S GRAFTON STREET CAFE
INTERNATIONAL €

Map p240 (☑01-672 7720; Bewley's Bldg, Grafton St; mains €10-14; ⊙breakfast, lunch & dinner; ☐all city centre) Dublin's most famous cafe was founded in 1840 and is a tourist attraction in its own right, drawing visitors in with its elegant main room and its magnificent set of stained-glass windows by Harry Clarke (1889–1931). The food – a selection of pizzas, burgers and sandwiches – is decent, but it's really just about savouring a nice cup of tea.

SIMON'S PLACE
CAFE €

Map p240 (George's St Arcade, South Great George's St; sandwiches €5; ⊙9am-5.30pm Mon-Sat; ☑) Simon hasn't had to change the menu of doorstep sandwiches and wholesome vegetarian soups since he first opened shop more than two decades ago – and why should he? His grub is as heartening and legendary as he is. It's a great place to sip a coffee and watch life go by in the old-fashioned arcade.

Seated at its wooden tables you'll usually find a fine and interesting selection of the city's bohemian set: downstairs is dingy and appropriately popular with Goths and other types with an aversion to sunlight.

LISTONS
SANDWICHES €

Map p238 (www.listonsfoodstore.ie; 25 Camden St; lunch €5-12; ⊗9am-6.30pm Mon-Fri, 10am-6pm Sat) The lunchtime queues streaming out the door of this place are testament to its reputation as Dublin's best deli. Its sandwiches (with fresh and delicious fillings), roasted-vegetable quiches, rosemary potato cakes and sublime salads will have you coming back again and again – the only problem is there's too much choice! On fine days, take your gourmet picnic to the nearby Iveagh Gardens.

GREEN NINETEEN
IRISH €

Map p238 (⊋01-478 9626; www.green19.ie; 19 Lower Camden St; mains €10-14; ⊗10am-11pm Mon-Sat, noon-6pm Sun) A firm favourite on Camden St's corridor of cool is this sleek restaurant that specialises in locally sourced, organic grub – without the fancy price tag. Braised lamb chump, corned beef, pot roast chicken and the ubiquitous burger are but the meaty part of the menu, which also includes salads and vegie options. We love it.

SILK ROAD CAFÉ
MIDDLE EASTERN €

Map p238 (Chester Beatty Library, Dublin Castle; mains €11; ⊗11am-4pm Mon-Fri) Museum cafes don't often make you salivate, but this vaguely Middle Eastern–North African–Mediterranean gem on the ground floor of the Chester Beatty Library is the exception. Complementing the house specialities including Greek moussaka and spinach lasagne are daily specials such as *djaj mehshi* (chicken stuffed with spices, rice, dried fruit, almonds and pine nuts). All dishes are halal and kosher.

BRETZEL BAKERY
FOOD €

Map p238 (⊋01-475 2724; www.bretzel.ie; 1a Lennox St; ⊗8.30am-3pm Mon, 8.30am-6pm Tue, Wed & Fri, 8.30am-7pm Thu, 9am-5pm Sat, 9am-1pm Sun; ⌷14, 15, 65 or 83) The bagels might be a bit on the chewy side, but they've got their charms – as do the scrumptious selections of breads, savoury snacks, cakes and biscuits that have locals queuing out the door on weekends. Recertified as kosher since 2003, the bakery has been on this Portobello site since 1870.

GOURMET BURGER KITCHEN
BURGERS €

Map p240 (www.gbkinfo.com; burgers €9-13) With three city-centre branches – including **South Anne St** and Temple Bar (p95) – GBK's assault on the burger market is almost complete, as customers can't get enough of its various offerings. Try the Kiwiburger – a beef burger topped with beetroot, egg, pineapple, cheese, salad and relish. They also have decent vegie options.

DAMSON DINER
AMERICAN FUSION €€

Map p240 (www.damsondiner.com; 52 South William St; mains €12.50-25; ⊗noon-midnight) Behind the glass-fronted entrance is a superb new eatery, where the menu offers up a mix of Asian dishes (fennel *bhaji*, *ssam* duck or pork) and American classics (Boston chowder, chilli con carne). Damson is also home to the best cheeseburger in town, where the beef is *stuffed* with cheese. Great food, great fun and superb music.

FADE STREET SOCIAL
MODERN IRISH €€

Map p240 (⊋01-604 0066; www.fadestreet social.com; Fade St; mains €19-29, tapas €8-12; ⊗lunch & dinner Mon-Fri, dinner Sat & Sun) Two eateries in one, courtesy of renowned chef Dylan McGrath: at the front, the buzzy Gastro Bar, which serves up gourmet tapas from a beautiful open kitchen. At the back, the more muted Restaurant does Irish cuts of meat – from veal to rabbit – served with home-grown, organic vegetables. Designed to impress; it does. Reservations suggested.

COPPINGER ROW
MEDITERRANEAN €€

Map p240 (www.coppingerrow.com; Coppinger Row; mains €18-25; ⊗noon-5.30pm & 6-11pm Mon-Sat, 12.30-4pm & 6-9pm Sun) Virtually all of the Mediterranean basin is represented on the ever-changing, imaginative menu. Choices include the likes of pan-fried sea bass with roast baby fennel, tomato and olives; or rump of lamb with spiced aubergine and dried apricots. A nice touch are the filtered still and sparkling waters (€1), where 50% of the cost goes to cancer research.

777
MEXICAN €€

Map p240 (www.777.ie; 7 Castle House, South Great George's St; mains €16-28; ⊗5.30-10pm Mon-Wed, 5.30-11pm Thu, 5pm-midnight Fri & Sat, 2-10pm Sun) You won't eat better, more authentic Mexican cuisine than here – the *tostados* and *taquitos* are great nibbles, or the perfect accompaniment for a tequila fest (they serve 22 different types); the mains are all prepared on a wood-burning grill and include a sensation tuna steak and a mouth-watering Iberico pork flank.

DUNNE & CRESCENZI
ITALIAN €€

Map p240 (www.dunneandcrescenzi.com; 14-16 South Frederick St; 3-course evening menu €30; 7.30am-10pm Mon-Sat, 9am-10pm Sun) This exceptional Italian eatery delights its regulars with a basic menu of rustic pleasures, such as panini, a single pasta dish and a superb plate of mixed antipasto drizzled in olive oil. It's always full, and the tables are just that little bit too close to one another, but the coffee is perfect and the desserts are sinfully good.

YAMAMORI
JAPANESE €€

Map p240 (01-475 5001; www.yamamorinoodles.ie; 71 South Great George's St; mains €16-25, lunch bento €9.95; 12.30-11pm;) Hip, inexpensive and generally pretty good, Yamamori rarely disappoints with its bubbly service and vivacious cooking that swoops from sushi and sashimi to whopping great plates of noodles, with plenty in between. The lunch bento is one of the best deals in town and draws them in from offices throughout the area.

It's a great spot for a sociable group – including vegetarians – although you'll have to book at the weekend to be one of the happy campers. There's another branch north of the river.

WAGAMAMA
JAPANESE €€

Map p240 (South King St; mains €11-17; 11am-11pm) There's ne'er a trace of raw fish to be seen, but this popular chain dishes up some terrific Japanese food nonetheless. Production-line rice and noodle dishes served pronto at canteen-style tables mightn't seem like the most inviting way to dine, but boy this food is good, and the basement it's served up in is surprisingly light and airy – for a place with absolutely no natural light.

AVOCA
CAFE €€

Map p240 (www.avoca.ie; 11-13 Suffolk St; mains €11-14) The waiters are easy on the eye for a reason: the upstairs cafe of the city's best designer crafts store has long been the favourite spot of the Ladies Who Lunch. Designer bags can get very heavy, so there's nothing better to restore flagging energy than the simple, rustic delights on offer: organic shepherd's pie, roast lamb with couscous, or sumptuous salads from the Avoca

kitchen. There's also a takeaway salad bar and hot-food counter in the basement.

INDIE DHABA
INDIAN €€

Map p240 (www.dhaba.ie; Anne's La, 21-26 South Anne St; tapas €7.25-14.25; lunch & dinner;) This is Indian food like you've never had it before, mouth-watering tapas served in an airy, modern setting. Which is the real surprise, given you're two floors below ground. The menu is incredibly broad – we enjoyed the *sigriwala bhateyr* (tamarind-and-peanut-stuffed quail) and the *hiran ka soola* (venison tenderloin). There's plenty of vegetarian options too.

GOOD WORLD
CHINESE €€

Map p240 (18 South Great George's St; dim sum €4-6, mains €12-19; 12.30pm-2.30am) The hands-down winner of our best-Chinese-restaurant competition, the Good World has two menus, but to really get the most of this terrific spot, steer well clear of the Western menu and its unimaginative dishes. With listings in two languages, the Chinese menu is packed with dishes and delicacies that keep us coming back for more.

PICHET
FRENCH €€

Map p240 (01-677 1060; www.pichetrestaurant.ie; 14-15 Trinity St; mains €17-29; lunch & dinner) TV chef Nick Munier and Stephen Gibson (formerly of L'Ecrivain) deliver their version of modern French cuisine to this elongated dining room replete with blue leather chairs and lots of windows to stare out of. The result is pretty good indeed, the food excellent – we expected nothing less – and the service impeccable. Sit in the back for atmosphere.

ODESSA
MEDITERRANEAN €€

Map p240 (01-670 7634; www.odessa.ie; 13 Dame Ct; dinner mains €15-28 ; lunch & dinner) Odessa and the hangover brunch go hand in hand like Laurel and Hardy. But this stylish eatery's dining credentials have long been maintained by its excellent dinner menu, which combines solid favourites including the homemade burger with more adventurous dishes such as roast fillet of hake served with chorizo, clams, white-bean stew and serrano ham.

SABA
ASIAN FUSION €€

Map p240 (01-679 2000; www.sabadublin.com; 26-28 Clarendon St; mains €13-23; lunch & dinner) The name means 'happy meeting place' and this Thai-Vietnamese fusion restaurant is just that, a very popular eatery with Dubliners who tuck into a wide selection of Southeast Asian dishes and test the limits of the cocktail menu. The atmosphere is all designer cool, the fare a tad shy of being genuinely authentic, but it's a good night out.

CAFÉ MAO
VIETNAMESE, THAI €€

Map p240 (☎01-670 4899; www.cafemao.com; 2-3 Chatham St; mains €12-19; ⊙to 10.30pm; ▣all city centre) Mao's often spicy mix of Vietnamese and Thai specialities, cooked to order and served with a musical soundtrack that declares its super-cool credentials, is one of the city's most successful restaurants. You can feast on the likes of *nasi goreng* and *bulkoko* here or at its other spots in the **Dundrum Town Centre** (☎01-296 2802; The Mill Pond, Dundrum Town Centre) and **Dun Laoghaire** (☎01-214 8090; The Pavilion Seafront).

BITE
SEAFOOD €€

Map p240 (www.bitedublin.com; 29 South Frederick St; mains €15-23; ⊙5-11pm Tue-Sat, noon-4.30pm & 5-11pm Fri-Sat) Locally sourced fish and shellfish are the main draw at this elegant little restaurant; the other is the relatively small menu, which means that the appropriate amount of care and attention is given to everything they serve – start with the popcorn laced in squid oil and work your way up to Malcolm Starmer's fresh lobster burger.

GREEN HEN
FRENCH €€

Map p240 (☎01-670 7238; www.greenhen.ie; 33 Exchequer St; mains €19-26; ⊙lunch & dinner Mon-Fri, brunch & dinner Sat & Sun) New York's Soho meets Parisian brasserie at this stylish eatery, where elegance and economy live side-by-side. If you don't fancy gorging on oysters or tucking into a divine Irish Hereford rib-eye, you can opt for the *plat du jour* or avail of the early-bird menus; watch out for their killer cocktails. Reservations recommended for dinner.

CHEZ MAX
FRENCH €€

Map p240 (☎01-633 7215; 1 Palace St; mains €13-19; ⊙from 7.30am; ▣50, 54, 56A, 77 or 77A) Guarding the main gate to Dublin Castle is a French cafe that is Gallic through and through, from the fixtures imported from gay Paree to the beautiful, sultry staff who ignore you until they're ready and then turn the sexy pout into a killer smile. The lunchtime *tartines* – basically open sandwiches –

are good enough to get us misty-eyed for Montmartre. They've recently opened a sister restaurant on Baggot St (p88).

BRASSERIE SIXTY6
FUSION €€

Map p240 (www.brasseriesixty6.com; 66 South Great George's St; mains €18-31; ⊙8am-11.30pm Mon-Sat, from 11am Sun) This New York–style brasserie's speciality is rotisserie chicken, done four different ways at any given time. Its meat-heavy menu also includes the likes of lamb shank and a particularly good bit of liver. For that special occasion, there's a whole roast pig (€300), but you need to order seven days in advance and be in a group of eight.

L'GUEULETON
FRENCH €€

Map p240 (www.lgueuleton.com; 1 Fade St; mains €19-26; ⊙12.30-4pm & 6-10pm Mon-Sat, 1-4pm & 6-9pm Sun) Dubliners have a devil of a time pronouncing the name (which means 'a gluttonous feast' in French) and have had their patience tested with the no-reservations-get-in-line-and-wait policy, but they just can't get enough of this restaurant's robust (read: meaty and filling) take on French rustic cuisine that makes twisted tongues and sore feet a small price to pay.

PIG'S EAR
MODERN IRISH €€

Map p240 (☎01-670 3865; www.thepigsear.com; 4-5 Nassau St; mains €18-26; ⊙lunch & dinner Mon-Sat; ▣all city centre) Looking over the playing fields of Trinity College – which counts as a view in Dublin – this fashionably formal restaurant is spread over two floors and is renowned for its exquisite and innovative Irish cuisine, including dishes such as slow-cooked pig belly and ox cheek cooked in stout. Trust us, it tastes better than it sounds.

THORNTON'S
FRENCH €€€

Map p240 (☎01-478 7000; www.thorntonsres taurant.com; 128 West St Stephen's Green; midweek 3-course lunch €45, dinner tasting menus €76-120; ⊙12.30-2pm & 7-10pm Tue-Sat) Chef Kevin Thornton's culinary genius is to take new French cuisine and give it a theatrical, Irish once-over: the result is a Michelin-starred, wonderful mix of succulent seafood dishes and meatier fare including noisette of milk-fed Wicklow lamb. A nice touch is when Kevin himself comes out to greet his guests and explain his creations. Reservations are essential.

TWO FOR TEA

You can get a cup of tea anywhere, but these are places where tea – in all its myriad infusions – is that little bit special (and they do a great coffee too).

CLEMENT & PEKOE · CAFE

Map p240 (www.clementandpekoe.com; 50 South William St; ⊙8am-7pm Mon-Fri, 10am-6pm Sat, noon-6pm Sun) Our favourite cafe in town is this hipster version of an Edwardian tearoom. Walnut floors, art-deco chandeliers and wall-to-wall displays of handsome tea jars are the perfect setting to enjoy the huge selection of loose leaf teas and carefully made coffees, all for around €3. It's the kind of place you'd find in Brooklyn.

WALL & KEOGH · CAFE

Map p238 (www.wallandkeogh.ie; 45 Richmond St South; ⊙8.30am-8.30pm Mon-Fri, 11am-7pm Sat & Sun) The Irish love their tea, and this marvellous new cafe is the place to enjoy your choice of 150 different types of them, served in ceramic Japanese teapots with all the care of a traditional tea ceremony. They also serve fabulous coffee and, if you're peckish, sandwiches, baked goods and even sushi.

SHANAHAN'S ON THE GREEN · STEAKHOUSE €€€

Map p238 (☏01-407 0939; www.shanahans.ie; 119 West St Stephen's Green; mains €46-49; ⊙from 6pm Sat-Thu, from noon Fri) 'American-style steakhouse' hardly does justice to this elegant restaurant where JR Ewing and his cronies would happily have done business. Although the menu features seafood, this place is all about meat, notably the best cuts of impossibly juicy and tender Irish Angus beef you'll find anywhere. The mountainous onion rings are the perfect accompaniment, while the sommeliers are experts.

CLIFF TOWNHOUSE · IRISH €€€

Map p238 (☏01-638 3939; www.theclifftownhouse.com; 22 North St Stephen's Green; mains €19-35; ⊙noon-2.30pm & 6-11pm Mon-Sat, noon-4pm & 6-10pm Sun) Sean Smith's menu is a confident expression of the very best of Irish cuisine – Warrenpoint fish pie, organic fillet of pork and a loin of venison share the menu with a masterful fish and chips.

TROCADERO · INTERNATIONAL €€€

Map p240 (☏01-677 5545; www.trocadero.ie; 3 St Andrew's St; mains €19-31.50; ⊙dinner Mon-Sat; ☐all city centre) As old school as a Dublin restaurant gets, this art-deco classic has been the social hub of the city's theatrical world for 50 years, a favourite of thespians and other luminaries. It's more of a nostalgia trip now, but the food remains uniformly good – a bunch of classics solidly made – as does the terrific atmosphere.

 # DRINKING & NIGHTLIFE

Amid the designer shops and trendy eateries of the Grafton St area, a few top-notch Victorian pubs combine elegance and traditional style to pull in punters from far and near. Dawson St is popular with straight professional types, the area immediately west of Grafton St has something for everyone, and trendy Wexford and Camden Sts tick the arty, alternative box.

STAG'S HEAD · PUB

Map p240 (1 Dame Ct) The Stag's Head was built in 1770, remodelled in 1895 and thankfully not changed a bit since then. It's a superb pub: so picturesque that it often appears in films and also featured in a postage-stamp series on Irish bars. A bloody great pub, no doubt.

NO NAME BAR · BAR

Map p240 (3 Fade St) A low-key entrance just next to the trendy French restaurant L'Gueuleton leads upstairs to one of the nicest bar spaces in town, consisting of three huge rooms in a restored Victorian townhouse plus a sizeable heated patio area for smokers. There's no sign or a name – folks just refer to it as the No Name Bar or, if you're a real insider, Number 3.

37 DAWSON ST · CONTEMPORARY BAR

Map p240 (☏01-672 8231; www.37dawsonstreet.ie; 37 Dawson St; ☐all city centre) Antiques, eye-catching art and elegant bric-a-brac adorn this new bar that has quickly established itself as a favourite with the trendy crowd. At the back is the new Whiskey Bar, a '50s-style bar that Don Draper would feel comfortable sipping a fine scotch at; upstairs is an elegant restaurant that serves a terrific brunch.

ANSEO
BAR

Map p238 (28 Lower Camden St) Unpretentious, unaffected and incredibly popular, this cosy alternative bar – which is pronounced 'an-*shuh*', the Irish for 'here' – is a favourite with those who live by the credo that to try too hard is far worse than not trying at all. Wearing cool like a loose garment, the punters thrive on the mix of chat and terrific DJs, who dig into virtually every crate to provide the soundtrack, whether it be Peggy Lee or Lee Perry.

HOGAN'S
BAR

Map p240 (35 South Great George's St) Once an old-style traditional bar, Hogan's is now a gigantic boozer spread across two floors. Midweek it's a relaxing hang-out for young professionals and restaurant and bar workers on a night off. But come the weekend the sweat bin downstairs pulls them in for some serious music courtesy of the usually excellent DJs.

LONG HALL
PUB

Map p240 (51 South Great George's St) Luxuriating in full Victorian splendour, this is one of the city's most beautiful and best-loved pubs. Check out the ornate carvings in the woodwork behind the bar and the elegant chandeliers. The bartenders are experts at their craft, an increasingly rare attribute in Dublin these days.

PYGMALION
CONTEMPORARY BAR

Map p240 (☎01-674 6712; www.bodytonicmusic. com; Powerscourt Townhouse Shopping Centre, 59 South William St; ☐all city centre) Currently one of the busiest bars in town, the 'Pyg' caters to a largely student crowd with its €10 pitchers, pounding music and labyrinthine nooks and crannies (perfect for a naughty hideaway). The owner thought it best to line the wall with carpet – perhaps they're worried that the action on the dance floor might get a little too crazy?

GROGAN'S CASTLE LOUNGE
PUB

Map p240 (15 South William St) This place is known simply as Grogan's (after the original

owner), and it is a city-centre institution. It has long been a favourite haunt of Dublin's writers and painters, as well as others from the alternative bohemian set, most of whom seem to be waiting for the 'inevitable' moment when they are finally recognised as geniuses.

DRAGON
GAY BAR

Map p240 (64-65 South Great George's St) High-concept, high-octane and simply loaded with attitude, the Dragon is the slightly trendier alternative to the long-established George down the street (George and the Dragon; get it?). It's more popular with guys than girls, and even then with a certain type of guy – young, brash and unafraid to express themselves...on the dance floor or in the arms of another.

MERCANTILE
CONTEMPORARY BAR

Map p240 (☎01-670 1700; 28 Dame St; ☐all city centre) A big, sprawling bar spread across three floors, the Mercantile's stock-in-trade has been tourists, mostly of the stag-and-hen type, who fill the place at weekends and lend it a party atmosphere, which then attracts local lads and lasses looking for a bit of 'fun'. The music is as loud as the atmosphere is boisterous – you know what to expect!

MARKET BAR
BAR

Map p240 (Fade St) An architectural beauty, this giant redbrick-and-iron-girder room that was once a Victorian sausage factory is now a large, breezy bar that stands as a far more preferable alternative to many of the city's superbars. Unlike virtually every other new pub in town, there's no music. It also does a roaring trade in Spanish-influenced pub grub.

GEORGE
GAY BAR

Map p240 (www.thegeorge.ie; 89 South Great George's St) The purple mother of Dublin's gay bars is a long-standing institution, having lived through the years when it was the only place in town where the gay crowd could, well, be gay. There are other places to go, but the George remains the best, if only for tradition's sake. Shirley's legendary Sunday night bingo is as popular as ever.

GLOBE
BAR

Map p240 (☎01-671 1220; www.globe.ie; 11 South Great George's St; ☐all city centre) The grand-daddy of the city's hipster bars, the Globe has held on to its groover status by virtue of tradition and the fact that the formula is brilliantly simple: wooden floors, plain brick walls and a no-attitude atmosphere that you just can't fake.

BERNARD SHAW
BAR

Map p238 (www.bodytonicmusic.com; 11-12 South Richmond St) This deliberately ramshackle boozer is probably the coolest bar in town for its marvellous mix of music – courtesy of its owners, the Bodytonic production crew, that also runs Twisted Pepper (p139) – and diverse menu of events such as afternoon car-boot sales, storytelling nights and fun competitions, including having a 'tag-off' between a bunch of graffiti artists. This place looks like a dump, but it works because it is the effortless embodiment of the DIY, low-cost fun that is very much the city's contemporary zeitgeist.

BRUXELLES
PUB

Map p240 (7-8 Harry St) Although it has largely shed its heavy metal and alternative skin, Bruxelles is still a raucous, fun place to hang out and there are different music areas. It's comparatively trendy on the ground floor, while downstairs is a great, loud and dingy rock bar with live music each weekend. Just outside, a **bronze Phil Lynott** (Map p240) is there to remind us of Bruxelles' impeccable rock credentials.

DAWSON LOUNGE
PUB

Map p240 (25 Dawson St) To see *the* smallest bar in Dublin, go through a small doorway, down a narrow flight of steps and into two tiny rooms that always seem to be filled with a couple of bedraggled drunks who look like they're hiding. Psst, here's a secret: a certain sunglassed lead singer of a certain ginormous Irish band is said to love unwinding in here from time to time.

INTERNATIONAL BAR
PUB

Map p240 (23 Wicklow St) This tiny pub with a huge personality is a top spot for an afternoon pint. It has a long bar, stained-glass windows, red velour seating and a convivial atmosphere. Some of Ireland's most celebrated comedians stuttered through their first set in the **Comedy Cellar**, which is, of course, upstairs.

KEHOE'S
PUB

Map p240 (9 South Anne St) This is one of the most atmospheric pubs in the city centre and a favourite with all kinds of Dubliners.

It has a beautiful Victorian bar, a wonderful snug, and plenty of other little nooks and crannies. Upstairs, drinks are served in what was once the publican's living room – and looks it!

MCDAID'S
TRADITIONAL PUB

Map p240 (01-679 4395; 3 Harry St; all city centre) One of Dublin's best-known literary pubs, this classic boozer was Brendan Behan's 'local' (until he was barred) and it still oozes character. The pints are perfect, and best appreciated during the day when it's not full of our type. Thankfully, there's no music – just conversation and raucous laughter.

NEARY'S
TRADITIONAL PUB

Map p240 (01-677 8596; 1 Chatham St; all city centre) One of a string of classic Victorian boozers off Grafton St once patronised by Dublin's legless literati, Neary's is a perfect stop-off day or night. It combines great service, a bohemian atmosphere and attractively worn furnishings, and is popular with actors from the nearby Gaiety Theatre.

OLD STAND
TRADITIONAL PUB

Map p240 (01-677 7220; 37 Exchequer St; all city centre) Refreshingly unreconstructed, this is one of the oldest pubs in Dublin and seems to be just sauntering along at the same pace it did 10 years ago, as if the whole Celtic Tiger thing never happened. It's named after the old stand at Lansdowne Rd Stadium, and is a favourite with sports fans and reporters.

PETER'S PUB
TRADITIONAL PUB

Map p240 (01-677 8588; 1 Johnston Pl; all city centre) A pub for a chat and a convivial catch up, this humble and friendly place is more like Peter's Living Room, and is one of the few remaining drinking dens in this area that hasn't changed personality in recent years, and is all the better (and popular) for it.

SWAN
TRADITIONAL PUB

Map p238 (01-647 5272; 70 Aungier St; all city centre) John Lynch's pub (known to all as the Swan) is home to two kinds of punter: the in-for-a-pint-and-a-chat tippler that doesn't venture far from the Victorian front bar; and the more animated younger person, who finds solace and music in the side bar. A beautiful marriage that works because neither troubles the other.

CAFÉ EN SEINE
BAR

Map p240 (01-677 4369; 40 Dawson St; all city centre) The wildly extravagant art-nouveau style of this huge bar has been a massive hit since it first opened in 1995, and while it may not be the 'in' place it once was, it is still very popular with suburbanites, the after-work crowd and out-of-towners. Maybe it's the glass panelling, or the real 12m-high trees; but most likely it's the beautiful people propping up the wood-and-marble bar.

☆ ENTERTAINMENT

WHELAN'S
LIVE MUSIC

Map p238 (01-478 0766; www.whelanslive.com; 25 Wexford St) The traditional pub attached to the popular live-music venue was one of the best places to wind down over a pint and a chat, until it closed its doors for a major refurb. What it'll become is anyone's guess – we just hope that it keeps its old-fashioned ambience.

DEVITT'S
LIVE MUSIC

Map p238 (01-475 3414; 78 Lower Camden St; ⊙from 9.30pm Thu-Sat) Devitt's – aka the Cussak Stand – is one of the favourite places for the city's talented musicians to display their wares, with sessions as good as any you'll hear in the city centre. Highly recommended.

COPPER FACE JACKS
CLUB

Map p238 (www.copperfacejacks.ie; 29-30 Harcourt St, Jackson Court Hotel; admission free-€10; ⊙10.30pm-3am) In rural Ireland you don't go clubbing; you go to 'the disco', and Copper's is the capital's very own version of it, offering unvarnished mayhem to the throngs that want to spend the evening drinking, dancing to familiar tunes and – hopefully – going home accompanied. Purists may scoff, but it's a formula that works a treat judging by its popularity.

LOST SOCIETY
CLUB

Map p240 (01-677 0014; www.lostsociety.ie; Powerscourt Town Centre, South William St; admission €6-10; all city centre) Part of the magnificent 18th-century Powerscourt complex, Lost Society offers two distinct nightlife experiences for the price of one ticket. Upstairs, spread across three levels and a host of rooms, the music is eclectic and the crowd beautifully self-aware. Downstairs is

🏃 Neighbourhood Walk
A Retail Stroll

START GEORGE'S ST ARCADE
FINISH MOLLY MALONE STATUE
LENGTH 1.1KM, TWO HOURS

Dubliners mightn't shop with the same ferocity as they did during the Celtic Tiger, but walk around the Grafton St area on any weekend and you'll bear witness to a city still very much in love with the retail experience.

Start your retail adventure in the ❶ **George's St Arcade** (p77), with its range of interesting stalls selling all kinds of alternative wares. In the midst of all this bohemia, take a look at the beautiful pieces in Barry Doyle Design Jewellers and browse the shelves of Stokes Books.

Exit at the Drury St side and cross onto Castle Market, stopping to browse the high-end women's fashions in ❷ **Costume** (p125) or, if you prefer, the vintage secondhand clothing of ❸ **Harlequin** (p127) next door or ❹ **Jenny Vander** (p127) back around the corner on Drury St.

From Castle Market, cross South William St and enter the ❺ **Powerscourt Townhouse Shopping Centre** (p77), the city's most elegant retail space – inside you'll find cafes, restaurants and a host of wonderful shops, including Article, for homewares and gifts; Bow Boutique, which is run by Irish designers; and, on the top floor, the Design Centre, a top-end boutique.

With arms laden with shopping bags exit the centre back onto South William St and walk south, taking the first left onto Coppinger Row. If it's Thursday, this narrow lane will be lined with ❻ **stalls** selling delicious produce and ready-made goodies; if not, ❼ **Coppinger Row restaurant** (p66) is a great spot for a little lunch refuelling.

Continue east and cross Clarendon St. At the corner with Johnson's Court is ❽ **Magills** (p125), a proper old-fashioned grocer selling cheeses and cold cuts. On Johnson's Court itself, the southern side is lined with jewellery stores, including ❾ **Appleby** (p126);

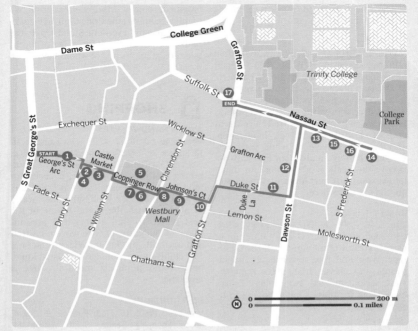

you'll surely find something sparkly worth coveting in the elegant window displays.

Take a left on Grafton St – if you like, you can stop for coffee at the historic **10 Bewley's** (p115) on the corner. Turn right onto Duke St: about 150 yards down on your left is **11 Cathach Books** (p125), the city's most illustrious bookseller, where for the price of a small house you can get your hands on a first edition folio of James Joyce's *Ulysses* (as well as a host of other books). If you want more recently published books, the biggest bookshop in town is **12 Hodges Figgis** (p125), around the corner on Dawson St.

From here walk down to Nassau St and take a right; **13 Blarney Woollen Mills** (p76) is immediately on your right if you're

looking for classic and contemporary Irish woollens; while, further down on the same side is the famous **14 Kilkenny Shop** (p125), which has all kinds of locally produced handicrafts, knits, glassware and silverware.

If you still need to pick up some typically Irish gifts, retrace your tracks back along Nassau St, stopping at **15 House of Names** (p126) where you can get coasters with your family's coat of arms, and **16 Knobs & Knockers** (p76), for that replica Georgian door handle that will go perfectly with your city centre apartment! And finish your walk in sight of Dublin's most famous retailer, **17 Molly Malone**, a statue of which stands at the bottom of Grafton St.

the Bassment, where the music is thumping and the dancing is hot and sweaty.

KRYSTLE — CLUB

Map p238 (☑01-478 4066; www.krystlenight club.com; Russell Court Hotel, 21-25 Harcourt St; ☉Thu-Sat; ☑all city centre, ☑Harcourt/St Stephen's Green) The favourite venue of many a Celtic cub, Krystle (annoyingly pronounced 'cris-*tal*' by its snootiest devotees) is where you'll most likely find the current crop of celebrities and their hangers-on, although you'll have to wade your way through the huge main floor and gain access to the upstairs VIP lounge for maximum exposure. Chart hits and club classics are the mainstay here.

GAIETY THEATRE — THEATRE

Map p240 (☑01-677 1717; www.gaietytheatre.com; South King St) The Gaiety's program of plays is strictly of the fun-for-all-the-family type: West End hits, musicals, Christmas pantos and classic Irish plays keep the more serious-minded away, but it leaves more room for those simply looking to be entertained.

UKIYO — KARAOKE

Map p240 (☑01-633 4071; www.ukiyobar.com; 7-9 Exchequer St; per hr €25; ☑all city centre) The basement rooms of this trendy sake bar can fit up to 10 people each for a night of singalong fun from the 30,000-odd songs on the menu (in a variety of languages).

LILLIE'S BORDELLO — CLUB

Map p240 (☑01-679 9204; www.lilliesbordello.ie; Adam Ct; admission €10-20; ☉11pm-3am) The snootiest club in town prides itself on being the venue of choice for whatever Cristal-swilling superstar is in town. Not that you'll rub shoulders with them, as they'll be safely ensconced in the ultra-VIP Jersey Lil's private members' bar. Take comfort though in having made it past the club's selective door policy. Bad music, bad attitude.

ANDREW'S LANE THEATRE — CLUB

Map p240 (ALT; www.facebook.com/andrews-lanetheatre; 9-17 St Andrews Lane; ☉11pm-3am Thu-Sat) A full-on club venue that is popular with students and younger clubbers. The music is loud, fast and overwhelming.

BANKER'S — COMEDY

Map p240 (☑01-679 3697; 16 Trinity St; admission €8; ☉9-11pm Fri & Sat; ☑all city centre) The basement room of this decent bar hosts two nights of comedy: the Craic Club on Fridays and the usually excellent Stand Up at the Bankers on Saturday nights. There's decent talent on stage – some of whom have made it onto TV.

 # SHOPPING

AVOCA HANDWEAVERS — IRISH CRAFTS

Map p240 (☑01-677 4215; www.avoca.ie; 11-13 Suffolk St; ☉9.30am-6pm Mon-Wed & Sat, 9.30am-7pm Thu & Fri, 11am-6pm Sun) Combining clothing, homewares, a basement food hall and an excellent top-floor cafe, Avoca promotes a stylish but homey brand of modern Irish life – and is one of the best places to find an original present. Many of the garments are woven, knitted and naturally dyed at its Wicklow factory. The children's section, with unusual knits, bee-covered gumboots and dinky toys, is fantastic.

BOW BOUTIQUE — CLOTHING

Map p240 (☑01-707 1763; Powerscourt Townhouse Shopping Centre, South William St; ☉10am-6pm Mon-Wed & Fri, 10am-8pm Thu, 9am-6pm Sat, noon-6pm Sun) The collective brainchild of four Irish designers – Eilis Boyle, Matthew Doody, Margaret O'Rourke and Wendy Crawford – this beautiful new boutique showcases original designs and made-to-measure items, and promotes 'eco-fashion' by stocking fairtrade labels from around the globe such as People Tree and Camilla Nordback.

ARTICLE — HOMEWARES

Map p240 (1st fl, Powerscourt Townhouse Shopping, South William St Centre; ☉10.30am-6pm Mon-Wed, Fri & Sat, 10.30am-7pm Thu, 1-5pm Sun) Beautiful tableware and decorative home accessories all made by Irish designers. Ideal for unique, tasteful gifts.

DESIGN CENTRE — CLOTHING

Map p240 (☑01-679 5718; www.designcentre.ie; Powerscourt Townhouse Shopping Centre, South William St; ☉10am-6pm Mon-Wed & Fri, 10am-8pm Thu, 9.30am-6pm Sat; ☑all city centre) Mostly dedicated to Irish designer womenswear, featuring well-made classic suits, evening wear and knitwear. Irish labels include John Rocha, Philip Treacy, Catherine Deane and Roisín Linnane.

KILKENNY SHOP
IRISH CRAFTS

Map p240 (☑01-677 7066; www.kilkennyshop. com; 6 Nassau St; ⊛8.30am-7pm Mon-Wed & Fri, 8.30am-8pm Thu, 8.30am-6pm Sat, 10am-6pm Sun) A large, long-running repository for contemporary, innovative Irish crafts, including multicoloured, modern Irish knits, designer clothing, Orla Kiely bags and lovely silver jewellery. The glassware and pottery is beautiful and sourced from workshops around the country. A great place to buy presents.

CATHACH BOOKS
BOOKS

Map p240 (☑01-671 8676; www.rarebooks.ie; 10 Duke St; ⊛9.30am-5.45pm Mon-Sat) Our favourite bookshop in the city stocks a rich and remarkable collection of Irish-interest books, with a particular emphasis on 20th-century literature and a large selection of first editions, including rare ones by the big guns: Joyce, Yeats, Beckett and Wilde.

COSTUME
CLOTHING

Map p240 (☑01-679 5200; www.costumedublin. ie; 10 Castle Market) Costume is considered a genuine pacesetter by Dublin's fashionistas; it has exclusive contracts with some of Europe's most innovative designers, such as Isabel Marant and Anna Sui. It also has the city's best range of Tempereley and American Retro. Local designers include Helen James, whose Japanese-influenced obis are enormously popular, and Leighlee.

MAGILLS
FOOD

Map p240 (☑01-671 3830; 14 Clarendon St; ⊛9.30am-5.45pm Mon-Sat; ⊒all city centre) With its characterful old facade and tiny dark interior Magills' old-world charm reminds you how Clarendon St must have once looked. At this family-run place, you get the distinct feeling that every Irish and French cheese, olive oil, packet of Italian pasta and salami was hand-picked.

DUBRAY BOOKS
BOOKS

Map p240 (☑01-677 5568; 36 Grafton St; ⊛9am-7pm Mon-Wed & Sat, 9am-9pm Thu & Fri, 11am-6pm Sun) Three roomy floors devoted to bestsellers, recent releases, coffee-table books and a huge travel section make this one of the better bookshops in town. It can't compete with its larger, British-owned rivals, but it holds its own with a helpful staff and a lovely atmosphere that encourages you to linger.

HODGES FIGGIS
BOOKS

Map p240 (☑01-677 4754; 56-58 Dawson St; ⊛9am-7pm Mon-Wed & Fri, 9am-8pm Thu, 9am-6pm Sat, noon-6pm Sun) The mother of all Dublin bookstores has books on every conceivable subject for every kind of reader spread across its three huge floors, including a substantial Irish section on the ground floor.

STOKES BOOKS
BOOKS

Map p240 (☑01-671 3584; 19 George's St Arcade; ⊛11am-6pm Mon-Sat; ⊒all city centre) A small bookshop specialising in Irish history books, both old and new. Other titles, covering a range of subjects, include a number of beautiful, old, leather-bound editions.

GREAT OUTDOORS
CAMPING & OUTDOORS

Map p240 (☑01-679 4293; www.greatoutdoors.ie; 20 Chatham St; ⊛9.30am-5.30pm Mon-Wed, Fri & Sat, 9.30am-8pm Thu; ⊒all city centre) This is Dublin's best outdoors store, with gear for hiking, camping, surfing, mountaineering, swimming and more. Fleeces, tents, inflatable dinghies, boots and gas cookers – they're all here as well as an info-laden noticeboard and superbly patient staff.

BROWN THOMAS
DEPARTMENT STORE

Map p240 (☑01-605 6666; www.brownthomas. com; 92 Grafton St; ⊛9.30am-8pm Mon, Wed & Fri, 10am-8pm Tue, 9.30am-9pm Thu, 9am-8pm Sat, 11am-7pm Sun) Soak up the Jo Malone–laden rarefied atmosphere of Dublin's most exclusive store, where presentation is virtually artistic. Here you'll find fantastic cosmetics, shoes to die for, exotic homewares and a host of Irish and international fashion labels such as Balenciaga, Stella McCartney, Lainey Keogh and Philip Treacy. The 3rd-floor Bottom Drawer outlet stocks the finest Irish linen you'll find anywhere.

ALIAS TOM
CLOTHING

Map p240 (☑01-671 5443; Duke Lane; ⊛9.30am-6pm Mon-Wed, Fri & Sat, 9.30am-8pm Thu; ⊒all city centre) Dublin's best designer menswear store, where friendly staff guide you through casuals by bling labels Burberry, Prada and whatever else makes for a classy fit. Downstairs it's classic tailored suits and designer shoes.

BT2
CLOTHING

Map p240 (☑01-605 6666; 88 Grafton St; ⊛9.30am-8pm Mon, Wed & Fri, 10am-8pm Tue,

9.30am-9pm Thu, 9am-8pm Sat, 11am-7pm Sun)
The kiddies' table in Brown Thomas' exquisitely laid-out dining room, BT2 is the annexe shop for the city's trendy young things,
targeting an audience that wants to look
the contemporary part and set the tone for
tomorrow. Brands include DKNY, Custom,
Diesel, Ted Baker and Tommy Hilfiger.

LOUIS COPELAND · CLOTHING

Map p240 (☑01-872 1600; www.louiscopeland.
com; 18-19 Wicklow St; ☺9am-5.30pm Mon-Wed,
Fri & Sat, 9am-7.30pm Thu; ☐all city centre) Dublin's answer to the famed tailors of London's
Saville Row, this shop makes fabulous suits
to measure, and stocks plenty of ready-to-
wear suits by international designers.

SHERIDAN'S CHEESEMONGERS · FOOD

Map p240 (☑01-679 3143; www.sheridans
cheesemongers.com; 11 South Anne St; ☺10am-
6pm Mon-Fri, from 9.30am Sat; ☐all city centre)
If heaven were a cheese shop, this would be
it. Wooden shelves are laden with rounds of
farmhouse cheeses, sourced from around
the country by Kevin and Seamus Sheridan,
who have almost single-handedly revived
cheese-making in Ireland. You can taste
any one of the 60 cheeses on display and
pick up some wild Irish salmon, Italian pastas and olives while you're at it.

BLARNEY WOOLLEN MILLS · IRISH CRAFTS

Map p240 (☑01-671 0068; www.blarney.com; 27
Nassau St; ☺9am-6pm Mon-Sat, 11am-6pm Sun;
☐all city centre) This is the Dublin branch of
the best-known Irish shop in the country –
the actual mills are located in County Cork,
within sight of the famous castle and its
gab-bestowing rock. This branch shouldn't
disappoint, with a particularly wide range
of cut crystal, porcelain presents and its
trademark woolly things.

DESIGNYARD · IRISH CRAFTS

Map p240 (☑01-474 1011; 48-49 Nassau St;
☺10am-5.30pm Mon-Wed & Fri, 10am-8pm
Thu, 10am-6pm Sat) A high-end, craft-as-
art shop where everything you see – glass,
batik, sculpture, painting – is one-off and
handmade in Ireland. It also showcases
contemporary jewellery stock from young
international designers. Perfect for that
bespoke engagement ring or a very special
present.

DANKER ANTIQUES · IRISH CRAFTS

Map p240 (☑01-677 4009; www.dankerantiques.
com; 4-5 Royal Hibernian Way; ☺9.30am-5pm
Mon-Sat; ☐all city centre) Chock-full of exquisite treasures, this shop specialises in Irish
and English antique silver, jewellery and
objets d'art. You can find period suites of
antique cutlery, candlesticks and candela-
bra as well as unusual items such as potato
rings – dish rings to insulate tables from
hot bowls.

HOUSE OF NAMES · IRISH CRAFTS

Map p240 (☑01-679 7287; www.houseofnames.
ie; 26 Nassau St; ☺10am-6pm Mon-Wed, Fri &
Sat, 10am-8pm Thu, 11am-6pm Sun; ☐all city
centre) Impress your friends by serving
them drinks on coasters emblazoned with
your family's coat of arms, matching the
sweatshirt you're wearing and, of course,
the glasses or mugs the drinks are served
in. All this and more can be yours from the
House of Names, so long as you have a surname with Irish roots.

KNOBS & KNOCKERS · IRISH CRAFTS

Map p240 (☑01-671 0288; www.knobsandknock
ers.ie; 19 Nassau St; ☺10am-6pm Mon-Wed, Fri
& Sat, 10am-8pm Thu, 11am-6pm Sun; ☐all city
centre) Replica Georgian door knockers
are a great souvenir of your Dublin visit,
but there are plenty of other souvenir door
adornments to look at here.

ANGLES · JEWELLERY

Map p240 (☑01-679 1964; Westbury Mall,
Clarendon St; ☺10am-6pm Mon-Wed, Fri & Sat,
10am-7pm Thu; ☐all city centre) You won't
find Claddagh rings or charm bracelets
here, just cabinets full of handmade, contemporary Irish jewellery, most of it by
up-and-coming Dublin craftspeople. Com-
missions are taken and can be sent on to
you abroad.

APPLEBY · JEWELLERY

Map p240 (☑01-679 9572; 5-6 Johnson's Ct;
☺9.30am-5.30pm Mon-Wed & Fri, 9.30am-7pm
Thu, 9.30am-6pm Sat; ☐all city centre) The best
known of the jewellery shops that line narrow Johnson's Ct, Appleby is renowned for
the high quality of its gold and silver jewellery, which tends towards more conven-
tional designs. This is the place for serious
stuff – diamond rings, sapphire-encrusted
cufflinks and Raymond Weil watches.

BARRY DOYLE
DESIGN JEWELLERS   JEWELLERY
Map p240 (☎01-671 2838; 30 George's St Arcade; ⊗10am-6pm Mon-Wed, Fri & Sat, 10am-7pm Thu; 🚇all city centre) Goldsmith Barry Doyle's upstairs shop is one of the best of its kind in Dublin. The handmade jewellery – using white gold, silver, and some truly gorgeous precious and semiprecious stones – is exceptional in its beauty and simplicity. Most of the pieces have Afro-Celtic influences.

RHINESTONES   JEWELLERY
Map p240 (☎01-679 0759; 18 St Andrew's St; ⊗9am-6.30pm Mon-Wed, Fri & Sat, 9am-8pm Thu, noon-6pm Sun; 🚇all city centre) Exceptionally fine antique and quirky costume jewellery from the 1920s to 1970s, with pieces priced from €25 to €2000. Victorian jet, 1950s enamel, art-deco turquoise, 1930s mother-of-pearl, cut-glass and rhinestone necklaces, bracelets, brooches and rings are displayed in old-fashioned cabinets.

WEIR & SON'S   JEWELLERY
Map p240 (☎01-677 9678; www.weirandsons.ie; 96-99 Grafton St; ⊗9am-5.30pm Mon-Wed, Fri & Sat, 9am-8pm Thu; 🚇all city centre) The largest jeweller in Ireland, this huge store on Grafton St first opened in 1869 and still has its original wooden cabinets and a workshop on the premises. There's new and antique Irish jewellery (including Celtic designs) and a huge selection of watches, Irish crystal, porcelain, leather and travel goods.

WALTON'S   MUSIC
Map p240 (☎01-475 0661; 69-70 South Great George's St; ⊗9am-6pm Mon-Wed, Fri & Sat, 9am-7pm Thu; 🚇all city centre) This is the place to go if you're looking for your very own *bodhrán* (goat-skin drum) or any other musical instrument associated with Irish traditional music. It also has an excellent selection of sheet music and recorded music.

GEORGE'S ST ARCADE   ARCADE
Map p240 (www.georgesstreetarcade.ie; btwn South Great George's St & Drury St; ⊗9am-6.30pm Mon-Wed, Fri & Sat, 9am-8pm Thu, noon-6pm Sun) Dublin's best nonfood market (there's sadly not much competition) is sheltered within an elegant Victorian Gothic arcade. Apart from shops and stalls selling new and old clothes, secondhand books, hats, posters, jewellery and records, there's a fortune teller, some gourmet nibbles and a fish and chipper who does a roaring trade.

WESTBURY MALL   SHOPPING ARCADE
Map p240 (Clarendon St; ⊗10am-6pm Mon-Sat, noon-5pm Sun; 🚇all city centre) Wedged between the five-star Westbury Hotel and the expensive jewellery stores of Johnson's Court, this small mall has a handful of pricey, specialist shops selling everything from Persian rugs to buttons and lace or tasteful children's wooden toys.

POWERSCOURT TOWNHOUSE
SHOPPING CENTRE   SHOPPING MALL
Map p240 (☎01-679 4144; 59 South William St; ⊗10am-6pm Mon-Wed & Fri, 10am-8pm Thu, 9am-6pm Sat, noon-6pm Sun) This absolutely gorgeous and stylish centre is in a carefully refurbished Georgian townhouse, built between 1741 and 1744. These days it's best known for its cafes and restaurants but it also does a top-end, selective trade in high fashion, art, exquisite handicrafts and other chichi sundries.

ST STEPHEN'S GREEN
SHOPPING CENTRE   SHOPPING MALL
Map p240 (☎01-478 0888; West St Stephen's Green; ⊗9am-7pm Mon-Wed, Fri & Sat, 9am-9pm Thu, 11am-6pm Sun) A 1980s version of a 19th-century shopping arcade, the dramatic, balconied interior and central courtyard are a bit too grand for the nondescript chain stores within. There's a Boots, Benetton and large Dunnes Store with supermarket, as well as last-season designer warehouse TK Maxx.

HARLEQUIN   VINTAGE CLOTHING
Map p240 (☎01-671 0202; 13 Castle Market; ⊗10.30am-6pm Mon-Wed, Fri & Sat, 10.30am-7pm Thu; 🚇all city centre) A fantastically cluttered shop, jam-packed with authentic vintage clothing gems from the 1920s onwards, as well as satin gloves, top hats, snakeskin bags and jet-beaded chokers.

JENNY VANDER   CLOTHING
Map p240 (☎01-677 0406; 50 Drury St) This secondhand store oozes elegance and sophistication. Discerning fashionistas and film stylists snap up the exquisite beaded handbags, fur-trimmed coats, richly patterned dresses and costume jewellery priced as if it were the real thing.

Merrion Square & Around

Neighbourhood Top Five

1 Exploring **Merrion Square** (p83), an oasis of calm steeped in Irish history.

2 Perusing the collection at the **National Gallery** (p82).

3 Visiting the antiquated **National Museum of Ireland – Natural History** (p86), which will captivate young and old.

4 Uncovering the fascinating treasures at the **National Museum of Ireland – Archaeology** (p80).

5 A night of music and beer in **O'Donoghue's** (p91) pub

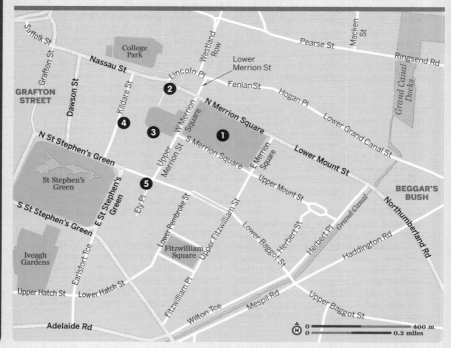

For more detail of this area see Map p244 ➡

Explore Merrion Square & Around

Ireland's national collections of art, history and natural history are to be found in the imposing neoclassical buildings that line the elegant Georgian streets and parks of the city's best-maintained 18th-century neighbourhood. Depending on your level of interest you'll need to devote as much as half a day to each, or just an hour or two if you're only interested in an overview. You'll also want to spend some time looking at the private residences that line Merrion and Fitzwilliam Squares – the many plaques on these Georgian buildings remind us that it was behind these brightly coloured doors that the likes of Oscar Wilde and William Butler Yeats hung their hats. These streets also house the offices of some of the country's most important businesses, so when there's even a hint of sunshine, workers pour out into the various parks, or follow the lead of poet Patrick Kavanagh and lounge along the banks of the Grand Canal. When they clock off, these same workers head to the wonderfully atmospheric and historical pubs of Baggot St and Merrion Row for a couple of scoops of chips and some unwinding banter. There are also some smart restaurants, including several of Dublin's best.

Local Life

⇒ **High Art** The Jack B Yeats collection in the National Gallery (p82) soothes a Dubliner's troubled soul, while the Royal Hibernian Academy (p87) is an excellent showcase of contemporary art. For something a little more affordable, the weekend art market (p83) along the railings of Merrion Square displays surprisingly good-quality work.

⇒ **Beer Power** Follow the power brokers, politicians and business crowd as they unwind in some of the city's best traditional boozers: Toner's (p91) and Doheny & Nesbitt's (p91) are established favourites, but O'Donoghue's (p91) of Merrion Row is in a league of its own.

⇒ **Fine Dining** The critics regularly praise Restaurant Patrick Guilbaud (p88) as the best in the country; whatever debate there is exists as a result of restaurants such as L'Ecrivain (p90). Either way, Messrs Michelin love them both.

Getting There & Away

⇒ **Bus** Most cross-city buses will get you here (or near enough).

⇒ **Train** The most convenient DART stop is Pearse St, with the station entrance on Westland Row.

Lonely Planet's Top Tip

The Vaughan Collection of watercolours by JMW Turner at the **National Gallery** (p82) is only displayed during the month of January, when the light is just right to appreciate the delicacy and beauty of these masterpieces.

 MERRION SQUARE & AROUND

Best Places to Eat

⇒ Restaurant Patrick Guilbaud (p88)
⇒ L'Ecrivain (p90)
⇒ Unicorn (p90)
⇒ Dax (p90)

For reviews, see p88 ⇒

Best Places to Drink

⇒ O'Donoghue's (p91)
⇒ James Toner's (p91)
⇒ Doheny & Nesbitt's (p91)
⇒ Hartigan's (p91)

For reviews, see p90 ⇒

 Best Examples of Irish Art

⇒ Yeats Room (p82)
⇒ Treasury (p80)
⇒ Royal Hibernian Academy (RHA) Gallagher Gallery (p87)

For reviews, see p80 ⇒

TOP SIGHT
NATIONAL MUSEUM OF IRELAND – ARCHAEOLOGY

The mother of all Irish museums and the country's most important cultural institution was established in 1977 as the primary repository of the nation's archaeological treasures.

The collection is so big, however, that it has expanded beyond the walls of this superb purpose-built building next to the Irish parliament into two other separate museums – the **decorative arts and history museum** (p126) at Collins Barracks and a **country life museum** in County Mayo, on Ireland's west coast. They're all fascinating, but the star attractions are to be found here, mixed up in Europe's finest collection of Bronze- and Iron-Age gold artefacts, the most complete collection of medieval Celtic metalwork in the world, fascinating prehistoric and Viking artefacts, and a few interesting items relating to Ireland's fight for independence. If you don't mind groups, the themed guided tours will help you wade through the myriad exhibits.

The Treasury

The Treasury is perhaps the most famous part of the collection, and its centrepieces are Ireland's two most famous crafted artefacts, the **Ardagh Chalice** and the **Tara Brooch**. The 12th-century Ardagh Chalice is made of gold, silver, bronze, brass, copper and lead; it measures 17.8cm high and 24.2cm in diameter and, put simply, is the finest example of Celtic art ever found. The equally renowned Tara Brooch was crafted around AD 700, primarily in white bronze, but with traces of gold, silver, glass, copper, enamel and wire beading, and was used as a clasp for a cloak. It was discovered on a beach in Bettystown, County Meath, in 1850, but later came into the hands of an art dealer who named it after the hill of Tara, the historic seat of the ancient high kings. It doesn't have quite the same ring to it, but it was the Bettystown Brooch that sparked a revival

DON'T MISS...

➡ Tara Brooch
➡ Ardagh Chalice
➡ Loughnasade War Trumpet
➡ Road to Independence Exhibition

PRACTICALITIES

➡ Map p244
➡ www.museum.ie
➡ Kildare St
➡ ⊙10am-5pm Tue-Sat, 2-5pm Sun

of interest in Celtic jewellery that hasn't let up to this day. There are many other pieces that testify to Ireland's history as the land of saints and scholars.

Ór-Ireland's Gold

Elsewhere in the Treasury is the Ór-Ireland's Gold exhibition, featuring stunning jewellery and decorative objects created by Celtic artisans in the Bronze and Iron Ages. Among them are the **Broighter Hoard**, which includes a 1st-century-BC large gold collar, unsurpassed anywhere in Europe, and an extraordinarily delicate gold boat. There's also the wonderful **Loughnasade bronze war trumpet**, which dates from the 1st century BC. It is 1.86m long and made of sheets of bronze, riveted together, with an intricately designed disc at the mouth. It produces a sound similar to the Australian didgeridoo, though you'll have to take our word for it. Running alongside the wall is a **15m log boat**, which was dropped into the water to soften, abandoned and then pulled out 4000 years later, almost perfectly preserved in the peat bog.

Road to Independence

On the same level is the Road to Independence exhibition, which features the **army coat worn by Michael Collins** on the day he was assassinated (there's still mud on the sleeve). In the same case is the cap purportedly also worn by Collins on that fateful day, complete with a bullet hole in its side – somehow, however, we think if the authorities had any confidence in this claim, the exhibit wouldn't be on the floor of the cabinet without even a note.

Elsewhere in the Museum

If you can cope with any more history, upstairs are **Medieval Ireland 1150–1550**, **Viking Age Ireland** – which features exhibits from the excavations at Wood Quay, the area between Christ Church Cathedral and the river – and our own favourite, the aptly named **Clothes from Bogs in Ireland**, a collection of 16th- and 17th-century woollen garments recovered from the bog. Enthralling stuff!

WHAT'S IN A NAME?

Virtually all of the treasures held here are named after the location in which they were found. It's interesting to note that most of them were discovered not by archaeologists' trowels but by bemused farmers out ploughing their fields, cutting peat or, in the case of the Ardagh Chalice, digging for spuds.

The museum was founded by an act of (British) Parliament on 14 August, 1877 as the Museum of Science and Art, Dublin. Its original purview was to house the expanding collection of the Royal Dublin Society, which were duly transferred to state ownership along with important collections owned by Trinity College and the Royal Irish Academy.

TOP SIGHT
NATIONAL GALLERY

A stunning Caravaggio and a room full of pieces by Ireland's pre-eminent artist, Jack B Yeats, are just a couple of highlights from this fine collection.

Its original collection of 125 paintings has grown, mainly through bequests, to over 13,000 artworks, including oils, watercolours, sketches, prints and sculptures.

The Building & Galleries

The building itself was designed by Francis Fowke (1823–65), whose architectural credits also include London's Victoria & Albert Museum. The entire building comprises 54 galleries; works are divided by history, school, geography and theme. There are four wings: the original Dargan Wing, the Milltown Wing (1899–1903), the Beit Wing (1964–68) and the Millennium Wing (2002).

The collection spans works from the 14th to the 20th centuries and includes all the major Continental schools.

Irish Art & Jack Butler Yeats

Obviously there is an emphasis on Irish art, and among the works to look out for are William Orpen's *Sunlight*, Roderic O'Conor's *Reclining Nude* and *Young Breton Girl*, and Paul Henry's *The Potato Diggers*. But the highlight, and one you should definitely take time to explore, is the **Yeats Room**, devoted to and containing more than 30 paintings by Jack B Yeats, a uniquely Irish Impressionist and arguably the country's greatest artist. Some of his finest moments are *The Liffey Swim*, *Men of Destiny* and *Above the Fair*.

The European Masters

The absolute star exhibit from a pupil of the European schools is Caravaggio's sublime **The Taking of Christ**, in which the troubled Italian genius attempts to light the scene figuratively and metaphorically (the artist himself is portrayed holding the lantern on the far right). The masterpiece lay undiscovered for more than 60 years in a Jesuit house in nearby Leeson St, and was found accidentally by the chief curator of the gallery, Sergio Benedetti, in 1992. Fra Angelico, Titian and Tintoretto are all in this neighbourhood. Facing Caravaggio, way down the opposite end of the gallery, is *A Genovese Boy Standing on a Terrace* by Van Dyck. Old Dutch and Flemish masters line up in between, but all defer to Vermeer's **Lady Writing a Letter**, which is lucky to be here at all, having been stolen by Dublin gangster Martin Cahill in 1992, as featured in the film *The General*.

The French section contains Jules Breton's famous 19th-century *The Gleaner*s, along with works by Monet, Degas, Pisarro and Delacroix, while Spain chips in with an unusually scruffy *Still Life with Mandolin* by Picasso, as well as paintings by El Greco and Goya, and an early Velázquez. There is a small British collection with works by Reynolds, Hogarth and Gainsborough (*The Cottage Girl* is especially beautiful).

Joseph Turner Exhibition

One of the most popular exhibitions occurs only in January, when the gallery hosts its annual display of the **Gainsborough collection**, featuring watercolours by Joseph Turner. The 35 works in the collection are best viewed at this time due to the particular quality of the winter light.

DON'T MISS...

➜ The Yeats Room
➜ The Taking of Christ
➜ Lady Writing a Letter
➜ Gainsborough collection

PRACTICALITIES

➜ Map p244
➜ www.national gallery.ie
➜ West Merrion Sq
➜ ⊘9.30am-5.30pm Mon-Wed, Fri & Sat, 9.30am-8.30pm Thu, noon-5.30pm Sun
➜ 🚌7 & 44 from city centre

TOP SIGHT
MERRION SQUARE

St Stephen's Green may win the popularity contest, but elegant Merrion Sq snubs its nose at such easy praise and remains the most prestigious of Dublin's squares.

Its well-kept lawns and beautifully tended flower beds are flanked on three sides by gorgeous Georgian houses with colourful doors, peacock fanlights, ornate door knockers and, occasionally, foot-scrapers, used to remove mud from shoes before venturing indoors.

The square, laid out in 1762, is bordered on its remaining side by the National Gallery (p82) and Leinster House (p86) – all of which, apparently, isn't enough for some. One former resident, WB Yeats (1865–1939), was less than impressed and described the architecture as 'grey 18th century'; there's just no pleasing some people.

DON'T MISS

➡ Oscar Wilde Statue
➡ Sunday Open Art Gallery
➡ Georgian houses

PRACTICALITIES

➡ Map p244
➡ admission free
➡ ⊙dawn-dusk
➡ 🚌7 & 44 from city centre

Oscar Wilde Statue

Just inside the southeastern corner of the square is a flamboyant **statue of Oscar Wilde** (Map p244), who grew up across the street at **No 1**. This was the first residence built on the square (1762) and during the Wilde tenancy was renowned for the literary salon hosted by his mother, Lady 'Speranza' Wilde. Alas, you can't visit the restored house (used exclusively by students of the American College Dublin) so you'll have to make do with the statue of Wilde, wearing his customary smoking jacket and reclining on a rock. Wilde may well be sneering at Dublin and his old home, although the expression may have more to do with the artist's attempt to depict the deeply divided nature of the man: from one side he looks to be smiling and happy; from the other, gloomy and preoccupied. Atop one of the plinths, daubed with witty one-liners and Wildean throwaways, is a small green statue of Oscar's pregnant mother.

Troubled Times

Despite the air of affluent calm, life around here hasn't always been a well-pruned bed of roses. During the Famine, the lawns of the square teemed with destitute rural refugees who lived off the soup kitchen organised here. The British Embassy was at 39 Merrion Sq East until 1972, when it was burnt out in protest against the killing of 13 civilians on Bloody Sunday in Derry.

Damage to fine Dublin buildings hasn't always been the prerogative of vandals, terrorists or protesters. East Merrion Sq once continued into Lower Fitzwilliam St in the longest unbroken series of Georgian houses in Europe. Despite this, in 1961 the Electricity Supply Board (ESB) knocked down 26 of them to build an office block – just another in a long list of crimes against architectural aesthetics that plagued the city in the latter half of the 20th century. The Royal Institute of the Architects of Ireland is rather more respectful of its Georgian address and hosts regular exhibitions.

Sunday Open Art Gallery

At weekends, the wrought-iron fences of Merrion Sq convert to gallery wall for the traditional open-air **art market** (Map p244; ⊙10am-6pm Sat & Sun). At any given time you'll find the work of 150 artists, mostly Sunday-painter types with a penchant for landscapes and still lifes, some of whom are very talented indeed.

1

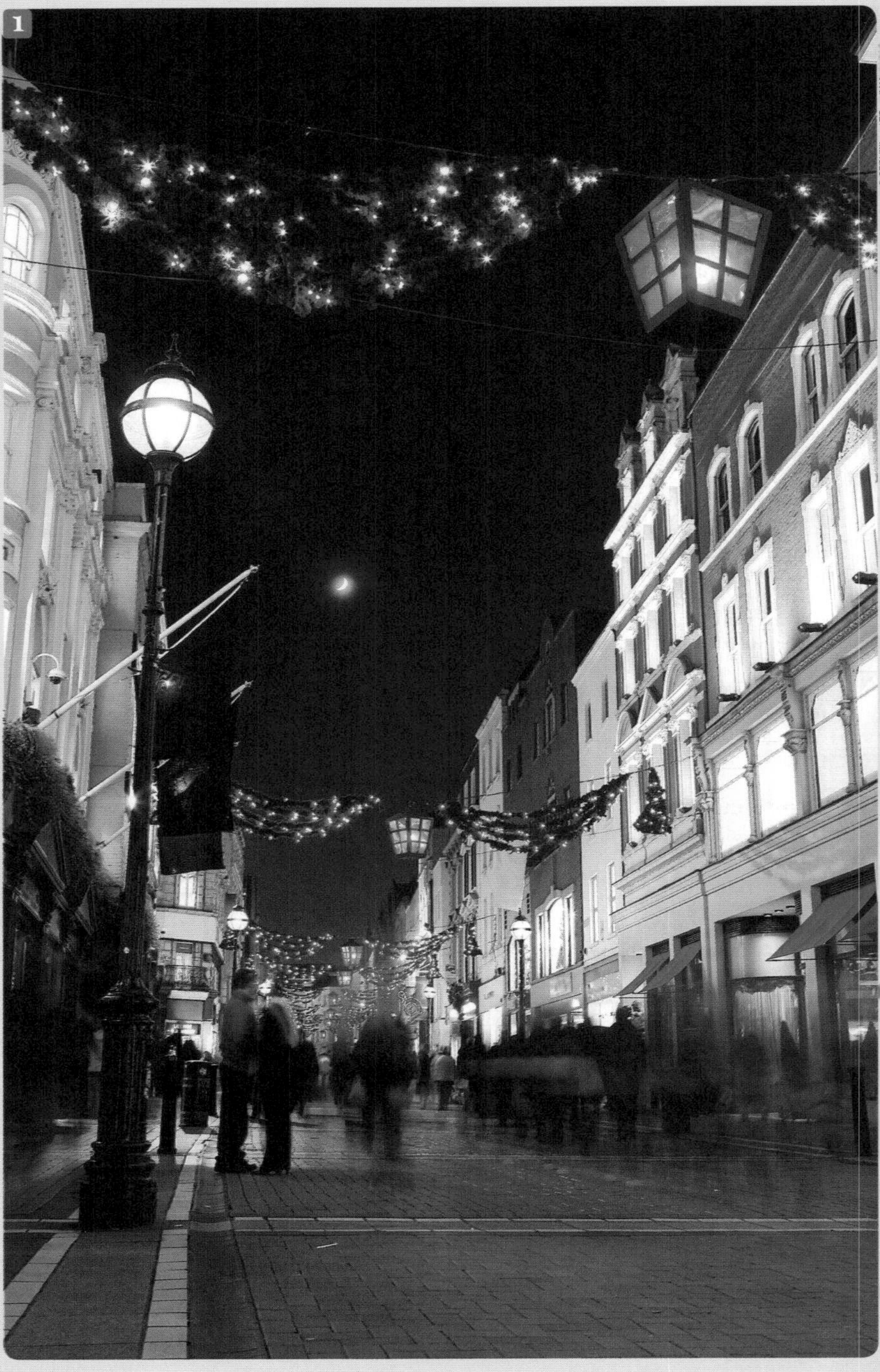

CHRIS HILL / GETTY IMAGES ©

MARTIN MOOS / GETTY IMAGES © ARTIST: DANNY OSBORNE

1. Grafton Street (p50)
Christmas on Grafton Street.

2. Leinster House (p86)
Built by Richard Cassels in 1748, Leinster House is the seat of the Oireachtas Éireann (Irish Parliament).

3. Oscar Wilde statue (p83)
Famed writer and poet, Oscar Wilde grew up at No 1 Merrion Square, just opposite this statue.

4. Merrion Square (p83)
The houses around Merrion Square are renowned for their Georgian architecture, featuring brightly coloured doors and peacock fanlights.

LUKASZ KULICKI / GETTY IMAGES ©

◉ SIGHTS

MERRION SQUARE   PARK
See p83.

NATIONAL MUSEUM OF IRELAND –
ARCHAEOLOGY   MUSEUM
See p80.

NATURAL HISTORY MUSEUM   MUSEUM
Map p244 (www.museum.ie; Merrion St; ⊗10am-5pm Tue-Sat, 2-5pm Sun; ⊒7 & 44 from the city centre) FREE Dusty, weird and utterly compelling, this window into Victorian times has barely changed since Scottish explorer Dr David Livingstone opened it in 1857 – before disappearing into the African jungle for a meeting with Henry Stanley. Which was perfectly fine until July 2007 when a large section of the original stone staircase collapsed, injuring 10 people and forcing the closure of one of the city's most beloved museums for a major restoration. It reopened in 2010, once again allowing us into explore its (slightly less) creaking interior crammed with some two million stuffed animals, skeletons and other specimens from around the world, ranging from West African apes to pickled insects in jars. Some are free-standing, others behind glass, but everywhere you turn the animals of the 'dead zoo' are still and staring.

Compared to the multimedia this and interactive that of virtually every modern museum, this is a beautifully preserved example of Victorian charm and scientific wonderment. It is usually full of fascinated kids, but it's the adults who seem to make the most noise as they ricochet like pinballs between displays. The **Irish Room** on the ground floor is filled with mammals, sea creatures, birds and some butterflies all found in Ireland at some point, including the skeletons of three 10,000-year-old Irish elk that greet you as you enter. The **World Animals Collection**, spread across three levels, has as its centrepiece the skeleton of a 20m-long fin whale found beached in County Sligo. Evolutionists will love the line-up of orang-utan, chimpanzee, gorilla and human skeletons on the 1st floor. A new addition here is the **Discovery Zone**, where visitors can do some first-hand exploring of their own, handling taxidermy and opening drawers. Other notables include the Tasmanian tiger (an extinct Australian marsupial, mislabelled as a Tasmanian wolf), a giant panda from China, and several African and Asian rhinoceroses. The wonderful **Blaschka Collection** comprises finely detailed glass models of marine creatures whose zoological accuracy is incomparable.

NATIONAL GALLERY   MUSEUM
See p82.

LEINSTER HOUSE   NOTABLE BUILDING
Map p244 (☑tour information 01-618 3271; www.oireachtas.ie; Kildare St; ⊗observation gallery 2.30-8.30pm Tue, 10.30am-8.30pm Wed, 10.30am-5.30pm Thu Nov-May, tours 10.30am, 11.30am, 2.30pm & 3.30pm Mon-Fri when parliament is in session; ⊒7 & 44 from the city centre) All the big decisions are made – or rubber-stamped – at Oireachtas Éireann (Irish Parliament). It was built by Richard Cassels in the Palladian style between 1745 and 1748. Its Kildare St facade looks like a townhouse (which inspired Irish architect James Hoban's designs for the US White House), whereas the Merrion Sq frontage was made to resemble a country mansion.

The first government of the Irish Free State moved in from 1922, and both the Dáil (lower house) and Seanad (senate) still meet here to discuss the affairs of the nation and gossip at the exclusive members bar. The 60-member Seanad meets for fairly low-key sessions in the north-wing saloon, while there are usually more sparks and tantrums when the 166-member Dáil bangs heads in a less-interesting room, formerly a lecture theatre, which was added to the original building in 1897. Parliament sits for 90 days a year. You get an entry ticket to the lower- or upper-house **observation galleries** from the Kildare St entrance on production of photo identification. Free, pre-arranged **guided tours** are available when parliament is in session.

The obelisk in front of the building is dedicated to Arthur Griffith, Michael Collins and Kevin O'Higgins, the architects of independent Ireland.

NO 29 LOWER
FITZWILLIAM ST   NOTABLE BUILDING
Map p244 (www.esb.ie/numbertwentynine; 29 Lower Fitzwilliam St; adult/student/child €6/3/free; ⊗10am-5pm Tue-Sat, 1-5pm Sun, closed late Dec; ⊒7 & 44 from the city centre) In an effort to atone at least partly for its sins against Dublin's Georgian heritage – it broke up Europe's most perfect Georgian row to build its headquarters – the Electricity Supply Board (ESB) carefully restored this home to

LITERARY ADDRESSES

Merrion Sq has long been the favoured address of Dublin's affluent intelligentsia. Oscar Wilde spent much of his youth at 1 North Merrion Sq, now the campus of the American College Dublin. Grumpy WB Yeats (1865–1939) lived at 52 East Merrion Sq and later, from 1922 to 1928, at 82 South Merrion Sq. George (AE) Russell (1867–1935), the self-described 'poet, mystic, painter and cooperator', worked at No 84. The great Liberator, Daniel O'Connell (1775–1847) was a resident of No 58 in his later years. Austrian Erwin Schrödinger (1887–1961), co-winner of the 1933 Nobel Prize for Physics, lived at No 65 from 1940 to 1956. Dublin seems to attract writers of horror stories, and Joseph Sheridan Le Fanu (1814–73), who penned the vampire classic *Camilla*, was a resident of No 70.

give an impression of genteel family life at the beginning of the 18th century.

From rat traps in the kitchen basement to handmade wallpaper and Georgian cabinets, the attention to detail is impressive, but the regular tours (dependent on numbers) are disappointingly dry.

GOVERNMENT BUILDINGS NOTABLE BUILDING

Map p244 (www.taoiseach.gov.ie; Upper Merrion St; ☉tours 10.30am-1.30pm Sat; ☐7 & 44 from the city centre) **FREE** This gleaming Edwardian pile was the last building (almost) completed by the British before they were booted out; it opened as the Royal College of Science in 1911. When the college vacated in 1989, Taoiseach Charles Haughey and his government moved in and spent a fortune refurbishing the complex.

Among the improvements made at the time was a private lift from Haughey's office that went up to a rooftop helipad and down to a limo in the basement.

Free 40-minute guided **tours** take you through the taoiseach's office, the Cabinet Room, the ceremonial staircase with a stunning stained-glass window – designed by Evie Hone (1894–1955) for the 1939 New York Trade Fair – and many fine examples of modern Irish arts and crafts.

Directly across the road from here, and now part of the Merrion Hotel, 24 Upper Merrion St is thought to be the birthplace of Arthur Wellesley (1769–1852), the first Duke of Wellington, who downplayed his Irish origins and once said 'being born in a stable does not make one a horse'. It is also possible that the cheeky bugger was born in Trim, County Meath.

FITZWILLIAM SQUARE PARK

Map p244 (☉closed to public; ☐10, 11, 13B or 46A from city centre) The smallest and the last of

Dublin's great Georgian squares was completed in 1825. It's also the only one where the central garden is still the private domain of the square's residents. William Dargan (1799–1867), the railway pioneer and founder of the National Gallery, lived at No 2, and the artist Jack B Yeats (1871–1957) lived at No 18.

Look out for the attractive 18th- and 19th-century metal coal-hole covers. The square is now a centre for the medical profession.

ROYAL HIBERNIAN ACADEMY (RHA) GALLAGHER GALLERY GALLERY

Map p244 (☎01-661 2558; www.royalhibernianacademy.ie; 15 Ely Pl; ☉11am-5pm Mon-Wed, Fri & Sat, 11am-9pm Thu, 2-5pm Sun; ☐10, 11, 13B or 51X from city centre) **FREE** This large, well-lit gallery at the end of a serene Georgian street has a grand name to fit its exalted reputation as one of the most prestigious exhibition spaces for modern and contemporary art in Ireland – although it's worked hard to shrug off a reputation for being a little dowdy and conservative in its tastes.

The big event is the Annual Exhibition, held in May, which shows the work of those artists deemed worthy enough by the selection committee, made up of members of the academy (easily identified amid the huge throng that attends the opening by the scholars' gowns). The show is a mix of technically proficient artists, Sunday painters and the odd outstanding talent.

NATIONAL LIBRARY HISTORIC BUILDING

Map p244 (www.nli.ie; Kildare St; ☉9.30am-9pm Mon-Wed, 10am-5pm Thu & Fri, 10am-1pm Sat; ☐all city centre) **FREE** Suitably sedate and elegant, the National Library was built from 1884 to 1890 by Sir Thomas Newenham Deane, at the same time and to a similar design as the National Museum. Its extensive collection has many valuable early manuscripts, first editions and maps.

Parts of the library are open to the public, including the domed reading room where Stephen Dedalus expounded his views on Shakespeare in *Ulysses*. For those prints that are worth a thousand words, you'll have to head down to Temple Bar to the National Photographic Archive (p94) extension of the library. There's a **Genealogy Advisory Service** on the 2nd floor, where you can obtain free information on how best to trace your Irish roots.

ST STEPHEN'S 'PEPPER CANISTER' CHURCH   CHURCH

Map p244 (☎01-288 0663; www.peppercanister. ie; Upper Mount St; ☐10, 11, 13B or 51X from city centre) **FREE** Built in 1825 in Greek Revival style and commonly known as the 'pepper canister' on account of its appearance, St Stephen's is one of Dublin's most attractive and distinctive churches, and looks particularly fetching at twilight when its exterior lights have just come on.

It occasionally hosts classical concerts, but don't go out of your way to see the interior. It's only open during services, usually held at 11am Sunday and 11.30am Wednesday, with an extra one at 11am on Friday in July and August.

🍴 EATING

CHEZ MAX   FRENCH €€

Map p244 (☎01-661 8899; www.chezmax.ie; 133 Baggot St; mains €13-20; ⊙from 10am Mon-Sat; ☐all city centre) Following the success of its sister restaurant by the gates of Dublin Castle, this version of Chez Max has taken pretty much the same formula (brasserie-style dining room, authentic French cuisine) and thrown in a tree-filled yard for extra measure. And it works a treat. If you're looking for a top-notch midrange bite, this could be the one.

RESTAURANT PATRICK GUILBAUD   FRENCH €€€

Map p244 (☎01-676 4192; www.restau rantpatrickguilbaud.ie; 21 Upper Merrion St; 2-/3-course set lunch €40/50, dinner mains €38-56; ⊙12.30-2.30pm & 7.30-10.30pm Tue-Sat; ☐7 & 44 from the city centre) Its devotees have long proclaimed this exceptional restaurant

🚶 Neighbourhood Walk
A Georgian Block

START KILDARE ST
FINISH NATIONAL GALLERY
LENGTH 1.7KM/ONE HOUR

Although Dublin is rightfully known as a Georgian city and many of its buildings were built between 1720 and 1814, the style cast such a tall shadow over Dublin design that for more than a century afterwards it was still being copied.

Begin your perambulation at the bottom (northern) end of Kildare St, opposite the walls of Trinity College Dublin. This street is named after James Fitzgerald, Duke of Leinster and the Earl of Kildare, who broke with 18th-century convention and opted to build his city mansion on the south side of the Liffey, away from the elegant neighbourhoods of the north side where most of his aristocratic peers lived. 'Where I go,' he confidently predicted, 'society will follow.'

He was right, and over the following century the street was lined with impressive buildings. On the left-hand side as you begin is the old Kildare Street Lords Club, a members' club famous for 'aristocracy, claret and whist' that was founded in 1782. In 1860 the original building was replaced by this Byzantine-style construction, designed by Thomas Newenham Deane, where it remained until 1976. It is now the home of the ❶**Alliance Francaise**.

On the same side a little further up is the ❷**National Library** (p87), another one of Deane's designs; immediately after the library, the imposing black gates and police presence protect ❸**Leinster House** (p108), the Palladian city pile that Fitzgerald commissioned Richard Cassels to build for him in 1745–48. It is now the seat of both houses of the Irish Parliament. From this side American visitors might think the building oddly familiar: the townhouse look is what inspired James Hoban, 1780 winner of the Duke of Leinster's medal for drawings of 'brackets, stairs and roofs,' to submit a design that won the competition to build the White House in 1792.

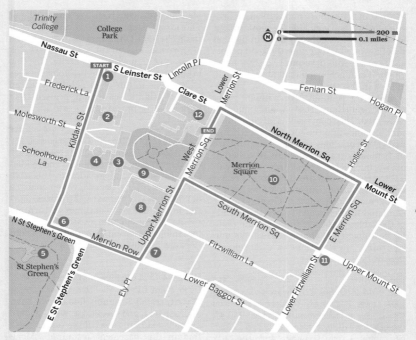

The next building along the street is the **4 National Museum of Ireland** (p80), another Deane building, which opened in 1890 and has since been the repository of the state's most valuable cultural treasures. As you reach the top of the street, the greenery in front of you is that of **5 St Stephen's Green** (p61), the city's best-loved public square. Once a common used for punishments and hangings, the green was landscaped with Guinness money in the mid-18th century and quickly became the aristocracy's favourite spot to take a walk.

Turn left and walk along the green, passing the **6 Shelbourne** (p172), onto Merrion Row, taking another left onto Merrion St. On your right, No 24 in the row of elegant Georgian houses is reputed to be the birthplace of Arthur Wellesley, the Duke of Wellington, who dealt with jibes about being born in Ireland by snippily responding that 'being born in a stable doesn't make one a horse'. That 'stable' is now part of the city's most elegant hotel, the **7 Merrion** (p172).

On your left-hand side you'll pass the **8 Government Buildings** (p87), where the current government runs its day-to-day affairs, and just past it, the rear entrance to Leinster House; from here it looks more like a country mansion. The smaller building wedged in between Government Buildings and Leinster House is the **9 Natural History Museum** (p86), opened in 1857.

On your right is **10 Merrion Square** (p107), the most elegant of Dublin's public spaces. The park itself is gorgeous, while the houses that surround it are magnificent: their doorways and fanlights are the most photographed of the city's Georgian heritage and a disproportionate number of Dublin's most famous residents lived on it at one point or another. If you want to see inside a typical Georgian home, **11 No 29 Lower Fitzwilliam St** (p86), at the square's southeastern corner, has been carefully restored.

Walk around or through Merrion Sq, making your way back to West Merrion Sq and the **12 National Gallery** (p82), which opened in 1864 and was built by Francis Fowke after a design by Charles Lanyon. For the sake of symmetry, the facade is a copy of that of the Natural History Museum.

the best in the country and Guillaume Lebrun's French haute cuisine the most exalted expression of the culinary arts, an opinion that has found favour with the good people at Michelin, who have put two stars in its crown. The lunch menu is an absolute steal, at least in this stratosphere.

The food is innovative without being fiddly, beautifully cooked and superbly presented. The room itself is all contemporary elegance and the service expertly formal yet surprisingly friendly – the staff are meticulously trained and are as skilled at answering queries and addressing individual requests as they are at making sure not one bread crumb lingers too long on the immaculate table cloths. Owner Patrick Guilbaud himself usually does the rounds of the tables in the evening to salute regular customers and charm first-timers into returning. Reservations are absolutely necessary.

L'ECRIVAIN
FRENCH €€€

Map p244 (☑01-661 1919; www.lecrivain.com; 109A Lower Baggot St; 3-course lunch menu €35, 10-course tasting menu €90, mains €40-47; ⊙lunch Mon-Fri, dinner Mon-Sat; ☐38 & 39 from city centre) A firm favourite with the bulk of the city's foodies, L'Ecrivain trundles along with just one Michelin star to its name, but the plaudits just keep coming. Head chef Derry Clarke is considered a gourmet god for the exquisite simplicity of his creations, which put the emphasis on flavour and the use of the best local ingredients – all given the French once over and turned into something that approaches divine dining.

UNICORN
ITALIAN €€€

Map p244 (☑01-676 2182; www.unicornrestaurant.com; 12b Merrion Ct, Merrion Row; mains €20-28; ⊙Mon-Sat; ☐all city centre) Saturday lunch at this Italian restaurant in a laneway off Merrion Row is a tradition for Dublin's media types, socialites, politicos and their cronies who guffaw and clink glasses in conspiratorial rapture. The extensive lunchtime antipasto bar is popular, but we still prefer the meaty á la carte menu – but there are pastas and fish dishes to cater to all palates.

DAX
FRENCH €€€

Map p244 (☑01-676 1494; www.dax.ie; 23 Upper Pembroke St; mains €19-31; ⊙lunch & dinner Tue-Fri, dinner Sat; ☐all city centre) Olivier Meisonnave, convivial ex-maître d' of Thornton's, stepped out on his own with Irish chef Pól ÓhÉannraich to open this posh-rustic restaurant named after his home town, north of Biarritz. In this bright basement venue, serious foodies will be able to sate their palate on seared fillet of Atlantic sea bream, braised Irish pork cheek or mushroom risotto.

BANG CAFÉ
MODERN EUROPEAN €€€

Map p244 (☑01-400 4229; www.bangrestaurant.com; 11 Merrion Row; mains €25-29; ⊙lunch & dinner; ☐all city centre) Fashionistas and foodies alike have been aficionados of this stylish spot for over a decade, which changed hands a few years ago (legal troubles, don't you know) but still continues to turn out top-notch contemporary Irish fare, including smoked venison loin and a delicious Wicklow Mountain woodpigeon.

ELY
WINE BAR €€€

Map p244 (☑01-676 8986; www.elywinebar.ie; 22 Ely Pl; mains €15-29; ⊙lunch & dinner Mon-Sat; ☐all city centre) Scrummy homemade burgers, bangers and mash, or wild smoked salmon salad are some of the dishes you'll find in this basement restaurant. Meals are prepared with organic and free-range produce from the owner's family farm in County Clare, so you can rest assured of the quality. There's a large wine list to choose from, with more than 70 sold by the glass. There are two more branches on either side of the Liffey.

DOBBINS
FRENCH €€€

Map p244 (☑01-676 4679; www.dobbins.ie; 15 Stephen's Lane; mains €19-31; ⊙lunch Mon-Fri, dinner Mon-Sat; ☐all city centre) Completely refurbished after 25 years as a stalwart of the city's top-end dining scene, Dobbins 2.0 is still a classy spot for an elegant dinner of established favourites – fish, chicken, duck and a good steak. Nothing too radical, just popular dishes done well. The service is excellent.

🍷 DRINKING & NIGHTLIFE

Away from the city centre there are a number of fine pubs that are worthy of the trek. Many fill up with office workers

straight after (or just before) clocking-off time and then get quieter as the night progresses.

O'DONOGHUE'S
PUB

Map p244 (15 Merrion Row; all city centre) Once the most renowned traditional music bar in all Dublin, this is where the world-famous folk group the Dubliners refined their rasp-ish brand of trad in the 1960s. On summer evenings a young, international crowd spills out into the courtyard beside the pub. It's also a famous rugby pub and the Dublin HQ for many Irish and visiting fans.

DOHENY & NESBITT'S
TRADITIONAL PUB

Map p244 (01-676 2945; 5 Lower Baggot St; all city centre) A standout, even in a city of wonderful pubs, Nesbitt's is equipped with antique snugs and is a favourite place for high-powered gossip among politicians and journalists; Leinster House is only a short stroll away.

HARTIGAN'S
PUB

Map p244 (100 Lower Leeson St; all city centre) This is about as spartan a bar as you'll find in the city, and is the daytime home to some serious drinkers, who appreciate the quiet, no-frills surroundings. In the evening it's popular with students from the medical faculty of University College Dublin (UCD).

JAMES TONER'S
PUB

Map p244 (139 Lower Baggot St; all city centre) Toner's, with its stone floors and antique snugs, has changed little over the years and is the closest thing you'll get to a country pub in the heart of the city. The shelves and drawers are reminders that it once doubled as a grocery shop.

The writer Oliver St John Gogarty once brought WB Yeats here, after the upper-class poet – who only lived around the corner – decided he wanted to visit a pub. After a silent sherry in the noisy bar, Yeats turned to his friend and said, 'I have seen the pub, now please take me home'. We always suspected he was a little too precious for normal people, and he would probably be horrified by the good-natured business crowd making the racket these days too. His loss.

BAGGOT INN
BAR

Map p244 (143 Lower Baggot St) This long-established watering hole famous for its live music has dressed itself up and is now more of a convivial sports bar (it's very popular during rugby weekends). It also offers customers the chance to pull their own pint – from a beer tower (€24 to €29) at their table.

MERRION SQUARE & AROUND DRINKING & NIGHTLIFE

Temple Bar

Neighbourhood Top Five

1 Watching a summertime **outdoor film** in Meeting House Sq (p96).

2 The always excellent exhibits at the **Gallery of Photography** (p94).

3 Radical fashions and oddball knick-knacks at the weekend **Cow's Lane Designer Mart** (p98).

4 Dropping the kids off at the **Ark Children's Cultural Centre** (p94), where their inner performer may be awakened.

5 Shopping for new titles and old classics at **Gutter Bookshop** (p99), one of the best in town.

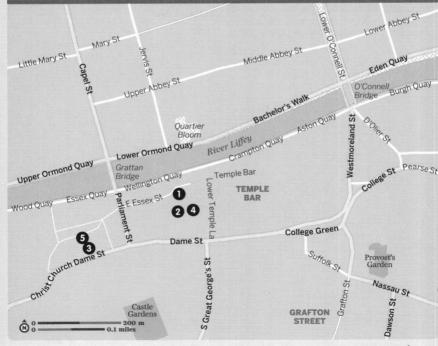

For more detail of this area see Map p236 ➡

Explore Temple Bar

You can visit all of Temple Bar's attractions in less than half a day, but that's not really the point: this cobbled neighbourhood, for so long the city's most infamous party zone, is really more about ambience than attractions. If you visit during the day, the district's bohemian bent is on display. You can browse for vintage clothes, get your nipples pierced, nibble on Mongolian barbecue, buy organic food, pick up the latest musical releases and buy books on every conceivable subject. You can check out the latest art installations, watch an outdoor movie or join in a pulsating drum circle. By night – or at the weekend – it's a different story altogether, as the area's bars are packed to the rafters with revellers looking to tap into their inner Bacchus: it's loud, raucous and usually a lot of fun. Temple Bar is also Dublin's official 'cultural quarter', so you shouldn't ignore its more high-minded offerings such as the progressive Project Arts Centre, Temple Bar Gallery & Studios and the Irish Film Institute (IFI).

Local Life

➡ **Markets** The Meeting House Square Market (p98) is all about gourmet goodies and organic foodstuffs; the Cow's Lane Designer Mart (p98) is a showcase of local art and clothing; while the Book Fair (p98) is the place to pick up secondhand novels and CDs.

➡ **Nightlife** A live music gig at the Button Factory (p97) or the Workman's Club (p97) is always a great night out, and you can really get your grind on at Mother (p97) on a Saturday night.

➡ **Brunch** Soaking up the excesses of the night before is a favourite weekend activity, and we recommend the marvellous mayhem at the Elephant & Castle (p95), or the more demure charms of Eden (p95), where in warm weather you can eat your eggs Benedict alfresco on the edge of Meeting House Sq.

Getting There & Away

➡ **Bus** As Temple Bar is right in the heart of the city, all cross-city buses will deposit you by the cobbled, largely pedestrianised streets, making access – and escape – that bit easier.

Lonely Planet's Top Tip

Unless you're in for a no-holds barred, knees-up weekend and don't care too much about sleeping, don't stay overnight in Temple Bar – hotel rooms are generally more cramped and noisier here than elsewhere. Temple Bar's central location and the city's size means you can get in and out of here with relative ease.

Best Places to Eat

➡ Crackbird (p94)

➡ Zaytoon (p94)

➡ Eden (p95)

➡ Elephant & Castle (p95)

For reviews, see p94➡

Best Places to Drink

➡ Vintage Cocktail Club (p96)

➡ Palace Bar (p96)

➡ Front Lounge (p96)

For reviews, see p96➡

Best Places to Shop

➡ Cow's Lane Designer Mart (p98)

➡ Gutter Bookshop (p99)

➡ Claddagh Records (p99)

For reviews, see p98➡

TEMPLE BAR

◉ SIGHTS

GALLERY OF PHOTOGRAPHY   GALLERY
Map p236 (www.galleryofphotography.ie; ⊙11am-6pm Mon-Sat; ☐all city centre) **FREE** This small gallery devoted to the photograph is set in an airy three-level space overlooking Meeting House Sq. It features a constantly changing menu of local and international work, and while it's a little too small to be considered a really good gallery, the downstairs shop is well stocked with all manner of photographic tomes and manuals.

TEMPLE BAR GALLERY & STUDIOS   GALLERY
Map p236 (☑01-671 0073; www.templebargallery.com; 5 Temple Bar; ⊙10am-6pm Tue, Wed, Fri & Sat, 10am-7pm Thu; ☐all city centre) **FREE** This multistoried gallery showcases the works of dozens of up-and-coming Irish artists at any one time, and is a great spot to see cutting-edge Irish art across a range of media. The gallery runs occasional open days when you can explore the work of artists beavering away in the studios that are part of the complex.

ARK CHILDREN'S
CULTURAL CENTRE   CULTURAL CENTRE
Map p236 (www.ark.ie; 11A Eustace St; ☐all city centre) Aimed at youngsters between the ages of three and 14, the Ark is enormously popular – and perpetually booked out. The centre runs age-specific activities aimed at stimulating participants' interests in science, the environment and the arts. The centre also has an open-air stage for summer events.

HANDEL WITH CARE

In 1742 the nearly broke GF Handel conducted the very first performance of his epic work *Messiah* in the since-demolished **Neal's Music Hall** (Map p236) on Fishamble St, the city's oldest street. Ironically, Jonathon Swift – author of *Gulliver's Travels* and dean of St Patrick's Cathedral – suggested the choirs of St Patrick's and Christchurch participate, but then he revoked his invitation, vowing to 'punish such vicars for their...rebellion, disobedience, perfidy and ingratitude.' The concert went ahead nonetheless, and the celebrated work is now performed in Dublin annually at the original spot – now a hotel that bears the composer's name.

NATIONAL PHOTOGRAPHIC
ARCHIVES   MUSEUM
Map p236 (⊙10am-4.45pm Mon-Sat, noon-4.45pm Sun; ☐all city centre) **FREE** What should be a wonderful resource putting a face on all facets of Irish history is actually a sadly disappointing archive of photographs taken from the 19th century onwards. Its visitor-friendly catalogue is computer accessible and the eager staff are always willing to help with queries, but the available material is not nearly as extensive as we'd hoped.

NATIONAL WAX MUSEUM PLUS   MUSEUM
Map p236 (www.waxmuseumplus.ie; The Armoury, Foster Pl; adult/child/concession €12/8/10; ☐all city centre) More a mini history museum in wax than Dublin's version of Madame Tussaud's, the quality of the waxworks is inconsistent – some look like the result of a hastily conceived school project. Still, the Chamber of Horrors (Dracula has a starring role) is pretty good. The 'plus' in the name refers to the interactive use of video and music.

ORIGINAL PRINT GALLERY   GALLERY
Map p236 (☑01-677 3657; www.originalprint.ie; Black Church Studio, 4 Temple Bar; ⊙10.30am-5.30pm Mon-Sat, 2-5pm Sun; ☐all city centre) **FREE** This gallery specialises in original, limited-edition prints, including etchings, lithographs and silk-screens, mostly by Irish artists.

EATING

CRACKBIRD   CHICKEN €
Map p236 (www.joburger.ie; 60 Dame St; mains €10; ⊙lunch & dinner; ☐all city centre) A buzzy, trendy spot that only serves chicken, dipped in batter and breadcrumbs and then deep-fried...sounds a bit limited, right? But the chicken is excellent, and the sides – choose from the likes of potato salad, chipotle baked beans or carrot and cranberry salad – add taste and variety to what might otherwise just be fancy chicken in a bucket.

ZAYTOON   MIDDLE EASTERN €
Map p236 (14-15 Parliament St; meals €11; ☐all city centre) It's the end of the night and you've got a desperate case of the munchies. Head straight for this terrific kebab joint and gobble the house speciality: the chicken shish-kebab meal, complete with chips and a soft drink.

LA DOLCE VITA
ITALIAN €

Map p236 (Cow's Lane; plates for 2 €13-22; ⊙8.30am-11pm Mon-Sat, from 10am Sun; 🚇all city centre) This relatively new place serves proper Italian antipasti, dished up in sharing plates and named after Fellini movies. You can get mixed cheese platters (Il Viaggio di Mastorna), prosciutto samplers (Amarcord) or a mix of both (La Strada). Wash it all down with a selection of wines by the glass.

GOURMET BURGER KITCHEN
BURGERS €

Map p236 (📞01-670 8343; Temple Bar Sq; burgers €9-13; ⊙noon-11pm Mon-Sat, noon-10pm Sun; 🚇all city centre) The Temple Bar branch of this popular and tasty burger restaurant is perfectly placed to feed the party crowd – after all, you really shouldn't drink on an empty stomach! By closing relatively early it avoids those same people with the post-club munchies.

QUEEN OF TARTS
CAFE €

Map p236 (4 Cork Hill; snacks from €4; ⊙7.30am-6pm Mon-Fri; 🚇all city centre) Diet dodgers rejoice, for this little cafe is to cakes what Willie Wonka was to chocolate, and you'll think you're in a dream when you see the displays of tarts, meringues, crumbles, cookies and brownies, never mind taste them. There are also great brekkies – such as potato-and-chive cake with mushroom and egg, plus the coffee is splendid and the service sweet. This is a treasure so popular that they opened a bigger version around the corner on **Cow's Lane** (Map p236; www. queenoftarts.ie; 3-4 Cow's Lane; mains €5-10; ⊙8am-7pm Mon-Fri, 9am-7pm Sat, 10am-6pm Sun; 🚇all cross-city).

EDEN
MODERN IRISH €€

Map p236 (📞01-670 5372; www.edenrestaurant. ie; Meeting House Sq; mains €16-28; ⊙noon-2.30pm & 6-10.30pm Mon-Fri, noon-3pm & 6-11pm Sat & Sun; 🚇all city centre) A long-standing Temple Bar favourite, Eden serves up generous helpings of modern Irish cuisine in a stylish setting – it's designed to look like the interior of an (empty) pool. Beef, chicken, duck and venison all feature on the menu, but our favourite is weekend brunch, where you can linger with the papers and refills of coffee.

ELEPHANT & CASTLE
DINER €€

Map p236 (📞01-679 3121; www.elephantand castle.ie; 18 Temple Bar; mains €12-26; ⊙8am-11.30pm Mon-Fri, 11.30am-11.30pm Sat & Sun; 🚇all city centre) If it's massive New York–style sandwiches or sticky chicken wings you're after, this bustling upmarket diner is just the joint. Be prepared to queue though, especially at weekends when the place heaves with the hassled parents of wandering toddlers and 20-somethings looking for for a carb-cure for the night before.

LARDER
CONTEMPORARY IRISH €€

Map p236 (8 Parliament St; dinner mains €16-25; ⊙8am-11pm; 🚇all city centre) This welcoming cafe-restaurant has a positively organic vibe to it, what with its wholesome porridge breakfasts, gourmet sandwiches with fillings such as serrano ham, gruyere and rocket, and speciality Suki teas (try the China gunpowder). The evening menu offers a range of well-prepared Irish dishes including a great rib-eye and crackling pork belly.

TEA ROOMS
MODERN IRISH €€

Map p236 (📞01-670 7766; www.theclarence.ie; Clarence, 6-8 Wellington Quay; 2-/3-course menu €24/28; ⊙dinner Thu-Sat, noon-4pm Sun; 🚇all city centre) Mathieu Melin is performing small miracles in this elegant restaurant, its soaring ceiling and double-height windows designed to resemble a church. There are few places in all of Dublin where you'll get such superb fare – an ambitious marriage of classic French cuisine and typically Irish produce – at such reasonable prices.

IL BACCARO
ITALIAN €€

Map p236 (📞01-671 4597; www.ilbaccarodublin. com; Meeting House Sq; mains €14-25; ⊙dinner daily, lunch Sat; 🚇all city centre) Want a free Italian lesson? Drop into this fabulous trattoria and eavesdrop in this rustic piece of the Old Boot, where the food is exuberantly authentic, and includes bruschetta, homemade pasta, Italian sausage and the like. The Italian wines are *buonissimi*.

TANTE ZOÉ'S
CAJUN, CREOLE €€

Map p236 (📞01-679 4407; 1 Crow St; mains €16-26; ⊙Mon-Sat; 🚇all city centre) Get your Mardi Gras on any night of the week at this old favourite, with its menu of gumbos, jambalayas, bayou steaks, Cajun-blackened this and Creole-infused that. It ain't subtle and it won't win a lot of gourmet foodie awards, but the crowd couldn't care less: they come to *laisser rouler les bons temps* and that's exactly what they get.

CHAMELEON INDONESIAN €€

Map p236 (📞01-671 0362; www.chameleon restaurant.com; 1 Lower Fownes St; mains €16.50-19.50; 🕙dinner Tue-Sun; 🖳all city centre) Friendly, cute and full of character, Chameleon is draped in exotic fabrics and serves up perky renditions of Indonesian classics, such as satay, gado gado and nasi goreng. If you can't decide what dish to have, you can always plump for the *rijsttaffel*, a selection of several dishes with rice. The top floor has low seating on cushions, which is perfect for intimate group get-togethers.

DRINKING & NIGHTLIFE

Temple Bar's loud and busy pubs are a far cry from authentic, but they're undoubtedly fun – that is if your idea of fun is mixing it with a bunch of lads and lasses from the north of England, egging each other on to show off their family jewels and daring one another to drain 10 Fat Frogs in a row, in front of a bemused audience of Spanish and Italian tourists, all sharing three glasses of Guinness. You've been warned!

PALACE BAR PUB

Map p236 (21 Fleet St; 🖳all city centre) With its mirrors and wooden niches, the Palace (established in 1823) is one of Dublin's great Victorian pubs and a stubborn stalwart against the modernising influences of the last half century. Patrick Kavanagh and Flann O'Brien were once regulars and it was for a long time the unofficial head office of the *Irish Times*.

VINTAGE COCKTAIL CLUB BAR

Map p236 (Crown Alley; 🖳all city centre) Behind the inconspicuous, unlit doorway initialled with the letters 'VCC' is one of the coolest bars in Dublin, a '60s-style London members' club or Vegas Rat Pack hang-out. The emphasis is on expertly made cocktails served in a super-stylish setting: the 2nd-floor smoking lounge is easily the most elegant place in town to light a Lucky in. All-round class.

FRONT LOUNGE BAR

Map p236 (33 Parliament St; 🖳all city centre) The unofficially gay 'Flounge' is a sophisticated and friendly bar that stands out from other gay joints in that it is quieter, more demure

MOVIES IN THE SQUARE

Every Saturday night throughout the summer (from June to August), Temple Bar's Meeting House Sq hosts free screenings of films beginning at 8pm. The movies on offer are usually classics and are often preceded by an Irish short.

and popular with a mixed crowd. Sexual orientation here is strictly secondary to having a drink and a laugh with friends, even though the 'Back Lounge' toward the back of the bar is traditionally predominantly gay.

PORTERHOUSE BAR

Map p236 (16-18 Parliament St; 🖳all city centre) The second-biggest brewery in Dublin, the Porterhouse looks like a cross between a Wild West bar and a Hieronymus Bosch painting – all wood and full of staircases. We love it, and although it inevitably gets crowded, this pub on the fringe of Temple Bar is for the discerning drinker and has lots of its own delicious brews, including its Plain Porter (some say it's the best stout in town) as well as unfamiliar imported beers.

TURK'S HEAD CONTEMPORARY BAR

Map p236 (📞01-679 9701; 27-30 Parliament St; 🖳all city centre) This superpub is decorated in two completely different styles – one really gaudy, the other a re-creation of LA c 1930 – and is one of the oddest and most interesting in Temple Bar. It pulsates nightly with a young pumped-up crowd of mainly tourists, out to boogie to chart hits. Be mindful of hidden steps all over the place.

THOMAS READ'S CONTEMPORARY BAR

Map p236 (📞01-670 7220; 1 Parliament St; 🖳all city centre) The clientele at this spacious and airy bar, spread across two levels, seems to favour a selection of wine and coffee over beer. During the day, it's a great place to relax and read a newspaper. For a more traditional setting its annexe, the Oak, is a great place for a pint.

OLIVER ST JOHN GOGARTY PUB

Map p236 (58-59 Fleet St; 🖳all city centre) You won't see too many Dubs ordering drinks in this bar, which is almost entirely given over to tourists who come for the carefully manufactured slice of authentic traditionalism...

and the knee-slappin', toe-tappin' sessions that run throughout the day. The kitchen serves up dishes that most Irish cooks have consigned to the culinary dustbin.

FITZSIMONS
CONTEMPORARY BAR

Map p236 (✐01-677 9315; www.fitzsimonshotel. com; 21-22 Wellington Quay; ▢all city centre) The epitome of Temple Bar's commitment to a kind of loud and wonderfully unsophisticated nightlife is this sprawling hotel bar, which serves booze, sports and cheesy music to a throbbing crowd of pumped revellers. At weekends, it gets so busy that the bouncers don't even try to keep the crowd from spilling out onto the cobbled streets. If you want a no-nonsense night out, this is the place for you.

MESSRS MAGUIRE
CONTEMPORARY BAR

Map p236 (✐01-670 5777; 1-2 Burgh Quay; ▢all city centre) This uber-bar and microbrewery just outside Temple Bar's eastern edge is spread across three levels, connected by a truly imperious staircase, and is a disconcerting mix of young and old, intimate and brash. Its own beers are worth contemplating, but not on the weekend when the place is absolutely jammed.

TEMPLE BAR
BAR

Map p236 (✐01-677 3807; 48 Temple Bar; ▢all city centre) The most photographed pub facade in Dublin, perhaps the world, the Temple Bar (aka Flannery's) is smack bang in the middle of the tourist precinct and is usually chock-a-block with visitors. It's good craic though, and presses all the right buttons, with traditional musicians, a buzzy atmosphere and even a beer garden. It's also one of the most expensive pubs in Dublin.

AULD DUBLINER
TRADITIONAL PUB

Map p236 (✐01-677 0527; 17 Anglesea St; ▢all city centre) Predominantly patronised by tourists, 'the Auld Foreigner', as locals have dubbed it, has a carefully manicured 'old-world' charm that has been preserved – or refined – after a couple of renovations. It's a reliable place for a singsong and a laugh, as long as you don't mind taking 15 minutes to get to and from the jax (toilets).

BROGAN'S
TRADITIONAL PUB

Map p236 (✐01-679 9570; 75 Dame St; ▢all city centre) Only a couple of doors down from the Olympia Theatre (p98), this is a wonderful old-style bar where conversation – not loud music – is king. The beer is also pretty good.

OCTAGON BAR
CONTEMPORARY BAR

Map p236 (✐01-670 9000; www.theclarence. ie; Clarence Hotel, 6-8 Wellington Quay; ▢all city centre) Temple Bar's trendiest watering hole is where you'll find many of Dublin's celebrities (including mates of the owners, who just happen to be U2) and their hangers-on, swaggering and sipping expertly made cocktails in front of stylish wood panelling amid perpetual daylight. Drinks are expensive, but if such things concern you, don't even try getting past the bouncers.

⭐ ENTERTAINMENT

MOTHER
CLUB

Map p236 (Copper Alley, Exchange St; cover €10; ☺11pm-3.30am Sat; ▢all city centre) The best club night in the city is ostensibly a gay night but does not discriminate: clubbers of every sexual orientation come for the sensational DJs who throw down a mixed bag of disco, synth-pop and other danceable styles.

WORKMAN'S CLUB
LIVE MUSIC

Map p236 (✐01-670 6692; www.theworkmans club.com; 10 Wellington Quay; ▢all city centre) A 300-capacity venue and bar in the former workingmen's club of Dublin, this new spot puts the emphasis on keeping away from the mainstream, which means a broad range of performers, from singer-songwriters to electronic cabaret.

BUTTON FACTORY
LIVE MUSIC

Map p236 (✐01-670 0533; Curved St; ▢all city centre) This venue offers a wide selection of musical acts, from traditional Irish music to drum and bass (and all things in between), to a non-image-conscious crowd. One night you might be shaking your glow light to a thumping live set by a top DJ and the next you'll be shifting from foot to foot as an esoteric Finnish band drag their violin bows over their electric guitar strings.

NEW THEATRE
THEATRE

Map p236 (✐01-670 3361; www.thenewtheatre. com; 43 East Essex St; adult/child €15/8; ▢all city centre) This small theatre's location above a left-wing bookshop should be a guide to the kind of thinking that informs most of the performances taking place on its small stage. It's all about having a social conscience, whether by promoting new work by emerging playwrights or putting on established works that highlight society's injustices.

HA'PENNY BRIDGE INN

TRADITIONAL & FOLK

Map p236 (⌁01-677 0616; 42 Wellington Quay; adult/concession €6/5; ▣all city centre) A traditional old bar that has Irish music downstairs on Sunday and Wednesdays, and comedy upstairs at the long-established **Capital Comedy Club** (⌁01-677 0616; adult/concession €6/5; ◷9-11pm Fri), which features local comics on the rise.

IRISH FILM INSTITUTE

CINEMA

Map p236 (IFI; ⌁01-679 5744; www.ifi.ie; 6 Eustace St; ▣all city centre) The Irish Film Institute has a couple of screens and shows classics and new art-house films, although we question some of their selections: weird and controversial can be a little tedious. The complex also has a bar, a cafe and a bookshop.

Weekly (€3) or annual (€25) membership is required for some uncertified films that can only be screened as part of a 'club' – the only way to get around the censor's red pen. It's a great cinema, but sometimes it can be a little pretentious.

OLYMPIA THEATRE

THEATRE

Map p236 (⌁01-677 7744; 72 Dame St; ▣all city centre) This beautiful Victorian theatre generally puts on light plays, musicals and pantomime, but also caters to a range of midlevel performers and fringe talents that are often far more interesting than the superstar acts – this is one of the best places for a more intimate gig.

PROJECT ARTS CENTRE

THEATRE

Map p236 (⌁1850 260 027; www.project.ie; 39 East Essex St; ▣all city centre) This is the city's most interesting venue for challenging new work – be it drama, dance, live art or film. Three separate spaces, none with a restricting proscenium arch, allow for maximum versatility. You never know what to expect, which makes it all that more fun: we've seen some awful rubbish here, but we've also seen some of the best shows in town.

 SHOPPING

Dublin's most touristy neighbourhood has a pretty diverse mix of shops. Apart from the usual wares you find in any tourist trap, Temple Bar's stores traditionally specialise in peddling secondhand clothing and flogging the weird and the (sometimes) wonderful; it's a place where you can get everything from a Celtic-design wall-hanging to a handcrafted bong. In recent years, the western end of the quarter has been developed and a number of new shops have opened up, mostly of the high-end luxury design kind, with prices to boot. A couple of Dublin's best markets take place in this area on Saturday.

TEMPLE BAR MARKETS

Temple Bar's markets are a weekend blitz of design, books and gourmet cuisine.

Book Fair Map p236 (Temple Bar Sq; ◷10am-5pm Sat; ▣all city centre) Bad, secondhand potboilers, sci-fi books, picture books and other assorted titles invite you to rummage about on Saturday afternoons. If you look hard enough, you're bound to find something worthwhile.

Cow's Lane Designer Mart Map p236 (Cow's Lane; ◷10am-5pm Sat; ▣all city centre) A real market for hipsters, on the steps of Cow's Lane, this market brings together more than 60 of the best clothing, accessory and craft stalls in town. Buy cutting-edge designer duds from the likes of Drunk Monk, punky T-shirts, retro handbags, costume jewellery by Kink Bijoux and even clubby babywear. It's open from June to September; the rest of the year it moves indoors to **St Michael's & St John's Banquet Hall** (Map p236), just around the corner.

Meeting House Square Market Map p236 (Meeting House Sq; ◷10am-5pm Sat; ▣all cross-city) From sushi to salsa, this is the city's best open-air food market, a compact stroll through gourmet lane where you can pick, prod and poke your way through the organic foods of the world. There are tastes of everywhere, from cured Spanish chorizos and paellas to Irish farmhouses cheeses, via handmade chocolates and freshly made crêpes, homemade jams and freshly squeezed juices.

GUTTER BOOKSHOP
BOOKS

Map p236 (☑01-679 9206; www.gutterbookshop.com; Cow's Lane; ☺10am-6.30pm Mon-Wed, Fri & Sat, 10am-7pm Thu, 11-6pm Sun; ◻all city centre) Taking its name from Oscar Wilde's famous line from *Lady Windermere's Fan,* 'we are all in the gutter, but some of us are looking at the stars', this fabulous bookshop is flying the flag for the downtrodden independent bookstore, stocking a mix of new novels, children's books, travel literature and other assorted titles.

URBAN OUTFITTERS
FASHION, MUSIC

Map p236 (☑01-670 6202; www.urbanoutfitters.com; 4 Cecilia St; ◻all city centre) With a blaring techno soundtrack, the only Irish branch of this American chain sells ridiculously cool clothes to discerning young buyers. Besides clothing, the shop stocks all kinds of interesting gadgets, accessories and furniture. On the 2nd floor you'll find a hypertrendy record shop (hence the techno).

CLADDAGH RECORDS
MUSIC STORE

Map p236 (☑01-677 0262; 2 Cecilia St; ◻all city centre) An excellent collection of good-quality traditional and folk music is the mainstay at this centrally located record shop. The profoundly knowledgable staff should be able to locate even the most elusive recording for you.

FLIP
CLOTHING & ACCESSORIES

Map p236 (☑01-671 4299; 4 Upper Fownes St; ☺10am-6pm Mon-Wed & Fri, 10am-7pm Thu & Sat, 1.30-6pm Sun; ◻all city centre) This hip Irish label takes the best male fashion moods of the 1950s and serves them back to us, minus the mothball smell. US college shirts, logo T-shirts, Oriental and Hawaiian shirts, Fonz-style leather jackets and well-cut jeans mix it with the genuine secondhand gear upstairs.

SPORTS & ACTIVITES

MELT
HEALTH & FITNESS

Map p236 (☑01-679 8786; www.meltonline.com; 2 Temple Lane; full body massage 30min/1hr €60/90; ☺9am-7pm Mon-Sat; ◻all city centre) A full range of massage techniques – from Swedish to shiatsu and many more in between – are doled out by expert practitioners at Melt, aka the Temple Bar Healing Centre. Also available are a host of other left-of-centre healing techniques, including acupuncture, Reiki and polarity therapy. They have also set up shop in the **Westin** (☑01-679 9352; Westin Dublin, Westmoreland St; ◻all city centre).

Kilmainham & the Liberties

Neighbourhood Top Five

1 Taking a trip through Ireland's troubled history at **Kilmainham Gaol** (p111).

2 Sampling a pint of the black stuff at the **Guinness Storehouse** (p102).

3 Exploring the Norman treasures of **Christ Church Cathedral** (p108).

4 Visiting Jonathan Swift's tomb in **St Patrick's Cathedral** (p105).

5 Admiring modern art in exquisite surroundings at the **Irish Museum of Modern Art** (p112)

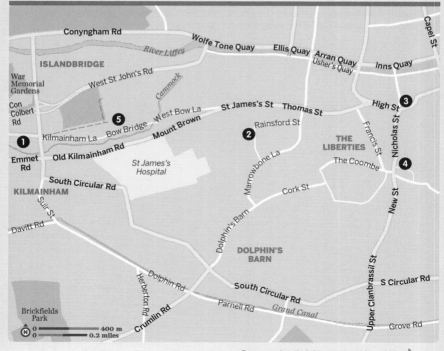

For more detail of this area see Map p246 ➡

Explore Kilmainham & the Liberties

Stretching westward along the Liffey from the city centre, you'll need a little bit of planning to get the most out of these two historic neighbourhoods. Coming from the heart of the city centre, you'll first stumble into the Liberties, on the edge of which are Dublin's two medieval cathedrals, built when the Liberties was a vibrant centre of industry. The area has been beset by myriad social problems in the last couple of centuries, yet it retains the passionate pride of a community that has been knitted together over many centuries, and many Dubliners are increasingly looking nostalgically towards the area as an example of their city 'in the rare auld times'.

Their nostalgia is usually expressed over a few pints, and the western border of the Liberties is where you'll find the source of their favourite nectar, the Guinness brewery at St James's Gate, where an old storehouse has been converted into the city's most visited museum. Further west again, just as the Liffey becomes more of a pastoral river in the riverside burg of Kilmainham, you'll come across the country's greatest modern-art museum and Kilmainham Gaol, which has played a key role in the tormented history of a country's slow struggle to gain its freedom. Both are well worth the westward trek (which can be made easier by bus). This is strictly day-trip territory – there's almost nothing in the way of accommodation and just a couple of decent eating options.

Local Life

➡ **Garden Walks** The Italianate garden at the Irish Museum of Modern Art (p112) is beautiful for a gentle amble, but one of the city's best-kept open secrets is the War Memorial Gardens (p118) in Kilmainham, which runs along the Liffey.

➡ **Markets** The Dublin Food Co-op (p119) in Newmarket is one of the city's best, and an excellent example of socially responsible retailing; it thrives thanks to the dedication of its many customers.

➡ **Hangout** The Fumbally Cafe (p118) is bringing cafe life to the Liberties.

Getting There & Away

➡ **Bus** Nos 50, 50A or 56A from Aston Quay and the 55 or 54A serve the cathedrals and the Liberties; for Kilmainham (including the Irish Museum of Modern Art) use bus nos 23, 51, 51A, 78 or 79 from Aston Quay.

Lonely Planet's Top Tip

The most convenient way to explore the area is as part of a hop-on, hop-off bus tour, all of which stop at the Guinness Storehouse, Irish Museum of Modern Art and Kilmainham Gaol. When your visit is done you can get back on and return to the city centre without hassle.

Best Places to Eat

➡ Lock's Brasserie (p118)
➡ Fumbally Cafe (p118)

For reviews, see p118 ➡

Best Places to Drink

➡ Fallon's (p118)
➡ Old Royal Oak (p119)
➡ Gravity Bar (p102)

For reviews, see p118 ➡

Best Places to Amble

➡ Irish Museum of Modern Art (p112)
➡ War Memorial Gardens (p118)

For reviews, see p112 ➡

KILMAINHAM & THE LIBERTIES

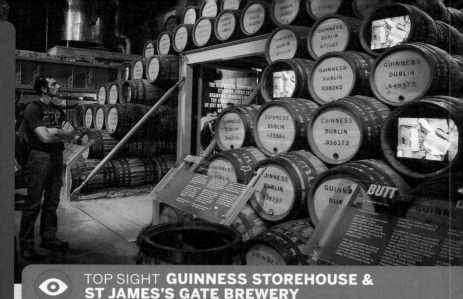

TOP SIGHT **GUINNESS STOREHOUSE & ST JAMES'S GATE BREWERY**

More than any beer produced anywhere in the world, Guinness has transcended its own brand and is not just the best-known symbol of the city but a substance with near spiritual qualities, according to its legions of devotees the world over.

The mythology of Guinness is remarkably durable: it doesn't travel well; its distinctive flavour comes from Liffey water; it is good for you – not to mention the generally held belief that you will never understand the Irish until you develop a taste for the black stuff. All absolutely true, of course, so it should be no surprise that the Guinness Storehouse, in the heart of the St James's Gate Brewery, is the city's most visited tourist attraction, an all-singing, all-dancing extravaganza that combines sophisticated exhibits, spectacular design and a thick, creamy head of marketing hype.

From Humble Beginnings to World Domination

In the 1770s, while other Dublin brewers fretted about the popularity of a new English beer known as porter – which was first created when a London brewer accidentally burnt his hops – Arthur Guinness started making his own version. By 1799 he had decided to concentrate all his efforts on this single brew. He died four years later, aged 83, but the foundations for world domination were already in place.

At one time a Grand Canal tributary was cut into the brewery to enable special Guinness barges to carry consignments out onto the Irish canal system or to the Dublin port. When the brewery extensions reached the Liffey in 1872, the fleet of Guinness barges became a familiar sight. Pretty soon Guinness was being

DON'T MISS...

➡ A drink of Guinness
➡ Gravity Bar view
➡ Advertising exhibit

PRACTICALITIES

➡ Map p246
➡ www.guinness-storehouse.com
➡ St James's Gate, South Market St
➡ adult/student/child €16.50/10.50/6.50, Conoisseur Experience €25, discounts apply for online bookings
➡ ⏰9.30am-5pm Sep-Jun, 9.30am-7pm Jul-Aug
➡ 🚌21A, 51B, 78, 78A or 123 from Fleet St, 🚃St James's

exported as far afield as Africa and the West Indies. As the barges chugged their way along the Liffey towards the port, boys used to lean over the wall and shout 'bring us back a parrot'. Dubliners still say the same thing to each other when they're going off on holiday.

The Essential Ingredients

One link with the past that hasn't been broken is the yeast used to make Guinness, essentially the same living organism that has been used since 1770. Another vital ingredient is a hop by the name of fuggles, which used to be grown exclusively around Dublin but is now imported from Britain, the US and Australia (everyone take a bow).

Guinness Storehouse

The brewery is far more than just a place where beer is manufactured. It is an intrinsic part of Dublin's history and a key element of the city's identity. Accordingly, the quasi-mythical stature of Guinness is the central theme of the brewery's museum, the Guinness Storehouse, which opened in 2000 and is the only part of the brewery open to visitors.

While inevitably overpriced and over-hyped, this paean to the black gold is done exceptionally well. It occupies the old Fermentation House, built in 1904. As it's a listed building, the designers could only adapt and add to the structure without taking anything away. The result is a stunning central atrium that rises seven storeys and takes the shape of a pint of Guinness. The head is represented by the glassed Gravity Bar, which provides panoramic views of Dublin to savour with your complimentary half-pint.

Before you race up to the top, however, you might want to check out the **museum** for which you've paid so handsomely. Actually, it's designed as more of an 'experience' than a museum. It has nearly four acres of floor space, featuring a dazzling array of audiovisual, interactive exhibits that cover most aspects of the brewery's story and explain the brewing process in overwhelming detail.

On the ground floor, a copy of Arthur Guinness' original lease lies embedded beneath a pane of glass in the floor. Wandering up through the various exhibits, including 70-odd years of advertising, you can't help feeling that the now wholly foreign-owned company has hijacked the mythology Dubliners attached to the drink, and it has all become more about marketing and manipulation than mingling and magic.

BEST DEAL IN TOWN

When Arthur started brewing in Dublin in 1759, he couldn't have had any idea that his name would become synonymous with Dublin around the world. Or could he? Showing extraordinary foresight, he had just signed a lease for a small disused brewery under the terms that he would pay just £45 annually for the next 9000 years, with the additional condition that he'd never have to pay for the water used.

The company was once the city's biggest employer – in the 1930s up to 5000 people made their living at the brewery. Today, the brewery is no longer the prominent employer it once was; a gradual shift to greater automation has reduced the workforce to around 450.

Gravity Bar

Whatever reservations you may have, however, can be more than dispelled at the top of the building in the circular **Gravity Bar**, where you get a complimentary glass of Guinness. The views from the bar are superb, but the Guinness itself is as near-perfect as a beer can be.

Real aficionados can opt for the **Conoisseur Experience**, where you sample the four different kinds of Guinness – Draught, Original, Foreign Extra Stout and Black Lager – whilst hearing their story from your designated bartender.

Getting to St James's Gate Brewery

To get here, head westwards beyond Christ Church, and you'll end up in the area known as the Liberties, home of the historic 26-hectare St James's Gate Brewery, which stretches along St James's St and down to the Liffey. On your way you'll pass **No 1 Thomas St**, where Arthur Guinness used to live, across the road from the 40m-tall **St Patrick's Tower**, built around 1757 and the tallest surviving windmill tower outside the Netherlands.

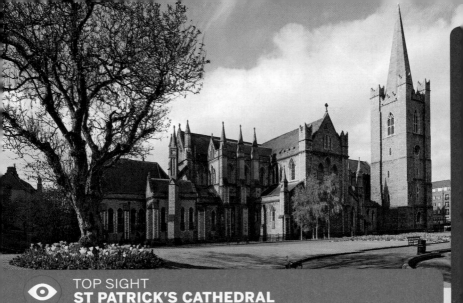

TOP SIGHT
ST PATRICK'S CATHEDRAL

Situated on the very spot that St Paddy supposedly rolled up his sleeves and dunked the heathen Irish into a well and thereby gave them a fair to middling shot at salvation, this is one of Dublin's earliest Christian sites and a most hallowed chunk of real estate.

Although a church has stood here since the 5th century, this building dates from the turn of the 12th century and has been altered several times, most notably in 1864 when it was saved from ruin and, some might say, over-enthusiastically restored. The interior is as calm and soothing as the exterior is sombre. The picturesque **St Patrick's Park**, adjoining, was a crowded slum until it was cleared in the early 20th century.

It's likely that St Patrick's was intended to replace Christ Church as the city's cathedral but the older church's stubborn refusal to be usurped resulted in the two cathedrals being virtually a stone's throw from one another. Separated only by the city walls (with St Patrick's outside), each possessed the rights of cathedral of the diocese. While St Pat's isn't as photogenic as its neighbour, it probably one-ups its sexier-looking rival in historical terms.

History

Following Henry VIII's 16th-century hissy fit and the dissolution of the monasteries, St Patrick's was ordered to hand over all of its estates, revenues and possessions. The chapter (bureaucratic head of the church) was imprisoned until they 'agreed' to the handover, the cathedral's privileges were revoked and it was demoted to the rank of parish church. It was not restored to its previous position until 1560.

DON'T MISS...

➡ Swift's Tomb
➡ Black James' Door
➡ Boyle's Monument

PRACTICALITIES

➡ Map p246
➡ www.stpatricks cathedral.ie
➡ St Patrick's Close
➡ adult/child €5.50/ free
➡ ⊙9am-5pm Mon-Sat, 9-10.30am & 12.30-2.30pm Sun year-round, longer hrs Mar-Oct
➡ 🚌50, 50A or 56A from Aston Quay, 54 or 54A from Burgh Quay

TO CHANCE YOUR ARM

Towards the north transept is a door that has become a symbol of peace and reconciliation since it helped resolve a scrap between the earls of Kildare and Ormond in 1492. After a feud, supporters of the squabbling nobles ended up in a pitched battle inside the cathedral, during which Ormond's nephew – one Black James – barricaded himself in the chapterhouse. Kildare, having calmed down, cut a hole in the door between them and stuck his arm through it to either shake his opponent's hand, or lose a limb in his attempt to smooth things over. James chose mediation over amputation and took his hand. The term 'to chance your arm' entered the English lexicon and everyone lived happily ever after – except Black James, who was murdered by Kildare's son-in-law four years later.

The cathedral had been built twice by 1254 but succumbed to a series of natural disasters over the following century. Its spire was taken out in a 1316 storm, while the original tower and part of the nave were destroyed by fire in 1362.

Further indignity arrived with Cromwell in 1649, when the nave was used as a stable for his horses. In 1666 the Lady Chapel was given to the newly arrived Huguenots and became known as the French Church of St Patrick. It remained in Huguenot hands until 1816. The northern transept was known as the parish church of St Nicholas Without (meaning outside the city), essentially dividing the cathedral into two distinct churches.

Such confusion led to the building falling into disrepair as the influence of the deanery and chapter waned. Although the church's most famous dean, Jonathan Swift (author of *Gulliver's Travels*, who served here from 1713 to 1745), did his utmost to preserve the integrity of the building, by the end of the 18th century it was close to collapse. It was just standing when the benevolent Guinness family stepped in to begin a massive restoration in 1864.

Baptistry & Swift's Grave

Fittingly, the first Guinness to show an interest in preserving the church, Benjamin, is commemorated with a **statue** at the main entrance. Inside to your left is the oldest part of the building, the **baptistry**, which was probably the entrance to the original building. It contains the original **12th-century floor tiles** and **medieval stone font**, which is still in use. Inside the cathedral proper, you come almost immediately to the **graves of Jonathan Swift** and his long-term companion Esther Johnson, better known as Stella. The Latin epitaphs are both written by Swift, and assorted Swift memorabilia lies all over the cathedral, including a pulpit and a death mask.

Boyle Monument

You can't miss the huge **Boyle Monument**, erected in 1632 by Richard Boyle, Earl of Cork. It stood briefly beside the altar until, in 1633, Dublin's viceroy, Thomas Wentworth, Earl of Strafford, had it shifted from its prominent position because he felt he shouldn't have to kneel to a Corkman. Boyle took his revenge in later years by orchestrating Wentworth's impeachment and execution. A figure in a niche at the bottom left of the monument is the earl's son Robert, a noted scientist who discovered Boyle's Law, which sets out the relationship between the pressure and the volume of a gas.

St Patrick's Well

In the opposite corner, there is a cross on a stone slab that once marked the position of **St Patrick's original well**, where the patron saint of Ireland rolled up his sleeves and got to baptising the natives.

ST PATRICK'S CATHEDRAL

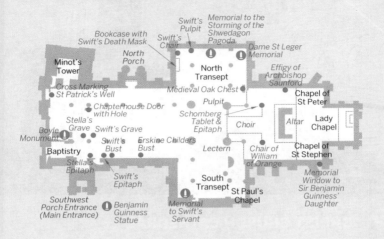

Minot's Tower
Cross Marking St Patrick's Well
Chapterhouse Door with Hole
Bookcase with Swift's Death Mask
North Porch
Swift's Chair
Swift's Pulpit
Memorial to the Storming of the Shwedagon Pagoda
Dame St Leger Memorial
North Transept
Effigy of Archbishop Saunford
Chapel of St Peter
Medieval Oak Chest
Pulpit
Schomberg Tablet & Epitaph
Choir
Altar
Lady Chapel
Chapel of St Stephen
Stella's Grave
Swift's Grave
Erskine Childers Bust
Lectern
Chair of William of Orange
Boyle Monument
Baptistry
Swift's Bust
Stella's Epitaph
Swift's Epitaph
South Transept
St Paul's Chapel
Memorial Window to Sir Benjamin Guinness' Daughter
Southwest Porch Entrance (Main Entrance)
Benjamin Guinness Statue
Memorial to Swift's Servant

North Transept & Northern Choir Aisle

The north transept contains various military memorials to Royal Irish Regiments, while the northern choir aisle has a tablet marking the **grave of the Duke of Schomberg**, a prominent casualty of the Battle of the Boyne in 1690. Swift provided the duke's epitaph, caustically noting on it that the duke's own relatives couldn't be bothered to provide a suitable memorial. On the opposite side of the choir is a chair used by William of Orange when he came to give thanks to God for his victory over the Catholic James II during the same battle.

South Transept & South AIsle

Passing through the south transept, which was once the chapterhouse where the Earl of Kildare chanced his arm, you'll see magnificent **stained-glass windows** above the funerary monuments. The south aisle is lined with memorials to prominent 20th-century Irish Protestants, including Erskine Childers, who was president of Ireland from 1973 to 1974, and whose father was executed by the Free State during the Civil War. The son never spoke of the struggle for Irish independence because, on the eve of his death, his father made him promise never to do anything that might promote bitterness among the Irish people.

Living Stones

On your way around the church, you will also take in the four sections of the permanent exhibition, **Living Stones**, which explores the cathedral's history and the contribution it has made to the culture of Dublin.

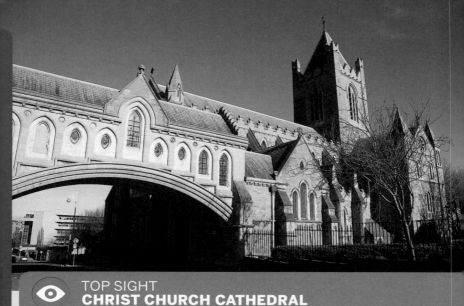

TOP SIGHT
CHRIST CHURCH CATHEDRAL

Its hilltop location and eye-catching flying buttresses make this the most photogenic of Dublin's three cathedrals as well as one of the capital's most recognisable symbols.

Early Beginnings

A wooden church was first erected here by Dunán, the first bishop of Dublin, and Sitric, the Viking king, around 1030, at the southern edge of Dublin's Viking settlement. In 1163, however, the secular clergy was replaced by a group of Augustinian monks installed by the patron saint of Dublin, Archbishop Laurence O'Toole. Six years later, Strongbow's Normans blew into town and got themselves into the church-building business, arranging with O'Toole (and his successor John Cumin) for the construction of a new stone cathedral that would symbolise Anglo-Norman glory. The new cathedral opened its doors late in the 12th century, by which time Strongbow, O'Toole and Cumin were long dead.

Above ground, the north wall, the transepts and the western part of the choir are almost all that remain from the original. It has been restored several times over the centuries and, despite its apparent uniformity, is a hotchpotch of different styles, ranging from Romanesque to English Gothic.

Hard Times

Until the disestablishment of the Church of Ireland in 1869, senior representatives of the Crown all swore their allegiance here. The church's fortunes, however, were not guaranteed. By the turn of the 18th century its popularity waned along with the district as the upper echelons of Dublin

DON'T MISS...

➡ Mummified Cat & Rat

➡ The Treasury

➡ Strongbow Monument

PRACTICALITIES

➡ Church of the Holy Trinity

➡ Map p246

➡ www.cccdub.ie

➡ Christ Church Pl

➡ adult/child €6/2

➡ 9.30am-5pm Mon-Sat & 12.30-2.30pm Sun year-round, longer hrs Jun-Aug

➡ 50, 50A or 56A from Aston Quay, 54 or 54A from Burgh Quay

society fled north, where they attended a new favourite, St Mary's Abbey. Through much of its history, Christ Church vied for supremacy with nearby St Patrick's Cathedral, but both fell on hard times in the 18th and 19th centuries. Christ Church was virtually derelict – the nave had been used as a market and the crypt had earlier housed taverns – by the time restoration took place. Whiskey distiller Henry Roe donated the equivalent of €30 million to save the church, which was substantially rebuilt from 1871 to 1878. Ironically, both of the great Church of Ireland cathedrals are essentially outsiders in a Catholic nation today, dependent on tourist donations for their very survival.

From its inception, Christ Church was the State Church of Ireland, and when Henry VIII dissolved the monasteries in the 16th century, the Augustinian priory that managed the church was replaced with a new Anglican clergy, which still runs the church today.

Chapterhouse & Northern Wall
From the southeastern entrance to the churchyard you walk past ruins of the **chapterhouse**, which dates from 1230. The **main entrance** to the cathedral is at the southwestern corner and as you enter you face the ancient **northern wall**. This survived the collapse of its southern counterpart but has also suffered from subsiding foundations (much of the church was built on a peat bog) and, from its eastern end, it leans visibly.

Monument to Strongbow
The southern aisle has a **monument to the legendary Strongbow**. The armoured figure on the tomb is unlikely to be of Strongbow (it's more probably the Earl of Drogheda), but his internal organs may have been buried here. A popular legend relates an especially visceral version of the daddy-didn't-love-me tale: the half-figure beside the tomb is supposed to be Strongbow's son, who was cut in two by his loving father when his bravery in battle was suspect – an act that surely would have saved the kid a fortune in therapist's bills.

South Transcept
The south transept contains the super baroque **tomb of the 19th earl of Kildare**, who died in 1734. His grandson, Lord Edward Fitzgerald, was a member of the United Irishmen and died in the abortive 1798 Rising. The entrance to the **Chapel of St Laurence** is off the south transept and contains two effigies, one of them is reputed to be of either Strongbow's wife or sister.

EVENSONG AT THE CATHEDRALS

In a rare coming together, the choirs of St Patrick's Cathedral and Christ Church Cathedral both participated in the first-ever performance of Handel's *Messiah* in nearby Fishamble St in 1742, conducted by the great composer himself. Both houses of worship carry on their proud choral traditions, and visits to the cathedrals during evensong will provide enchanting and atmospheric memories. The choir performs evensong in St Patrick's at 5.45pm Monday to Friday (not on Wednesday in July and August), while the Christ Church choir performs at 5.30pm on Sunday, 6pm on Wednesday and Thursday, and 5pm Saturday. If you're going to be in Dublin around Christmas, do not miss the carols at St Patrick's; call ahead for the hard-to-get tickets on ☎01-453 9472.

In March 2012, the heart of St Laurence O'Toole, which had been kept in the church for 890 years, was stolen by a gang linked to the international trade of rhino horns.

CHRIST CHURCH CATHEDRAL

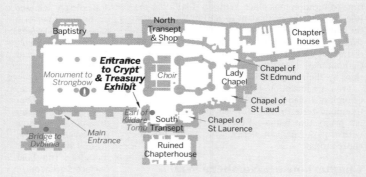

Crypt

An entrance by the south transept descends to the unusually large arched **crypt**, which dates back to the original Viking church. Curiosities in the crypt include a glass display-case housing a mummified cat in the act of chasing a mummified rat (aka Tom & Jerry), frozen midpursuit inside an organ pipe in the 1860s. Also on display are the stocks from the old 'liberty' of Christ Church, used when church authorities meted out civil punishments to wrongdoers. The **Treasury** exhibit includes rare coins, the Stuart coat of arms and gold given to the church by William of Orange after the Battle of the Boyne. From the main entrance, a **bridge**, part of the 1871–78 restoration, leads to Dvblinia.

TOP SIGHT
KILMAINHAM GAOL

If you have *any* interest in Irish history, especially the juicy bits about resistance to British rule, you will be shaken and stirred by a visit to this infamous prison.

It was the stage for many of the most tragic and heroic episodes in Ireland's recent past, and the list of its inmates reads like a who's who of Irish nationalism. Solid and sombre, its walls absorbed the barbarism of British occupation and recount it in whispers to visitors.

History

It took four years to build, and the prison opened – or rather closed – its doors in 1796. The Irish were locked up for all sorts of misdemeanours, some more serious than others. A six-year-old boy spent a month here in 1839 because his father couldn't pay his train fare, and during the Famine it was crammed with the destitute imprisoned for stealing food and begging. But it is most famous for incarcerating 120 years of Irish nationalists, from Robert Emmet in 1803 to Éamon de Valera in 1923. All of Ireland's botched uprisings ended with the leaders' confinement here, usually before their execution.

It was the treatment of the leaders of the 1916 Easter Rising that most deeply etched the gaol into the Irish consciousness. Fourteen of the rebel commanders were executed in the stone breakers' yard, including James Connolly who was so badly injured at the time of his execution that he was strapped to a chair at the opposite end of the yard, just inside the gate. The places where they were shot are marked by two simple black crosses. The executions turned an apathetic nation on a course towards violent rebellion.

The gaol's final function was as a prison for the newly formed Irish Free State, an irony best summed up with the story of Ernie O'Malley, who escaped from the gaol when incarcerated by the British but was locked up again by his erstwhile comrades during the Civil War. This chapter is played down on the tour, and even the passing comment that Kilmainham's final prisoner was the future president, Éamon de Valera, doesn't reveal that he had been imprisoned by his fellow Irish citizens. The gaol was decommissioned in 1924.

Guided Tours

Visits are by guided tour and start with a stirring audiovisual introduction, screened in the chapel where 1916 leader Joseph Plunkett was wed to his beloved just 10 minutes before his execution. The thought-provoking (but too crowded) tour takes you through the old and new wings of then prison, where you can see the former cells of famous inmates, read graffiti on the walls and immerse yourself in the atmosphere of the execution yards.

Asgard & Museum

Incongruously sitting outside in the yard is the *Asgard*, the ship that successfully ran the British blockade to deliver arms to nationalist forces in 1914. It belonged to, and was skippered by, Erskine Childers, father of the future president of Ireland. He was executed by Michael Collins' Free State army in 1922 for carrying a revolver, which had been a gift from Collins himself. There is also an outstanding museum dedicated to Irish nationalism and prison life. On a lighter note, real U2 fans will recognise the prison as the setting for the video for their 1982 single 'A Celebration'.

DON'T MISS...

➡ Prison Museum
➡ Stone Breakers' Yard
➡ Prison Cells

PRACTICALITIES

➡ Map p246
➡ www.heritage ireland.com
➡ Inchicore Rd
➡ adult/child €6/2
➡ ◷9.30am-6pm Apr-Sep, 9.30am-5.30pm Mon-Sat, 10am-6pm Sun Oct-Mar

TOP SIGHT **ROYAL HOSPITAL KILMAINHAM & IRISH MUSEUM OF MODERN ART**

IMMA is the country's foremost gallery for contemporary Irish art, although it takes second billing to the majestic building in which it is housed.

The Royal Hospital Kilmainham was built between 1680 and 1684 as a retirement home for veteran soldiers, a function it fulfilled until 1928, after which it was left to languish for half a century before being saved in a 1980s restoration; another refurb in 2012–13 saw the upgrade of the museum's lighting and fire safety systems.

Royal Hospital Kilmainham

The inspiration for the design came from James Butler, duke of Ormonde and Charles II's viceroy, who had been so impressed by Les Invalides on a trip to Paris that he commissioned William Robinson to knock up a Dublin version. What the architect designed was Dublin's finest 17th-century building and the highpoint of the Anglo-Dutch style of the day. It consists of an unbroken range enclosing a vast, peaceful courtyard with arcaded walks. A chapel in the centre of the northern flank has an elegant clock tower and spire. This was the first truly classical building in Dublin and was a precursor for the grand Georgian constructions of the 18th century. Christopher Wren began building London's Chelsea Royal Hospital two years after work commenced here.

The spectacularly restored hospital was unveiled in 1984, on the 300th anniversary of its construction. The next year it received the prestigious Europa Nostra award for 'distinguished contribution to the conservation of Europe's architectural heritage'.

Guided Tours

There are free guided tours of the museum's exhibits at 2.30pm on Wednesday, Friday and Sunday throughout the year, but we strongly recommend the free, seasonal heritage itinerary 50-minute **tour** (⊙hourly 11am-4pm Tue-Sat, 1-4pm Sun Jun-Sep) run by the Office of Public Works. It shows off some of the building's treasures, including the **Banqueting Hall**, with 22 specially commissioned portraits, and the stunning **baroque chapel**, with papier-mâché ceilings and a set of exquisite Queen Anne gates. Also worth seeing are the fully restored **formal gardens**.

Irish Museum of Modern Art

In 1991 it became home to IMMA and the best of modern and contemporary Irish art. The blend of old and new works wonderfully, and you'll find contemporary Irish artists such as Louis Le Brocquy, Sean Scully, Barry Flanagan, Kathy Prendergrass and Dorothy Cross featured here, as well as a film installation by Neil Jordan. The permanent exhibition also features paintings from heavy-hitters Pablo Picasso and Joan Miró, and is topped up by regular temporary exhibitions. There's a good cafe and **bookshop** (Map p246) on the grounds.

DON'T MISS...
- ➡ The Madden Arnholz Collection
- ➡ Formal Gardens

PRACTICALITIES
- ➡ IMMA
- ➡ Map p246
- ➡ www.imma.ie
- ➡ Military Rd
- ➡ ⊙10am-5.30pm Tue & Thu-Sat, 10.30am-5.30pm Wed, noon-5.30pm Sun, tours 2.30pm Tue-Sun, noon Sat
- ➡ 🚆Heuston

⦿ SIGHTS

**GUINNESS STOREHOUSE &
ST JAMES'S BREWERY**   BREWERY, MUSEUM
See p102.

ST PATRICK'S CATHEDRAL   CHURCH
See p105.

CHRIST CHURCH CATHEDRAL   CHURCH
See p108.

KILMAINHAM GAOL   MUSEUM
See p111.

**ROYAL HOSPITAL KILMAINHAM &
IRISH MUSEUM OF MODERN ART**   MUSEUM
See p112.

MARSH'S LIBRARY   LIBRARY
Map p246 (www.marshlibrary.ie; St Patrick's
Close; adult/child €2.50/free; ◷9.30am-1pm &
2-5pm Mon & Wed-Fri, 10am-1pm Sat; ▣50, 50A or
56A from Aston Quay, 54 or 54A from Burgh Quay)
It mightn't have the immediate appeal of a
brewery or a big old church, but this mag-
nificently preserved scholars' library, virtually unchanged in three centuries, is one of
Dublin's most beautiful open secrets, and
an absolute highlight of any visit. Few think
to scale its ancient stairs to see its beautiful, dark oak bookcases, each topped with
elaborately carved and gilded gables, and
crammed with books. Here you can savour
the atmosphere of three centuries of learning, slow into synch with the tick-tocking of
the 19th-century grandfather clock, listen
to the squeaky boards and absorb the scent
of leather and learning. It's amazing how
many people visit St Patrick's Cathedral
next door and overlook this gem.

Founded in 1701 by Archbishop Narcissus
Marsh (1638–1713) and opened in 1707, the
library was designed by Sir William Robinson, the man also responsible for the Royal

---

Hospital Kilmainham. It's the oldest public
library in the country, and contains 25,000
books dating from the 16th to the early 18th
century, as well as maps, manuscripts (including one in Latin dating back to 1400)
and a collection of incunabula (books
printed before 1500). In its one nod to the
21st century, the library's current 'keeper',
Dr Muriel McCarthy, is the first woman to
hold the post.

Apart from theological books and bibles
in dozens of languages, there are tomes on
medicine, law, travel, literature, science, navi-
gation, music and mathematics. One of the
oldest and finest books is a volume of *Cicero's
Letters to His Friends,* printed in Milan in
1472. The most important of the four main
collections is the 10,000-strong library of Edward Stillingfleet, bishop of Worcester.

Most of Marsh's own extensive collection is also here, and there are various
items that used to belong to Jonathan Swift
(dean of St Patrick's Cathedral), including
his copy of *History of the Great Rebellion.*
His margin notes include a number of comments vilifying Scots, of whom he seemed
to have a low opinion.

Like the rest of the library, the three al-
coves, in which scholars were once locked
to peruse rare volumes, have remained virtually unchanged for three centuries. Don't
worry though: the skull in the furthest
one doesn't belong to some poor forgotten scholar, it's a cast of the head of Stella,
Swift's other half. The library is also home
to Delmas Conservation Bindery, which
repairs and restores rare old books, and
makes an appearance in Joyce's *Ulysses.*

DVBLINIA & THE VIKING WORLD   MUSEUM
Map p246 (☎01-679 4611; www.dublinia.ie; adult/
student/child €7.50/6.50/5; ◷10am-5pm Apr-
Sep, 11am-4pm Mon-Sat & 10am-4.30pm Sun
Oct-Mar; ▣50, 50A or 56A from Aston Quay, 54
or 54A from Burgh Quay) A must for the kids,
the old Synod Hall, added to Christ Church
Cathedral during its late-19th-century restoration, is home to the seemingly peren-
nial **Dvblinia**, a lively and kitschy attempt
to bring medieval Dublin to life. Models,
streetscapes and somewhat old-fashioned
interactive displays do a fairly decent job of
it, at least for kids. The model of a medieval
quayside and a cobbler's shop are both excellent, as is the scale model of the medieval
city. Up one floor is **Viking World**, which
has a large selection of objects recovered
from Wood Quay, the world's largest Viking

VIKING TRACES

Fishamble St, Dublin's oldest street,
dates back to Viking times. Brass
symbols in the pavement direct you
towards a **mosaic** (Map p246), just
southwest of the overpass between
Christ Church Cathedral and Dvblinia,
laid out to show the ground plan of the
sort of Viking dwelling excavated here
in the early 1980s.

114

RICHARD I'ANSON / GETTY IMAGES ©

1. Temple Bar (p92)
Street art in Temple Bar.

2. Marsh's Library (p113)
Founded in 1701 by Archbishop Narcissus Marsh, Marsh's Library is the oldest public library in Ireland.

3. Royal Hospital Kilmainham (p112)
This former retirement home for veteran soldiers now houses the Irish Museum of Modern Art.

4. Auld Dubliner (p97)
The Auld Dubliner is a renowned traditional pub (and tourist magnet) in Temple Bar.

archaeological site. Interactive exhibits tell the story of Dublin's 9th- and 10th-century Scandinavian invaders, but the real treat is exploring life aboard the recreated longboat. Finally, you can climb neighbouring **St Michael's Tower** and peek through its grubby windows for views over the city to the Dublin hills. There is also a pleasant cafe and the inevitable souvenir shop. Your ticket gets you into Christ Church Cathedral free, via the link bridge.

KILMAINHAM GATE
LANDMARK

Map p246 (☐23, 51, 51A, 78 or 79 from Aston Quay) The Kilmainham Gate was designed by Francis Johnston (1760–1829) in 1812 and originally stood at the Watling St junction with Victoria Quay, near the Guinness brewery, where it was known as the Richmond Tower. It was moved to its current position opposite the prison in 1846 as it obstructed the increasingly heavy traffic to the new Kingsbridge Station (now Heuston Station), which opened in 1844.

ST AUDOEN'S CHURCHES
CHURCH

It was only right that the newly arrived Normans would name a church after their patron saint Audoen (the 7th-century bishop of Rouen, aka Ouen), but they didn't quite figure on two virtually adjacent churches bearing his name, just west of Christ Church Cathedral. The more interesting of the two is the **Church of Ireland** (Map p246; ⊘9.30am-4.45pm Jun-Sep) **FREE**, the only medieval parish church in the city that's still in use. It was built between 1181 and 1212, although a 9th-century burial slab in the porch suggests that it was built on top of an even older church. Its tower and door date from the 12th century and the aisle from the 15th century, but the church today is mainly a product of a 19th-century restoration.

As part of the tour you can explore the ruins as well as the present church, which has funerary monuments that were beheaded by Cromwell's purists. Through the heavily moulded Romanesque Norman door you can also touch the 9th-century 'lucky stone' that was believed to bring good luck to business.

St Anne's Chapel, the visitor centre, houses a number of tombstones of leading members of Dublin society from the 16th to the 18th centuries. At the top of the chapel is the tower, which holds the three oldest bells in Ireland, dating from 1423. Although

---

🏃 Neighbourhood Walk
Viking & Medieval Dublin

START ESSEX GATE, PARLIAMENT ST
FINISH DUBLIN CASTLE
DISTANCE 2.5KM/TWO HOURS

Begin your walk in Temple Bar, at the corner of Parliament St and Essex Gate, once a main entrance gate to the city. A ❶ **bronze plaque** on a pillar marks the spot where the gate once stood. Further along, you can see the original foundations of Isolde's Tower through a grill in the pavement, in front of the pub of the same name.

Head west down Essex Gate and West Essex St until you reach Fishamble St; turn right towards the quays and left into Wood Quay. Cross Winetavern St and proceed along Merchant's Quay. To your left you'll see the ❷ **Church of St Francis**, otherwise known as Adam & Eve's, after a tavern through which worshippers gained access to a secret chapel during Penal Law times during the 17th and 18th centuries.

Further down Merchant's Quay you'll spot the ❸ **Father Mathew Bridge**, built in 1818 on the spot of the fordable crossing that gave Dublin its Irish name, Baile Átha Cliath (Town of the Hurdle Ford). Take a left onto Bridge St and stop for a drink at Dublin's oldest pub, the ❹ **Brazen Head** (p117), dating from 1198 (although the present building dates from a positively youthful 1668).

Take the next left onto Cook St, where you'll find ❺ **St Audoen's Arch**, one of the only remaining gates of 32 that were built into the medieval city walls, dating from 1240. Climb through the arch up to the ramparts to see one of the city's oldest existing churches, ❻ **St Audoen's** (p116). It was built around 1190, and is not to be confused with the newer Catholic church next door.

Leave the little park, join High St and head east until you reach the first corner. Here on your left is the former Synod Hall, now ❼ **Dvblinia** (p115), where medieval Dublin has been interactively re-created. Turn left and walk under the Synod Hall Bridge, which links

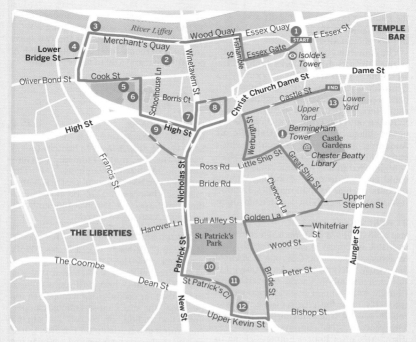

Dvblinia to one of the city's most important landmarks – 8 **Christ Church Cathedral** (p108) – and, in medieval times, the most important church inside the city walls.

Exit the cathedral onto Christ Church Pl, cross over onto Nicholas St and turn right onto Back Lane. Proceed to 9 **Tailor's Hall**, Dublin's oldest surviving guild hall, built between 1703 and 1707 (though it says 1770 on the plaque) for the Tailors Guild. It's now the headquarters of An Taisce, the National Trust for Ireland.

Do an about-turn, head back along the lane and turn right into Nicholas St, which becomes Patrick St. To your left you'll see 10 **St Patrick's** (p107), Dublin's most important cathedral, which stood outside the

city walls. Along St Patrick's Close, beyond the bend on the left, is the stunningly beautiful 11 **Marsh's Library** (p115), named after Archbishop Narcissus Marsh, dean of St Patrick's. Further along again on your left is the 12 **Dublin Metropolitan Police** building, once the Episcopal Palace of St Sepulchre.

Finally, follow our route up Bride St, Golden Lane and Great Ship St, and finish up with a long wander around 13 **Dublin Castle**. Be sure not to miss the striking powder-blue Bermingham Tower and the nearby Chester Beatty Library, south of the castle, which houses one of the city's most fascinating collections of rare books and manuscripts, and is well worth a visit.

the church's exhibits are hardly spectacular, the building itself is beautiful and a genuine slice of medieval Dublin.

The church is entered from the south off High St through **St Audoen's Arch**, which was built in 1240 and is the only surviving reminder of the city gates. The adjoining park is pretty but attracts many unsavoury characters, particularly at night.

Joined onto the Protestant church is the newer, bigger, 19th-century **Catholic St Audoen's**, an expansive church in which Father 'Flash' Kavanagh used to read Mass at high speed so that his large congregation could head off to more absorbing Sunday pursuits, such as football matches. In 2006 it was handed over to the Polish chaplaincy.

ST WERBURGH'S CHURCH
CHURCH

Map p246 (☎01-478 3710; Werburgh St; ⊗services 1st & 3rd Sunday of the month at 11am, call for access at other times; 🚌50, 50A or 56A from Aston Quay, 54 or 54A from Burgh Quay) Lying west of Dublin Castle, St Werburgh's Church stands upon ancient foundations (probably from the 12th century), but was rebuilt several times during the 17th and 18th centuries. The church's tall spire was dismantled after Robert Emmet's rising in 1803, for fear that future rebels might use it as a vantage point for snipers. Interred in the vault is Lord Edward Fitzgerald, who turned against Britain, joined the United Irishmen and was a leader of the 1798 Rising. In what was a frequent theme of Irish uprisings, compatriots gave him away and his death resulted from the wounds he received when captured. Coincidentally, Major Henry Sirr, the man who captured him, is buried out in the graveyard. On the porch you will notice two fire pumps that date from the time when Dublin's fire department was composed of church volunteers. The interior is rather more cheerful than the exterior, although the church is rarely used. Phone, or see the caretaker at 8 Castle St, to see inside. Donations welcome.

WAR MEMORIAL GARDENS
PARK

(www.heritageireland.ie; South Circular Rd, Islandbridge; ⊗8am-dusk Mon-Fri, from 10am Sat & Sun; 🚌25, 25A, 26, 68 or 69 from city centre) Hardly anyone ever ventures this far west, but they're missing a lovely bit of landscaping in the shape of the War Memorial Gardens. By our reckoning as pleasant a patch of greenery as any you'll find in the heart of the Georgian centre. Designed by Sir Edwin

Lutyens, the memorial commemorates the 49,400 Irish soldiers who died during WWI – their names are inscribed in the two huge granite bookrooms that stand at one end. A beautiful spot and a bit of history to boot.

EATING

FUMBALLY CAFE
CAFE €

Map p246 (Fumbally Lane; mains €5-8; ⊗8am-5pm Mon-Sat; 🚌49, 54A & 77X from city centre) Part of the new, trendy Fumbally Development is this terrific warehouse cafe. The superb menu has a range of pastries, homemade sandwiches, healthy breakfasts and daily lunch specials. The avocado sandwich is divine. A cut above the rest.

LEO BURDOCK'S
FISH & CHIPS €

Map p246 (2 Werburgh St; cod & chips €9.50; ⊗noon-midnight Mon-Sat, 4pm-midnight Sun; 🚌all city centre) You will often hear that you haven't eaten in Dublin until you've queued in the cold for cod 'n' chips wrapped in paper from the city's most famous chipper. Total codswallop, of course, but there's something about sitting on the street, balancing the bag on your lap and trying to eat the chips quickly before they go cold that smacks of Dublin in a bygone age.

LOCK'S BRASSERIE
CONTEMPORARY IRISH €€€

(☎01-420 0555; www.locksbrasserie.com; 1 Windsor Tce; mains €25-32; ⊗dinner daily, lunch Thu-Sun; 🚌128, 14, 142, 14A, 15, 15A, 15B, 15E, 15F, 65, 65B, 74, 74A, 83 from city centre) The most discreet of Dublin's Michelin-starred restaurants is this wonderful canalside brasserie, where head chef Sebastian Masi has wowed diners with his limited menu of old favourites. The six mains are evenly split between fish and meat, but each is a bit of culinary magic – the John Dory with squid ink and anchovy pappardelle, purple sprouting broccoli, broccoli puree and garlic foam is so good that you'll eat it especially slowly.

DRINKING & NIGHTLIFE

FALLON'S
TRADITIONAL PUB

Map p246 (☎01-454 2801; 129 The Coombe; 🚌123, 206 or 51B from city centre) Just west of the city centre, in the heart of medieval Dublin, this is a fabulously old-fashioned bar that has been serving a great pint of Guinness since the end of the 17th century. Prize fighter Dan Donnelly, the only boxer ever to be knighted, was head bartender here in 1818. It's a genuine Irish bar filled with Dubs.

OLD ROYAL OAK TRADITIONAL PUB
Map p246 (11 Kilmainham Lane; 🚌68, 69 & 79 from city centre) Locals are fiercely protective of this gorgeous traditional pub, which opened in 1845 to serve the patrons and staff of the Royal Hospital (now the Irish Museum of Modern Art). The clientele has changed, but everything else has remained the same, which makes this one of the nicest pubs in the city to enjoy a few pints.

BRAZEN HEAD TRADITIONAL PUB
Map p246 (📞01-679 5186; 20 Lower Bridge St; 🚌51B, 78A or 123 from city centre) Reputedly Dublin's oldest pub, the Brazen Head has been serving thirsty patrons since 1198 when it set up as a Norman tavern. It's a bit away from the city centre, and the clientele is made up of foreign-language students, tourists and some grizzly auld locals.

Though its history is uncertain, the sunken level of the courtyard indicates how much street levels have altered since its construction. Robert Emmet was believed to have been a regular visitor, while in *Ulysses*, James Joyce reckoned 'you get a decent enough do in the Brazen Head'.

ENTERTAINMENT

VICAR STREET LIVE MUSIC
Map p246 (📞01-454 5533; www.vicarstreet.com; 58-59 Thomas St) Smaller performances take place at this intimate venue near Christ Church Cathedral. It has a capacity of 1000, between its table-serviced group seating downstairs and theatre-style balcony. Vicar Street offers a varied program of performers, with a strong emphasis on soul, folk, jazz and foreign music.

TIVOLI THEATRE THEATRE
Map p246 (📞01-454 4472; 135-136 Francis St; adult/child & student €15/10; 🚌51B, 51C, 78A or 123 from city centre) This commercial theatre offers a little bit of everything, from a good play with terrific actors to absolute nonsense with questionable comedic value.

SHOPPING

Some of the most interesting, and wackiest, shopping is done along Francis St in the Liberties, home of art dealers and antiquarians of every hue.

DUBLIN FOOD CO-OP MARKET
Map p246 (www.dublinfoodcoop.com; 12 Newmarket; ⏲2-8pm Thu, 9.30am-4.30pm Sat; 🚌49, 54A & 77X from city centre) From dog food to detergent, everything in this market hall is organic and/or eco-friendly. Thursdays has a limited selection of local and imported fairtrade products, but Saturday is when it's all on display – Dubliners from all over drop in for their responsible weekly shop. There's an on-the-premises baker and even baby-changing facilities.

FLEURY ANTIQUES ANTIQUES
Map p246 (📞01-473 0878; 57 Francis St; ⏲9.30am-6pm Mon-Sat; 🚌123, 206 or 51B from city centre) This blue-fronted antiques shop does a steady connoisseur's trade in all manner of oil paintings (there's something for virtually every taste), vases, candelabras, silverware, porcelain and decorative pieces from the 18th century right up to the 1930s.

O'SULLIVAN ANTIQUES ANTIQUES
Map p246 (📞01-454 1143; 43-44 Francis St; ⏲10am-5pm Mon-Sat; 🚌123, 206 or 51B from city centre) Fine furniture and furnishings from the Georgian, Victorian and Edwardian eras are the speciality of this respected antiques shop, where a rummage might also reveal some distinctive bits of ceramic and crystal, not to mention medals and uniforms from a bygone era that will win you first prize at the costume ball.

OXFAM HOME HOMEWARES
Map p246 (📞01-402 0555; 86 Francis St; ⏲10am-5.30pm Mon-Fri, to 1pm Sat; 🚌123, 206 or 51B from city centre) They say charity begins at home so get rummaging among the veneer cast-offs in this furniture branch of the charity chain where you might stumble across the odd 1960s Subbuteo table or art-deco dresser. Esoteric vinyl from the '80s is another speciality of the house.

North of the Liffey

Neighbourhood Top Five

1 Nodding sagely at the art collection in the **Dublin City Gallery – The Hugh Lane** (p122).

2 Sampling a snifter of the hard stuff at the **Old Jameson Distillery** (p126) – that's whiskey to you and me.

3 Spending a night at the **Abbey Theatre** (p137), the spiritual home of the Irish theatrical experience.

4 Wandering about the glorious yard of Collins Barracks, without forgetting the collection of the **National Museum of Ireland – Decorative Arts & History** (p126).

5 Tantalising your tastebuds by eating in the north side's new breed of restaurants, like **Musashi Noodles & Sushi Bar** (p135), as good as any you'll find south of the river.

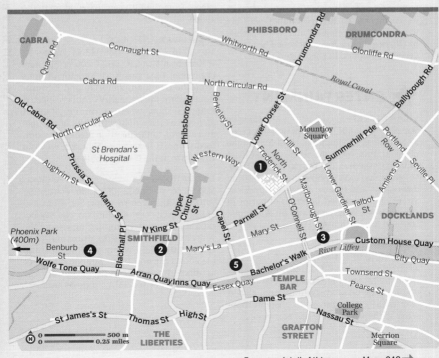

For more detail of this area see Map p248

Explore North of the Liffey

With the biggest geographical spread of any neighbourhood, a little planning and a bit of transport will be required to fully explore Dublin north of the Liffey. O'Connell St and its attractions are pretty straightforward and can be explored with ease on foot, with the biggest demand on your time being the fabulous collection at the Hugh Lane gallery. The north side's other attractions are to the west, and the best way to get to them is by Luas (www.luas.ie), which will reduce your journey to mere minutes. The Old Jameson Distillery and Collins Barracks are within walking distance of each other, on either side of Smithfield, but you might need the services of the Phoenix Park shuttle bus to explore Europe's largest enclosed city park, home to the president, the US Ambassador, the zoo and a herd of red deer, not to mention visiting Dubliners when the weather is good.

Beyond the Royal Canal, which encloses the northern edge of the city centre, are a bunch of attractions that are well worth the effort: you could devote the guts of half a day each visiting the Croke Park museum, Glasnevin cemetery and the National Botanic Gardens; an excursion to Marino to see the famous Casino is also worthwhile, and you can get there via the DART suburban train.

Local Life

➡ **Hangout** Go to Brother Hubbard (p134) on Capel St for great coffee and an easy-going atmosphere; equally good is Third Space (p134) in Smithfield.

➡ **Food** The northside's culinary credentials are elevated by the likes of Musashi (p135) on Capel St, Wuff (p135) on Benburb St or L Mulligan (p136) nearby.

➡ **Park Life** Do as Dubliners do on a fine day and take in the massive expanse of the Phoenix Park (p123), where you can run, cycle, play, walk or just lie down, depending on your fancy.

Getting There & Away

➡ **Bus** All city centre buses stop on O'Connell St or the nearby quays. City buses serve Glasnevin and Croke Park.

➡ **Tram** The Luas runs east to west parallel to the Liffey from Abbey St to Heuston Station

➡ **Train** The DART runs from Connolly Station northeast to Clontarf Rd, which is handy for the Casino at Marino.

Lonely Planet's Top Tip

The area between the northern end of O'Connell St and Gardiner St to the east as far up as Dorset St is best avoided late at night, as the potential for drug- or alcohol-fuelled trouble is heightened in a neighbourhood beset by the ills of urban deprivation.

 ## Best Places to Eat

➡ Musashi Noodles & Sushi Bar (p135)

➡ Chapter One (p136)

➡ Wuff (p135)

➡ L Mulligan Grocer (p136)

➡ The Hot Stove (p136)

For reviews, see p134➡

Best Places to Drink

➡ Kavanagh's (p137)

➡ Walshe's (p136)

➡ Dice Bar (p137)

➡ Pantibar (p137)

For reviews, see p136➡

Best Places to Shop

➡ Penney's (p141)

➡ Jervis St Centre (p141)

➡ Arnott's (p141)

➡ Clery's (p141)

For reviews, see p141➡

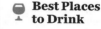

NORTH OF THE LIFFEY

TOP SIGHT
DUBLIN CITY GALLERY – THE HUGH LANE

Whatever reputation Dublin may have as a repository of top-class art is in large part due to the collection at this magnificent gallery, home to Impressionist masterpieces, the best of modern Irish work from 1950 onward, and the actual studio of Francis Bacon.

The Gallery

Founded in 1908, the gallery's home since 1933 has been the stunning **Charlemont House**, designed by the Georgian superstar architect, William Chambers, in 1763. A modernist extension, which opened in 2006, has seen the addition of 13 bright galleries spread across three floors.

Sir Hugh Lane & his Bequest

The gallery owes its origins to one Sir Hugh Lane (1875–1915). Born in County Cork, Lane worked in London art galleries before setting up his own gallery in Dublin. He had a connoisseur's eye and a good nose for the directions of the market, which enabled him to build up a superb collection, particularly strong in Impressionists.

Unfortunately for Ireland, neither his talents nor his collection were much appreciated. Irish rejection led him to rewrite his will and bequeath some of the finest works in his collection to the National Gallery in London. Later he relented and added a rider to his will leaving the collection to Dublin. However, he failed to have it witnessed, thus causing a long legal squabble over which gallery had rightful ownership.

The collection (known as the **Hugh Lane Bequest 1917**) was split in a complicated 1959 settlement that sees some of the paintings moving back and forth. The conditions of the exchanges are in the midst of negotiation, but for now the gallery has Manet's *La Musique Aux Tuileries*, Degas' *Bains de Mer*, and *Lavacourt under Snow* by Monet.

Francis Bacon Studio

Impressionist masterpieces notwithstanding, the gallery's most popular exhibit is the **Francis Bacon Studio**, which was painstakingly moved, in all its shambolic mess, from 7 Reece Mews, South Kensington, London, where the Dublin-born artist (1909–92) lived for 31 years. The display features some 80,000 items madly strewn about the place, including slashed canvases, the last painting he was working on, tables piled with materials, walls daubed with colour samples, portraits with heads cut out, favourite bits of furniture and many assorted piles of crap. It's a teasing and tantalising, riveting and ridiculous masterpiece that provides the viewer no real sense of the artist himself. Far more revealing is the 10-minute profile of him with Melvyn Bragg and the immensely sad photographs of Bacon's immaculately tidy bachelor pad, which suggest a deep, personal loneliness.

Elsewhere in the Gallery

The new wing is also home to a permanent collection of seven abstract paintings by Irish-born, New York–based **Sean Scully**, probably Ireland's most famous living painter.

You can round off a satisfying visit with lunch in the superb cafe (p135) in the basement, before making a stop in the well-stocked **gift shop** (Map p248; Parnell Sq N, Charlemont House, Northside).

DON'T MISS

➡ The Hugh Lane Bequest 1917 paintings
➡ The Francis Bacon Studio
➡ The Sean Scully collection
➡ The Irish collection

PRACTICALITIES

➡ Map p248
➡ ☏01-222 5550
➡ www.hughlane.ie
➡ 22 North Parnell Sq
➡ admission free
➡ ⊘10am-6pm Tue-Thu, 10am-5pm Fri & Sat, 11am-5pm Sun
➡ ☐3,7, 10, 11, 13, 16, 19, 46A, 123

DESIGN PICS / PATRICK SWAN / GETTY IMAGES ©

TOP SIGHT
PHOENIX PARK

Dubliners are rightly proud of this humongous patch of greenery at the northwestern edge of the city centre, a short skip from Heuston Station and the Liffey quays.

The hugely impressive 709 hectares that comprise the park make up one of the largest set of inner-city green lungs in the world. The park is a magnificent playground for all kinds of activities, from running to polo, and it's a fitting home to the president of Ireland, the American ambassador and a shy herd of fallow deer who are best observed – from a distance – during the summer months. It is also where you'll find Europe's oldest zoo, not to mention dozens of playing fields for all kinds of sport. How's that for a place to stretch your legs?

The Lay of the Land

Chesterfield Ave runs northwest through the length of the park from the Parkgate St entrance to the Castleknock Gate. Near the Parkgate St entrance is the 63m-high **Wellington Monument** obelisk, which was completed in 1861. Nearby is the **People's Garden**, dating from 1864, and the bandstand in the Hollow. Across Chesterfield Ave from the Áras an Uachtaráin – and easily visible from the road – is the massive **Papal Cross**, which marks the site where Pope John Paul II preached to 1.25 million people in 1979. In the centre of the park the **Phoenix Monument**, erected by Lord Chesterfield in 1747, looks so unlike a phoenix that it's often referred to as the Eagle Monument.

Dublin Zoo

Established in 1831, the 28-hectare **Dublin Zoo** (www.dublinzoo.ie; Phoenix Park; adult/child/family €16/11.50/45.50; ⏰9.30am-6pm Mar-Sep, 9.30am-dusk Oct-Feb; 🚌10 from O'Connell St, 25

DON'T MISS

➡ Wellington Monument
➡ Tour of Áras an Uachtaráin
➡ Dublin Zoo
➡ The deer herd

PRACTICALITIES

➡ www.phoenixpark.ie
➡ admission free
➡ ⏰24hr
➡ 🚌10 from O'Connell St, 25 or 26 from Middle Abbey St then Phoenix Park Shuttle Bus from Parkgate St entrance.

FARMLEIGH HOUSE

Situated in the north-west corner of the Phoenix Park, opulent Farmleigh House (www.farmleigh.ie) can only be visited by joining one of the 30-minute house tours. However, the real highlight of the 32-hectare estate is the garden, where regular shows are held. There is also an extensive program of cultural events in summer, ranging from food fairs to classical concerts.

At 709 hectares, the Phoenix Park dwarfs the measly 337 hectares of New York's Central Park and is larger than all of the major London parks put together.

& 26 from Middle Abbey St) just north of the Hollow is one of the oldest in the world. It is well known for its lion-breeding program, which dates back to 1857, and includes among its offspring the lion that roars at the start of MGM films. You'll see these tough cats, from a distance, on the 'African Savanna', just one of several habitats created in the last few years.

The zoo is home to roughly 400 animals from 100 different species, and you can visit all of them across the eight different habitats that range from an Asian jungle to a family farm, where kids get to meet the inhabitants up close and even milk a (model) cow. There are restaurants, cafes and even a train to get you round.

Áras an Uachtaráin

The residence of the Irish president is a Palladian **lodge** that was built in 1751 and enlarged a couple of times since, most recently in 1816. It was home to the British viceroys from 1782 to 1922, and then to the governors general until Ireland cut ties with the British Crown and created the office of president in 1937. Queen Victoria stayed here during her visit in 1849, when she appeared not to even notice the Famine. The candle burning in the window is an old Irish tradition, to guide 'the Irish diaspora' home.

Tickets for the free one-hour **tours** (Phoenix Park; ⊙guided tours hourly 10am-4pm Sat) **FREE** can be collected from the **Phoenix Park Visitor Centre** (⊙10am-5.45pm daily Mar-Sep, 9.30-5.30pm Wed-Sun Oct-Feb), the converted former stables of the papal nunciate, where you'll see a 10-minute introductory video before being shuttled to the Áras itself to inspect five state rooms and the president's study. If you can't make it on a Saturday, just become the elected president of your own country or a Nobel laureate or something, and then wrangle a personal invite.

Ashtown Castle

Next door to Áras an Uachtaráin is the restored four-storey Ashtown Castle, a 17th-century tower house 'discovered' inside the 18th-century nuncio's mansion when the latter was demolished in 1986 due to dry rot. You can visit the castle only on a guided tour from the visitor centre.

Elsewhere in the Park

The southern part of the park has many **football** and **hurling pitches**; although they actually occupy about 80 hectares (200 acres), the area is known as the **Fifteen Acres**. To the west, the rural-looking **Glen Pond** corner of the park is extremely attractive.

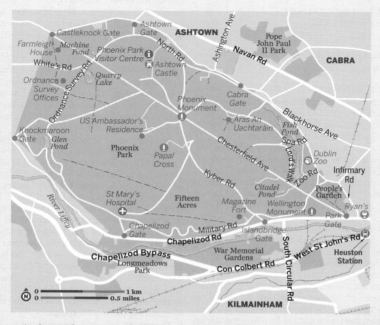

At the northwestern end of the park, near the White's Gate entrance, are the offices of **Ordnance Survey Ireland**, the government mapping department. This building was originally built in 1728 by Luke Gardiner, who was responsible for the architecture in O'Connell St and Mountjoy Sq in north Dublin.

Back towards the Parkgate St entrance is the **Magazine Fort** (closed to the public) on Thomas's Hill. The fort was no quick construction, the process taking from 1734 to 1801. It provided useful target practice during the 1916 Easter Rising, and was raided by the Irish Republican Army (IRA) in 1940 when the entire ammunition reserve of the Irish army was nabbed (it was recovered a few weeks later).

◉ SIGHTS

DUBLIN CITY GALLERY – THE HUGH LANE   GALLERY
See p122.

PHOENIX PARK   PARK
See p123.

OLD JAMESON DISTILLERY   MUSEUM

Map p248 (www.jamesonwhiskey.com; Bow St; adult/child €14/7.70; ⊙9am-6pm Mon-Sat, 10am-6pm Sun; 🚌25, 66, 67 or 90 from city centre, 🚇Smithfield) Smithfield's biggest draw is devoted to *uisce beatha* (*ish*-kuh ba-ha, 'the water of life'). The whowhatnow? It's whiskey, which doesn't quite bestow life, but, if drunk enough, will undoubtedly take it away. Here, in the original home of one of its most famous and renowned distillers, you can get an introduction to the history and culture of this most potent of drinks.

The museum occupies a section of the old distillery, which kept the capital in whiskey from 1780 to 1971 (after which the remaining distillers moved to a new ultra-modern distillery in Midleton, County Cork). The museum can only be visited on guided tours, which run every 35 minutes. They start with a short film and then, with the aid of models and exhibitions, explain everything you ever wanted to know about Irish whiskey, from its fascinating history to how it's made and why it differs from Scotch – ex-footballer (and Scot) Ally McCoist once joked that the Irish thought of everything, including putting an 'e' in whiskey. At the end of the tour you'll be invited into the **Jameson Bar** for a dram of complimentary whiskey. Stay alert and make sure to volunteer for the tasting tour, where you get to sample whiskeys from all around the world and train your palate to identify and appreciate the differences between each.

At the end of the tour, you're deposited in the shop, which was kinda the whole point of the tour in the first place. If you do want to bring a bottle or two home, make sure you buy one that you can't get in your local. There are some 100 brands of Irish whiskey (not all sold here) but only three – Jameson, Bushmills and Tullamore Dew – are widely available. Our tip is Red Breast, pure pot still, the way all Irish whiskey used to be made, although the swashbuckling Power's is numero uno in Ireland and difficult to get elsewhere.

There's also a good cafe and restaurant.

NATIONAL MUSEUM OF IRELAND – DECORATIVE ARTS & HISTORY   MUSEUM

(www.museum.ie; Benburb St; ⊙10am-5pm Tue-Sat, 2-5pm Sun; 🚌25, 66, 67 or 90 from city centre, 🚇Smithfield) **FREE** No wonder the British army were so reluctant to pull out of Ireland when they were occupying this magnificent space, the oldest army barracks in Europe. The collection features fashion, furniture, weaponry, folk life, silver, ceramics and glassware in an attempt to offer a bird's-eye view of Ireland's social, economic and military history over the last millennium.

But you cannot ignore the surroundings, as magnificent as any structure you'll see in Ireland. The building was completed in 1704 according to the design of Thomas Burgh, whose CV also includes the Old Library in Trinity College and St Michan's Church. Its central square held six entire regiments and is a truly awesome space, surrounded by arcaded colonnades and blocks linked by walking bridges. Following the handover to the new Irish government in 1922, the barracks was renamed to honour Michael Collins, a hero of the struggle for independence, who was killed that year in the Civil War; to this day most Dubliners refer to the museum as the **Collins Barracks**.

Decorative arts is a tough thing to get right, especially if you want to offer a broad appeal, but the well-designed displays, interactive multimedia and a dizzying array of disparate artefacts make for an interesting and valiant effort. On the 1st floor is the museum's Irish silver collection, one of the largest collections of silver in the world; on the 2nd floor you'll find Irish period furniture and scientific instruments, while the 3rd floor has simple and sturdy Irish country furniture. Modern-furniture-and-design lovers will enjoy the exhibition on iconic Irish designer **Eileen Gray** (1878–1976), one of the museum's highlights. One of the most influential designers of the 20th century, Gray's life and work are documented in the exhibit, which shows examples of her most famous pieces. The fascinating **Way We Wore exhibit** displays Irish clothing and jewellery from the past 250 years. An intriguing sociocultural study, it highlights the symbolism jewellery and clothing had in bestowing messages of mourning, love and identity.

An exhibition chronicling Ireland's **1916 Easter Rising** is on the ground floor. Visceral memorabilia, such as first-hand accounts of the violence of the Black and Tans

O'CONNELL STREET

The grand dame of Dublin thoroughfares is the imperially wide O'Connell St, a street that has played a central role in key episodes of Dublin's – and the nation's – history. None more so than the 1916 Easter Rising, when the proclamation announcing Ireland's independence was read out to a slightly bemused crowd from the steps of the General Post Office (p130).

History

The street owes its existence to the efforts of Luke Gardiner, Dublin's premier Georgian developer, who laid out plans for a grand boulevard to reflect the exalted status of the neighbourhood. The whole project was completed in 1794 – just seven short years before the Act of Union closed the doors on an independent Irish parliament and led many of the city's aristocrats to leave Dublin for good. For much of the next two centuries Sackville St (as it was called until 1924) fell into decline. Its handsome residences were partly converted into slum dwellings for the city's burgeoning poor.

The destruction of 1916 didn't do the street any favours, but the real damage to O'Connell St occurred in the decades after WWII, when the street fell into the care of fast-food outlets, ugly shops and amusement arcades. A huge program of redevelopment has seen the street restored to something approaching its former grandeur, including the construction of new, pedestrian-friendly pavements, a central mall and refurbished shopfronts.

Statuary

O'Connell St is lined with statues of Irish history's good and great. The big daddy of them all is the 'Liberator' himself, **Daniel O'Connell** (Map p248; 1775–1847), completed in 1880, whose massive bronze bulk soars above the street at the bridge end. The four winged figures at his feet represent O'Connell's supposed virtues: patriotism, courage, fidelity and eloquence. Dubs began to refer to the street as O'Connell St soon after the monument was erected; its name was officially changed after independence.

Heading away from the river, past a monument to **William Smith O'Brien** (1803–64), leader of the Young Irelanders, is a statue that easily rivals O'Connell's for drama: just outside the GPO is the spread-armed figure of trade-union leader **Jim Larkin** (Map p248; 1876–1947). His big moment came when he helped organise the general strike in 1913 – the pose catches him in full flow, urging workers to rise up for their rights. We're with you, comrade.

Next up and difficult to miss is the Spire (p130), but just below it, on pedestrianised North Earl St, is the detached figure of **James Joyce** (Map p248; 1882–1941), looking on the fast and shiny version of 21st-century O'Connell St with a bemused air. Dubs have lovingly dubbed him the 'prick with the stick' and we're sure Joyce would have loved the vulgar rhyme.

Further on is **Father Theobald Mathew** (Map p248; 1790–1856), the 'apostle of temperance'. There can't have been a tougher gig in Ireland, but he led a spirited campaign against 'the demon drink' in the 1840s and converted hundreds of thousands to teetotalism.

The top of the street is completed by the imposing statue of **Charles Stewart Parnell** (Map p248; 1846–91), the 'uncrowned king of Ireland', who was an advocate of Home Rule and became a political victim of Irish intolerance.

and post-Rising hunger strikes, the handwritten death certificates of the republican prisoners and their postcards from Holloway prison, bring to life this poignant period of Irish history.

Some of the best pieces are gathered in the **Curator's Choice exhibition**, which is a collection of 25 objects hand-picked by different curators, and displayed alongside an account of why they were chosen.

BARRY MASON / ALAMY ©

1. Dublin City Gallery – The Hugh Lane (p122)

Charlemont House is home to a stunning art collection bequeathed to Dublin by Sir Hugh Lane (1875–1915).

2. Northside (p120)

Explore north over the River Liffey via O'Connell Bridge to Dublin's grandest thoroughfare.

3. Old Jameson Distillery (p126)

Now the site of a museum devoted to whiskey, the Jameson Distillery produced 'the water of life' in Dublin between 1780 and 1971.

4. Phoenix Park (p123)

Home to Europe's oldest zoo, the Phoenix Park is one of the world's largest inner city parks.

GENERAL POST OFFICE HISTORIC BUILDING

Map p248 (www.anpost.ie; O'Connell St; ⊙8am-8pm Mon-Sat; 🚃all city centre, 🚇Abbey) Not just the country's main post office, or an eye-catching neoclassical building: the General Post Office is at the heart of Ireland's struggle for independence as it served as command HQ for the rebels during the Easter Rising of 1916. As a result, it has become the focal point for all kinds of protests, parades and remembrances.

The fateful events of 1916 resulted in a week-long bombardment by the British Army which left Francis Johnston's 1818-masterpiece a smouldering wreck: you can still see pockmarks and bullet holes in the huge pillars supporting the Ionic portico, which spans the five central bays and is topped by three statues representing Fidelity, Hibernia and Mercury. The damage was so bad that it didn't reopen until 1929.

In the spacious and light-filled interior there's a beautiful bronze statue, the *Death of Cuchulainn* (1935), depicting the legendary hero of Ulster, whose spirit was evoked in the poetry of Pádraig Pearse. He was an awesome warrior slain at the age of 27 after being tricked into an unfair fight. Even as he lay dead, nobody dared approach the body for fear of attack, and it wasn't until ravens landed on him that they were convinced he was dead. The statue is dedicated to those who died in the Rising. Also inside is a series of communist noble-worker–style paintings depicting scenes from the Easter Rising. There are also lots of people going about the everyday business of buying stamps and posting letters. Finally, among all the flags hanging in here, notice that the Union Jack is hung behind the counter and out of reach? It had to be moved there because people kept setting it alight.

SPIRE MONUMENT

Map p248 (O'Connell St; 🚃all city centre, 🚇Abbey) The city's most visible landmark soars over O'Connell St and is an impressive bit of architectural engineering that was erected in 2001: from a base of only 3m in diameter, it soars more than 120m into the sky and tapers into a 15cm-wide beam of light...it's tall and shiny and it does the trick rather nicely.

The brainchild of London-based architect Ian Ritchie, it is apparently the highest sculpture in the world, but much like the Parisian reaction to the construction of the Eiffel Tower, Dubliners are divided as to its aesthetic value and have regularly made fun of it. Among other names, we like 'the erection in the intersection', the 'stiletto in the ghetto', and the altogether brilliant 'eyeful tower'.

NATIONAL LEPRECHAUN MUSEUM MUSEUM

Map p248 (www.leprechaunmuseum.ie; Twilfit House, Jervis St; adult/child €12/8; ⊙9.30am-6.30pm Mon-Sat, from 10.30am Sun; 🚃all city centre, 🚇Jervis) Abandon all cynicism ye who enter here, otherwise you won't get through the exhibits of this museum dedicated to the history of the 'little people' without finding it all completely ridiculous. If you can suspend judgement, you'll discover that there is a folklore element to the place, and that kids will find it a lot of fun.

In truth, you get little more than an introductory glimpse at the leprechaun story, from the (largely American) image of a gold-burying, good-luck-bringing, lucky charms–type figure to the creature associated with the mythical Tuatha dé Danann people that preceded the Celts. There's the optical illusion tunnel (which makes you appear smaller to those at the other end), the room full of oversized furniture, the wishing wells and, invariably, the pot of gold; all of which is strictly for the kids. But if Walt Disney himself went on a leprechaun hunt when visiting Ireland during the filming of *Darby O'Gill and the Little People* in 1948, what the hell do we know?

FOUR COURTS HISTORIC BUILDING

Map p248 (Inns Quay; ⊙9am-5pm Mon-Fri; 🚃25, 66, 67 or 90 from city centre, 🚇Four Courts) James Gandon's (1743–1823) masterpiece is a mammoth complex stretching 130m along Inns Quay. It is as fine an example of Georgian public architecture as there is in Dublin and – despite the construction of a brand new criminal courts building further west along the Liffey – still the enduring symbol of Irish law going about its daily business.

Construction on the Four Courts began in 1786, soon engulfing the Public Offices (built a short time previously at the western end of the same site), and continued until 1802. By then it included a Corinthian-columned central block connected to flanking wings with enclosed quadrangles. The ensemble is topped by a diverse collection of statuary. The original four courts – Exchequer, Common Pleas, King's Bench and Chancery – branch off the central rotunda.

The Four Courts played a brief role in the 1916 Easter Rising without suffering damage, but it wasn't so lucky during the Civil War. When anti-Treaty forces seized the building and refused to leave, Free State forces led by Michael Collins shelled it from across the river. As the occupiers retreated, the building was set on fire and many irreplaceable early records were burned. These were the opening salvos in the Irish Civil War. The building wasn't restored until 1932.

Visitors are allowed to wander through, but not to enter the courts or other restricted areas. In the lobby of the central rotunda you'll see bewigged barristers conferring and police officers handcuffed to their charges waiting to enter court.

JAMES JOYCE
CULTURAL CENTRE   CULTURAL CENTRE

Map p248 (www.jamesjoyce.ie; 35 North Great George's St; adult/student/child €5/4/free; ⊙10am-5pm Tue-Sat; ☐3, 10, 11, 11A, 13, 16, 16A, 19, 19A, 22 from city centre) Denis Maginni, the exuberant, flamboyant dance instructor and 'confirmed bachelor' immortalised by James Joyce in *Ulysses,* taught the finer points of dance out of this beautifully restored Georgian house, now a centre devoted to promoting and preserving the Joycean heritage.

Although Jimmy probably never set foot in the house, he lived in the 'hood for a time, went to a local school and lost his virginity a stone's throw away in what was once Europe's largest red-light district. We couldn't imagine a more fitting location for the centre.

The centre owes its existence to the sterling efforts of Senator David Norris, a charismatic Joycean scholar and gay-rights activist who bought the house in 1982 and oversaw its restoration and conversion into the centre that it is today.

What it is today is more of a study centre than a museum, although there are a handful of exhibits that will pique the interest of a Joyce enthusiast. These include some of the furniture from Joyce's Paris apartment, which was rescued from falling into German hands in 1940 by Joyce's friend Paul Léon; a life-size re-creation of a typical Edwardian bedroom (not Joyce's, but one similar to what James and Nora would have used); and the original door of 7 Eccles St, the home of Leopold and Molly Bloom in *Ulysses,* which was demolished in real life to make way for a private hospital.

It's not much, but the absence of period stuff is more than made up for by the superb interactive displays, which include three short documentary films on various aspects of Joyce's life and work, and – the highlight of the whole place – computers that allow you to explore the content of *Ulysses* episode by episode and trace Joyce's life year by year. It's enough to demolish the myth that Joyce's works are an impenetrable mystery and render him as he should be to the contemporary reader: a writer of enormous talent who sought to challenge and entertain his audience with his breathtaking wit and use of language.

While here, you can also admire the fine plastered ceilings, some of which are restored originals while others are meticulous reproductions of Michael Stapleton's designs. Senator Norris fought a long, unrewarding battle for the preservation of Georgian Dublin, and it's wonderful to see others have followed his example – the street has been given a much-needed facelift and now boasts some of the finest Georgian doorways and fanlights in the city.

DUBLIN WRITERS MUSEUM   MUSEUM

Map p248 (www.writersmuseum.com; 18 North Parnell Sq; adult/child €7.50/4.70; ⊙10am-5pm Mon-Sat, 11am-5pm Sun; ☐3, 10, 11, 11A, 13, 16, 16A, 19, 19A, 22 from city centre) Memorabilia aplenty and lots of literary ephemera line the walls and display cabinets of this elegant museum devoted to preserving the city's rich literary tradition up to 1970. A curious decision to omit living writers limits its appeal and no account at all is given to contemporary writers, who would arguably be more popular with today's readers.

Although the busts and portraits of the greats in the gallery upstairs are worth more than a cursory peek, the real draws are the ground-floor displays, which include Samuel Beckett's phone (with a button for excluding incoming calls, of course), a letter from the 'tenement aristocrat' Brendan Behan to his brother, and a first edition of Bram Stoker's *Dracula.*

The building, comprising two 18th-century houses, is worth exploring on its own. Dublin stuccodore Michael Stapleton decorated the upstairs gallery. The **Gorham Library** next door is worth a peek and there's also a calming Zen garden. The museum cafe is a pleasant place to linger, while the basement restaurant, Chapter One (p136), is one of the city's best.

Admission includes taped guides in English and other languages, which have the annoying habit of repeating quotes with actor's voices.

While the museum focuses on the dearly departed, the **Irish Writers Centre** (Map p248; ☑01-872 1302; 19 North Parnell Sq) next door provides a meeting and working place for their living successors.

ST MICHAN'S CHURCH   CHURCH

Map p248 (Lower Church St; adult/child/student €5/3.50/4; ☉10am-12.45pm & 2-4.45pm Mon-Fri, to 12.45pm Sat ; ☑Smithfield) Macabre remains are the main attraction at this church, which was founded by the Danes in 1096 and named after one of their saints. Among the 'attractions' is an 800-year-old Norman crusader who was so tall that his feet were lopped off so he could fit in a coffin. Visits are by guided tour only.

The oldest architectural feature is the 15th-century battlement tower; otherwise the church was rebuilt in the late 17th century, considerably restored in the early 19th century and again after the Civil War. The interior of the church, which feels more like a courtroom, is worth a quick look as you wait for your guide. It contains an organ from 1724, which Handel may have played for the first-ever performance of his *Messiah*. The organ case is distinguished by the fine oak carving of 17 entwined musical instruments on its front. A skull on the floor on one side of the altar is said to represent Oliver Cromwell. On the opposite side is the Stool of Repentance, where 'open and notoriously naughty livers' did public penance.

The tours of the underground vaults are the real draw, however. The bodies within are aged between 400 and 800 years, and have been preserved by a combination of methane gas coming from rotting vegetation beneath the church, the magnesium limestone of the masonry (which absorbs moisture from the air), and the perfectly constant temperature. The corpses have been exposed because the coffins in the vaults were stacked on top of one another and some toppled over and opened when the wood rotted. The guide sounds like he's been delivering the same, albeit fascinating, spiel for too long, but you'll definitely be glad you're not alone down there.

ARBOUR HILL CEMETERY   CEMETERY

(☑01-821 3021; www.heritageireland.ie; Arbour Hill; ☉8am-4pm Mon-Fri, 11am-4pm Sat, 9.30am-4pm

Sun; ☑25, 25A, 37, 38, 39, 66, 67, 90 or 134 from city centre, ☑Museum) **FREE** Just north of Collins Barracks, this small cemetery is the final resting place of all 14 of the executed leaders of the 1916 Easter Rising. The burial ground is plain, with the 14 names inscribed in stone. Beside the graves is a cenotaph bearing the Easter Proclamation, a focal point for official and national commemorations.

The front of the cemetery incongruously, but poignantly, contains the graves of British personnel killed in the War of Independence. Here, in the oldest part of the cemetery, as the gravestones toppled, they were lined up against the boundary walls where they still stand solemnly today.

KING'S INNS   HISTORIC BUILDING

Map p248 (www.kingsinns.ie; Henrietta St; ☑25, 25A, 66, 67, 90 or 134 from city centre, ☑Four Courts) Home to Dublin's legal profession (and where barristers are still trained), King's Inns occupies a classical building built by James Gandon between 1795 and 1817 on Constitution Hill, with Francis Johnston chipping in with the cupola. A fine example of Georgian public architecture, the building itself is alas only open to members and their guests.

GARDEN OF REMEMBRANCE   PARK

Map p248 (Parnell Sq; ☉8.30am-6pm Apr-Sep, 9.30am-4pm Oct-Mar; ☑3, 10, 11, 13, 16, 19 or 22 from city centre) This rather austere little park was opened by President Éamon de Valera in 1966 for the 50th anniversary of the Easter Rising. The most interesting feature in the garden is a bronze statue of the **Children of Lir** (Map p248) by Oisín Kelly; according to Irish legend the children were turned into swans by their wicked stepmother.

It is still known to some Dubs as the 'Garden of Mature Recollection', mocking the linguistic gymnastics employed by former favourite for president Brian Lenihan, who was caught out lying in a minor political scandal and used the phrase to try and wiggle his way out of it.

BELVEDERE HOUSE   SCHOOL

Map p248 (6 Great Denmark St; 🚌3, 10, 11, 13, 16, 19 or 22 from city centre) The home of Jesuit Belvedere College since 1841, James Joyce studied here between 1893 and 1898 (and described his experiences in *A Portrait of the Artist*), and we can only wonder if he ever took a moment to admire the magnificent plasterwork by master stuccodore Michael Stapleton in between catechism classes and arithmetic homework? It's closed to the public.

ROTUNDA HOSPITAL   HOSPITAL

Map p248 (✆01-873 0700; Parnell Sq; ⊙visiting hours 6-8pm; 🚌3, 10, 11, 13, 16, 19 or 22 from city centre) Irish public hospitals aren't usually attractions, but this one – founded in 1748 as the first maternity hospital in the British Isles – makes for an interesting walk-by or an unofficial wander inside if you're interested in Victorian plasterwork. It shares its basic design with Leinster House (p86) because the architect of both, Richard Cassels, used the same floor plan to economise.

The hospital was established by Dr Bartholomew Mosse and was for a time the world's largest hospital devoted to maternity care – at a time when the burgeoning urban population was enduring shocking infant mortality rates. To the main building Cassels added a three-storey tower, which Mosse intended to use for fundraising purposes (charging visitors an entry fee). He also laid out pleasure gardens, which were fashionable among Dublin's high society for a time, and built the Rotunda Assembly Hall to raise money. The hall is now occupied by the **Ambassador Theatre** (Map p248; ✆1890 925 100; O'Connell St), and the Supper Rooms house the Gate Theatre (p139).

Inside, the public rooms and staircases give some idea of how beautiful the hospital once was, and they lead to one of Dublin's largely hidden gems, the sumptuous **Rotunda Chapel**, built in 1758, and featuring superb coloured plasterwork by German stuccodore Bartholomew Cramillion. The Italian artist Giovanni Battista Capriani was supposed to supplement the work but his paintings were never installed, which is probably just as well because you can't imagine how this little space would have looked with even more decoration. If you intend visiting, you have to bear in mind that this is still a functioning hospital and you must be very quiet when coming to see the chapel. It's not terribly well signposted inside and is often locked outside visiting hours (although if you ask kindly or look like you're in desperate need of a prayer, somebody will let you in).

ST MARY'S ABBEY   MUSEUM

Map p248 (✆01-833 1618; www.heritageireland.ie; Meeting House Lane; ⊙10am-5pm Tue-Thu Jun-Sep; 🚌11, 16 or 41 from city centre) Where now the glories of Babylon? All that remains of what was once Ireland's wealthiest and most powerful monastery is the chapterhouse, so forgotten that most Dubliners are unaware of its existence. Visitors can enjoy a small exhibition and view a model of what the abbey looked like in its heyday. From March to September, tours can be booked through the Casino at Marino (p140).

Founded in 1139, this Cistercian abbey ran the show when it came to Irish church politics for much of the Middle Ages, although its reputation with the authorities was somewhat sullied when it became a favourite meeting place for rebels against the crown. On 11 June 1534, 'Silken' Thomas Fitzgerald, the most important of Leinster's Anglo-Norman lords, entered the chapterhouse flanked by 140 horsemen with silk fringes on their helmets (hence his name) and flung his Sword of State on the ground in front of the awaiting King's Council – a ceremonial two-fingered salute to King Henry VIII and his authority. Fitzgerald's abbey antics feature in the 'Wandering Rocks' chapter of Joyce's *Ulysses*.

ST MARY'S CHURCH   CHURCH

Map p248 (Mary St; 🚌11, 16 or 41 from city centre) Designed by William Robinson in 1697, this is the most important church to survive from that period (although it's no longer in use and is closed to the public). John Wesley, founder of Methodism, delivered his first Irish sermon here in 1747 and it was the preferred church of Dublin's 18th-century social elite. Many famous Dubliners were baptised in its font, and Arthur Guinness was married here in 1793.

ST MARY'S PRO-CATHEDRAL CHURCH

Map p248 (Marlborough St; ⊘8am-6.30pm; ⊠all city centre, ⊠Abbey) FREE Dublin's most important Catholic church is not quite the showcase you'd expect. It's in the wrong place for starters. The large neoclassical building, built between 1816 to 1825, was intended to stand where the GPO is, but Protestant objections resulted in its current location, on a cramped street that was then at the heart of Monto, the red-light district.

In fact, it's so cramped for space around here that you'd hardly notice the church's six Doric columns, which were modelled on the Temple of Theseus in Athens, much less be able to admire them. The interior is fairly functional, and its few highlights include a carved altar by Peter Turnerelli and the alto relief representation of the Ascension by John Smyth. The best time to visit is 11am on Sunday when the Latin Mass is sung by the Palestrina Choir, with whom Ireland's most celebrated tenor, John McCormack, began his career in 1904.

The design of the church is shrouded in some mystery. In 1814 John Sweetman won a competition held to find the best design for the church, a competition that had actually been organised by his brother William. It's not certain whether John actually designed the building, since he was living in Paris at the time and may have bought the plans from the French architect Auguste Gauthier, who designed the similar Notre Dame de Lorette in northern France. The only clue as to the church's architect is in the ledger, which lists the builder as 'Mr P'.

Finally, a word about the term 'pro' in the title. It implies, roughly, that it is an 'unofficial cathedral'. More accurately it was built as a sort of interim cathedral to be replaced when sufficient funds were available. Church leaders never actually got around to it, leaving the capital of this most Catholic of countries with two incredible-but-underused Protestant cathedrals and one fairly ordinary Catholic one. Irony one, piety nil.

ST GEORGE'S CHURCH CHURCH

Map p248 (Hardwicke Pl; ⊠11, 16 or 41 from city centre) One of Dublin's most beautiful buildings is this deconsecrated church, built by Francis Johnston between 1802 and 1813 in Greek Ionic style. It is topped by an eye-catching, 60m-high steeple modelled on that of St Martin-in-the-Fields in London. Alas, it has fallen into serious disrepair and

has been shrouded in scaffolding for more than a decade.

Although this was one of Johnston's finest works, and the Duke of Wellington was married here, the building's neglect is largely to do to the fact that it's Church of Ireland and not Roman Catholic – the Protestant (and largely moneyed) community for whom it was built has shrunk to the point of disappearance. The bells that Leopold Bloom heard in that book were removed, the ornate pulpit was carved up and used to decorate the pub Thomas Read's (p96), and the spire is in danger of crumbling, which has resulted in the scaffolding. The church is not open to the public.

EATING

THIRD SPACE CAFE €

Map p248 (Unit 14, Block C, Smithfield Market; ⊘8am-7pm Mon-Tue & Fri, to 9.30pm Wed-Thu, 9.30am-5pm Sat; ⊠Smithfield) One of the most welcoming cafes in town is this wonderful spot in Smithfield, which serves gorgeous sandwiches, wraps and baps, as well a tart of the day (€5.95) and wines by the glass. Sit in the window, take out a book and just relax. The staff are fabulous.

BROTHER HUBBARD CAFE €

Map p248 (153 Capel St; ⊘8am-5.30pm Mon-Fri, 10am-5pm Sat; ⊠all city centre, ⊠Jervis) When did the art of coffee become, well, an art? When the likes of this terrific little cafe began serving up its specialist beans (procured from coffee experts 3FE), turning each cappuccino into the perfect creation. For solid sustenance, the scones are excellent and the sandwiches as good as you'll find anywhere. The perfect hangout spot.

SOUP DRAGON TAKEAWAY €

Map p248 (www.soupdragon.com; 168 Capel St; soups €5-10; ⊘8am-5pm Mon-Fri, 10am-4pm Sat; ⊠all city centre, ⊠Jervis) Queues are a regular feature outside this fabulous spot that specialises in soups-on-the-go, but they also do excellent curries, stews, pies and salads. The all-day breakfast options are excellent – we especially like the mini-breakfast quiche of sausage, egg and bacon. Bowls come in three different sizes and prices include fresh bread and a piece of fruit.

THE EVOLUTION OF A GEORGIAN STREET

Dublin's first example of Georgian urban design was **Henrietta Street** (Map p248; ☐25, 25A, 37, 38, 39, 66, 67, 90 or 134 from city centre, ☐Courts), laid out in the 1720s at the behest of Luke Gardiner, who was to become the city's pre-eminent Georgian developer. Wider than most 18th-century streets, it was lined with a series of large, red-bricked Palladian mansions. Gardiner himself lived at No 10, in a house designed by Richard Cassels. The street was originally known as Primate's Hill, as the Archbishop of Armagh owned one of the houses; it was later demolished (along with two others) to make way for the Law Library of King's Inns (p132; still there at the street's western end). The name Henrietta was inspired by either the wife of Charles FitzRoy, the Duke of Grafton, or the wife of Charles Paulet, the 2nd Duke of Bolton (after whom nearby Bolton St is named).

The street was Dublin's most fashionable address until the Act of Union in 1801, after which it fell into disrepair. For most of the 20th century it was a tenement street, with each house crammed with as many as 70 residents. Recent restorations have restored the 13 remaining houses to something approaching their elegant best, and the cul-de-sac remains a wonderful insight into the evolution of Georgian residential architecture.

TASTE OF EMILIA ITALIAN €

Map p248 (28 Lower Liffey St; mains €4-10; ⊙noon-10.30pm Wed-Sat, from 5pm Tue, from 3.30pm Sun; ☐all city centre) This warm, buzzing locale does a wonderful trade in cured meats and cheeses from all over Italy, paying particular attention to the produce of the true heartland of Italian cuisine, Emilia-Romagna. The sandwiches are made with homemade *piadina* bread or *tigelle,* and you can wash it down with a light sparkling wine from the north of Italy.

PANEM CAFE €

Map p248 (21 Lower Ormond Quay; mains €7-10; ⊙9am-5pm Mon-Sat; ☐all city centre) Pasta, focaccia and salads are the standard fare at this diminutive quay-side cafe, but the specialties are wickedly sweet and savoury pastries, which are all made on-site. The croissants and brioche – filled with Belgian chocolate, almond cream or hazelnut amaretti – are the perfect snack for a holiday stroll along the Liffey Boardwalk. Lunchtimes are chaotic.

LA TAVERNA DI BACCO ITALIAN €

Map p248 (☑01-873 0040; Quartier Bloom; salads & sandwiches €5-8, mains €8-9; ⊙closed lunch Sun; ☐all city centre) Right in the heart of Quartier Bloom is this pleasant Italian eatery that serves simple pastas, antipasti and cheeses from the home country. Just a few steps away is its sister spot, the **Enoteca Delle Langhe** (Map p248; Bloom's Lane; mains €8-10; ⊙lunch & dinner), which mostly specialises in wines and cold cuts.

**DUBLIN CITY GALLERY –
THE HUGH LANE** INTERNATIONAL €

Map p248 (☑01-874 1903; www.hughlane.ie; 22 North Parnell Sq; mains €8-12; ⊙10am-6pm Mon-Thu, to 5pm Fri-Sun; ☐3, 10, 11, 13, 16, 19 or 22 from city centre) There's hardly a better way to ruminate over the art in the gallery (p122) than over lunch in the new gallery cafe, an airy room in the basement next to a small garden. The menu tends largely towards the healthy-eating side of things, offering a range of scrumptious tarts and exotic seasonal salads.

**MUSASHI NOODLES &
SUSHI BAR** JAPANESE €€

Map p248 (☑01-532 8057; www.musashidublin.com; 15 Capel St; mains €15-25; ⊙lunch & dinner; ☐all city centre, ☐Jervis) A lovely, low-lit room, this new spot is the most authentic Japanese restaurant in the city, serving up freshly crafted sushi to an ever-growing number of devotees. The lunch bento deals are a steal, and if you don't fancy raw fish they also do a wide range of other Japanese specialties. It's BYO (corkage charged). Evening bookings recommended.

WUFF INTERNATIONAL €€

(23 Benburb St; mains €14-24; ⊙7.30am-4pm Mon-Wed, to 10pm Thu-Fri, 10am-10pm Sat, to 4pm Sun; ☐25, 25A, 66, 67 from city centre, ☐Museum) This neighbourhood bistro does excellent breakfasts and brunches – the truffle-infused poached eggs with Gruyère on toast are divine – as well as fine

NORTH OF THE LIFFEY EATING

dinner mains that feature fish, duck, beef and a couple of veggie options. The name is inspired by the catcall used by bears to attract the men they fancy.

L MULLIGAN GROCER CONTEMPORARY IRISH €€
(18 Stoneybatter; mains €14-21; ◻25, 25A, 66, 67 from city centre, ▣Museum) It's a great traditional pub, but the main reason to come here is for the food, all sourced locally and made by expert hands. The menu includes dishes like slow-cooked free-range pork belly and herb-crumbed haddock, as well as particularly tasty lamb burger. There are about a dozen craft beers on draught and as many again in a bottle.

HOT STOVE MODERN IRISH €€
Map p248 (www.thehotstoverestaurant.com; 38-39 Parnell Sq West; mains €17-22; ◷lunch & dinner Tue-Fri, dinner Sat; ◻3, 10, 11, 13, 16, 19 or 22 from city centre) An elegant new restaurant that may one day vie for the northside's best, the Hot Stove serves locally sourced, beautifully prepared Irish dishes including pork belly, a changing selection of fish dishes and the ubiquitous steak. The pretheatre menu (two/three courses €23/28) is a steal, the wine list is excellent and the service top-notch.

YAMAMORI SUSHI JAPANESE €€
Map p248 (www.yamamorinoodles.ie; 38-39 Lower Ormond Quay; sushi €3-3.50, mains €17-35; ◷lunch & dinner ; ▣all city centre) A sibling of the long-established Yamamori (p67) on South Great George's St, this large restaurant – spread across two converted Georgian houses and including a bamboo garden – does Japanese with great aplomb, serving up all kinds of favourites from steaming bowls of ramen to a delicious *nami moriawase*. Like its sister restaurant, the lunchtime bento boxes are a popular choice.

CHAPTER ONE MODERN IRISH €€€
Map p248 (✆01-873 2266; www.chapterone restaurant.com; 18 North Parnell Sq; 2-course lunch €29, 4-course dinner €65; ◷12.30-2pm Tue-Fri, 6-11pm Tue-Sat; ◻3, 10, 11, 13, 16, 19 or 22 from city centre) Michelin-starred Chapter One is our choice for the city's best eatery because it successfully combines flawless haute cuisine with a relaxed, welcoming atmosphere that is at the heart of Irish hospitality. The food is French-inspired contemporary Irish, the menus change regularly and the service

is top-notch. The three-course pre-theatre menu (€36.50) is a favourite with those heading to the Gate around the corner.

WINDING STAIR MODERN IRISH €€€
Map p248 (✆01-873 7320; winding-stair.com; 40 Lower Ormond Quay; mains €23-27; ◷noon-5pm & 5.30-10.30pm; ▣all city centre) Housed within a beautiful Georgian building that was once home to the city's most beloved bookshop (the ground floor still is one), the Winding Stair's conversion to elegant restaurant has been faultless. The wonderful Irish menu – creamy fish pie, bacon and organic cabbage, steamed mussels, and Irish farmyard cheeses – coupled with an excellent wine list makes for a memorable meal.

MORRISON GRILL INTERNATIONAL €€€
Map p248 (✆01-878 2999; www.morrisonhotel. ie; Morrison Hotel, Lower Ormond Quay; mains €18-30; ◷dinner; ▣all city centre) The main eatery of the newly refurbished Morrison Hotel is really a very fancy grill whose specialties are meats cooked in Ireland's only Josper indoor barbecue oven. If you don't fancy steaks, burgers or grilled fish, there's a selection of other main courses, but the real treat here is food cooked at over 500 degrees.

🍷 DRINKING & NIGHTLIFE

The north side's pubs just don't get the same numbers of visitors as their south side brethren, which means that if you're looking for a truly authentic pub experience, you're more likely to get it here. Around O'Connell St you'll also get the rough with the smooth, and we suggest you keep your wits about you late at night so as to avoid the potential for trouble that can sadly beset the city's main thoroughfare after dark.

WALSHE'S PUB
(6 Stoneybatter; ◻25, 25A, 66, 67 from city centre, ▣Museum) If the snug is free, a drink in Walshe's is about as pure a traditional experience as you'll have in any pub in the city; if it isn't, you'll have to make do with the old-fashioned bar, where the friendly staff and brilliant clientele (a mix of locals and hipster imports) are a treat. A proper Dublin pub.

ONE FOOT IN THE GRAVE

A contender for best pub in Dublin is **John Kavanagh's** (Gravediggers; ✆01-830 7978; 1 Prospect Sq; 🚌13, 19 or 19A from O'Connell St) of Glasnevin, more commonly known as the Gravediggers because the employees from the adjacent cemetery had a secret serving hatch so that they could drink on the job. Founded in 1833, it is reputedly Dublin's oldest family-owned pub: the current owners are the sixth generation of Kavanaghs to be in charge. Inside, it's as traditional a boozer as you could hope: stone floors, lacquered wooden wall panels and all. In summer time the green of the square is full of drinkers basking in the sun, while inside the hardened locals ensure that ne'er a hint of sunshine disturbs some of the best Guinness in town. An absolute classic.

DICE BAR
BAR

(✆01-674 6710; 79 Queen St; 🚌25, 25A, 66, 67 from city centre, 🚉Museum) Co-owned by Huey from the Fun Lovin' Criminals, the Dice Bar looks like something you might find on New York's Lower East Side. Its dodgy locale, black-and-red painted interior, dripping candles and stressed seating, combined with rocking DJs most nights, make it a magnet for Dublin hipsters. It has Guinness and local microbrews.

PANTIBAR
GAY BAR

Map p248 (www.pantibar.com; 7-8 Capel St; 🚌all city centre) It's not as big as the George (p70) or as in-your-face as the Dragon (p70), but Pantibar is just as bold and brash as both, mostly because its owner, the eponymous Panti, is an outrageous entertainer and goes to great lengths to make sure that a night in her bar is going to be one to remember. The floor shows – both on and off the stage – are fabulous. It's open late Friday and Saturday.

RYAN'S
PUB

(✆01-677 6097; 28 Parkgate St; 🚉Heuston) Near the Phoenix Park, this is one of only a handful of city pubs that has retained its Victorian decor virtually intact, complete with ornate bar and snugs. An institution among Dublin's public houses, this is truly worth the trip.

FLOWING TIDE
PUB

Map p248 (9 Lower Abbey St; 🚌all city centre, 🚉Abbey) This beautiful, atmospheric old pub is directly opposite the Abbey (p137) and is popular with theatre-goers – it can get swamped around 11pm, after the curtain comes down. They blend in with some no-bullshit locals who give the place a vital edge, and make it a great place for a drink and a natter.

NEALON'S
TRADITIONAL PUB

Map p248 (✆01-872 3247; 165 Capel St; 🚌all city centre, 🚉Jervis) The warm and cosy decor of this traditional pub is matched by the exceptionally friendly staff. There's live jazz on Sunday.

OVAL
TRADITIONAL PUB

Map p248 (✆01-872 1259; 78 Middle Abbey St; 🚌all city centre, 🚉Abbey) This is a great little pub, where young and old come together in conversation and rich, creamy pints go down a treat. The Tardis effect is evident once you walk through the door: it is much bigger than it looks from the outside, spreading over three floors.

SACKVILLE LOUNGE
PUB

Map p248 (Sackville Pl; 🚌all city centre) This tiny 19th-century, one-room, wood-panelled bar lies just off O'Connell St and is popular with actors from the nearby Abbey (p137) and Peacock (p139) theatres, as well as a disproportionate number of elderly drinkers. It's a good pub for a solitary pint.

⭐ ENTERTAINMENT

ABBEY THEATRE
THEATRE

Map p248 (✆01-878 7222; www.abbeytheatre.ie; Lower Abbey St; 🚌all city centre, 🚉Abbey) Ireland's renowned national theatre, founded by WB Yeats in 1904, has been reinvigorated in recent years by director Fiach MacConghaill, who has introduced lots of new blood to what was in danger of becoming a moribund corpse. The current programme has a mix of Irish classics (Synge, O'Casey etc), established international names (Shepard, Mamet) and new talent (O'Rowe, Carr et al).

Debate over the theatre's home – an ugly, purpose-built box from 1966 – has been silenced by economic realities, and so the city's theatregoers have had to make do

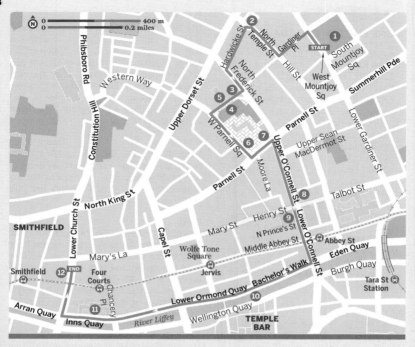

🏃 Neighbourhood Walk
Take A Walk on the North Side

START MOUNTJOY SQ
FINISH ST MICHAN'S CHURCH
LENGTH 2.5KM; TWO HOURS

Take a left at the northwestern corner of
1 Mountjoy Sq and walk down Gardiner
Pl, turning right onto North Temple St. Up
ahead is the fine, but now deconsecrated
Georgian **2 St George's Church** (p134),
designed by architect Francis Johnston.

Take a left onto Hardwicke St and left
again onto North Frederick St. On your right
you'll spot the distinctive **3 Abbey Pres-
byterian Church**, built in 1864.

The northern slice of Parnell Sq houses
the **4 Garden of Remembrance** (p132),
opened in 1966 to commemorate the 50th
anniversary of the 1916 Easter Rising. North
of the square, facing the park, is the excellent **5 Dublin City Gallery – The Hugh
Lane,** (p122) home to some of the best
modern art in Europe.

In the southern part of Parnell Sq is the
6 Rotunda Hospital (p133), a wonderful

example of public architecture in the Georgian style. The southeastern corner of the
square has the **7 Gate Theatre** (p119),
one of the city's most important theatres.

Head south down O'Connell St, passing
by the 120m-high **8 Spire** (p110). Erected
in 2001, it is an iconic symbol of the city. On
the western side of O'Connell St, the stunning neoclassical **9 General Post Office**
(p130) towers over the street.

When you hit the river, turn right and
walk along the boardwalk until you reach
the city's most distinctive crossing point,
the **10 Ha'Penny Bridge** (named for the
charge levied on those who used it).

Continue west along Ormond Quay to
one of James Gandon's Georgian masterpieces, the **11 Four Courts** (p110), home
to the most important law courts in Ireland.
Finally take a right onto Church St to admire **12 St Michan's Church** (p132), a
beautiful Georgian construction with grisly
vaults populated by the remains of the long
departed.

DA NORT'SOYID & THE SOUTHSYDE

It is commonly assumed that the south side is totally posh and the north side is a derelict slum – it means the jokes are easier to make and the prejudices easier to maintain. But the truth is a little more complex. The 'south side' generally refers to Dublin 4 and the fancy suburbs immediately west and south – conveniently ignoring the traditionally working-class neighbourhoods in southwestern Dublin like Bluebell and Tallaght. North Dublin is huge, but the north side tag is usually applied to the inner suburbs, where incomes are lower, accents are more pronouncedly Dublin and – most recently – the influx of foreign nationals is more in evidence. All Dubliners are familiar with the posh twit stereotype born and raised on the south side, but there's another kind of Dubliner, usually from the middle-class districts of northern Dublin, who affects a salt-of-the-earth accent while talking about the 'gee-gees' and says things like 'tis far from sushi we was rared' while tucking into a *maki* roll.

with an acoustic makeover that has improved the experience of going to a play. Monday performances are cheaper. Work by up-and-coming writers and more experimental theatre is staged in the adjoining **Peacock Theatre** (Map p248; ☎01-878 7222; ◫all city centre, ◳Abbey).

GATE THEATRE
THEATRE

Map p248 (☎01-874 4045; www.gatetheatre.ie; 1 Cavendish Row) The city's most elegant theatre, housed in a late-18th-century building, features a generally unflappable repertory of classic American and European plays. Orson Welles' first professional performance was here, and James Mason played here early in his career. Even today it is the only theatre in town where you might see established international movie stars work on their credibility with a theatre run.

TWISTED PEPPER
NIGHTCLUB

Map p248 (☎01-873 4800; www.bodytonic music.com/thetwistedpepper; 54 Middle Abbey St; ◷bar 4pm-late, cafe 11am-6pm; ◫all city centre, ◳Abbey) Dublin's hippest venue comes in four parts: DJs spin great tunes in the Basement; the Stage is for live acts; the Mezzanine is a secluded bar area above the stage; and the Cafe is where you can get an Irish breakfast all day. All run by the Bodytonic crew, one of the most exciting music and production crowds in town.

COBBLESTONE
PUB

Map p248 (North King St; ◳Smithfield) This pub in the heart of Smithfield has a great atmosphere in its cosy upstairs bar, where there are superb nightly music sessions performed by traditional musicians (especially Thursday) and up-and-coming folk acts.

GRAND SOCIAL
CONTEMPORARY BAR

Map p248 (☎01-874 0076; www.thegrandsocial. ie; 35 Lower Liffey St; ◫all city centre, ◳Jervis) This multipurpose venue hosts club nights, comedy and live music gigs as well as being a decent bar for a drink. It's spread across three floors, each of which has a different theme: The Parlour downstairs is a cozy, old-fashioned bar; the mid-level Ballroom is where the dancing is; the upstairs Loft hosts a variety of events.

LAUGHTER LOUNGE
COMEDY

Map p248 (☎1800 266 339; www.laughterlounge. com; 4-8 Eden Quay; admission from €25; ◷doors open 7.30pm; ◫all city centre) Dublin's only specially designated comedy theatre is where you'll find those comics too famous for the smaller pub stages but not famous enough to sell out the city's bigger venues. Think comedians on the way up (or on the way down).

ACADEMY
LIVE MUSIC

Map p248 (☎01-877 9999; www.theacademy dublin.com; 57 Middle Abbey St; ◫all city centre, ◳Abbey) A terrific midsized venue, the Academy's stage has been graced by an impressive list of performers, from Nick Cave's Bad Seeds to '80s superstar Nik Kershaw. It's also the place to hear those unknown names who stand a better-than-evens chance of making it somewhere.

CINEWORLD MULTIPLEX
CINEMA

Map p248 (☎0818 304 204; www.cineworld.ie; Parnell Centre, Parnell St; ◫all city centre) This 17-screen cinema shows only commercial releases. The seats are comfy, the concession stand is huge and the selection of pick 'n' mix could induce a sugar seizure. It lacks the style of older cinemas, but we like it anyway.

BEYOND THE ROYAL CANAL

The Royal Canal, constructed from 1790, marks the traditional boundary of the city centre's northern edge, and beyond it, amidst the semi-detached suburban dwellings, are a handful of sights that are well worth a visit.

Croke Park Experience

The Gaelic Athletic Association (GAA) considers itself not just the governing body of a bunch of Irish games but also the stout defender of a cultural identity that is ingrained in Ireland's sense of self. To get an idea of just how important the GAA is, a visit to the **Croke Park Experience** (www.crokepark.ie; Clonliffe Rd, New Stand, Croke Park; adult/child/student museum €6/4/5, museum & tour €12/8/9; ⊙9.30am-5pm Mon-Sat, noon-5pm Sun Apr-Oct, 10am-5pm Tue-Sat, noon-4pm Sun Nov-Mar) is a must. The twice-daily tours (except match days) of the impressive Croke Park stadium are excellent, and well worth the extra cost. The stadium's newest attraction is the **Skyline** (www.skylinecrokepark.ie; Croke Park; adults/students/children €25/20/15; ⊙11am & 2pm May-Sep, Fri-Sun only Oct-Apr), a guided tour around the stadium roof.

Glasnevin Cemetery

The tombstones at Ireland's largest and most historically important burial **site** (www.glasnevin-cemetery.ie; Finglas Rd; ⊙24hr; 🚌40, 40A or 40B from Parnell St) **FREE** read like a 'who's who' of Irish history, as most of the leading names of the last 150 years are buried here.

A modern replica of a round tower acts as a handy landmark for locating the tomb of Daniel O'Connell, who died in 1847. Charles Stewart Parnell's tomb is topped with a large granite rock, on which only his name is inscribed – a remarkably simple tribute to a figure of such historical importance. Other notable people buried here include Sir Roger Casement, Republican leader Michael Collins, docker and trade unionist Jim Larkin, and poet Gerard Manley Hopkins.

The history of the cemetery is told in wonderful, award-winning detail in the **museum** (museum & tour €12, museum only €6; ⊙10am-5pm Mon-Fri, 11am-6pm Sat & Sun), which tells the social and political story of Ireland through the lives of the people known and unknown who are buried here. The best way to visit the cemetery is to take one of the daily **tours** (11.30am, 12.30pm & 2.30pm).

National Botanic Gardens

Founded in 1795, the 19.5-hectare **botanic gardens** (Botanic Rd; ⊙9am-6pm Mon-Sat, 11am-6pm Sun Apr-Oct, 10am-4.30pm Mon-Sat, 11am-4.30pm Sun Nov-Mar; 🚌13, 13A or 19 from O'Connell St, or bus 34 or 34A from Middle Abbey St) **FREE** are home to a series of curvilinear glasshouses, dating from 1843 to 1869, created by Richard Turner. Within these Victorian masterpieces you will find the latest in botanical technology, including a series of computer-controlled climates reproducing the environments of different parts of the world. Among the pioneering botanical work conducted here was the first attempt to raise orchids from seed, back in 1844.

Casino at Marino

It's not the roulette-wheel kind of casino but the original Italian kind, the one that means 'summer home', and this particular **casino** (www.heritageireland.ie; Malahide Rd; adult/child/senior €3/1/2; ⊙10am-5pm May-Sep; 🚌20A, 20B, 27, 27B, 42, 42C or 123 from city centre) is one of the most enchanting constructions in all of Ireland. It was built in the mid-18th century for the Earl of Charlemont, who returned from his grand tour of Europe with more art than he could store in his own home, Marino House. He also came home with a big love of the Palladian style – hence the architecture of this wonderful folly.

Entrance is by guided tour only. The exterior of the building, with a huge entrance doorway, and 12 Tuscan columns forming a templelike facade, creates the expectation that its interior will be a simple single open space. But instead it is an extravagant convoluted maze. A variety of statuary adorns the outside but it's the amusing fakes that are most enjoyable.

LIGHTHOUSE CINEMA CINEMA

Map p248 (☑01-879 7601; www.lighthouse cinema.ie; Smithfield Plaza; ☐all city centre, ⓢSmithfield) The most impressive cinema in town is this snazzy four-screener in a stylish building just off Smithfield Plaza. The menu is strictly art house, and the cafe-bar on the ground floor is perfect for discussing the merits of German Expressionism.

SAVOY CINEMA

Map p248 (☑01-874 6000; Upper O'Connell St; ⊗from 2pm; ☐all city centre) The Savoy is a five-screen, first-run cinema, and has late-night shows at weekends. Savoy Cinema 1 is the largest in the country and its enormous screen is the perfect way to view really spectacular blockbuster movies.

 SHOPPING

With only a handful of exceptions, northside shopping is all about the high-street chain store and the easy-access shopping centre, which is mighty convenient for Dubliners looking for everyday wear at decent prices, but will hardly make for a satisfying long-distance retail pilgrimage. But if you want to do as Dubliners do...

EASON'S BOOKS

Map p248 (☑01-873 3811; www.easons.ie; 40 Lower O'Connell St; ☐all city centre) The biggest selection of magazines and foreign newspapers in the whole country can be found on the ground floor of this huge bookshop near the GPO, along with literally dozens of browsers leafing through mags with ne'er a thought of purchasing one.

WINDING STAIR BOOKS

Map p248 (☑01-873 3292; 40 Lower Ormond Quay; ⊗9.30am-6pm Mon-Sat; ☐all city centre) There was a public outcry when this creaky old place closed a few years ago. It's just reopened its doors and Dublin's bohemians, students and literati can once more thumb the fine selection of new and secondhand books crammed into heaving bookcases. After browsing, head up the winding stairs to the excellent restaurant (p136).

ARNOTT'S DEPARTMENT STORE

Map p248 (☑01-805 0400; 12 Henry St; ☐all city centre) Occupying a huge block with entrances on Henry, Liffey and Abbey Sts, this is our favourite of Dublin's department stores. It stocks virtually everything, from garden furniture to high fashion, and it's all relatively affordable.

CLERY'S & CO DEPARTMENT STORE

Map p248 (☑01-878 6000; O'Connell St; ☐all city centre) This elegant department store is Ireland's most famous retailer, and a real Dublin classic. Recently restored to its graceful best, Clery's has sought to shed its conservative reputation by filling its shelves with funkier labels to attract younger buyers.

PENNEY'S DEPARTMENT STORE

Map p248 (☑01-888 0500; www.primark.co.uk; 47 Mary St; ☐all city centre) Ireland's cheapest department store is a northside favourite, a place to find all kinds of everything without paying a fortune for it – it's the best place in town for men's socks and jocks. True, the stuff you'll find here isn't guaranteed to last, but at prices like these, why quibble over quality?

WALTON'S MUSIC

Map p248 (☑01-874 7805; 2 North Frederick St; ☐36 or 36A from city centre) The main branch of the well-known music store.

MOORE STREET MARKET MARKET

Map p248 (Moore St; ⊗8am-4pm Mon-Sat; ☐all city centre) An open-air, steadfastly 'Old Dublin' market, with fruit, fish and flowers. Traditional vendors hawk cheap cigarettes, tobacco and chocolate amongst the new wave of Chinese and Nigerians selling phonecards and hair extensions. Don't try to buy just one banana though – if it says 10 for €1, that's what it is.

JERVIS STREET CENTRE SHOPPING CENTRE

Map p248 (☑01-878 1323; Jervis St; ☐all city centre) This modern, domed mall is a veritable shrine to the British chain store. Boots, Topshop, Debenhams, Argos, Dixons, M&S and Miss Selfridge all get a look-in.

Docklands & the Grand Canal

Neighbourhood Top Five

1 A visit aboard the **Jeanie Johnston** (p144), a working replica of a 19th-century coffin ship.

2 Contemplating the Famine amongst Rowan Gillespie's thought-provoking bronze **statues** (p144).

3 Attending a gig at the **Bord Gáis Energy Theatre** (p147)

4 A walk to the **Poolbeg Lighthouse** (p147), enjoying the stunning views of the bay and city.

5 Sightseeing while cruising on a **Sea Safari** (p212) historical tour.

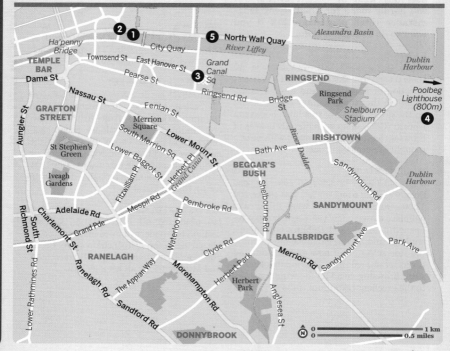

For more detail of this area see Map p252 and p254 ➡

Explore Docklands

Although much of the Docklands development that transformed the eastern end of the Liffey towards Dublin Port is given over to office and apartment blocks, there are parts of 'Canary Dwarf' that are worth exploring at ground level. The aesthetic highlight of the area is the 10,000-sq-metre Grand Canal Square, designed by American landscape architect Martha Schwartz. Flanking its northwestern side is the magnificent Bord Gáis Energy Theatre (2010), designed by Daniel Libeskind and named after its primary sponsor, one of Ireland's leading energy providers. Stretching across the square from its entrance is a red 'carpet' – a series of red, resin-glass angled sticks that glow – and a green one – made up of polygon-shaped planters filled with marshlike vegetation.

On the north banks of the Liffey, the standout buildings are the snazzy National Convention Centre (2010), designed by Kevin Roche; the Custom House (1781–91), a colossal Georgian building topped by a copper dome; and the city's premier indoor venue, the O2, which is the main attraction in the Point Village, a development that also includes a cinema and a hotel.

Local Life

⇒ **Sustenance** For proper Neapolitan-style pizza, Paulie's Pizza (p145) is easily the best in town; just around the corner (and owned by the same two brothers) is the equally popular Juniors (p145), which attracts the trendy crowd with its version of a Brooklyn eatery.

⇒ **Imbibe** If you want to celebrate (or commiserate) with fans after a game at the Aviva Stadium, you'll find plenty of company in The Chophouse (p147) and across the street in the more traditional Slattery's (p147). A short walk south of here on Haddington Rd is the Beggar's Bush (p147), aka Jack Ryan's, which is also a popular sporting pub.

Getting There & Away

⇒ **Bus** The most convenient public transport option is the bus – Nos 1, 47, 56A and 77A go from Dame St to the edge of Grand Canal Square. For the north side, bus 151 goes from Bachelor's Walk to the Docklands.
⇒ **Tram** The Luas Red Line terminus is at the Point Village.
⇒ **Train** The DART stops at Grand Canal Quay.

Lonely Planet's Top Tip

To quell your hunger or quench your thirst, head southwest off the Grand Canal Dock to the junction of Haddington Rd, Upper Grand Canal St and Bath Ave, where you'll find a handful of terrific restaurants and popular pubs.

Best Places to Eat

⇒ Juniors (p145)
⇒ Paulie's Pizza (p145)
⇒ Herbstreet (p145)
⇒ Ely Gastro Pub (p145)

For reviews, see p145 ⇒

Best Places to Drink

⇒ Beggar's Bush (p147)
⇒ Slattery's (p147)
⇒ Kennedy's (p147)

For reviews, see p147 ⇒

Best for Design

⇒ National Convention Centre
⇒ Bord Gáis Energy Theatre (p147)
⇒ The Marker (p177)

For reviews, see p147 ⇒

⊙ SIGHTS

Take in the sights on a historical tour of the River Liffey and Dublin Port with Sea Safaris (p212).

CUSTOM HOUSE
MUSEUM

Map p252 (⊙10am-5pm Mon-Fri, 2-5pm Sat-Sun; 🚇all city centre) Georgian genius James Gandon (1743–1823) announced his arrival on the Dublin scene with this magnificent building (1781–91), constructed just past Eden Quay at a wide stretch in the River Liffey. It's a colossal, neoclassical pile that stretches for 114m topped by a copper dome, beneath which the visitor centre features a small museum on Gandon and the history of the building.

When it was being built, angry city merchants and dockers from the original Custom House further upriver in Temple Bar were so menacing that Gandon often came to work wielding a broadsword. He was supported by the era's foremost property developer, Luke Gardiner, who saw the new Custom House as a major part of his scheme to shift the axis of the city eastwards from medieval Capel St to what was then Gardiner's Mall (now O'Connell St).

Best appreciated from the south side of the Liffey, its fine detail deserves closer inspection. Arcades, each with seven arches, join the centre to the end pavilions and the columns along the front have harps carved in their capitals. Motifs alluding to transport and trade include the four rooftop statues of Neptune, Mercury, Plenty and Industry, destroyed when the building was gutted in a five-day fire during the independence struggle in 1921, then replaced in 1991. The interior was extensively redesigned after 1921 and again in the 1980s. Below the frieze are heads representing the gods of Ireland's 13 principal rivers, and the sole female head, above the main door, represents the River Liffey. The cattle heads honour Dublin's beef trade, and the statues behind the building represent Africa, America, Asia and Europe. Set into the dome are four clocks and, above that, a 5m-high statue of Hope.

FAMINE MEMORIAL
MEMORIAL

Map p252 (Custom House Quay; 🚇all city centre) Just east of Custom House is one of Dublin's most thought-provoking examples of public art: the set of life-sized bronze figures (1997) by Rowan Gillespie known simply as 'Famine'. Designed to commemorate the ravages of the Great Hunger (1845–51): their haunted, harrowed look testifies to a journey that was both hazardous and unwelcome.

The location of the sculptures is also telling, for it was from this very point in 1846 that one of the first 'coffin ships' (as they quickly came to be called) set sail for the United States. Steerage fare on the *Perseverence* was £3 and 210 passengers made that first journey, landing in New York on 18 May 1846, with all passengers and crew intact.

In June 2007, a second series of Famine sculptures by Rowan Gillespie was unveiled on the quayside in Toronto's Ireland Park by Irish president Mary McAleese to commemorate the arrival of Famine refugees in the New World.

JEANIE JOHNSTON
MUSEUM, SHIP

Map p252 (www.jeaniejohnston.ie; Custom House Quay; adult/child €8.50/4.50; ⊙tours 11am, noon & hourly 2-4pm; 🚇all city centre) One of the city's most original tourist attractions is an exact working replica of a 19th-century coffin ship, as the sailing boats that transported starving emigrants away from Ireland during the Famine were gruesomely known. A small on-board museum details the harrowing plight of a typical journey, which usually took around 47 days.

This particular ship, a three-masted barque originally built in Québec in 1847, made 16 transatlantic voyages, carrying more than 2500 people, and never suffered a single death. The ship also operates as a Sail Training vessel, with journeys taking place from May to September. If you are visiting during these times, check the website for details of when it will be in dock.

NATIONAL PRINT MUSEUM
MUSEUM

Map p254 (✆01-660 3770; www.nationalprintmuseum.ie; Haddington Rd, Garrison Chapel, Beggar's Bush; adult/concession €3.50/2; ⊙9am-5pm Mon-Fri, 2-5pm Sat & Sun; 🚌7, 8 or 45 from city centre, 🚇DART to Grand Canal Dock) You don't have to be into printing to enjoy this quirky little museum, where personalised guided tours are offered in a delightfully casual and compelling way. A video looks at the history of printing in Ireland and then you wander through the various (still working) antique presses amid the smell of ink and metal.

HERE TODAY, GONE TOMORROW?

As part of the ongoing repercussions of Ireland's banking and financial crisis, most of the snazzy developments that spearheaded the city's urban regeneration program have encountered massive financial difficulties as the loans incurred to build them have come due with the owners simply incapable of repaying them. And so it is with the Docklands' biggest developments, the Bord Gáis Energy Theatre and the Point Village, which in mid-2013 were taken over by the National Asset Management Agency (NAMA), a government body set up in 2009 to manage the enormous shortfalls incurred by property developers and speculators. The good news is that NAMA are slow to close anything down, preferring instead to find some way to turn the distressed business into a more profitable enterprise, which may mean reduced or slimmed-down trading rather than a total shutdown.

The guides are excellent and can tailor the tours to suit your special interests – for example, anyone interested in history can get a detailed account of the difficulties encountered by the rebels of 1916 when they tried to get the proclamation printed. Upstairs, there are lots of old newspaper pages recording important episodes in Irish history over the last century.

WATERWAYS VISITOR CENTRE　　MUSEUM
Map p252 (✆01-677 7510; www.waterways ireland.org; Grand Canal Quay; adult/child €4/2; ☉10am-6pm Wed-Sun; ⬚Grand Canal Dock) Recently renovated, this snazzy centre documents the history of Ireland's waterways and includes exhibits on the city's two canals, as well as an interactive display that allows visitors to 'drive' a barge. You can also hear the stories of the monsters that reside in the canal locks.

✗ EATING

PAULIE'S PIZZA　　ITALIAN €€
Map p254 (www.juniors.ie; 58 Upper Grand Canal St; pizzas €12-17; ☉dinner; ⭑) In July 2010 the brothers who created Juniors (just around the corner) imported a traditional Neapolitan pizza oven and set about introducing Dubliners to proper, thin-crusted pizza from the city of its birthplace. Margheritas, *biancas* (no tomato sauce), calzone and other Neapolitan specialities are the real treat, but there's also room for a classic New York slice as well as a few local creations.

JUNIORS　　ITALIAN €€
Map p254 (✆01-664 3648; www.juniors.ie; 2 Bath Ave; mains €16-24; ☉lunch & dinner) Cramped and easily mistaken for any old cafe, Juniors

is anything but ordinary: designed to imitate a New York deli, the food (Italian-influenced, all locally sourced produce) is delicious, the atmosphere always buzzing (it's often hard to get a table) and the ethos top-notch, which is down to the two brothers who run the place.

ELY BAR & BRASSERIE　　FUSION €€
Map p252 (www.elywinebar.ie; Custom House Quay; mains €13-21; ☉noon-3pm & 6-10pm Mon-Fri, 1-4pm & 6-10pm Sat) Scrummy homemade burgers, bangers and mash, and wild smoked salmon salad are some of the meals you'll find in this restaurant, which is contained within a converted tobacco warehouse in the heart of the International Financial Services Centre (IFSC). Dishes are prepared with organic and free-range produce from the owner's family farm in County Clare, so you can be assured of the quality. There's a large wine list to choose from, with over 70 sold by the glass.

ELY GASTRO PUB　　INTERNATIONAL €€
Map p252 (Grand Canal Quay; ☉lunch & dinner) Amid the exposed brick, designer lampshades and comfortable seating is a terrific bar (30 craft beers on tap) that also doubles as an excellent restaurant, serving well-made classics (chicken, burger, steak and a particularly good fish-and-cheddar pie) that will more than satisfy if you're preparing for a gig at the Bord Gáis Energy Theatre or are just out for the night.

HERBSTREET　　FUSION €€
Map p252 (www.herbstreet.ie; Hanover Quay; mains €13-19; ☉lunch & dinner Mon-Fri, dinner Sat) Low-power hand driers, 1-watt LED bulbs, secondhand furniture and strictly European wines: this eatery is taking its green responsibilities seriously. The fish used here is farmed locally, and all of the other dishes –

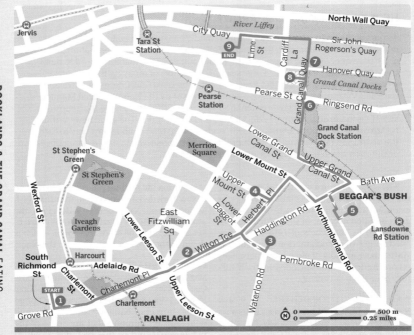

Neighbourhood Walk
Along the Grand Canal

START PORTOBELLO PUB, SOUTH RICHMOND ST
FINISH CITY QUAY
LENGTH 5KM; 2½ HOURS

Begin at the **1 Portobello** pub, a popular watering hole built to service the solid hungers of workers building the canal.

Turn left at the Grand Canal and begin your stroll along the towpath. About 200m past Leeson St Bridge is the **2 Patrick Kavanagh statue**, relaxing on a bench. The Monaghan-born poet is immortalised in the spot he loved most in Dublin – where he couldn't get barred.

When you get to Baggot St Bridge take a right onto Baggot St and refuel at **3 Searson's** (42–44 Upper Baggot St), a popular bar. Return to the canal and continue eastwards, diverting left at Mount St for **4 St Stephen's Church**, a Greek Revival structure known as the 'pepper canister' on account of its curious shape.

Back on the towpath, turn right at Northumberland Rd and left onto Haddington Rd

for the **5 National Print Museum** (p144). Housed in the old Beggar's Bush barracks, this is a surprisingly interesting museum, especially if you're a fan of old books.

Turn left onto Upper Grand Canal St, then right into Grand Canal Quay for the **6 Waterways Visitor Centre** (p145), where you can find out everything you could possibly want to know about the construction of the country's canals and waterways.

Before heading back to the city, stop for a drink at the trendy **7 Ely Gastro Pub** (p105) overlooking Grand Canal Quay; sit outside and take in Daniel Libeskind's **8 Bord Gáis Energy Theatre** (p147).

Walk north to Sir John Rogerson's Quay, turn left and left again at Windmill Lane. Here you'll find **9 Windmill Lane Studios**, where U2 have their offices and recorded all of their early records up to *The Unforgettable Fire*. Back on Rogerson's Quay, walk west along the quays and back into the city.

fine, delicious portions of sandwiches, burgers and salads – are sourced as close to the restaurant as possible.

QUAY 16 FUSION €€€

Map p252 (☑01-817 8760; www.mvcillairne.com; MV Cill Airne, North Wall Quay; bar food €12-14, mains €23-30; ☉noon-3pm Mon-Fri, 6-10pm Mon-Sat) The MV *Cill Airne*, commissioned in 1961 as a passenger liner tender, is now permanently docked along the north quays, where it serves the public as a bar, bistro and fine restaurant. The food in this restaurant is surprisingly good – dishes such as Himalayan salt-aged fillet steak and pan-roasted sea bass are expertly prepared and served alongside an excellent variety of wines.

DRINKING & NIGHTLIFE

While you wouldn't traipse all the way out here just to get a drink, if you're in the neighbourhood there are plenty of good spots to enjoy a pint or two.

BEGGAR'S BUSH TRADITIONAL PUB

Map p254 (Jack Ryan's; 115 Haddington Rd) A staunch defender of the traditional pub aesthetic, Ryan's (as it's referred to by its older clientele) has adjusted to the modern age by adding an outside patio for good weather. Everything else, though, has remained the same, which is precisely why it's so popular with flat-capped pensioners and employees from nearby Google.

SLATTERY'S TRADITIONAL PUB

Map p254 (62 Upper Grand Canal St) A decent boozer that is a favourite with rugby fans who didn't get tickets to the match – they congregate around the TVs and ebb and flow with each passage of the game. It's also popular on Friday and Saturday nights.

KENNEDY'S TRADITIONAL PUB

Map p252 (☑01-677 0626; 10 George's Quay; ☐all city centre, ☒Tara St) This is a proper traditional pub where literally nothing has changed in 50 years, including some of the clientele. Tread softly and speak even quieter so as not to disturb the contemplative atmosphere of a bar that seems oblivious to what's happened to Dublin in the last 20 years.

WORTH A DETOUR

POOLBEG LIGHTHOUSE

One of the city's most rewarding walks is a stroll along the South Wall to the Poolbeg Lighthouse (that red tower visible in the middle of Dublin Bay). To get there, you'll have to make your own way from Ringsend (which is reachable by bus 1, 2 or 3 from the city centre), past the power station to the start of the wall (it's about 1km). It's not an especially long walk – about 800m or so – but it will give you a stunning view of the bay and the city behind you, a view best enjoyed just before sunset on a summer's evening.

JOHN MULLIGAN'S PUB

Map p252 (8 Poolbeg St; ☐all city centre) This brilliant old boozer was established in 1782 and has barely changed over the years. In fact, the last time it was renovated was when Christy Brown and his rowdy clan ran amok here in the film *My Left Foot*. It has one of the finest pints of Guinness in Dublin and a colourful crew of regulars. It's just off Fleet St, outside the eastern boundary of Temple Bar.

CHOPHOUSE BAR

Map p254 (2 Shelbourne Rd) A big sprawling bar with a variety of lounges that get packed when there's something on at the Aviva.

☆ ENTERTAINMENT

BORD GÁIS ENERGY THEATRE THEATRE

Map p252 (☑01-677 7999; www.grandcanaltheatre.ie; Grand Canal Sq) Forget the uninviting sponsored name: Daniel Libeskind's masterful design is a three-tiered, 2000-capacity auditorium where you're as likely to be entertained by the Bolshoi or a touring state opera as you are to see Disney on Ice or Barbra Streisand. It's a magnificent venue – designed for classical, paid for by the classics.

O2 LIVE MUSIC

Map p252 (☑01-819 8888; www.theo2.ie; East Link Bridge, North Wall Quay) The premier indoor venue in the city has a capacity of around 10,000 and plays host to the very brightest stars in the firmament: Rihanna,

Bryan Adams and the cast of Glee are just some of the acts that have brought their magic to its superb stage.

ODEON CINEMA CINEMA
Map p252 (www.odeoncinemas.ie; Point Village) A six-screen multiplex showing all the latest releases.

SHOPPING

Isn't there enough shopping for you around Grafton St? For a long time the Docklands development crowd didn't think so and imagined a new shopping oasis by the banks of the Liffey. Things didn't _quite_ go as planned and the Docklands remains largely bereft of the kind of retail distractions envisaged, with one notable exception.

TOWER CRAFT DESIGN CENTRE IRISH CRAFTS
Map p252 (☏01-677 5655; Pearse St; ☺9.30am-6pm Mon-Sat, 9.30am-8pm Thu; ▣all city centre) Housed in a 19th-century warehouse that was Dublin's first iron-structured building, this design centre has studios for local craftspeople. They produce jewellery in both contemporary and Celtic-inspired designs, and work with Irish pewter, ceramics, silk and other fabrics. Besides jewellery they produce pottery, rugs, wall hangings, cards, leather bags and various other handcrafted items. It's immediately opposite the Waterways Visitors Centre, off Lower Grand Canal St.

SPORTS & ACTIVITIES

MARKIEVICZ LEISURE CENTRE HEALTH & FITNESS
Map p252 (☏01-672 9121; www.dublincity.ie; Townsend St; adult/child €6/3; ☺7am-10pm Mon-Thu, to 9pm Fri, 9am-6pm Sat, 10am-4pm Sun; ▣all city centre, ▣Tara St) This excellent fitness centre has a swimming pool, a workout room (with plenty of gym machines) and a sauna. You can swim for as long as you please, but children are only allowed at off-peak times (10am to 5.30pm Monday to Saturday).

Day Trips from Dublin

Brú Na Bóinne p150
Neolithic passage tombs that are a highlight of any visit to Ireland.

Glendalough p154
The remains of an early Christian monastic settlement nestled in a beautiful glacial valley.

Howth p158
Seaside village with terrific restaurants at the foot of a bulbous head with fine walks.

Enniskerry & Powerscourt Estate p160
A Palladian mansion with a stunning garden and even better views of the surrounding countryside.

Castletown House & Around p161
Ireland's largest Palladian home, built for the 18th-century's richest man.

Dalkey & Around p165
Compact village by the sea with a nice harbour and coastal walks.

TOP SIGHT
BRÚ NA BÓINNE

The vast Neolithic necropolis known as Brú na Bóinne (the Boyne Palace), a thousand years older than Stonehenge, is one of the most extraordinary sites in Europe and a powerful testament to the achievements of prehistoric humans.

The area, 40km northwest of Dublin, consists of many different sites, with the three principal ones being New-grange, Knowth and Dowth. Allow plenty of time to visit: an hour for the interpretive centre alone, two hours if you wish to include a trip to Newgrange or Knowth, and a half-day to visit the interpretive centre and sites (Dowth is not open to tourists).

To get here, take the M1 north to Drogheda and then N51 west to Brú na Bóinne. Bus Éireann (return €12.90, 1½ hours, one daily) and Newgrange Shuttlebus run to the Brú na Bóinne visitor centre from central Dublin.

Visitor Centre

The superb **interpretive centre**, whose spiral design echoes that of Newgrange, features an excellent series of inter-active exhibits on all aspects of pre-Celtic history, includ-ing a full-scale replica of the burial chamber at Newgrange. There's a good film introducing the complex, a decent **cafe** (dishes €4.50-12; ⊘breakfast & lunch; 🖼) and a bookshop.

Newgrange

The star attraction is **Newgrange**, with its white round stone walls topped by a grass dome. Just the size is impres-sive – 80m in diameter and 13m high – but underneath it gets even better: here lies the finest Stone Age passage tomb in Ireland, and one of the most remarkable prehistoric sites in Europe. It dates from around 3200 BC, predating the pyramids by some six centuries.

No one is quite sure of its original purpose. It could have been a burial place for kings or a centre for ritual – although the tomb's precise alignment with the sun at the time of the winter solstice also suggests it was designed to act as a calendar. Over time, Newgrange, like Dowth and Knowth, deteriorated and was at one stage even used as a quarry. The site was extensively restored in 1962 and again in 1975.

A superbly carved **kerbstone** with double and triple spirals guards the tomb's main entrance, but the area has been reconstructed so that tourists don't have to clamber in over it. Above the entrance is a slit, or roof box, which lets light in. Another beautifully decorated kerbstone stands at the exact opposite side of the mound. Some experts say that a **ring of standing stones** encircled the mound, forming a great circle about 100m in diameter, but only 12 of these stones remain, with traces of others below ground level.

Holding the whole structure together are the 97 boulders of the **kerb ring**, designed to stop the mound from collapsing outwards. Eleven of these are decorated with motifs similar to those on the main entrance stone, although only three have extensive carvings.

The white quartzite that decorates the tomb was originally obtained from Wicklow, 70km to the south – in an age before horse and wheel, it was transported by sea and then up the River Boyne – and there is also some granite from the Mourne Mountains in North-ern Ireland. Over 200,000 tonnes of earth and stone also went into the mound.

You can walk down the narrow 19m passage, lined with 43 stone uprights (some of them engraved), which leads into the **tomb chamber** about one-third of the way into the

DON'T MISS

➡ Newgrange
➡ Brú na Bóinne Visitor Centre

PRACTICALITIES

➡ ☏041-988 0300
➡ www.heritage ireland.ie
➡ Donore
➡ adult/child visitor centre €3/2; visitor centre & Newgrange €6/3; visitor centre & Knowth €5/3; visitor centre, Newgrange & Knowth €11/6
➡ ⊘9am-5pm Nov-Jan, 9.30am-5.30 Feb-Apr, 9am-6.30pm May, 9am-7pm Jun-Sep, 9.30am-5.30pm Oct

colossal mound. The chamber has three recesses, and in these are large **basin stones** that held cremated human bones. As well as the remains, the basins would have held funeral offerings of beads and pendants, but these were stolen long before archaeologists arrived.

Above, the massive stones support a 6m-high **corbel-vaulted roof**. A complex drainage system means that not a drop of water has penetrated the interior in 40 centuries.

Knowth

Northwest of Newgrange, the burial mound of **Knowth** was built around the same time and seems set to surpass its better-known neighbour in both its size and the importance of the discoveries made here. It has the greatest collection of passage-grave art ever uncovered in Western Europe, and has been under excavation since 1962; you may see archaeologists at work when you visit.

Soon after excavations began a **passage** leading to the central chamber was cleared; at 34m it is much longer than the one at Newgrange. In 1968 a 40m passage was unearthed on the opposite side of the mound. Also in the mound are the remains of six early-Christian **souterrains** (underground chambers) built into the side. Some 300 **carved slabs** and 17 **satellite graves** surround the main mound.

Human activity at Knowth continued for thousands of years after its construction, which accounts for the site's complexity. The Beaker folk, so called because they buried their dead with drinking vessels, occupied the site in the Bronze Age (c 1800 BC), as did the Celts in the Iron Age (c 500 BC). In 965 it was the seat of Cormac MacMaelmithic, later Ireland's high king for nine years, and in the 12th century the Normans built a motte and bailey (a raised mound with a walled keep) here. The site was finally abandoned around 1400.

Dowth

The circular mound at **Dowth** is similar in size to Newgrange – about 63m in diameter – but is slightly taller at 14m high. It has suffered badly at the hands of everyone from road builders and treasure hunters to amateur archaeologists, who scooped out the centre of the tumulus in the 19th century. Relatively untouched by modern archaeologists, Dowth shows what Newgrange and Knowth looked like for most of their history. Because it's unsafe, Dowth is closed to visitors, though the mound can be viewed from the road between Newgrange and Drogheda. Excavations will continue for years to come.

GUIDED TOURS

Highly recommended are the **Mary Gibbons Tours** (☎086 355 1355; www.newgrangetours. com; adult/student €35/30), which depart from numerous Dublin hotels beginning at 9.30am Monday to Saturday, and take in the whole of the Boyne Valley. The expert guides offer a fascinating insight into Celtic and pre-Celtic life and you'll get access to Newgrange even on days when all visiting slots are filled. **Bus Éireann** (www.buseireann.ie; adult/child €32.50/23.75; ☺Thu & Sat, Apr-Sep) runs Newgrange and the Boyne Valley tours, departing from Busáras in Dublin at 10am and returning at approximately 5.45pm.

In summer it gets very crowded and you are not guaranteed a visit to either of the passage tombs – there are only 750 tour slots and on peak days 2000 people show up. Tickets are sold on a first-come, first-served basis (no advance bookings) so arrive early and be prepared for a wait.

Brú na Bóinne

All visits start at the visitor centre **1**, which has a terrific exhibit that includes a short context-setting film. From here, you board a shuttle bus that takes you to Newgrange **2**, where you'll go past the kerbstone **3** into the main passage **4** and the burial chamber **5**. If you're not a lucky lottery winner for the solstice, fear not – there's an artificial illumination ceremony that replicates it. If you're continuing on to tour Knowth **6**, you'll need to go back to the visitor centre and get on another bus; otherwise, you can drive directly to Dowth **7** and visit, but only from outside (the information panels will tell you what you're looking at).

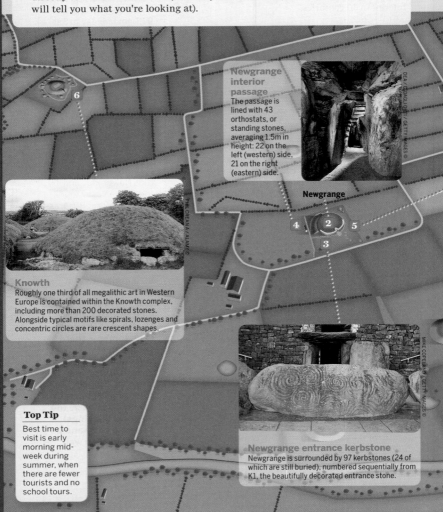

Newgrange interior passage

The passage is lined with 43 orthostats, or standing stones, averaging 1.5m in height: 22 on the left (western) side, 21 on the right (eastern) side.

Newgrange

Knowth

Roughly one third of all megalithic art in Western Europe is contained within the Knowth complex, including more than 200 decorated stones. Alongside typical motifs like spirals, lozenges and concentric circles are rare crescent shapes.

Top Tip

Best time to visit is early morning mid-week during summer, when there are fewer tourists and no school tours.

Newgrange entrance kerbstone

Newgrange is surrounded by 97 kerbstones (24 of which are still buried), numbered sequentially from K1, the beautifully decorated entrance stone.

Dowth
Like Newgrange, Dowth's passage grave is designed to allow for a solar alignment during the winter solstice. The crater at the top was due to a clumsy attempt at excavation in 1847.

FACT FILE

The winter solstice event is witnessed by a maximum of 60 people selected by lottery. In 2012, 29,570 people applied.

Newgrange burial chamber
The corbelled roof of the chamber has remained intact since its construction, and is considered one of the finest of its kind in Europe.

Brú na Bóinne Visitor Centre
Opened in 1997, the modern visitor centre was heavily criticised at first as being unsuitable but then gained plaudits for the way it integrated into the landscape.

TOP SIGHT
GLENDALOUGH

If you're looking for the epitome of rugged and romantic Ireland, you won't do much better than Glendalough, truly one of Ireland's most beautiful corners.

The substantial remains of this important monastic settlement are certainly impressive, but the real draw is the splendid setting: two dark and mysterious lakes tucked into a deep valley covered in forest. It is, despite its immense popularity, a deeply tranquil and spiritual place. Visit early or late in the day – or out of season – to avoid the big crowds, and remember that a visit here is all about walking, so wear comfortable shoes.

At the valley entrance, before the Glendalough Hotel, is **Glendalough Visitor Centre** (www.heritageireland.ie; adult/child €3/1; ☺9.30am-6pm mid-Mar–mid-Oct, to 5pm mid-Oct–mid-Mar). It has a high-quality 17-minute audiovisual presentation called *Ireland of the Monasteries*.

St Kevin & Glendalough

In AD 498 a young monk named Kevin arrived in the valley looking for somewhere to meditate and be at one with nature. He camped in what had been a Bronze Age tomb on the southern side of the Upper Lake and for the next seven years slept on stones, wore animal skins, maintained a near-starvation diet and befriended the birds and animals. Kevin's ecofriendly lifestyle soon attracted disciples and over the next couple of centuries his one-man operation mushroomed into a proper settlement. By the 9th century thousands of students studied and lived in a thriving community that spread over a considerable area.

Inevitably, Glendalough's success made it a key target for Viking raiders, who sacked the monastery at least four times between 775 and 1071. In 1398 English forces from Dublin almost completely destroyed it. Some life lingered on here as late as the 17th century, when, under renewed repression, the monastery finally died.

The Upper Lake

The original site of St Kevin's settlement, **Teampall na Skellig**, is at the base of the cliffs towering over the southern side of the Upper Lake, and is accessible only by boat; unfortunately, there's no boat service to the site and you'll have to settle for looking at it across the lake. The terraced shelf has the reconstructed ruins of a church and early graveyard. Rough wattle huts once stood on the raised ground nearby. Scattered around are some early grave slabs and simple stone crosses.

Just east of the lake and 10m above its waters is the 2m-deep artificial cave called **St Kevin's Bed**, said to be where Kevin lived. The earliest human habitation of the cave was long before St Kevin's era – there's evidence that people lived in the valley for thousands of years before the monks arrived. In the green area just south of the car park is a large circular wall thought to be the remains of an early-Christian *caher* (stone fort).

Follow the lakeshore path southwest from the car park until you find the considerable remains of **Reefert Church** above the tiny Poulanass River. This small, rather plain, 11th-century Romanesque nave-and-chancel church, was traditionally the burial site of the chiefs of the local O'Toole family. The surrounding **graveyard** contains a number of rough stone crosses and slabs.

Climb the steps at the back of the churchyard and follow the path to the west; at the top of a rise overlooking the lake you'll find the scant remains of **St Kevin's Cell**, a small beehive hut.

The Lower Lake

While the Upper Lake has the best scenery, the most fascinating buildings lie east of the Lower Lake.

Around the bend from the Glendalough Hotel is the stone arch of the **monastery gatehouse**, the only surviving example of a monastic entranceway in the country.

Beyond that lies a **graveyard**, which is still in use. The 10th-century **round tower** is 33m tall and 16m in circumference at the base. The upper storeys and conical roof were reconstructed in 1876. Near the tower, to the southeast, lies the **Cathedral of St Peter and St Paul**, with a 10th-century nave. The chancel and sacristy both date from the 12th century.

At the centre of the graveyard, to the south of the round tower, is the **Priest's House**, dating from 1170 but heavily reconstructed. During the 18th century it became a burial site for local priests – hence the name. The 10th-century **St Mary's Church**, 140m southwest of the round tower, probably stood outside the walls of the monastery and belonged to local nuns. A little to the east are the scant remains of **St Kieran's Church**, the smallest at Glendalough.

Glendalough's trademark is **St Kevin's Church** – or Kitchen – at the southern edge of the enclosure. With its miniature belfry, protruding sacristy and steep stone roof, it's a masterpiece. How it came to be known as a kitchen is a mystery as there's no indication that it was ever anything other than a church. The oldest parts of the building date from the 11th century – the structure has been remodelled since but it's still a classic early Irish church.

At the junction with Green Rd is the **Deer Stone**, in the middle of a group of rocks. Legend claims that when St Kevin needed milk for two orphaned babies, a doe stood here waiting to be milked. The stone is actually a *bullaun*, used as a grinding stone for medicines or food.

The road east leads to **St Saviour's Church**, with its detailed Romanesque carvings. To the west a nice **woodland trail** leads up the valley past the Lower Lake to the Upper Lake.

GUIDED TOURS

The award-winning **Wild Wicklow Tour** (☎01-280 1899; www.wildwicklow.ie; adult/student & child €28/25; ⊙departs 9am) of Glendalough, Avoca and the Sally Gap never fails to generate rave reviews for atmosphere and all-round fun, but so much craic has made a casualty of informative depth. Alternatively, **Bus Éireann** (☎01-836 6111; www.buseireann.ie; Busáras; adult/child/student €29/23/25; ⊙departs 10am mid-Mar–Oct) runs good but slightly impersonal whole-day tours of Glendalough and the Powerscourt Estate, which return to Dublin at about 5.45pm.

Many *bullaun*, such as the Deer Stone, were widely regarded as having supernatural properties; women who bathed their faces with water from the hollow were supposed to keep their looks forever. Early churchmen brought them into their monasteries, perhaps hoping to inherit some of the stones' powers.

Glendalough

WALKING TOUR

A visit to Glendalough is a trip through ancient history and a refreshing hike in the hills. The ancient monastic settlement founded by St Kevin in the 5th century grew to be quite powerful by the 9th century, but it started falling into ruin from 1398 onwards. Still, you won't find more evocative clumps of stones anywhere.

Start at the **Main Gateway** **1** to the monastic city, where you will find a cluster of important ruins, including the (nearly perfect) 10th-century **Round Tower** **2**, the **Cathedral** **3** dedicated to **Sts Peter and Paul**, and **St Kevin's Kitchen** **4**, which is really a church. Cross the stream past the famous **Deer Stone** **5**, where Kevin was supposed to have milked a doe, and turn west along the path. It's a 1.5km walk to the **Upper Lake** **6**. On the lake's southern shore is another cluster of sites, including the **Reefert Church** **7**, a plain 11th-century Romanesque church where the powerful O'Toole family buried their kin, and **St Kevin's Cell** **8**, the remains of a beehive hut where Kevin is said to have lived.

St Kevin's Cell
This beehive hut is reputedly where St Kevin would go for prayer and meditation; not to be confused with St Kevin's Bed, a cave where he used to sleep.

Deer Stone
The spot where St Kevin is said to have truly become one with the animals is really just a large mortar called a *bullaun*, used for grinding food and medicine.

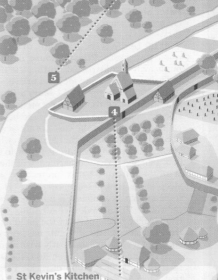

St Kevin's Kitchen
This small church is unusual in that it has a round tower sticking out of the roof – it looks like a chimney, hence the church's nickname.

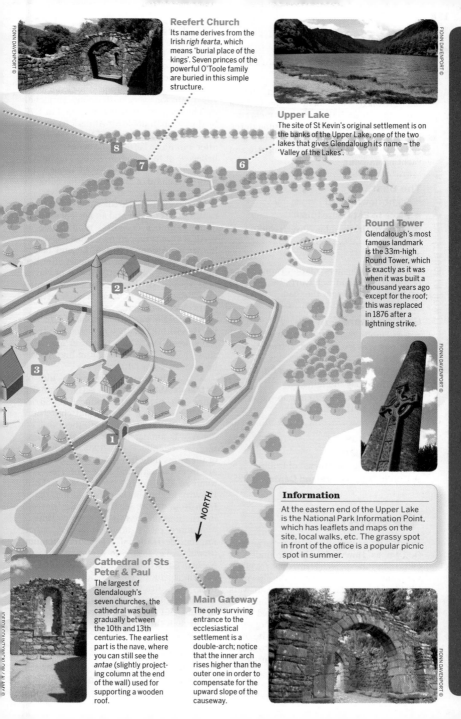

Reefert Church
Its name derives from the Irish *righ fearta*, which means 'burial place of the kings'. Seven princes of the powerful O'Toole family are buried in this simple structure.

Upper Lake
The site of St Kevin's original settlement is on the banks of the Upper Lake, one of the two lakes that gives Glendalough its name – the 'Valley of the Lakes'.

Round Tower
Glendalough's most famous landmark is the 33m-high Round Tower, which is exactly as it was when it was built a thousand years ago except for the roof; this was replaced in 1876 after a lightning strike.

NORTH

Information
At the eastern end of the Upper Lake is the National Park Information Point, which has leaflets and maps on the site, local walks, etc. The grassy spot in front of the office is a popular picnic spot in summer.

Cathedral of Sts Peter & Paul
The largest of Glendalough's seven churches, the cathedral was built gradually between the 10th and 13th centuries. The earliest part is the nave, where you can still see the *antae* (slightly projecting column at the end of the wall) used for supporting a wooden roof.

Main Gateway
The only surviving entrance to the ecclesiastical settlement is a double-arch; notice that the inner arch rises higher than the outer one in order to compensate for the upward slope of the causeway.

Howth

Explore

A popular excursion from Dublin, Howth has developed as a residential suburb. It is a pretty little town built on steep streets running down to the waterfront. Although the harbour's role as a shipping port has long ended, Howth remains a fishing centre and yachting harbour.

The Best...

➡ **Sight** Howth Head
➡ **Place to Eat** House (p159)
➡ **Place to Drink** Abbey Tavern (p160)

Top Tip

The weekend farmers' market is one of the best in the city and well worth the effort to get here, especially for the food.

Getting There & Away

➡ **Bus** Dublin bus 31, 31A or 31B (€2.80, 45 minutes, every 30 minutes) from Lower Abbey St.
➡ **Car** Northeast along Clontarf Rd; follow the northern bay shoreline.
➡ **Train** DART (€2.80, 20 minutes, every 20 minutes) to Howth.

Need to Know

➡ **Area Code** ☎01
➡ **Location** 9km northeast of Dublin
➡ **Dublin Discover Ireland Centre** (p212)

◉ SIGHTS

Howth is essentially a very large hill (known as Howth Head) surrounded by cliffs, and the peak (171m) has excellent views across Dublin Bay right down to Wicklow. From the summit you can walk to the top of the Ben of Howth, which has a cairn said to mark a 2000-year-old Celtic royal grave. The 1814 Baily Lighthouse, at the southeastern corner, is on the site of an old stone fort and can be reached by a dramatic cliff-top walk. There was an earlier hilltop beacon here in 1670.

HOWTH CASTLE   CASTLE

Most of the town backs onto the extensive grounds of Howth Castle, built in 1564 but much changed over the years, most recently in 1910 when Sir Edwin Lutyens gave it a modernist makeover. Today the castle is divided into four very posh private residences. The original estate was acquired in 1177 by the Norman noble Sir Almeric Tristram, who changed his surname to St Lawrence after winning a battle at the behest (or so he believed) of his favourite saint. The family has owned the land ever since, though the unbroken chain of male succession came to an end in 1909.

On the grounds are the ruins of the 16th-century **Corr Castle** and an ancient dolmen (tomb chamber or portal tomb made of vertical stones topped by a huge capstone) known as **Aideen's Grave**. Legend has it that Aideen died of a broken heart after her husband was killed at the Battle of Gavra near Tara in AD 184, but the legend is rubbish because the dolmen is at least 300 years older than that.

The **castle gardens** (◷24hr) FREE are worth visiting, as they're noted for their rhododendrons (which bloom in May and June), azaleas and a long, 10m-high beech hedge planted in 1710.

Also within the grounds are the ruins of **St Mary's Abbey** (Abbey St) FREE, originally founded in 1042 by the Viking King Sitric, who also founded the original church on the site of Christ Church Cathedral. The abbey was amalgamated with the monastery on Ireland's Eye in 1235. Some parts of the ruins date from that time, but most are from the 15th and 16th centuries. The tomb of Christopher St Lawrence (Lord Howth), in the southeastern corner, dates from around 1470. See the caretaker or read instructions on the gate for opening times.

A more recent addition is the rather ramshackle **National Transport Museum** (Howth Castle; adult/child & student €3.50/2; ◷2-5pm Sat & Sun), which has a range of exhibits including double-decker buses, a bakery van, fire engines and trams – most notably a Hill of Howth electric that operated from 1901 to 1959. To reach the museum, go through the castle gates and turn right just before the castle.

IRELAND'S EYE   BIRD SANCTUARY

(☎01-831 4200; return €12) A short distance offshore from Howth is Ireland's Eye, a

Howth

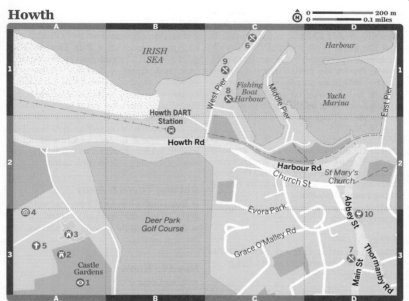

rocky sea-bird sanctuary with the ruins of a 6th-century monastery. There's a Martello tower at the northwestern end of the island, where boats from Howth land, while a spectacularly sheer rock face plummets into the sea at the eastern end. As well as the sea birds overhead, you can see young birds on the ground during the nesting season. Seals can also be spotted around the island.

Doyle & Sons (📞01-831 4200; return €14) takes boats out to the island from the East Pier of Howth Harbour during the summer, usually on weekend afternoons. Don't wear shorts if you're planning to visit the monastery ruins because they're surrounded by a thicket of stinging nettles. And bring your rubbish back with you – far too many island visitors don't.

✖ EATING & DRINKING

HOWTH FISHERMEN'S FARMER'S MARKET
MARKET €
(📞01-611 5016; www.irishfarmersmarkets.ie; West Pier, Howth Harbour; ◷10am-5pm Sun & bank holidays) One of the best in Dublin, this is the place to come not only for fresh fish (obviously) but also for organic meat, veg and homemade everything else, including jams,

Howth

◉ Sights
1 Castle Gardens	A3
2 Corr Castle	A3
3 Howth Castle	A3
4 National Transport Museum	A3
5 St Mary's Abbey	A3

✖ Eating
6 Aqua	C1
7 House	D3
8 Howth Fishermen's Farmer's Market	C1
9 Oar House	C1

◉ Drinking & Nightlife
| 10 Abbey Tavern | D3 |

cakes and breads. A great option for Sunday lunch.

★HOUSE
IRISH €€
(📞01-839 6388; www.thehouse-howth.ie; 4 Main St; mains €16-23; ◷9am-3pm Mon-Fri, 11.30am-3pm & 6pm-11pm Sat & Sun) Wonderful spot on the main street leading away from the harbour where you can feast on dishes like crunchy Bellingham blue cheese polenta or wild Wicklow venison stew as well as a fine selection of fish.

OAR HOUSE SEAFOOD €€

(☏01-839 4562; www.oarhouse.ie; 8 West Pier; mains €16-24; ☺12.30-10pm) A feast-o-fish is what the menu is all about at this newish restaurant – particularly the locally caught variety. Par for the course in a fishing village, but this place stands out both for the way the fish is prepared and because you can get everything on the menu in smaller, tapas-style portions as well as mains.

AQUA SEAFOOD €€€

(☏01-832 0690; www.aqua.ie; 1 West Pier; mains €29-32; ☺lunch & dinner Tue-Sat) Another contender for best seafood in Howth, Aqua serves top-quality fish dishes in its elegant dining room overlooking the harbour. The building was once home to the Howth Yacht Club.

ABBEY TAVERN PUB

(Abbey St) An old-style tavern popular with old salts and visitors looking to hang out with salt dogs.

Enniskerry & Powerscourt Estate

Explore

About 500m south of the charming village of Enniskerry is the entrance to the 64-sq-km Powerscourt Estate, Wicklow's grandest country pile. This is one of the most popular day trips from Dublin, and the village – built in 1760 by Richard Wingfield, Earl of Powerscourt, so that his labourers would have somewhere to live – is a terrific spot to while away an afternoon.

The Best...

➡ **Sight** Formal Gardens (p160)
➡ **Place to Eat** Poppies Country Cooking (p161)
➡ **Place to Stay** Summerhill House Hotel (p161)

Top Tip

You can visit Powerscourt and Glendalough together as part of a **Bus Éireann Tour** (☏01-836 6111; www.buseireann.ie; Busáras; adult/child/student €28/22/25; ☺10am mid-Mar/Oct), which departs from the Dublin Discover Ireland Centre (p212). Dublin Bus Tours (p212) includes a visit in its four-hour 'South Coast & Gardens' tour, which takes in the stretch of coastline between Dun Laoghaire and Killiney before turning inland to Wicklow and on to Enniskerry. Admission to the gardens is included.

Getting There & Away

➡ **Bus** Dublin bus 44 (€2.50, 1¼ hours, every 20 minutes) from city centre.
➡ **Car** South to Bray along N11 and west for 3km on R117.

Need to Know

➡ **Area Code** ☏01
➡ **Location** 18km south of Dublin
➡ **Dublin Discover Ireland Centre** (p212)

◉ SIGHTS

POWERSCOURT ESTATE HOUSE, GARDENS

(www.powerscourt.ie; near Enniskerry; admission to house free, gardens adult/child €8.50/5; ☺9.30am-5.30pm Mar-Oct, to dusk Nov-Feb) Powerscourt Estate has existed more or less since 1300 when the LePoer (later Anglicised to Power) family built themselves a castle here. The property then changed Anglo-Norman hands a few times before coming into the possession of Richard Wingfield, newly appointed Marshall of Ireland, in 1603; his descendants lived here for the next 350 years. In 1731 the Georgian wunderkind, Richard Cassels, turned his genius to building the stunning Palladian-style mansion, which he finished in 1743. An extra storey was added to the building in 1787 and other alterations were made in the 19th century. The house was restored after the Wingfields sold up in the 1950s, but the whole building was gutted by fire on the very eve of its reopening in 1974.

The estate has since come into the hands of the sporting-goods giants, the Slazengers, who have overseen a second restoration, as well as the addition of two **golf** courses, a cafe, a huge garden centre and a bunch of cutesy retail outlets. If you can deal with the crowds (summer weekends are the worst) or, better still, avoid them and visit midweek, you're in for a real treat.

Easily the biggest draw are the simply magnificent 20-hectare **formal gardens** and the breathtaking views that accompany them. Originally laid out in the 1740s, they were redesigned in the 19th century by Daniel Robinson, who had as much a fondness for the booze as he did for horticultural pursuits. Perhaps this influenced his largely informal style, which resulted in a magnificent blend of landscaped gardens, sweeping terraces, statuary, ornamental lakes, secret hollows, rambling walks and walled enclosures replete with over 200 types of trees and shrubs – all beneath the stunning natural backdrop of the Great Sugarloaf Mountain to the southeast. Tickets come with a map laying out 40-minute and hour-long tours of the gardens. Don't miss the exquisite **Japanese Gardens** or the **Pepperpot Tower**, modelled on a 3-inch actual pepperpot owned by Lady Wingfield. Our favourite, however, is the **animal cemetery**, final resting place of the Wingfield pets and even some of their best loved milking cows. Some of the epitaphs are astonishingly personal.

POWERSCOURT WATERFALL   WATERFALL
(adult/child €5/3.50; ☉9.30am-7pm May-Aug, 10.30am-5.30pm Mar-Apr & Sep-Oct, to 4.30pm Nov-Jan) A 7km walk to a separate part of the Powerscourt Estate takes you to the 130m Powerscourt Waterfall. It's the highest waterfall in Britain and Ireland, and is most impressive after heavy rain. You can also get to the falls by road, following the signs from the estate. A nature trail has been laid out around the base of the waterfall, taking you past giant redwoods, ancient oaks, beech, birch and rowan trees. There are plenty of birds in the vicinity, including the chaffinch, cuckoo, chiffchaff, raven and willow warbler.

 EATING

POPPIES COUNTRY COOKING   CAFE €
(☎01-282 8869; The Square; mains €9; ☉8.30am-6pm) If the service wasn't so slow and the organisation so frustratingly haphazard, this poky little cafe on the main square would be one of the best spots in Wicklow. The food – when you finally get a chance to eat it – is sensational: wholesome salads, filling sandwiches on doorstop-cut bread and award-winning ice cream will leave you plenty satisfied.

🛏 SLEEPING

SUMMERHILL HOUSE HOTEL   HOTEL €€
(☎01-286 7928; www.summerhillhousehotel.com; r from €90; ☎⃣☑) A truly superb country mansion about 700m south of Enniskerry, just off the N11, is the best place around to lay your head on soft cotton pillows surrounded by delicate antiques and pastoral views in oils. Everything about the place – including the top-notch breakfast – is memorable.

Castletown House & Around

Explore

In a country full of elegant Palladian mansions, it is no mean feat to be considered the grandest of the lot, but Castletown House simply has no peer. It is Ireland's largest and most imposing Georgian estate, and a testament to the vast wealth enjoyed by the Anglo-Irish gentry during the 18th century.

The Best...
➤ **Sight** Wonderful Barn (p164)
➤ **Place to Stay** Carton House (p164)

Top Tip

If you're going to play one of the two golf courses at Carton House, opt for the Montgomerie course over the one designed by Mark O'Meara – harder sure, but better.

Getting There & Away

➤ **Bus** Dublin buses 67 and 67A (one way €3.50, about one hour, hourly) depart from D'Olier St for Celbridge and stop at the gates of Castletown House.

➤ **Car** Take the N4 to Celbridge.

WOJTEK BUSS / GETTY IMAGES ©

1. Newgrange (p150)

The star attraction of the Neolithic necropolis Brú na Bóinne, Newgrange was built around 3200 BC, predating the pyramids by six centuries.

2. Howth (p158)

The 1814 Baily Lighthouse at Howth sits on the site of an old stone fortress and overlooks the Irish Sea.

3. Powerscourt Estate (p160)

The Palladian-style mansion at Powerscourt Estate was finished by Georgian wunderkind Richard Cassels in 1743.

4. Glendalough (p154)

The beautiful valley of Glendalough holds the ruins of a religious settlement established in AD 498.

Need to Know

➡ **Area Code** ☑01
➡ **Location** 21km west of Dublin
➡ **Dublin Discover Ireland Centre** (p212)

⊙ SIGHTS

CASTLETOWN HOUSE   HISTORIC BUILDING

(☑01-628 8252; www.castletownhouse.ie; Celbridge; adult/child €4.50/3.50; ⊙10am-4.45pm Tue-Sun Easter-Oct) The house was built between 1722 and 1732 for William Conolly (1662–1729), speaker of the Irish House of Commons and, at the time, Ireland's richest man.

In 1718 Italian architect Alessandro Galilei (1691–1737) designed the facade of the main block so as to resemble a 16th-century Italian palazzo. However, he left Ireland efore construction began and the project was entrusted to Sir Edward Lovett Pearce (1699–1733), who had returned from his grand tour of Italy in 1724. Inspired by the work of Andrea Palladio, Pearce enlarged the original design of the house and added the colonnades and the terminating pavilions.

The interior is as opulent as the exterior suggests. From the impressive, two-story entrance hall (with its two-tone, polished limestone floor and Kilkenny marble fireplace, you'll visit the Dining Hall (look for the Inigo Jones–inspired ceiling) and the various reception rooms, including the Red and Green drawing rooms, named after their dominant colour schemes. Probably the most impressive room in the house is the Long Gallery, replete with family portraits and exquisite stucco work by the Francini brothers. It was designed as a picture gallery, but was then converted into an informal space for entertainment in the 1760s by Lady Louisa Conolly (1743–1821) – wife of Thomas who had inherited the house from his father William, namesake and nephew of the original owner.

Upstairs, the various bedrooms give an insight as to how the 1% of the 18th and 19th centuries liked to sleep – or greet visitors: in the manner of the court at Versailles, William Conolly's own bedroom was designed so that he would receive guests while sitting up in bed.

The house remained in the Conolly family's hands until 1965, when it was purchased by Desmond Guinness. He spent vast amounts of money on restoring the house to its original splendour, an investment that was continued from 1979 by the Castletown Foundation. In 1994 Castletown House was transferred to state care and today it is managed by the Heritage Service.

WONDERFUL BARN   NOTABLE BUILDING

(☑01-624 5448; Leixlip; ⊙closed to the public) Immediately to the east of the grounds of Castletown House, and on private property that never belonged to the house, you will find the curious, conical Wonderful Barn. Standing 21m high, this extraordinary five-storey structure, which is wrapped by a 94-step winding staircase, was commissioned by Lady Conolly in 1743 to give employment to local tenants whose crops were ruined by the severe frosts in the winters of 1741 and 1742. The building was ostensibly a granary, but it was also used as a shooting tower – doves were considered a delicacy in Georgian times. Flanking the main building are two smaller towers, which were also used to store grain. Be warned however: the land surrounding the barn has been zoned for redevelopment and there is a plan to build 500-odd houses around it, so prepare to trundle through a building site.

LARCHILL ARCADIAN GARDENS   GARDENS

(☑01-628 7354; www.larchill.ie; Kilcock; adult/child €7.50/5.50; ⊙noon-6pm Tue-Sun Jun-Aug, noon-6pm Sat & Sun Sep) About 12km northwest of the Castletown House are the Larchill Arcadian Gardens, Europe's only example of a mid-18th-century *ferme ornée* (ornamental farm). A 40-minute walk takes you through beautiful landscaped parklands, passing eccentric follies (including a model of the Gibraltar fortress and a shell-decorated tower), gazebos and a lake. Children will be chuffed with the adventure playground, maze and rare-breed farm animals.

🛌 SLEEPING

CARTON HOUSE   HOTEL €€€

(☑01-505 2000; www.cartonhouse.com; r from €145; @🕤📶🏊) It really doesn't get any grander than this vast, early 19th-century estate set on over 1000 acres of lavish grounds. The interiors belie the Palladian exterior and are stylishly minimalist. As you'd expect, the beautiful rooms come equipped with all the latest high-tech gadgetry. To reach the hotel, follow the R148 east towards Leixlip along the Royal Canal.

Dalkey & Around

Explore

Dublin's most important medieval port, Dalkey, has long since settled into its role as an elegant dormitory village, but there are some revealing vestiges of its illustrious past, most notably the remains of three of the eight castles that once lorded over the area.

The Best...

➡ **Sight** Dalkey Castle & Heritage Centre

➡ **Place to Eat** Guinea Pig (p166)

Top Tip

The 3km walk over Dalkey Hill between Dalkey and Killiney offers terrific views of Killiney Bay and lots and lots of gorse bushes.

Getting There & Away

➡ **Bus** Dublin bus 8 (€2.20, one hour, every 25 minutes) from Burgh Quay to Dalkey.

➡ **Car** Take the N11 south to Dalkey.

➡ **Train** DART (€2.20, 20 minutes, every 10 to 20 minutes) south to Dalkey.

Need to Know

➡ **Area Code** ☑01

➡ **Location** 8km south of Dublin

➡ **Dublin Discover Ireland Centre** (p212)

⊙ SIGHTS

Facing each other on Castle St are the 15th-century Archibold's Castle and Goat Castle. Overlooking Bullock Harbour are the remains of Bulloch Castle, built by the monks of St Mary's Abbey in Dublin around 1150.

WORTH A DETOUR

KILLINEY

About 1km south of Dalkey is the super-affluent seaside suburb of Killiney, home to some of Ireland's wealthiest people and a handful of celebrities, including Bono, Enya and filmmaker Neil Jordan. The attraction is self-evident, from the long, curving sandy beach of Killiney Bay (which 19th-century residents felt resembled Naples' Sorrento Bay, hence the Italian names of all the local roads) to the gorse-covered hills behind it, which make for a great walk. Alas, for most of us, Killiney will always remain a place to visit; on the rare occasion that a house comes on the market, it would take a cool €5 million to get the seller to bite.

To the south there are good views from the small park at Sorrento Point as well as from Killiney Hill. Dalkey Quarry is a popular site for rock climbers, and originally provided most of the granite for the gigantic piers at Dun Laoghaire Harbour. A number of rocky swimming pools are also found along the Dalkey coast.

DALKEY CASTLE & HERITAGE CENTRE
HERITAGE CENTRE

(☑01-285 8366; www.dalkeycastle.com; Castle St, Dalkey; adult/child €7.95/5.95; ⊙10am-6pm Mon-Fri, from 11am Sat-Sun Jun-Aug; closed Tue Sep-May) Spread across Goat Castle and St Begnet's Church, this heritage centre has models, displays and exhibitions on Dalkey's history; a **Living History tour** in the format of a theatre performance; and a **Writers' Gallery** on the town's rich literary heritage – from Samuel Beckett (who was born here) to Joseph O'Connor (who lives here). The centre also organises **walking tours** (€7; ⊙11am & noon Wed & Fri Jun-Aug).

ST BEGNET'S HOLY WELL
CHRISTIAN SITE

(admission free, boat from Coliemore Harbour per hr €25) A few hundred metres offshore is Dalkey Island, home to **St Begnet's Holy Well**, the most important of Dalkey's so-called holy wells. This one is reputed to cure rheumatism, making the island a popular destination for tourists and the faithful alike. The island is easily accessible by boat from Coliemore Harbour; you can't book a boat, so just show up.

JAMES JOYCE MUSEUM   MUSEUM

(📋01-280 9265; www.visitdublin.com; Joyce Tower, Sandycove; ⊙10am-4pm) FREE About 1km north of Dalkey is Sandycove, with a pretty little beach and the **Martello Tower**, built by British forces to keep an eye out for a Napoleonic invasion and now home to the James Joyce Museum. This is where the action begins in James Joyce's epic novel *Ulysses*. The museum was opened in 1962 by Sylvia Beach, the Paris-based publisher who first dared to put *Ulysses* into print, and has photographs, letters, documents, various editions of Joyce's work and two death masks of Joyce on display.

FORTY FOOT POOL   POOL

(Sandycove) Below the Martello Tower is the Forty Foot Pool, an open-air sea-water bathing pool that took its name from the army regiment, the Fortieth Foot, that was stationed at the tower until the regiment was disbanded in 1904. At the close of the first chapter of *Ulysses*, Buck Mulligan heads off to the Forty Foot Pool for a morning swim. A morning wake-up here is still a local tradition, whether it's winter or summer. In fact, a winter dip isn't much braver than a summer one since the water temperature varies by only about 5°C between the two seasons. Basically, it's always bloody cold.

Pressure from female bathers eventually opened this public stretch of water, originally nudist and for men only, to both sexes despite strong opposition from the 'forty-foot gentlemen'. The men eventually compromised with the ruling that a 'Togs Must Be Worn' sign would now apply after 9am. Prior to that time nudity prevails and swimmers are still predominantly male.

EATING

CAVISTON'S SEAFOOD
RESTAURANT   SEAFOOD €€

(📋01-280 9245; Glasthule Rd, Sandycove; mains €19-24; ⊙noon-5pm Tue-Thu, noon-midnight Fri & Sat) Long-established seafood specialists Caviston's have made the fruit of the sea a cottage industry; well worth the 1km trek to Sandycove.

GUINEA PIG   SEAFOOD €€€

(📋01-285 9055; 17 Railway Rd, Dalkey; mains €25-35; ⊙dinner only) Despite the name, is this the best seafood restaurant in Dublin? Many a food critic seems to think so.

Sleeping

Hotel rooms in Dublin aren't as expensive as they were during the Celtic Tiger years, but demand is still high and booking is highly recommended, especially if you want to stay in the city centre or within walking distance of it.

Hotels

From basic chain hotels to luxurious lodgings, Dublin's hotels offer the same kind of choice and service you'd find in any European capital. The best hotels are advertised as five-star, and while they're generally very good and the service is usually excellent, they're really more like a four-star hotel in London or New York – with prices to match. Smaller boutique hotels offer fewer rooms but more personalised attention, while chain hotels are perfect if all you want is a clean, central bed to sleep in and a decent breakfast.

B&Bs, Guesthouses & Townhouses

For so long the bedrock of basic accommodation, the old-fashioned B&B, with worn, slightly chintzy decor, has largely been surpassed by the cheaper chain hotels, but their more upmarket cousins – the Georgian guesthouses and townhouses – are now the city's most interesting version of an authentic boutique experience. The best of these are beautifully decked out and extremely comfortable. Breakfast can range from home-baked breads, fruit and farmhouse cheeses to a traditional, fat-laden fry-up.

Hostels

Hostels are the only truly budget option within a stone's throw of the city centre. Thankfully, most of these maintain a pretty high standard of hygiene and comfort. Many offer various sleeping arrangements, from a bed in a large dorm to a four-bed room or a double. There are plenty to choose from, but they tend to fill up very quickly and stay full.

Serviced Apartments

There are central self-catering apartments for groups, families or those on extended stays who may prefer to do their own thing. These are usually equipped to the standard of a modern, suburban home, while at the upper end they are like luxury penthouse apartments.

Bookings

Getting the hotel of your choice without a reservation can be tricky in high season (May to September) so always book your room in advance. You can book directly with the hotel, or through Dublin Tourism's online booking service (www.visitdublin.com).

There are also great savings if you book online. These rates are generally available year-round, but are tougher to find during high season. Be sure to book ahead and ask for a pre-booking rate.

NEED TO KNOW

Price Ranges
The below categories indicate the cost per night of a standard double room in high season.

€	under €80
€€	€80–150
€€€	over €150

Booking Services
Advance internet bookings are your best bet for deals. These are just a handful of services that will get you a competitive rate.

All Dublin Hotels (www.irelandhotels.com/hotels/dublin)

Dublin City Centre Hotels (http://dublin.city-centre-hotels.com)

Dublin Hotels (www.dublinhotels.com)

Dublin Tourism (www.visitdublin.com)

Go Ireland (www.goireland.com)

Hostel Dublin (www.hosteldublin.com)

Discounted Rates
In these uncertain times it's unlikely you will ever have to pay the quoted rate, but you'll need flexibility to get the best deals, usually midweek specials outside the high season.

Check-In & Check-Out Times
Check-out at most establishments is noon, but some of the smaller guesthouses and B&Bs require that you check out a little earlier, usually around 11am. Check-in times are usually between noon and 2pm.

Lonely Planet's Top Choices

Aberdeen Lodge (p177) A wonderful hidden gem.

Grafton House (p170) Funky central beds.

Isaacs Hostel (p174) Best bunks in town.

Pembroke Townhouse (p177) Georgian luxury.

Merrion (p172) The city's best hotel.

Best by Budget

€
Trinity Lodge (p170) Comfy and central B&B.

Isaacs Hostel (p174) Best bunks in the city.

€€
Radisson Blu Royal Hotel (p170) Elegant and very stylish.

Cliff Townhouse (p170) Terrific boutique bolthole.

Aberdeen Lodge (p177) Hospitality at its best.

€€€
Merrion (p172) Sophisticated, elegant and central.

Westbury (p171) Where the stars like to sleep.

Best Hotel Bars

Central Hotel (p171) The Library Bar is discreet and elegant.

Radisson Blu Royal Hotel (p170) Bangkok-style bar.

Four Seasons (p178) Ice, baby, ice.

Westbury Hotel (p171) I recognise him/her/them!

Best for Comfy Pillows

Brooks Hotel (p170) Everyone needs a pillow menu.

Merrion (p172) Nestle your head in luxury.

Aberdeen Lodge (p177) Sublime sleeps.

Westin Dublin (p174) The beds are heavenly.

Best for Afternoon Tea

Merrion (p172) The most decadent petit fours.

Shelbourne (p172) A timeless experience.

Best for Boutique Beds

Cliff Townhouse (p170) Ten magnificent rooms.

Irish Landmark Trust (p173) A unique sleeping experience.

Number 31 (p172) Architect-designed marvel.

Where to Stay

Neighbourhood	For	Against
Grafton Street & Around	Close to sights, nightlife, everything; a good choice of midrange and top-end hotels.	Generally more expensive than elsewhere; not always good value for money.
Merrion Square & Around	Lovely neighbourhood, elegant hotels and town-house accommodation.	Not a lot of choice; virtually no budget accommodation.
Temple Bar	In the heart of the action; close to everything.	Noisy and touristy; not especially good value for money.
Kilmainham & the Liberties	Close to the old city.	No good accommodation.
North of the Liffey	Good range of choice; within walking distance of sights and nightlife.	Budget accommodation not always good quality; some locations not especially comfortable after dark.
Docklands & the Grand Canal	Excellent contemporary hotels with good service.	Isolated in a neighbourhood that doesn't have a lot of life after dark.

SLEEPING

🛏 Grafton Street & Around

Grafton St itself has only one hotel – one of the city's best – but you'll find a host of choices in the area surrounding it. Not surprisingly, being so close to the choicest street in town comes at a premium, but the competition for business is fierce, which ensures quality is top rate.

TRINITY LODGE
GUESTHOUSE €

Map p240 (📞01-617 0900; www.trinitylodge. com; 12 South Frederick St; s/d from €56/70; 📶; 🚌cross-city buses, 🚇St Stephen's Green) Martin Sheen's grin greets you upon entering this cosy, award-winning guesthouse, which he declared his favourite spot for an Irish stay. Marty's not the only one: this place is so popular that they've added a second townhouse across the road, which has also been kitted out to the highest standards. Room 2 of the original house has a lovely bay window.

AVALON HOUSE
HOSTEL €

Map p240 (📞01-475 0001; www.avalon-house. ie; 55 Aungier St; dm/s/d from €10/34/54; @📶; 🚌all cross-city, 🚇St Stephen's Green) One of the city's most popular hostels, welcoming Avalon House has pine floors, high ceilings and large, open fireplaces that create the ambience for a good spot of meet-the-backpacker lounging. Some of the cleverly designed rooms have mezzanine levels, which are great for families. Book well in advance.

RADISSON BLU ROYAL HOTEL
HOTEL €€

Map p238 (📞01-898 2900; www.radissonblu.ie/ royalhotel-dublin; Golden Lane; r €110-220; @📶; 🚌all cross-city, 🚇St Stephen's Green) Our favourite hotel in this price range is an excellent example of how sleek lines and muted colours combine beautifully with luxury, ensuring a memorable night's stay. From hugely impressive public areas to sophisticated bedrooms – each with flat-screen digital TV embedded in the wall to go along with all the other little touches – this hotel will not disappoint.

GRAFTON HOUSE
B&B €€

Map p240 (📞01-648 0010; www.graftonguest house.com; 26-27 South Great George's St; s/d from €79/109; @📶; 🚌all cross-city, 🚇St Stephen's Green) This slightly off-beat guesthouse in a Gothic-style building gets the nod in all three key categories: location, price and style. Just next to George's St Arcade, the Grafton offers the traditional friendly features of a B&B (including a terrific breakfast), coupled with a funky design – check out the psychedelic wallpaper. Hard to beat at this price.

CLIFF TOWNHOUSE
GUESTHOUSE €€

Map p238 (📞01-638 3939; www.theclifftown house.com; 22 St Stephen's Green North; r from €99; @📶; 🚇St Stephen's Green) As *pied-à-terres* go, this is a doozy: there are 10 exquisitely appointed bedrooms spread across a wonderful Georgian property whose best views overlook St Stephen's Green. Downstairs is Sean Smith's superb restaurant, Cliff Townhouse (p69).

BROOKS HOTEL
HOTEL €€

Map p240 (📞01-670 4000; www.sinnotthotels. com; 59-62 Drury St; r from €110; 🚌all cross-city, 🚇St Stephen's Green) About 120m west of Grafton St, this small, plush place has an emphasis on familial, friendly service. The decor is nouveau classic with high-veneer-panelled walls, decorative bookcases and old-fashioned sofas, while bedrooms are extremely comfortable and come fitted out in subtly coloured furnishings. The clincher for us though is the king- and super-king-size beds in all rooms, complete with...a pillow menu. Go figure.

BUSWELL'S HOTEL
HOTEL €€

Map p240 (📞01-614 6500; www.quinnhotels.com; 23-27 Molesworth St; r from €100; @; 🚌all cross-city, 🚇St Stephen's Green) This Dublin institution, open since 1882, has a long association with politicians, who wander across the road from Dáil Éireann to wet their beaks at the hotel bar. The 69 bedrooms have all been given the once-over, but have kept their Georgian charm intact.

HARRINGTON HALL
GUESTHOUSE €€

Map p238 (📞01-475 3497; www.harringtonhall. com; 69-70 Harcourt St; s/d from €89/119; @📶; 🚇Harcourt) Want to fluff up the pillows in the home of a former Lord Mayor of Dublin? The traditional Georgian style of Timothy Charles Harrington's home – he wore the gold chain from 1901 to 1903 – has thankfully been retained and this smart guesthouse stands out for its understated elegance. The 1st- and 2nd-floor rooms have their original fireplaces and ornamental ceilings.

Guests can avail themselves of the late bar and nightclub in the Harcourt Hotel next door.

STAUNTON'S ON THE GREEN HOTEL €€

Map p238 (✆01-478 2300; www.stauntonsonthe green.ie; 83 St Stephen's Green South; r from €109; 🖵all cross-city, 🚇St Stephen's Green) A perfect location on St Stephen's Green (next door to the Department of Foreign Affairs), this handsome Georgian house has clean rooms that are just a mite care-worn. The front-facing rooms have floor-to-ceiling windows overlooking the green. Any closer and you're sleeping with the Lord Mayor.

LA STAMPA HOTEL €€

Map p240 (✆01-677 4444; www.lastampa.ie; 35 Dawson St; r from €120; @🛜; 🖵all cross-city, 🚇St Stephen's Green) La Stampa is an atmospheric boutique hotel on trendy Dawson St with 29 Asian-influenced white rooms with rattan furniture and exotic velvet throws. The Mandala Day Spa is a luxurious, all-frills ayurvedic spa, but to fully benefit from your restorative treatments, ask for a top-floor bedroom away from the noise of the bar below.

GRAFTON CAPITAL HOTEL HOTEL €€

Map p240 (✆01-648 1221; www.capital-hotels. com; Lower Stephen's St; r from €125; 🖵all cross-city) It's hardly recognisable as such today, but this centrally located hotel just off Grafton St is actually a couple of converted Georgian townhouses. Its 75 modern rooms are designed along the lines of function before form, which makes them perfect for the weekend visitor who wants to bed down somewhere central and still keep some credit-card space for a good night out. Breakfast is included.

O'CALLAGHAN STEPHEN'S GREEN HOTEL €€

Map p238 (✆01-607 3600; www.stephensgreen hotel.ie; 1-5 Harcourt St; r from €159; @🛜; 🖵all cross-city, 🚇St Stephen's Green) Past the glass-fronted lobby are 75 thoroughly modern rooms that make full use of the visual impact of primary colours, most notably red and blue. This is a business hotel *par excellence;* everything here is what you'd expect from a top international hotel (including a gym and a business centre). There are extraordinary online deals available.

CENTRAL HOTEL HOTEL €€

Map p240 (✆01-679 7302; www.centralhotel dublin.com; 1-5 Exchequer St; s/d from €75/89; 🛜; 🖵all cross-city, 🚇St Stephen's Green) The rooms are a modern – if miniaturised – version of Edwardian luxury. Heavy velvet curtains and custom-made Irish furnishings (including beds with draped backboards) fit a little too snugly into the space afforded them, but they lend a touch of class. Note that street-facing rooms can get a little noisy. Location-wise, the name says it all.

HILTON HOTEL €€

Map p238 (✆01-402 9988; www.dublin.hilton. com; Charlemont Pl; r from €110; @🛜; 🚇Charlemont) Modern rooms with all mod cons is what you'd expect from the Hilton group, and this canalside property delivers precisely that. Comfortable and convenient (close to a Luas stop), it's also eminently forgettable – you've seen decor like this in cities all over the world.

CAMDEN COURT HOTEL HOTEL €€

Map p238 (✆01-475 9666; www.camdencourt hotel.com; Camden St; s/d from €79/110; @🛜; 🖵all cross-city, 🚇Harcourt) Big and bland ain't such a bad thing this close to St Stephen's Green, especially if the mainstay of your clientele is the business crowd. They like the standardised rooms but *love* the amenities, which include a 16m pool, health club (with jacuzzi, sauna and steam room) and fully equipped gym.

WESTBURY HOTEL HOTEL €€€

Map p240 (✆01-679 1122; www.doylecollec tion.com; Grafton St; r/ste from €199/299; @🛜; 🖵all cross-city) Visiting celebs looking for some quiet time have long favoured the Westbury's elegant suites, where they can watch TV from the jacuzzi before retiring to a four-poster bed. Mere mortals tend to make do with the standard rooms, which are comfortable enough but lack the sophisticated grandeur promised by the luxurious public spaces – which are a great spot for an afternoon drink.

FITZWILLIAM HOTEL HOTEL €€€

Map p240 (✆01-478 7000; www.fitzwilliam-hotel. com; St Stephen's Green West; r from €160; @🛜; 🖵all cross-city, 🚇Stephen's Green) You couldn't pick a more prestigious spot on the Dublin Monopoly board than this minimalist Terence Conrad–designed number overlooking the Green. Ask for a corner room on the

SLEEPING

5th floor (502 or 508), with balmy balcony and a view. The hotel is also home to one of the city's best restaurants, Thornton's (p68).

🛏 Merrion Square & Around

It's the most sought-after real estate in town, so it's hardly surprising that it's home to the lion's share of the city's top hotels. But although you'll pay for the privilege of bedding down in luxury, there are some excellent deals available at many of these well-located properties, which are within a gentle stroll of the best restaurants, bars and attractions the city has to offer.

DAVENPORT HOTEL HOTEL €€
Map p244 (🖉01-607 3500; www.davenport hotel.ie; Merrion Sq North; r from €110; @�; 🖵all cross-city) Housed within the old Merrion Hall, which was built in 1863 for the Plymouth Brethren, this is a solid business hotel with large rooms equipped with orthopaedic beds and big bathrooms. It's popular with both business and leisure visitors; if you book online you get free wi-fi for the duration of your stay.

SHELBOURNE HOTEL €€€
Map p244 (🖉01-676 6471; www.theshelbourne.ie; 27 St Stephen's Green North; r from €220; @�; 🖵all cross-city, 🚇St Stephen's Green) Dublin's most iconic hotel, founded in 1824, was bought out by the Marriott group, who

spent a ton of money restoring its rooms and public spaces to their former grandeur, a few years ago. The refurb was successful, but their management style has been criticised as being somewhat short of its five-star reputation.

Whatever your experiences, you're staying in a slice of history: it was here that the Irish Constitution was drafted in 1921, and this is the hotel in Elizabeth Bowen's eponymous novel. Afternoon tea in the refurbished Lord Mayor's Lounge remains one of the best experiences in town.

NUMBER 31 GUESTHOUSE €€€
Map p244 (🖉01-676 5011; www.number31. ie; 31 Leeson Close; s/d/tr incl breakfast €180/260/300; �; 🖵all cross-city) The city's most distinctive property is the former home of modernist architect Sam Stephenson, who successfully fused '60s style with 18th-century grace. Its 21 bedrooms are split between the retro coach house, with its fancy rooms, and the more elegant Georgian house, where rooms are individually furnished with tasteful French antiques and big comfortable beds.

Gourmet breakfasts with kippers, homemade breads and granola are served in the conservatory. Yeah, baby!

MERRION HOTEL €€€
Map p244 (🖉01-603 0600; www.merrionhotel. com; Upper Merrion St; r/ste from €485/995; @�🏊; 🖵all cross-city) This resplendent five-star hotel, in a terrace of beautifully

---

HOME AWAY FROM HOME

Self-catering apartments are a good option for visitors staying a few days, for groups of friends, or families with kids. Apartments range from one-room studios to two-bed flats with lounge areas, and include bathrooms and kitchenettes. A decent two-bedroom apartment will cost about €100 to €150 per night. Good, central places include the following:

Clarion Stephen's Hall Map p244 (🖉01-638 1111; www.premgroup.com; 14-17 Lower Leeson St; s/d €125/240; @; 🖵all cross-city) Deluxe studios and suites, with all mod cons; akin to an elegant hotel room.

Home From Home Apartments Map p252 (🖉01-678 1100; www.yourhomefromhome. com; The Moorings, Fitzwilliam Quay; €110-180) Deluxe one- to three-bedroom apartments in the south-side city centre. Minimum two-night stay in high season.

Latchfords Map p244 (🖉01-676 0784; www.latchfords.ie; 99-100 Lower Baggot St; €100-160) Studios and two-bedroom flats in a Georgian townhouse.

Oliver St John Gogarty's Penthouse Apartments Map p236 (🖉01-671 1822; www. gogartys.ie; 18-21 Anglesea St; 2 bedroom €99-189) Perched high atop the pub of the same name, these one- to three-bedroom places have views of Temple Bar.

restored Georgian townhouses, opened in 1988 but looks like it's been around a lot longer. Try to get a room in the old house (with the largest private art collection in the city), rather than the newer wing, to sample its truly elegant comforts.

Located opposite Government Buildings, its marble corridors are patronised by politicos, visiting dignitaries and the odd celeb. Even if you don't stay, come for the superb afternoon tea (€36), with endless cups of tea served out of silver pots by a raging fire.

CONRAD DUBLIN INTERNATIONAL
HOTEL €€€

Map p244 (☑01-602 8900; www.conradhotels. com; Earlsfort Tce; r €220; @🛜; 🖵all city centre) Dublin's first truly modern international business hotel has not just kept up with the pace of change but has set the standard for other newer hotels in its class. The king-size rooms are spotless and well equipped, the public areas elegant and the staff absolutely top notch.

There's a dizzying array of special discount rates – at the last minute, room prices are often slashed by half – for both business and leisure travellers.

🛏 Temple Bar

If you're here for a weekend of wild abandon and can't fathom anything more than a quick stumble into bed, then Temple Bar's choice of hotels and hostels will suit you perfectly. Generally speaking the rooms are small, the prices large and you should be able to handle the late-night symphonies of die-hard revellers.

BARNACLES
HOSTEL €

Map p236 (☑01-671 6277; www.barnacles.ie; 19 Lower Temple Lane; dm €19-22; 🛜; 🖵all city centre) If you're here for a good time and not a long time, then this Temple Bar hostel is the ideal spot to meet fellow revellers; tap up the helpful and knowledgeable staff for the best places to cause mischief; and sleep off the effects of said mischief while being totally oblivious to the noise outside, which is constant.

Rooms are quieter at the back. Top facilities include a comfy lounge with an open fire. Linen and towels are provided. A contender for the south side's best hostel, it also has a discount deal with a nearby covered car park.

GOGARTY'S TEMPLE BAR HOSTEL
HOSTEL €

Map p236 (☑01-671 1822; www.gogartys.ie/ hostel; 58-59 Fleet St; dm/d €14/50; 🛜; 🖵all city centre) Sleeping isn't really the activity of choice for anyone staying in this compact, decent hostel in the middle of Temple Bar, next to the pub of the same name. It tends to get booked up with stag and hen parties so, depending on your mood, bring either your earplugs or bunny ears. Six self-catering apartments are also available.

KINLAY HOUSE
HOSTEL €

Map p236 (☑01-679 6644; www.kinlaydublin.ie; 2-12 Lord Edward St; dm/d incl breakfast €18/60; 🛜; 🖵all city centre) An institution among the city's hostels, this former boarding house for boys has massive, mixed 24-bed dorms, as well as smaller rooms. Its bustling location next to Christ Church Cathedral and Dublin Castle is a bonus, but some rooms suffer from traffic noise. There are cooking facilities and a cafe, and breakfast is included. Not for the faint-hearted.

ASHFIELD HOUSE
HOSTEL €

Map p236 (☑01-679 7734; www.ashfieldhouse. ie; 19-20 D'Olier St; dm €9-18, d €48-60; @🛜; 🖵all city centre) A stone's throw from Temple Bar and O'Connell Bridge, this modern hostel in a converted church has a selection of tidy four- and six-bed rooms, one large dorm and 25 rooms with private bathrooms. It's more like a small hotel, but without the price tag. A Continental-style breakfast is included – a rare beast indeed for hostels. Maximum stay is six nights.

IRISH LANDMARK TRUST
SELF-CATERING €€€

Map p236 (☑01-670 4733; www.irishlandmark. com; 25 Eustace St; 2/3 nights for 7 people €600/875; 🖵all city centre) This 18th-century heritage house has been gloriously restored to the highest standard by the Irish Landmark Trust. Furnished with tasteful antiques and authentic furniture and fittings (including a grand piano in the drawing room), it sleeps up to seven in its three bedrooms, which must be booked for a minimum of two nights.

PARAMOUNT HOTEL
HOTEL €€

Map p236 (☑01-417 9900; www.paramounthotel. ie; cnr Parliament St & Essex Gate; s/d €69/120; @🛜; 🖵all city centre) Behind the Victorian facade, the lobby is a faithful re-creation of a 1930s hotel, complete with dark-wood floors, deep-red leather Chesterfield couches and heavy velvet drapes. The 70-odd rooms don't quite bring *The Maltese Falcon* to mind, but they're handsomely furnished and very comfortable. Downstairs is the Turk's Head (p96), one of the area's most popular bars.

MORGAN HOTEL   BOUTIQUE HOTEL €€
Map p236 (☏01-643 7000; www.themorgan.com; 10 Fleet St; r from €100; @ 🖥; 🖵all city centre) It was built to attract the Spice Girls, now it just caters to girls (and guys) on a spicy weekend in Dublin. No bad thing, of course, especially as the hotel has stood up well to the ravages of recession. Top-rate facilities, friendly staff and a bunch of online combo offers make this an attractive option.

DUBLIN CITI HOTEL   HOTEL €€
Map p236 (☏01-679 4455; www.dublincitihotel. com; 46-49 Dame St; r from €89; @; 🖵all cross-city) An unusual turreted 19th-century building right next to the Central Bank is home to this cheap and cheerful hotel. Rooms aren't huge but are simply furnished and have fresh white quilts. It's only a stagger (literally) from the heart of Temple Bar, hic.

ELIZA LODGE   GUESTHOUSE €€
Map p236 (☏01-671 8044; www.elizalodge.com; 23-24 Wellington Quay; s/d/ste from €79/99/119; 🖵all city centre) It's priced like a hotel, looks like a hotel, but it's still a guesthouse. The 18 rooms are comfortable, spacious and – due to its position right over the Millennium Bridge – come with great views of the Liffey. It has discounted parking rates with a nearby car park.

CLARENCE HOTEL   HOTEL €€€
Map p236 (☏01-407 0800; www.theclarence.ie; 6-8 Wellington Quay; r €109-259, ste €299-1499; @ 🖥; 🖵all city centre) Bono and the Edge's discreet little bolthole is no longer the hottest bedroom in town, which is a good thing because the reality never lived up to the hype. Instead, what's left is a handsome boutique hotel designed to reflect the aesthetic of a 1930s gentlemen's club, complete with an excellent bar and a fine restaurant.

WESTIN DUBLIN   HOTEL €€€
Map p240 (☏01-645 1000; www.thewestindub lin.com; Westmoreland St; r from €179; @ 🖥; 🖵all city centre) Formerly a grand branch of the Allied Irish Bank, this fine old building was gutted and reborn as a stylish upmarket hotel. The rooms, many of which overlook a beautiful atrium, are decorated in elegant mahogany and soft colours that are reminiscent of the USA's finest. You will sleep on 10 layers of the Westin's own trademark Heavenly Bed, which is damn comfortable indeed.

The hotel's most elegant room is the former banking hall, complete with gold-leaf plasterwork on the ceiling. It is now used for banquets. Breakfast will set you back €27.

🛏 North of the Liffey

There is a scattering of good midrange options between O'Connell St and Smithfield. Gardiner St, to the east of O'Connell St, is the the traditional B&B district of town, but you're better off sticking to the southern end of the street where the properties are better and the street is safer.

★ISAACS HOSTEL   HOSTEL €
Map p248 (☏01-855 6215; www.isaacs.ie; 2-5 Frenchman's Lane; dm/tw from €14/54; @ 🖥; 🖵all city centre, 🚆Connolly) The northside's best hostel – hell, for atmosphere alone it's the best in town – is in a 200-year-old wine vault just around the corner from the main bus station. With summer barbecues, live music in the lounge, internet access and colourful dorms, this terrific place generates consistently good reviews from backpackers and other travellers.

JACOB'S INN   HOSTEL €
Map p248 (☏01-855 5660; www.isaacs.ie; 21-28 Talbot Pl; dm/d from €12.50/74; 🖥; 🚆Connolly) Sister hostel to Isaacs around the corner, this clean and modern hostel offers spacious accommodation with private bathrooms and outstanding facilities, including some wheelchair-accessible rooms, a bureau de change, bike storage and a self-catering kitchen.

GLOBETROTTERS TOURIST HOSTEL   HOSTEL €
Map p248 (☏01-878 8088; www.globetrotters dublin.com; 46-48 Lower Gardiner St; dm €16; 🖵all city centre, 🚆Connolly) This is a really friendly place with 94 beds in a variety of dorms, all with bathrooms and under-bed storage. The funky decor is due to the fact

CAMPUS ACCOMMODATION

During the summer months, visitors can opt to stay in campus accommodation, which is both convenient and comfortable.

Trinity College Map p240 (☑01-896 1177; www.tcd.ie; Accommodations Office, Trinity College; s/d from €58/78; @ 🕾; 🖵all cross-city) The closest thing to living like a student at this stunningly beautiful university is crashing in their rooms when they're on holidays. Rooms and two-bed apartments in the newer block have their own bathrooms; those in the older blocks share facilities, though there are private sinks. Breakfast is included.

Mercer Court Campus Accommodation Map p240 (☑01-478 2179; www.mercer court.ie; Lower Mercer St; s/d 80/120; @ 🕾) Owned and run by the Royal College of Surgeons, this is the most luxurious student-accommodation option in the city. It's close to Grafton St and St Stephen's Green. The rooms are modern and up to hotel standard.

Dublin City University (DCU) (☑01-700 5736; www.summeraccommodation.dcu.ie; Larkfield Apartments, Campus Residences, Dublin City University; s/d from €50/84; ⊘mid-Jun–mid-Sep; 🖵11, 11A, 11B, 13, 13A, 19 or 19A from city centre) This accommodation is proof that students slum it in relative luxury. The modern rooms have plenty of amenities at hand, including a kitchen, common room and a fully equipped health centre. The Glasnevin campus is only 15 minutes by bus or car from the city centre.

that it shares the same artistic ethos (and dining room) as the Townhouse (p176) next door. There's a little patio garden to the rear for that elusive sunny day.

ABBEY COURT HOSTEL
HOSTEL €

Map p248 (☑01-878 0700; www.abbey-court. com; 29 Bachelor's Walk; dm/d €18/79; 🖵all cross-city) Spread over two buildings, this large, well-run hostel has 33 clean dorm beds with good storage. Its excellent facilities include a dining hall, conservatory and barbecue area. Doubles with bathroom are in the newer building where a light breakfast is provided in the adjacent cafe. Not surprisingly, this is a popular option for travellers. Reservations are advised.

ANCHOR GUESTHOUSE
B&B €€

Map p248 (☑01-878 6913; www.anchorhouse dublin.com; 49 Lower Gardiner St; r weekday/weekend from €71/143; 🖵all city centre, 🚇Connolly) Most B&Bs round these parts offer pretty much the same stuff: TV, half-decent shower, clean linen and tea- and coffee-making facilities. The Anchor does all of that, but it just has an elegance you won't find in many of the other B&Bs along this stretch. This lovely Georgian guesthouse, with its delicious wholesome breakfasts, comes highly recommended by readers. They're dead right.

CASTLE HOTEL
HOTEL €€

Map p248 (☑01-874 6949; www.castle-hotel.ie; 3-4 Great Denmark St; r from €80; 🕾; 🖵all city centre, 🚇Connolly) In business since 1809, the Castle Hotel may be slightly rough around the edges but it's one of the most pleasant hotels this side of the Liffey. The fabulous palazzo-style grand staircase leads to the 50-odd bedrooms, whose furnishings are traditional and a tad antiquated, but perfectly good throughout – check out the original Georgian cornicing around the high ceilings.

CLIFDEN GUESTHOUSE
GUESTHOUSE €€

Map p248 (☑01-874 6364; www.clifdenhouse. com; 32 Gardiner Pl; s/d/tr from €70/90/110; 🖵36 or 36A) The Clifden is a very nicely refurbished Georgian house with 14 tastefully decorated rooms. They all come with bathrooms, are immaculately clean and extremely comfortable. A nice touch is the free parking, even after you've checked out!

MALDRON HOTEL SMITHFIELD
HOTEL €€

Map p248 (☑01-485 0900; www.maldronhotels. com; Smithfield Village; r from €90; 🕾; 🖵25, 25A, 25B, 66, 66A, 66B, 67, 90, 151 to Upper Ormond Quay, 🚇Smithfield) With big bedrooms and plenty of earth tones to soften the contemporary edges, this functionally modern hotel is your best bet in this part of town. We love the floor-to-ceiling windows: great for checking out what's going on below in the square.

JURY'S INN PARNELL ST   HOTEL €€

Map p248 (☑01-878 4900; www.jurysinns.com; Moore St Plaza, Parnell St; r €109; @☎; ☐36 or 36A) Jury's hotels are nothing if not reliable, and this edition of Ireland's most popular hotel chain is no exception. What do you care that the furnishings were mass-produced and flat-packed and that the decor was created to be utterly inoffensive to everything save good taste? The location – just off Upper O'Connell St – is terrific.

BROWN'S HOTEL   HOTEL €€

Map p248 (☑01-855 0034; www.brownshotel ireland.com; 80-90 Lower Gardiner St; s/d €99/159; ☐Connolly Station) A popular hotel along the strip, Brown's 22 rooms are a fairly comfortable bunch even if they're a little shabby looking. They fill up quickly and there's usually a pretty lively atmosphere, although we could do without the noise from the hostel next door.

ACADEMY HOTEL   HOTEL €€

Map p248 (☑01-878 0666; www.academyhotel. ie; Findlater Pl; r from €60; @☎; ☐all city centre) Only a few steps from O'Connell St, this solidly three-star hotel is part of the Best Western group and as such offers the kind of comfortable, if unmemorable, night's sleep associated with the brand. The deluxe suites come with free wi-fi and flat-screen digital TVs. There's discounted parking at the covered car park next door.

MORRISON HOTEL   HOTEL €€€

Map p248 (☑01-887 2400; www.morrisonho tel.ie; Ormond Quay; r from €199; @☎; ☐all cross-city, ☐Jervis) A buyout by Russian billionaire Elena Baturina has breathed new life into this quayside hotel, courtesy of a €7m refurbishment that has seen the rooms given a contemporary makeover and the already elegant public spaces a facelift. King-size beds (with Serta mattresses), 40-inch LED TVs, free wi-fi and Crabtree & Evelyn toiletries are just some of the hotel's offerings.

Now operated by Hilton Doubletree, you won't sleep in more luxurious surroundings anywhere on the north side.

GRESHAM HOTEL   HOTEL €€€

Map p248 (☑01-874 6881; www.gresham-hotels.com; Upper O'Connell St; r from €200, ste €450-2500; @☎; ☐all cross-city) This landmark hotel shed its traditional granny's parlour look with a major overhaul some years ago. Despite its brighter, smarter, modern appearance and a fabulous open-plan foyer, its loyal clientele – elderly groups on shopping breaks to the capital and well-heeled Americans – continues to find it charming. Rooms are spacious and well serviced, though the decor is a little brash.

TOWNHOUSE HOTEL   INN €€€

Map p248 (☑01-878 8808; www.townhouseof dublin.com; 47-48 Lower Gardiner St; s/d/tr €140/199/219; ☐36 or 36A, ☐Connolly) The ghostly writing of Irish-Japanese author Lafcadio Hearn may have influenced the Gothic-style interior of his former home. A dark-walled, gilt-framed foyer with jingling chandelier leads into 82 individually designed comfy (but cramped) rooms. It shares a dining room with the Globetrotters Tourist Hostel (p174) next door.

🛏 Docklands

You'll be relying on public transport or a taxi to get you in and out of town for things to do.

GIBSON HOTEL   HOTEL €€

Map p252 (☑01-618 5000; www.thegibson hotel.ie; Point Village; r from €120; @☎; ☐151 from city centre, ☐Grand Canal Dock) Built for business travellers and out-of-towners taking in a gig at the O2 next door, the Gibson is undoubtedly impressive: 250-odd ultra-modern rooms decked out in snazzy Respa beds, flat-screen TVs and internet work stations. The public areas are bright, big and airy – lots of muted colours and floor-to-ceiling glass – and you might catch last night's star act having breakfast the next morning.

CLARION HOTEL IFSC   HOTEL €€

Map p252 (☑01-433 8800; www.clarionhotel ifsc.com; Custom House Quay; r from €140, ste €190; @☎☒) This swanky business hotel in the heart of the Irish Financial Services Centre has beautiful rooms decorated with contemporary light oak furnishings and a blue-and-taupe colour scheme that is supposed to soothe the mind after a long day of meetings.

MALDRON HOTEL CARDIFF LANE   HOTEL €€

Map p252 (☑01-643 9500; www.maldron hotels.com; Cardiff Lane; r/ste €159/209; @🗢🌊; 🚍56A & 77B, 🚇Grand Canal Dock) A good mid-range hotel with excellent amenities (two restaurants, a bar and a fitness centre), this hotel suffers only because of its location, on an isolated street far from the city-centre action. Its saving grace is the nearby Grand Canal Dock and its selection of bars and restaurants.

ABERDEEN LODGE   GUESTHOUSE €€

Map p254 (☑01-283 8155; www.aberdeen-lodge. com; 53-55 Park Ave; s/d €99/149; @🗢; 🚍2, 3, 🚈DART Sydney Parade) Not only is this absolutely one of Dublin's best guesthouses, but it's a carefully guarded secret, known only to those who dare stay a short train ride from the city centre. Their reward is a luxurious house with a level of personalised service as good you'll find in one of the city's top hotels.

Most of the stunning rooms have either a four-poster, a half-tester or a brass bed to complement the authentic Edwardian furniture and tasteful art on the walls. The suites even have fully working Adams fireplaces. As there is one member of staff for every two rooms, the service is exceptional, not to mention totally hands-on and very courteous.

PEMBROKE TOWNHOUSE   INN €€

Map p254 (☑01-660 0277; www.pembroketown house.ie; 90 Pembroke Rd; r from €99; 🗢🐾; 🚍5, 7, 7A, 8, 18 or 45 from city centre) This super-luxurious townhouse is a perfect example of what happens when traditional and modern combine to great effect. A classical Georgian house has been transformed into a superb boutique hotel, with each room carefully crafted and appointed to reflect the best of contemporary design and style, right down to the modern art on the walls and the handy lift to the upper floors. May we borrow your designer?

WATERLOO HOUSE   INN €€

Map p254 (☑01-660 1888; www.waterloohouse. ie; 8-10 Waterloo Rd; s/d €129/145; 🗢; 🚍5, 7, 7A, 8, 18 or 45 from city centre) Within walking distance of St Stephen's Green, this lovely guesthouse is spread over two ivy-clad Georgian houses off Baggot St. Rooms are tastefully decorated with high-quality furnishings in authentic Farrow & Ball Georgian colours, and all have cable TV and kettles. Home-cooked breakfast is served in the conservatory or in the garden on sunny days.

ARIEL HOUSE   INN €€

Map p254 (☑01-668 5512; www.ariel-house.net; 52 Lansdowne Rd; s/d from €99/139; 🗢; 🚍5, 7, 7A, 8, 18 or 45 from city centre) Somewhere between a boutique hotel and a luxury B&B, this highly rated Victorian-era property has 28 rooms with private bathrooms, all individually decorated in period furniture, which lends the place an air of genuine luxury. A far better choice than most hotels.

MARKER   HOTEL €€€

Map p252 (☑01-687 5100; www.themarkerhotel dublin.com; Grand Canal Sq; r from €200; @🗢; 🚍56a & 77A, 🚇Grand Canal Dock) Dublin's newest designer digs is impressive from the

---

BEDS BEYOND THE ROYAL CANAL

Just beyond the Royal Canal, about 3km east of Upper O'Connell St in the suburb of Drumcondra, are rows of late-Victorian and Edwardian houses, some of which offer comfortable B&B rooms: the attraction is that they're on the road to the airport and are served by all of the airport buses.

Griffith House (☑01-837 5030; www.griffithhouse.com; 125 Griffith Ave; s/d €40/60; 🚍41, 41B or 16A from city centre) Suburban elegance should never be underestimated, especially not if it comes in the shape of this handsome Victorian home with four elegant rooms, three of which have private bathrooms. It's a simple, traditional place that puts the emphasis on a warm welcome, a good night's sleep and a filling breakfast.

Croke Park Hotel (☑01-607 0000; www.doylecollection.com; Croke Park, Jones's Rd; r from €135; 🚍3, 11, 11A, 16, 16A or 123 from O'Connell St) Just across the street from the cathedral of Gaelic sports, this branch of the Jury's chain targets fans up for the match. The rooms are big, clean and characterless – but what does that matter when you're celebrating...or commiserating?

outside – the shell is a stunning building created by Manuel Aires Mateus. The recession put paid to it for a couple of years, but it finally opened in 2013 with 187 ultra-swish contemporary bedrooms, a ground-floor cocktail lounge and a decent restaurant. The rooftop bar has great views.

DYLAN   HOTEL €€€

Map p254 (☑01-660 3001; www.dylan.ie; Eastmoreland Pl; r from €200; @⊛; ☑5, 7, 7A, 8, 18, 27X or 44 from city centre) The Dylan's baroque-meets-Scandinavian-sleek designer look has been a big hit, a reflection perhaps of a time when too much was barely enough for the glitterati who signed contracts over cocktails before retiring to crisp Frette linen sheets in the wonderfully appointed rooms upstairs.

SCHOOLHOUSE HOTEL   BOUTIQUE HOTEL €€€

Map p254 (☑01-667 5014; www.schoolhouse hotel.com; 2-8 Northumberland Rd; r from €159; ⊛🐾; ☑5, 7, 7A, 8, 18, 27X or 44 from city centre)

A Victorian schoolhouse dating from 1861, this beautiful building has been successfully converted into an exquisite boutique hotel that is (ahem) ahead of its class. Its 31 cosy bedrooms, named after famous Irish people, all have king-sized beds, big white quilts and loudly patterned headboards. The Canteen bar and patio bustles with local business folk in summer.

FOUR SEASONS   HOTEL €€€

Map p254 (☑01-665 4000; www.fourseasons. com; Simmonscourt Rd; r from €225; @⊛🐾; ☑5, 7, 7A, 8, 18 or 45 from city centre) Like Alexis Carrington gliding down the stairs in *Dynasty,* you know you're in the presence of a diva when you step inside the grand lobby of this enormous hotel. To some, the effect is a little garish, a bit like Joan Collins herself – but to others, the combination of marble, chandeliers and marvellous bedrooms screams luxury. It's in the grounds of the Royal Dublin Showgrounds.

Understand Dublin

Dublin Today

Times are tough and austerity – a catch-all term for the unforgiving program of forced cuts and revenue increases that Ireland has been dealing with of late – is neither an abstract concept nor a temporary inconvenience. Dubliners, steeled by centuries of tough times, have adjusted accordingly, but the pain is profound and ongoing.

Best on Film

Adam and Paul (2004; Lenny Abrahamson) Mark O'Halloran and Tom Murphy put in compelling and convincing performances as two junkies from the inner-city projects desperate for a fix. It's funny, pithy and occasionally silly, but a great debut for Abrahamson nonetheless.

The Dead (1987; John Huston) Based on a short story from James Joyce's *Dubliners*, *The Dead* focuses on a dinner party in Dublin at the end of the 19th century and specifically the thoughts of one of the party goers. A difficult task for Huston in his last film, and he pulls it off with aplomb.

Best in Print

Dubliners (1914; James Joyce) In our humble opinion, one of the most perfectly written collections of short stories ever; 15 poignant and powerful tales of Dubliners and the moments that define their lives. Even if you never visit, read this book.

New Dubliners (2005; edited by Oona Frawley) The likes of Maeve Binchy, Dermot Bolger, Roddy Doyle, Colum McCann and Joseph O'Connor lend their respective talents to creating short stories about modern-day Dublin.

Economic Bailouts

Ever since the infamous bank guarantee of October 2008 – when the six Irish pillar banks left dangerously exposed by the Global Financial Crisis were given a blanket guarantee of all their liabilities (totalling €440 billion) by a panicked government – Ireland has been mired in a profound economic crisis. The guarantee expired in 2010 and the government was forced to turn to the EU, the European Financial Stability Fund and the International Monetary Fund (IMF) – commonly referred to as the 'troika' – for a bailout, totalling roughly €85 billion. This money has to be repaid, and the terms set by the troika – who show up every three months for a progress report – have resulted in one draconian budget after another.

Political Rhetoric

A change of government in 2011 – which saw Fianna Fáil decimated and the election of Fine Gael in coalition with the Labour Party – was initially greeted with cautious hope, but that hope soon gave way to despair when the pre-election rhetoric about creating jobs and making 'Ireland the best small country in the world to do business in' was revealed to be just that – rhetoric.

Doing More with Less

Spend any length of time in a Dubliner's company and you'll soon hear their version of what went wrong, who's to blame and what the future holds, but no matter which version you get, you'll quickly recognise how frustrated most people are. Unemployment is at a 20-year high, and with more than 3000 people leaving Ireland every month, emigration is now at its highest point since the Famine. Mortgage distress – the horrendous by-product of the burst property bubble – is a major theme, as an increasing number of Dubliners find themselves unable to make mortgage repayments on properties that in some cases have lost more than half their value.

'Doing more with less' is the dispiriting buzz phrase of the moment – whether it's feeding the family, paying off debt or running a business for ever-dwindling consumers. Dubliners are working harder than ever for less pay: salary cuts are the price they pay for the privilege of still having a job.

But just as they're frustrated and frightened by an uncertain future, they remain, for the most part, doggedly defiant, urged on by the idea that things are so bad they can only get better. Which might explain why Dubliners (and the Irish in general) are so reluctant to take to the streets with their discontent: there is sympathy and even admiration for Greek and Spanish defiance, but it's tempered by a pragmatism that inevitably concludes that protesting doesn't really fix anything and that as bad as the situation in Dublin undoubtedly is, it's still better than what's going on in Athens, Madrid or Nicosia.

Hope for the Future

Some pundits will point to the city's long history of tough times and declare there's nothing new, but there's a whole generation of Dubliners who've never known difficult times or recession: they grew up with the unfettered ambitions of the Celtic Tiger, where everything was possible so long as you were willing to chase it. Rather than surrender their ambitions many have opted to emigrate, but those that have stayed have endeavoured to find new opportunities amid the mayhem. New ventures are starting all the time, smaller in scale perhaps than a few years ago, but no less interesting. If you want proof, just try one of the slew of new restaurants, cafes and bars that have opened since the crisis began. If anything, they're a reminder that no matter how tough things get, Dubliners will always find a way to enjoy themselves.

if Dublin were 100 people

87 would be Irish
4 would be Asian
3 would be African
1 would be a visitor
5 would be other

age of Dubliners
(%)

0-14 years old   15-24   25-54

55-64   65 and over

population per sq km

DUBLIN   IRELAND

≈ 65 people

History

Until a couple of decades ago if you'd asked your average Dubliner the key to the city's complex and conflicted history, they'd most likely give you a version of the past punctuated with '800 years'. This refers to the duration of the English (or British) occupation, the *sine qua non* of everything that has ever happened to this city. If the past has a strong bearing on modern life, then the last two decades have seen a dramatic re-examination of the old narrative. As Dublin prospered and then crashed, Dubliners have dismissed '800 years' as old-fashioned and irrelevant: these days, the villains of the piece are the bankers, the IMF and the greed of their own.

Early Footprints & Celtic Highways

Celtic society was ruled by Brehon Law, the tenets of which still form the basis of Ireland's ethical code today.

Stone Age farmers who arrived in Ireland between 10,000 and 8000 BC provided the country's genetic stock and laid the foundations of its agricultural economy. During the following Bronze Age, in addition to discovering and crafting metals to stock the future National Museum, they also found time to refine their farming techniques and raise livestock.

Iron Age warriors from Eastern Europe, who were known as the Celts, arrived in the country around 500 BC and divided Ireland into provinces and a myriad of districts ruled by chieftains. Roads connecting these provinces converged at a ford over the River Liffey called Átha Cliath (Ford of the Hurdles) and the settlement that grew up at this junction during the 9th century was to give Dublin its Irish name, Baile Átha Cliath (Town of the Hurdle Ford).

The Coming of Christianity

St Patrick founded the See of Dublin sometime in the mid–5th century and went about the business of conversion in present-day Wicklow and Malahide, before laying hands on Leoghaire, the King of Ireland, using water from a well next to St Patrick's Cathedral. Or so the story goes. Irrespective of the details, Patrick and his monk buddies were successful because they managed to fuse the strong tradition of druidism and

TIMELINE

10,000 BC

Human beings arrive in Ireland during the mesolithic era, originally crossing a land bridge between Scotland and Ireland and later the sea in hide-covered boats.

AD 431–432

Pope Celestine I sends Bishop Palladius to Ireland to minister to those 'already believing in Christ'; St Patrick arrives the following year to continue the mission.

MANUEL VELASCO / GETTY IMAGES ©

Statue of St Patrick

pagan ritual with the new Christian teaching, which created an exciting hybrid known as Celtic, or Insular, Christianity.

Compared to new hot spots like Clonmacnoise in County Offaly and Glendalough in County Wicklow, Dublin was a rural backwater and didn't really figure in the Golden Age, when Irish Christian scholars excelled in the study of Latin and Greek learning and Christian theology. They studied in the monasteries that were, in essence, Europe's most important universities, producing brilliant students, magnificent illuminated books such as the *Book of Kells* (now housed in Trinity College) ornate jewellery and the many carved stone crosses that dot the island 'of saints and scholars'.

The nature of Christianity in Ireland was one of marked independence from Rome, especially in the areas of monastic rule and penitential practice, which emphasised private confession to a priest followed by penances levied by the priest in reparation – which is the spirit and letter of the practice of confession that exists to this day.

St Patrick showed a remarkable understanding of Celtic power structures by working to convert chieftains rather than ordinary Celts, who inevitably followed their leaders into adopting the new religion.

The Vikings

Raids by marauding Vikings had been a fact of Irish life for quite some time before a group of them decided to take a break from their hell-raising to build a harbour (or *longphort*, in Irish) on the banks of the Liffey in 837. Although a Celtic army forced them out some 65 years later, they returned in 917 with a massive fleet, established a stronghold by the black pool at Wood Quay, just behind Christ Church Cathedral, and dug their heels in. They went back to plundering the countryside but also laid down guidelines on plot sizes and town boundaries for their town of 'Dyflinn' (derived from the Irish for 'black pool', '*dubh linn*'), which became the most prominent trading centre in the Viking world.

But their good times came to an end in 1014 when an alliance of Irish clans led by Brian Ború decisively whipped them (and the Irish clans that *didn't* side with Brian Ború) at the Battle of Clontarf, forever breaking the Scandinavian grip on the eastern seaboard. However, rather than abandoning the place in defeat, the Vikings enjoyed Dublin so much that they decided to stay there and integrate.

Best Books

A Short History of Dublin (2000) Pat Boran

Cities of the Imagination: Dublin (2007) Siobhán Kilfeather

Dublin – A Celebration (2000) Pat Liddy

Dublin: A Cultural & Literary History (2005) Siobhán Kilfeather

Encyclopaedia of Dublin (2005) Douglas Bennett

Strongbow & the Normans

The next wave of invaders came in 1169, when an army of Cambro-Norman knights led by Richard de Clare (better known as Strongbow) landed in Wexford at the urging of Dermot MacMurrough, who needed help to regain his throne as the King of Leinster. As a gesture of thanks, MacMurrough made Strongbow his heir and gave him Aoife,

917	988	1169	1172
Plundering Vikings establish a new settlement at the mouth of the harbour and call it 'Dyfflin', which soon becomes a centre of economic power.	High King Mael Seachlainn II leads the permanent Irish conquest of Dyfflin, giving the settlement its modern name in Irish – Baile Átha Cliath, meaning 'Town at the Hurdle Ford'.	Henry II's Welsh and Norman barons capture Waterford and Wexford with the help of Dermot MacMurrough, beginning a 750-year occupation of Ireland by Britain.	King Henry II of England invades Ireland, forcing the Cambro-Norman warlords and some of the Gaelic Irish kings to accept him as their overlord.

Reputed 15th-century effigy of Richard 'Strongbow' de Clare

his daughter, as a wife. Strongbow and his knights then took Dublin in 1170 and decided to make it their new capital.

Meanwhile, King Henry II of England, concerned that the Normans might set up a rival power base in Ireland, organised his own invading force, and landed his army in 1171 – with the blessing of Pope Adrian IV, who wanted Henry to make Ireland's renegade monks toe the Roman line.

During the 12th century Dublin became a pilgrimage city, in part because it housed the Bachall Íosa (staff of Jesus), St Patrick's legendary crozier.

The Normans declared their fealty to the English throne and set about reconstructing and fortifying their new capital. In 1172 construction began on Christ Church Cathedral, and 20 years later work began on St Patrick's Cathedral, a few hundred metres to the south.

Henry II's son, King John, commissioned the construction of Dublin Castle in 1204 '…for the safe custody of our treasure…and the defence of the city'. As capital of the English 'colony' in Ireland, Dublin expanded.

1297	1315	1348	1350–1530
Dublin becomes the main seat of the Parliament of Ireland, comprised of merchants and landowners.	A Scottish army led by Edward de Bruce attacks the city; waning English interest in defending Dublin forces the Earls of Kildare to become the city's main protector.	Roughly half of the city's population of 30,000 succumbs to the Black Death; victims were buried in mass graves in an area of the Liberties still known as the 'Blackpitts'.	The Anglo-Norman barons establish power bases independent of the English crown. English control gradually extends to an area around Dublin known as 'the Pale'.

Trade was organised and craft guilds developed, although membership was limited to those of 'English name and blood'.

As Dublin grew bigger so did its problems, and over the next few centuries misery seemed to pile upon mishap. In 1317 Ireland's worst famine of the Middle Ages killed off thousands and reduced some to cannibalism. In 1348 the country was decimated by the Black Death, the devastating recurrence of which over the following century indicates the terrible squalor of medieval Dublin.

In the 15th century, the English extended their influence beyond the Pale by throwing their weight behind the dominant Irish lords. The atmosphere was becoming markedly cosier as the Anglo-Norman occupiers began to follow previous invaders by integrating into Irish culture.

The Tudors & the Protestant Ascendancy

Ireland presented a particular challenge to Henry VIII (r 1509–1547), in part due to the Anglo-Norman lords more or less unfettered power over the country, which didn't sit well with Henry's belief in strong monarchial rule. He decreed absolute royal power over Ireland, but the Irish lords weren't going to take it lying down.

In 1534 the most powerful of Leinster's Anglo-Normans, 'Silken' Thomas Fitzgerald, renounced his allegiance to the king, and Henry came at him ferociously: within a year Fitzgerald was dead and all his lands confiscated. Henry ordered the surrender of all lands to the English Crown and, three years later, after his spat with Rome, he dissolved the monasteries and all Church lands passed to the newly constituted Anglican Church. Dublin was declared an Anglican city and relics such as the Bachall Íosa were destroyed.

Elizabeth I (r 1558–1603) came to the throne with the same uncompromising attitude to Ireland as her father. Ulster was the most hostile to her, with the Irish fighting doggedly under the command of Hugh O'Neill, the Earl of Tyrone, but they too were finally defeated in 1603.

O'Neill's defeat signalled the end of Gaelic Ireland and the renewed colonisation of the country through plantation. Loyal Protestants from England and Scotland were awarded the rich agricultural, confiscated lands of Ulster, sowing the bitter seeds of division that blight the province to this day. Unlike previous arrivals, these new colonists kept very much apart from the native Irish, who were left disenfranchised, landless and reduced to a state of near misery.

All the while, Dublin prospered as the bulwark of English domination and became a bastion of Protestantism. A chasm developed between the 'English' city and the 'Irish' countryside, where there was continuing unrest and growing resentment. After winning the English

BEYOND THE PALE

For all their might, the Anglo-Normans' dominance was limited to a walled area surrounding what today is loosely Greater Dublin, and was then called 'the Pale'. Beyond the Pale – a phrase that entered the English language to mean 'beyond convention' – Ireland remained unbowed and unconquered.

1487	1487	1537	1584
Gerard Mór Fitzgerald, Earl of Kildare, occupies Dublin with help of troops from Burgundy, in direct defiance of King Henry VII.	Fitzgerald supports claims of Yorkist pretender Lambert Simnel, a 10-year-old who is crowned King Edward VI in Christ Church Cathedral.	'Silken' Thomas Fitzgerald, son of the Earl of Kildare, storms Dublin and its English garrisons. The rebellion is quashed; Thomas and his followers are executed.	Mayoress Margaret Ball dies following imprisonment for her Catholic sympathies. Archbishop Dermot O'Hurley is hanged for his support of a rebellion against the English crown.

Civil War, Oliver Cromwell came to Ireland to personally reassert English control and, while Protestant Dublin was left untouched (save the use of St Patrick's Cathedral as a stable for English horses), his troops were uncompromising in their dealing with rebellion up and down the eastern coast.

Georgian Dublin & the Golden Age

Following the Restoration of 1660 and the coronation of Charles II (r 1660–85), Dublin embarked upon a century of unparalleled development and essentially waved two fingers at the rest of Ireland, which was being brought to its knees. In 1690 the rest of Ireland backed the losing side when it took up arms for the Catholic king of England, James II (r 1685–1688), who was ultimately defeated by the Protestant William of Orange at the Battle of the Boyne, not far from Dublin, in 1690.

William's victory ushered in the punitive Penal Code, which stripped Catholics of most basic rights in a single, sweeping legislative blow. Again, however, the country's misfortune proved the capital's gain as the city was flooded with landless refugees willing to work for a pittance.

With plenty of cash to go around and an eagerness to live in a city that reflected their new-found wealth, the Protestant nobility overhauled Dublin during the reigns of the four Georges (1714–1830). Speculators bought up swaths of land and commissioned substantial projects of urban renewal, including the creation of new streets, the laying out of city parks and the construction of magnificent new buildings and residences.

It was impossible to build in the heart of the medieval city, so the nouveau riche moved north across the river, creating a new Dublin of stately squares surrounded by fine Georgian mansions. The elegantly made-over Dublin became the second city in the British Empire and the fifth largest in Europe.

Dublin's teeming, mostly Catholic, slums soon spread north in pursuit of the rich, who turned back south to grand new homes around Merrion Sq, St Stephen's Green and Fitzwilliam Sq.

Dublin Declines, Catholicism Rises

Constant migration from the countryside into Dublin meant that, by the end of the 18th century, the capital had a Catholic majority, most of whom lived in terrible conditions in ever-worsening slums. Inspired by the Enlightenment and the principles of the French Revolution of 1789, many leading Irish figures (nearly all of whom were Protestant) began to question the quality and legitimacy of British rule.

HUGUENOTS

The end of the 17th century saw an influx of Huguenot weavers, who settled in Dublin after fleeing anti-Protestant legislation in France and established a successful cloth industry, largely in the Liberties, that helped fuel the city's growth.

1594–1603	1592	1597	1603
The Nine Years' War between the English crown and Irish chieftains led by Hugh O'Neill brings English troops to Dublin, who force citizenry to house them.	Trinity College is founded on the grounds of a former monastery, on the basis of a charter granted by Elizabeth I to 'stop Ireland being infected by popery'.	An accidental explosion in a gunpowder store in Winetavern St kills 200 civilians.	Hugh O'Neill and the Irish fighting under his command in Ulster are defeated by Elizabeth I's forces. He and his fellow earls flee the country in what is known as the Flight of the Earls.

Rebellion was in the air by the turn of the century, starting with the abortive French invasion at the urging of Dubliner Wolfe Tone (1763–1798) and his United Irishmen in 1798. The 'Year of the French' resulted in defeat for the invaders and the death of Tone, but in 1803 the United Irishmen tried again, this time under the leadership of Robert Emmet (1778–1803), which also resulted in failure and Emmet's execution on Thomas St, near the Guinness Brewery.

It was only a matter of time before Dublin's bubble burst, and the pin came in the form of the 1801 Act of Union, which dissolved the Irish parliament (originally established in 1297) and reintroduced direct rule from Westminster. Many of the upper classes fled to London, the dramatic growth that had characterised Dublin in the previous century came to an almost immediate halt, and the city fell into a steady decline.

While Dublin was licking its wounds, a Kerry lawyer called Daniel O'Connell (1775–1847) launched his campaign to recover basic rights for Catholics, achieving much with the Catholic Emancipation Act of 1829. The 'Liberator', as he came to be known, became the first Catholic lord mayor of Dublin in 1841.

In 1745 when James Fitzgerald, the Earl of Kildare, started construction of Leinster House he was mocked for his move into the wilds. 'Where I go society will follow', he confidently predicted. He was right; today Leinster House is the seat of Irish parliament and is in modern Dublin's centre.

A Nation's Soup Kitchen

Rural Ireland had become overwhelmingly dependent on the easily grown potato. Blight – a disease that rots tubers – had always been an occasional hazard, but when three successive crops failed between 1845 and 1847, it spelt disaster. The human cost was cataclysmic: up to one million people died from disease and starvation, while more again fled the country for Britain and the United States. The damage was compounded by the British government's adoption of a laissez-faire economic policy, which opposed food aid for famine occurring within the empire. In Ireland, landowners refused to countenance any forbearance on rents, all the while exporting crops to foreign markets. Defaulters – starving or not – were penalised with incarceration in workhouses or prison.

The British government's uncompromising stance hardened the steel of opposition. The deaths and mass exodus caused by the Famine had a profound social and cultural effect on Ireland and left a scar on the Irish psyche that cannot be overestimated. Urban Dublin escaped the worst ravages, but desperate migrants flooded into the city looking for relief – soup kitchens were set up all over the city, including in the bucolic Merrion Sq, where presumably its affluent residents bore direct witness to the tragedy.

1640s–1682

Dublin's resurgence begins as the city's population grows from 10,000 in the mid-1640s to nearly 60,000 in 1682.

GEORGE MUNDAY / DESIGN PICS / GETTY IMAGES ©

1680

The architectural style known as Anglo-Dutch results in the construction of notable buildings such as the Royal Hospital Kilmainham, now the Irish Museum of Modern Art.

Royal Hospital Kilmainham (p112)

The horrors of the Famine and its impact on Dublin's centre saw the wealthy abandon the city for a new set of salubrious suburbs south of Dublin along the coast, now accessible via Ireland's first railway line, built in 1834 to connect the city to Kingstown (present-day Dun Laoghaire). The flight from the city continued for the next 70 years and many of the fine Georgian residences became slum dwellings. With such squalor came a host of social ills, including alcohol, which had always been a source of solace but now became a chronic problem.

By 1910 it was reckoned that 20,000 Dublin families each occupied a single room.

The Blossoming of National Pride

In the second half of the 19th-century, Dublin was staunchly divided along sectarian lines and, although Catholics were still partly second-class citizens, a burgeoning Catholic middle class provided the impetus for Ireland's march towards independence.

It was the dashing figure of Protestant landlord Charles Stewart Parnell (1846–91), from County Wicklow, that first harnessed the broad public support for Home Rule. Elected to Westminster in 1875, the 'Uncrowned King of Ireland' campaigned tirelessly for land reform and a Dublin parliament.

He appeared to have an ally in the British prime minister, William Gladstone, who lightened the burden on tenants by passing Land Acts enabling them to buy property. He was also converted to the cause of Home Rule, for both principled reasons and practical ones: the granting of some form of self-government would at least have the effect of reconciling Irish nationalism to the British state.

Charles Stewart Parnell suffered a swift fall from grace after it was made public that he had been having an affair with a married woman, Kitty O'Shea. He was ditched as leader of his own Irish Parliamentary Party in 1890 and died a broken man the following year. More than 200,000 people attended his funeral at Glasnevin Cemetery.

In the twilight of the 19th century there was a move to preserve all things Irish. The Gaelic Athletic Association (GAA) was set up in 1884 to promote Irish sports, while Douglas Hyde and Eoin McNeill formed the Gaelic League in 1893 to encourage Irish arts and language. The success of the Gaelic League paved the way for the Celtic Revival Movement, spearheaded by WB Yeats and Lady Gregory, who founded the Abbey Theatre in 1904.

Strife, Resistance & Home Rule

Although Irish culture was thriving at the start of the 20th century, the country's peaceful efforts to free itself from British rule were thwarted at every juncture. Dublin's slums were the worst in Europe, and the emergence of militant trade unionism introduced a socialist agenda to the struggle for self-determination.

In 1905 Arthur Griffith (1871–1922) founded a new political movement called Sinn Féin ('Ourselves Alone'), which sought to achieve Home Rule through passive resistance rather than political lobbying. It

1695	1757	1759	1801
Penal laws prohibit Catholics from owning a horse, marrying outside their religion and from buying or inheriting property; within 100 years Catholics will own only 5% of Irish land.	The Wide Street Commission is set up to design the framework of a modern city: new parks are laid out, streets widened and new public buildings commissioned.	Arthur Guinness buys a disused brewery on a plot of land opposite St James's Gate. Initially he brews only ale, but in the 1770s turns his expertise to a new beer called porter.	The Act of Union unites Ireland politically with Britain. The Irish Parliament votes itself out of existence following an intensive campaign of bribery.

NO·MAN·HAS·A·RIGHT·TO·FIX·THE·
BOUNDARY·TO·THE·MARCH·OF·A·NATION·
NO·MAN·HAS·A·RIGHT·
TO·SAY·TO·HIS·COUNTRY·
THUS·FAR·SHALT·THOU·
GO·AND·NO·FURTHER·
WE·HAVE·NEVER·
ATTEMPTED·TO·FIX·
THE·NE·PLUS·ULTRA·
TO·THE·PROGRESS·OF·
IRELANDS·NATIONHOOD·
AND·WE·NEVER·SHALL

Statue of Charles Stewart Parnell (p127)

urged the Irish to withhold taxes and its MPs to form an Irish government in Dublin.

Meanwhile, trade union leaders Jim Larkin and James Connolly agitated against low wages and corporate greed, culminating in the Dublin Lockout of 1913, where 300 employers 'locked out' 20,000 workers for five months. During this time, Connolly established the Irish Citizen Army (ICA) to defend striking workers from the police. Things were heating up.

Home Rule was finally passed by Westminster in 1914, but its provisions were suspended for the duration of WWI. Bowing to pressure from Protestant-dominated Ulster, where 140,000 members of the newly formed Ulster Volunteer Force (UVF) swore to resist any attempts to weaken British rule in Ireland, the bill also made provisions for the 'temporary' exclusion of the north from the workings of the future act.

British prime minister William Gladstone introduced Home Rule bills three times into the House of Commons between 1886 and 1895, but the House of Lords voted them down on each occasion.

1839	1840	1841	1845–51
Following a powerful campaign by Daniel O'Connoll, the 'Liberator', the Catholic Emancipation Act is passed, repealing the remaining Penal Laws.	The Corporation Act allows Catholics to vote in local elections for the first time since the 1690s, giving them a two to one majority.	Daniel O'Connell is elected the first Catholic mayor of Dublin in 150 years; one of his first acts is to found a multi-denominational cemetery in Glasnevin.	A mould called phytophthora ravages the potato harvest. The Great Famine is the single greatest catastrophe in Irish history, with the deaths of up to one million people.

WWI

When World War I ended in 1918, 50,000 Irish citizens had lost their lives.

How temporary was 'temporary' was anybody's guess – and it was in such political fudging that the seeds of trouble were sown. To counter the potential threat from the UVF, Irish nationalists formed the Irish Volunteer Force (IVF), but a stand-off was avoided when the vast majority of them enlisted in the British Army: if Britain was going to war 'in defence of small nations' then loyalty to the Allied cause would help Ireland's long-term aspirations.

The Easter Rising

The more radical factions within Sinn Féin, the IVF and the ICA saw Britain's difficulty as Ireland's opportunity, and planned to rise up against the Crown on Easter Sunday, 1916. In typical fashion, the rhetoric of the rebellion outweighed the quality of the planning. When the head of the IVF, Eoin McNeill, got wind of the plans, he published an advertisement in the newspaper cancelling the planned 'manoeuvres'. The leaders rescheduled the revolution for the following day but word never spread beyond the capital, where a motley band of about a thousand rebels assembled and seized strategic buildings. The main garrison was the General Post Office, outside which the poet and school teacher Pádraig Pearse read out the *Proclamation of the Republic*.

The British Army didn't take the insurgence seriously at first but after a few soldiers were killed, they sent a gunboat down the Liffey to rain shells on the rebels. After six days of fighting the city centre was ravaged and the death toll stood at 300 civilians, 130 British troops (many of whom were Irish) and 60 rebels.

The rebels, prompted by Pearse's fear of further civilian casualties, surrendered and were arrested. Crowds gathered to mock and jeer them as they were led away. Initially, Dubliners resented them for the damage they had caused in their futile rising, but their attitudes began to change following the executions of the leaders in Kilmainham Gaol. The hostility shown to the rebels turned to outright sympathy and support.

Many Dubliners were appalled at the sentences received by the leaders of the Rising, especially the fate suffered by 18-year-old Willie Pearse, whose main offence was that he was Pádraig's brother. James Connolly, the hero of the Dublin working classes, was so severely injured during the Rising that he was strapped to a chair and shot.

The War of Independence

In the 1918 general election, the more radical Sinn Féin party won three-quarters of the Irish seats. In May 1919, they declared independence and established the first Dáil Éireann (Irish Assembly) in Dublin's Mansion House, led by Éamon de Valera. This was effectively a declaration of war.

Mindful that they could never match the British on the battlefield, Sinn Féin's military wing – made up of Irish Volunteers now renamed the Irish Republican Army (IRA) – began attacking arms dumps and

1867	1882	1905	1913
Several thousand supporters of the Irish Republican Brotherhood (IRB) fight the police in Tallaght; they disperse and some 200 agitators are arrested.	An offshoot of the IRB, known as the Invincibles, assassinate the Chief Secretary and his assistant in the Phoenix Park.	Journalist Arthur Griffiths founds a new movement whose aim is independence under a dual monarchy; he names the movement Sinn Féin, meaning 'ourselves alone'.	The largest labour dispute in Irish history sees 25,000 Dublin workers 'locked out' for six months by defiant employers.

barracks in guerrilla strikes. The British countered by strengthening the Royal Irish Constabulary (RIC) and introducing a tough auxiliary force made up of returning WWI servicemen known as the Black and Tans (after the colour of their uniforms).

They met their match in Michael Collins, the IRA's commander and a master of guerrilla warfare. Although the British knew his name, Collins masterfully concealed his identity and throughout the war was able to freewheel around the city on his bicycle like he didn't have a care in the world.

On 10 November 1920, Collins learned that 14 undercover British intelligence operatives known as the 'Cairo Gang' had just arrived in Dublin. The following morning, he had his own crack squad ('the Apostles') assassinate each one of them as they lay in their beds. That afternoon, British troops retaliated by opening fire on the crowd at a hurling match in Croke Park, resulting in the deaths of 10 spectators and one player, Michael Hogan, whose death was later commemorated when the main stand at the stadium was named after him. The events of 'Bloody Sunday' galvanised both sides in the conflict and served to quash any moral doubts over what was becoming an increasingly brutal struggle.

Brutalities notwithstanding, the war resulted in relatively few casualties – 2014 in total – and by mid-1921 had ground to a kind of stalemate. Both sides were under pressure to end it: the international community was urging Britain to resolve the issue one way or another, while, unbeknownst to the British, the IRA was on the verge of collapse. A truce was signed on 11 July, 1921.

Civil War

The terms of – and the circumstances surrounding – the Treaty that ended the War of Independence make up the single most divisive episode in Irish politics, one that still breeds prejudice, inflames passions and shapes the political landscape in parts of the country.

After months of argument and facing the threat of, in the words of British Prime Minister Lloyd George, an 'immediate and terrible war', the Irish negotiating team, led by Michael Collins, signed the Anglo-Irish Treaty on 6 December 1921. Instead of establishing the Irish Republic for which the IRA had fought, it created an Irish Free State, effectively a British dominion, in which members of the newly constituted parliament would have to swear allegiance to the British Crown before they could participate in government. The six counties comprising Northern Ireland were given the choice of becoming part of the Free State or remaining in the United Kingdom; they chose the latter, sowing the seeds of discontent that would lead to further rounds of the

The Civil War began when anti-Treaty IRA forces occupied Dublin's Four Courts and were shelled by pro-Treaty forces, led by Michael Collins. Dublin, which escaped any real damage during the War of Independence, became a primary theatre of the Civil War, which cost the lives of 250 Dubliners.

Éamon de Valera, the leader of the first Dáil Éireann, was spared the firing squad in 1916 because of his US birth; killing him would have been a public-relations disaster.

1916	1919–21	1921–22	1948
Republicans take the GPO in Dublin and announce the formation of an Irish Republic. After less than a week of fighting, the rebels surrender and are summarily executed.	The Irish War of Independence begins in January 1919. Two years (and 2014 casualties) later, the war ends in a truce on 11 July 1921, leading to peace talks.	The Anglo-Irish Treaty is signed on 6 December. It gives 26 counties of Ireland independence and six Ulster counties the choice of opting out. The Irish Free State is founded in 1922.	Fine Gael, in coalition with the new Republican Clann na Poblachta, wins the 1948 general election and declares the Free State a republic.

General Post Office (p130)

Troubles in the North. Although Collins was dissatisfied with the deal, he hoped it would be the 'first real step' in the journey towards an Irish republic. Nevertheless, he also foresaw trouble and remarked prophetically that 'I've just signed my own death warrant'.

De Valera vehemently opposed the Treaty and the two erstwhile comrades were pitted against one another into pro-Treaty and anti-Treaty camps. Although the Dáil narrowly ratified the Treaty and the electorate accepted it by a large majority, Ireland slid into civil war during June 1922.

Ironically, the Civil War was more brutal than the struggle that preceded it. In 11 months roughly 3000 Irish died – including 77 state executions – but the vindictive nature of the fighting left indelible scars that have yet to be fully healed. The assassination of Michael Collins in his home county of Cork on 22 August, 1922 rocked the country;

1949	1960s	1969	1972
Ireland leaves the British Commonwealth, and the South cut its links to the North.	A construction boom sees the growth of new suburbs north and south of the city in an effort to re-house Dubliners removed from dangerous city-centre tenements.	Marches in Derry are disrupted by Loyalist attacks and heavy-handed police action, culminating in the 'Battle of the Bogside' (12–14 August). It marks the beginning of the 'Troubles'.	Angry demonstrators burn the British Embassy in Dublin in response to the killing of 13 civilians in Derry by British paratroopers.

500,000 people (almost one-fifth of the population) attended his funeral. The last few months of fighting were especially ugly, with both sides engaging in tit-for-tat atrocities. On May 24, 1923, de Valera ordered the anti-Treaty forces to drop their arms.

The Irish Republic

Ireland finally entered a phase of peace. Without an armed struggle to pursue – at least not one pursued by the majority – the IRA became a marginalised force in independent Ireland and Sinn Féin fell apart. In 1926, de Valera created a new party, Fianna Fáil (Soldiers of Destiny), which has been the dominant force in Irish politics ever since. Over the following decades, Fianna Fáil gradually eliminated most of the clauses of the Treaty with which it had disagreed (including the oath of allegiance).

In 1932, a freshly painted Dublin hosted the 31st Eucharistic Congress, which drew visitors from around the world. The Catholic Church began to wield disproportionate control over the affairs of the state; contraception was made illegal in the 1930s and the age of consent was raised from 16 to 17.

In 1936, when the IRA refused to disarm, de Valera had it banned. The following year the Civil War–tainted moniker 'Free State' was dropped in favour of Eire as the country's official name in a rewrite of the constitution.

Despite having done much of the groundwork, Fianna Fáil lost out to its rivals Fine Gael, descendants of the original pro-Treaty Free State government, on declaring the 26 counties a republic in 1949.

The Stroll to Modernisation

Sean Lemass succeeded de Valera as Taoiseach (prime minister) in 1959 and set about fixing the Irish economy, which he did so effectively that the rate of emigration soon halved. While neighbouring London was swinging in the '60s, Dublin was definitely swaying. Youngsters from rural communities poured into the expanding city and it seemed like the good times were never going to end. But, almost inevitably, the economy slid back into recession.

On the 50th anniversary of the 1916 Easter Rising, Nelson's Pillar on O'Connell St was partially blown up by the IRA and crowds cheered as the remainder was removed the following week. Republicanism was still prevalent and a new round of the 'Troubles' were about to flair up in the North.

Ireland joined the European Economic Community (EEC), a forerunner to the European Union (EU), in 1973 and got a significant leg-up from the organisation's coffers over the following decades. But the tides

Author and treaty negotiator, Robert Erskine Childers was executed by the government on November 24, 1922. Opposed to the final draft of the Treaty, Childers joined anti-Treaty forces during the Civil War when he was found to be in possession of a gun, the penalty for which was death.

Although Ireland remained neutral during WWII – as a way of pushing its independence – Dublin's North Strand was hit by a 227kg German bomb on 31 May, 1941, killing more than 30 and injuring 90.

HISTORY THE IRISH REPUBLIC

1974	1988	1990s	1993
Simultaneous bombings in Monaghan and Dublin on 17 May leave 33 dead and 300 injured, the biggest loss of life in any single day during the Troubles.	Dublin celebrates its millennium, even though the town was established long before 988.	Low corporate tax, decades of investment in higher education, transfer payments from the EU and a low-cost labour market lead to the 'Celtic Tiger' boom.	Twenty thousand demonstrators call for an end to IRA violence as a result of the bomb that killed two children in Warrington, England.

of change were once again on the rise. Political instability and an international recession did little to help hopes of economic recovery, and by the early '80s emigration was once again a major issue. But Ireland – and Dublin in particular – was growing increasingly liberal, and was straining at the shackles imposed on its social and moral mores by a largely conservative Catholic Church. Politicians too were seen in a new light as stories of corruption and cronyism became increasingly commonplace. Dublin was hardly touched by the sectarian tensions that would pull Northern Ireland asunder, although 25 people died after three Loyalist car bombs exploded in the city in 1974.

The Tiger's Roar

European aid was to prove instrumental in kick-starting the Irish economy in the early 1990s. Huge sums of money were invested in education and physical infrastructure, while the renewal of Lemass' industrial policy of incentivizing foreign investment through tax breaks and the provision of subsidies made Ireland very attractive to high-tech businesses looking for a door into EU markets. In less than a decade Ireland went from being one of the poorest countries in Europe to one of the wealthiest: unemployment fell from 18% to 3.5%, total exports quadrupled, the average industrial wage somersaulted to the top of the European league and GNP rose between 5% to 15% every year from 1991 to 2006. In a 1994 report for finance house Morgan Stanley, analyst Kevin Gardiner coined the term 'Celtic Tiger' to describe this unparalleled level of growth and the name (eventually) stuck, becoming a byword for economic prosperity.

Prosperity's twin was a more progressive attitude toward social policy. Challenges to the more conservative aspects of Catholic teaching became more trenchant, and from the 1980s onward, steady campaigning resulted in new laws protecting gay rights, access to contraception and a successful referendum on divorce.

The dramatic decline in the influence of the Church in Irish affairs cannot be overstated. Although prosperity and broader global trends are primary factors, the terrible revelations of widespread child abuse and the untidy and often stubborn efforts of Church authorities to sweep the truth under the carpet has provoked a seething rage amongst many Dubliners, who are appalled by the Church's insensitivity to the care of the most vulnerable of their flock. Many older believers feel an acute sense of betrayal, leading them to question a lifetime's devotion to their local parishes. The current Archbishop of Dublin, Diarmuid Martin, has nevertheless been especially forthright in acknowledging the culpability of the Church and has devoted much of his pastoral duty to rebuilding the reputation of his diocese.

POPE JOHN PAUL II

The visit of Pope John Paul II in 1979 – the first time for a pontiff – saw more than one million people flock to the Phoenix Park to hear him say mass.

2007	2008	2009	2011
The IRA ends its campaign of violence on July 28, ordering its units to assist 'the development of purely political and democratic programs through exclusively peaceful means'.	The Global Financial Crisis triggers the collapse of the Irish banking system and the property boom; Ireland's economy goes into financial free-fall.	The publication of the Murphy Report reveals a vast network of secrecy and cover-up of widespread crimes of sexual abuse by serving priests within the Dublin diocese.	National elections result in a coalition between Fine Gael and Labour; for the first time Fianna Fáil fail to win any seats in Dublin.

Literary Dublin

Dubliners know a thing or two about the written word. No other city of comparable size can claim four Nobel Prize winners for literature, but the city's impact on the English-reading world extends far beyond the fab four of Shaw, Yeats, Beckett and Heaney...one name, folks: James Joyce.

Literary Capital

Before Dublin was even a glint in a Viking's eye, Ireland was the land of saints and scholars, thanks to the monastic universities that sprang up around the country to foster the spread of Christianity and the education of Europe's privileged elite. But for our purposes, we need to fast-forward 1000 years to the 18th century and the glory days of Georgian Dublin, when the Irish and English languages began to cross-fertilise. Experimenting with English, using turns of phrase and expressions translated directly from Gaeilge, and combining these with a uniquely Irish perspective on life, Irish writers have dazzled and delighted readers for centuries. British theatre critic Kenneth Tynan summed it up thus: 'The English hoard words like misers: the Irish spend them like sailors.'

Dublin has as many would-be sailors as Hollywood has frustrated waitresses, and it often seems like a bottomless well of creativity. The section given over to Irish writers is often the largest and busiest in any local bookstore, reflecting not only a rich literary tradition and thriving contemporary scene, but also an appreciative, knowledgeable and hungry local audience that attends readings and poetry recitals like rock fans at a gig.

Indeed, Dublin has produced so many writers, and has been written about so much, that you could easily plan a Dublin literary holiday. *A Literary Guide to Dublin*, by Vivien Igoe, includes detailed route maps, a guide to cemeteries and an eight-page section on literary and historical pubs. A Norman Jeffares' *Irish Writers: From Swift to Heaney* also has detailed and accessible summaries of writers and their work.

> In 2010 Dublin was named a UNESCO City of Literature – one of six cities in the world to receive the accolade, along with Iowa City, Melbourne, Edinburgh, Norwich and Reykjavik.

Old Literary Dublin

Modern Irish literature begins with Jonathan Swift (1667–1745), the master satirist, social commentator and dean of St Patrick's Cathedral. He was the greatest Dublin writer of the early Georgian period and is most famous for *Gulliver's Travels,* a savage social satire that has morphed into a children's favourite. He was an 'earnest and dedicated champion of liberty', as he insisted on writing in his own epitaph.

He was followed by Oliver Goldsmith (1730–74), author of *The Vicar of Wakefield,* and Thomas Moore (1779–1852), whose poems formed the repertoire of generations of Irish tenors. Dublin-born Oscar Wilde (1854–1900) is renowned for his legendary wit, immense talent and striking sensitivity. Bram Stoker (1847–1912) created the most famous Gothic ghouls of them all, and his novel *Dracula* remains one of the world's most popular books. The name of the count may have come from the Irish *droch fhola* (bad blood).

> **Dublin's Nobel Laureates**
> ....
> *William Butler Yeats (1923)*
> ....
> *George Bernard Shaw (1925)*
> ....
> *Samuel Beckett (1969)*
> ....
> *Seamus Heaney (1995)*

Playwright and essayist George Bernard Shaw (1856–1950), author of *Pygmalion* (which was later turned into *My Fair Lady*), hailed from Synge St near the Grand Canal, while James Joyce (1882–1941), the city's most famous son and one of the greatest writers of all time, was born not far away in Rathgar.

William Butler (WB) Yeats (1865–1939) is best remembered as a poet, though he also wrote plays and spearheaded the late-19th-century Irish Literary Revival, which culminated in the founding of the Abbey Theatre in 1904. *Sailing to Byzantium* and *Easter 1916* are two of his finest poems – the latter, about the Easter Rising, ends with the famous line 'A terrible beauty is born'. His poetry is mostly tied up with his sense of Irish heroism, esoteric mysticism and the unrequited love he had for Maud Gonne.

Oliver St John Gogarty (1878–1957) is said to have borne a lifelong grudge against his one-time friend James Joyce because of his appearance as Buck Mulligan in the latter's *Ulysses*. He was a character in his own right and his views are presented in his memoirs *As I Was Going Down Sackville Street* (1937). He had a mean streak though, and took exception to a throwaway remark written by Patrick Kavanagh (1904–67) alluding to him having a mistress; he successfully sued the poet, whom he described as 'that Monaghan boy'.

Kavanagh, from farming stock in Monaghan, walked to Dublin (a very long way) in 1934 and made the capital his home. His later poetry explored Ireland's city-versus-country dynamic. He was fond of the Grand Canal, along the banks of which he is commemorated, with 'just a canal-bank seat for the passer-by', as he had wished.

You can't imagine the brooding Samuel Beckett (1906–89) hanging around in this company and, while his greatest literary contributions were as a dramatist in self-imposed exile, he did write a collection of short stories in Dublin, *More Pricks Than Kicks* (1934), about an eccentric local character. The book so irked the new Free State government that it was banned, no doubt hastening Beckett's permanent move to Paris.

One-time civil servant Brian O'Nolan (1911–66), also known as Flann O'Brien and Myles na Gopaleen, was a celebrated comic writer and career drinker. He wrote several books, most notably *At Swim-Two-Birds* (1939) and *The Third Policeman* (1940), but was most fondly remembered for the newspaper columns he penned for nearly three decades before his death.

He was eclipsed – at least in the drinking stakes – by novelist, playwright, journalist and quintessential Dublin hell-raiser, Brendan Behan (1923–64), who led a short and frantic life. In 1953, Behan began work as a columnist with the now-defunct *Irish Press,* and over the next decade wrote about his beloved Dublin, using wonderful, earthy satire and a keen sense of political commentary that set him apart from other journalists. A collection of his newspaper columns was published under the title *Hold Your Hour and Have Another*.

The Contemporary Scene

'I love James Joyce. Never read him, but he's a true genius.' And while this is certainly true of Dublin's greatest literary son, most Dubliners feel more or less the same about the other literary giants of yesteryear. Ask them for their favourite contemporary authors, though, and you'd kick off a knowledgeable debate peppered with dozens of worthy names.

Contemporary heavyweights include Roddy Doyle (1958–), made famous by the mega-successful Barrytown quartet (all of which were made into the films); his most recent novel is *The Dead Republic* (2010),

DUBLIN WRITERS MUSEUM

If you want to see Beckett's phone, Behan's union card and a first edition of *Dracula* all under the one roof, the Dublin Writers Museum has extensive collections of the city's most famous (dead) writers.

JAMES JOYCE

Foremost among Dublin writers is James Joyce, author of *Ulysses*, the greatest book of the 20th century – although we've yet to meet five people who've actually finished it. Still, Dubliners are immensely proud of the writer once castigated as a literary pornographer by locals and luminaries alike – even George Bernard Shaw dismissed him as vulgar. Joyce was so unappreciated that he left the city, never to reside in it again, though he continued to live here through his imagination and literature.

His Life

Born in Rathgar in 1882, the young Joyce had three short stories published in an Irish farmers' magazine under the pen name Stephen Dedalus in 1904. The same year he fled town with the love of his life, Nora Barnacle (when James' father heard her name he commented that she would surely stick to him). He spent most of the next 10 years in Trieste, now part of Italy, where he wrote prolifically but struggled to get published. His career was further hampered by recurrent eye problems and he had 25 operations for glaucoma, cataracts and other conditions.

The first major prose he finally had published was *Dubliners* (1914), a collection of short stories set in the city, including the three stories he had written in Ireland. Publishers began to take notice and his autobiographical *A Portrait of the Artist as a Young Man* (1916) followed. In 1918 the US magazine *Little Review* started to publish extracts from *Ulysses*, but notoriety was already pursuing his epic work and the censors prevented publication of further episodes after 1920.

Passing through Paris on a rare visit to Dublin, he was persuaded by Ezra Pound to stay a while in the French capital, and later said he 'came to Paris for a week and stayed 20 years'. It was a good move for the struggling writer for, in 1922, he met Sylvia Beach of the Paris bookshop Shakespeare & Co, who finally managed to put *Ulysses* (1922) into print. The publicity of its earlier censorship ensured instant success.

Buoyed by the success of the inventive *Ulysses*, Joyce went for broke with *Finnegans Wake* (1939), 'set' in the dreamscape of a Dublin publican. Perhaps not one to read at the airport, the book is a daunting and often obscure tome about eternal recurrence. It is even more complex than *Ulysses* and took the author 17 years to write.

In 1940 WWII drove the Joyce family back to Zürich, where the author died the following year.

Ulysses

Ulysses is the ultimate chronicle of the city in which Joyce once said he intended to 'give a picture of Dublin so complete that if the city suddenly one day disappeared from the earth it could be reconstructed out of my book'. It is set here on 16 June, 1904 – the day of Joyce's first date with Nora Barnacle – and follows its characters as their journeys around town parallel the voyage of Homer's *Odyssey*.

The experimental literary style makes it difficult to read, but there's much for even the slightly bemused reader to relish. It ends with Molly Bloom's famous stream of consciousness discourse, a chapter of eight huge, unpunctuated paragraphs. Because of its sexual explicitness, the book was banned in the US and the UK until 1933 and 1937, respectively.

In testament to the book's enduring relevance and extraordinary innovation, it has inspired writers of every generation since. Joyce admirers from around the world descend on Dublin every year on 16 June to celebrate Bloomsday and retrace the steps of its central character, Leopold Bloom. It is a slightly gimmicky and touristy phenomenon that appeals almost exclusively to Joyce fanatics and tourists, but it's plenty of fun and a great way to lay the groundwork for actually reading the book.

the third book about an IRA hitman called Henry. Sebastian Barry (1955–) started his career as a poet, made his name as a playwright but achieved his greatest success as a novelist. Favourites include the award-winning *The Secret Scripture* (2008), about a 100-year-old inmate of a mental hospital who decides to write an autobiography. More recently, *On Canaan's Side* (2011) was long-listed for Man Booker Prize.

Anne Enright (1962–) nabbed the Booker for *The Gathering* (2007), a Zeitgeist tale of alcoholism and abuse – she described it as 'the intellectual equivalent of a Hollywood weepie'. Another Booker Prize winner is heavyweight John Banville (1945–), who won it for *The Sea* (2009); we recommend either *The Book of Evidence* (1989) or the masterful *roman-á-clef The Untouchable* (1997), based loosely on the secret-agent life of art historian Anthony Blunt. Banville's precise and often cold prose divides critics, who consider him either the English language's greatest living stylist or an unreadable intellectual; if you're of the latter inclination then you should check out his immensely enjoyable (and highly readable) crime novels, written under the pseudonym of Benjamin Black: the most recent ones include *A Death in Summer* (2011), *Vengeance* (2012) and *Holy Orders* (2013). Other established favourites include Wexford-born but Dublin-based Colm Tóibín (1955–), author of nine novels including *Brooklyn* (2009) and the novella *The Testament of Mary* (2012), which deals with the life of Mary, mother of Jesus, in her old age.

Besides these established authors, the contemporary scene is benefiting from the arrival of a slew of new writers with a Generation Y perspective on life, love and growing up in Ireland. New themes are being explored to wonderful effect, including the experience of the migrant communities, the atomising effect of the Celtic Tiger and the struggle for sexual equality, which have all found their way onto the pages of books by new voices eager to tell the story of contemporary Ireland. Outstanding talents include the likes of Ciarán Collins, whose debut novel *The Gamal* (2013) is a wonderfully poignant and funny look at the pains of adolescence in a small Irish community. Gavin Corbett's *This is the Way* (2013) tells of the travails of a Traveller (a member of Ireland's indigenous itinerant community) in 21st century Dublin. Niamh Boyce won the Hennessy XO New Writer of the Year Award in 2012 and has followed it with her first novel, *The Herbalist* (2013), about an exotic stranger in a small Irish town whose presence uncovers the town's worst secrets. And in one of the most successful examples of self-publishing, debut novelist Helen Seymour's *Beautiful*

LIVING POET'S SOCIETY

Seamus Heaney (1939–) was born in Derry but now lives mostly in Dublin. He is the bard of all Ireland and evokes the spirit and character of the country in his poetry. He won the Nobel Prize for Literature in 1995, and the humble wordsmith compared all the attention to someone mentioning sex in front of their mammy. *Opened Ground – Poems 1966–1996* (1998) is our favourite of his books.

Dubliner Paul Durcan (1944–) is one of the most reliable chroniclers of changing Dublin. He won the prestigious Whitbread Prize for Poetry in 1990 for '*Daddy, Daddy*' and is a funny, engaging, tender and savage writer. Poet, playwright and Kerryman Brendan Kennelly (1936–) is an immensely popular character around town. He lectures at Trinity College and writes a unique brand of poetry that is marked by its playfulness, as well as historical and intellectual impact. Eavan Boland (1944–) is a prolific and much-admired writer, best known for her poetry, who combines Irish politics with outspoken feminism; *In a Time of Violence* (1994) and *The Lost Land* (1998) are two of her most celebrated collections.

If you're interested in finding out more about poetry in Ireland in general, visit the website of the excellent Poetry Ireland (www.poetryireland.ie), which showcases the work of new and established poets.

Noise (2013) – about a fictional group of friends in 1980s Dublin – had its movie rights bought by Irish director John Moore, whose latest film was *A Good Day to Die Hard* (2013).

Finally, authors may hate the label and publishers profess to disregard it, but chick lit is big business, and few have mastered it as well as the Irish. Doyenne of them all is Maeve Binchy (1940–2012) whose mastery of the style saw her outsell most of the literary greats – her last novel before she died was *A Week in Winter* (2012). Marian Keyes (1963–) is another author with a long line of best-sellers, including her latest, *The Mystery of Mercy Close* (2012). She's a terrific storyteller with a rare ability to tackle sensitive issues like alcoholism and depression, issues that she herself has suffered from and is admirably honest about. Former agony aunt Cathy Kelly turns out novels at the rate of one a year: a recent book is *The Honey Queen* (2013), about all not being well in the fictional town of Redstone...

If you want more substance to your reading, Nuala O'Faolain (1940–2008), former opinion columnist for the *Irish Times,* 'accidentally' wrote an autobiography when a small publisher asked her to write an introduction to a collection of her columns. Her irreverent, humorous and touching prose struck a chord with readers and the essay was republished as *Are You Somebody?* (1996), followed by *Almost There – the Onward Journey of a Dublin Woman* (2003), both of which became international best-sellers.

Musical Dublin

Dublin's literary tradition may have the intellectuals nodding sagely, but it's the city's musical credentials that have the rest of us bopping, for it's no cliché to say that music is as intrinsic to the local lifestyle as a good night out. Even the streets – well, OK, Grafton St and Temple Bar – are alive with the sounds of music, and you can hardly get around without stubbing your toe on the next international superstar busking their way to a record contract. One thing's for certain, you'll have the music of Dublin ringing in your ears long after your gig here is done.

Traditional & Folk

Irish music – commonly referred to as 'traditional' or simply 'trad' – has retained a vibrancy not found in other traditional European forms. This is probably because despite having retained many of its traditional aspects, Irish music has itself influenced many forms of music, most notably US country and western. Other reasons for its current success include the willingness of its exponents to update the way it's played – in ensembles rather than the customary *céilidh* (communal dance) bands – and the habit of pub sessions, introduced by returning migrants.

The pub session is still the best way to hear the music at its rich, lively best – and thanks largely to the tourist demand there are some terrific sessions in pubs throughout the city. Thankfully, though, the best musicians have also gone into the recording studio. If you want to hear musical skill that will both tear out your heart and restore your faith in humanity, go no further than the fiddle-playing of Tommy Peoples on *The Quiet Glen* (1998), the beauty of Paddy Keenan's uillean pipes on his eponymous 1975 album, or the stunning guitar playing of Andy Irvine on albums like *Compendium: The Best of Patrick Street* (2000).

The most famous traditional band are The Chieftains, who spend most of their time these days playing in the US and marked their 50th anniversary in 2012 with the ambitious *Voice of Ages*, a collaboration with the likes of Bon Iver and Paolo Nutini. More folksy than traditional were The Dubliners, founded in O'Donoghue's on Merrion Row the same year as The Chieftains. Most of the original members, including the utterly brilliant Luke Kelly and front-man Ronnie Drew, have died, but the group still plays the odd nostalgic gig in Dublin. In 2006 they released *Live at Vicar St*, which captures some of their brilliance.

Another band whose career has been stitched into the fabric of Dublin life is the Fureys, comprising four brothers originally from the travelling community (no, not like the Wilburys) along with guitarist Davey Arthur. And if it's rousing renditions of Irish rebel songs you're after, you can't go past the Wolfe Tones. Ireland is packed with traditional talent and we strongly recommend that you spend some time in a specialised traditional shop like Claddagh Records.

Since the 1970s, various bands have tried to blend traditional with more progressive genres with mixed success. The first band to pull it off was Moving Hearts, led by Christy Moore, who went on to become an important folk musician in his own right.

LUKE KELLY: THE ORIGINAL DUBLINER

With a halo of wiry ginger hair and a voice like hardened honey, Luke Kelly (1940–84) was perhaps the greatest Irish folk singer of the 20th century, a performer who used his voice in the manner of the American blues singers he admired so much – to express the anguish of being 'lonely and afraid in a world they never made' (to quote AE Housman). He was a founding member of The Dubliners along with Ronnie Drew (1934–2008), Barney McKenna (1939–) and Ciaran Burke (1935–88), but he treated Dublin's most famous folk group as more of a temporary cooperative enterprise. He shared the singing duties with Drew, lending his distinctive voice to classic drinking ditties such as 'Dirty Old Town' and rousing rebel songs like 'A Nation Once Again', but it was his mastery of the more reflective ballad that made him peerless. His rendition of 'Raglan Road', from a poem by Patrick Kavanagh which the poet himself insisted he sing, is the most beautiful song about Dublin we've ever heard; but it is his version of Phil Coulter's 'Scorn Not His Simplicity' that grants him his place among the immortals. Coulter wrote the song following the birth of a son with Down syndrome and even though it became one of Luke's best-loved songs, he had such respect for it that he rarely sang it at The Dubliners' boisterous gigs.

Popular Music

Like everywhere else, the '60s introduced Dublin to rock and pop, allowing local bands to believe they had a future beyond the stages of their local dance hall. Thin Lizzy, formed in 1969, were the most successful of these: led by the imperious Phil Lynott (1949–86), they dominated the '70s with their brand of Celtic-and-blues-infused rock. Albums like *Jailbreak* (1976) and *Live and Dangerous* (1978) are high points of a sterling career.

And then, in 1976, a supernova was born in North Dublin. The world and her sister have an opinion about U2 and, especially, their shy, unopinionated lead singer Bono, but U2 have not only eclipsed virtually every other band save the Rolling Stones for mega-stardom and longevity, but have come to represent Dublin on the international stage in a way that nobody – including James Joyce and Guinness – have done before. If we had to pick just one album, it would be the simply magnificent *The Joshua Tree* (1987), although *Achtung Baby* (1991) is quite something too. Their musical output of late has dipped, as inevitably it would with a band whose members are comfortably middle-aged: their last album, *No Line on the Horizon* (2009), was released to very mixed reviews.

U2's success cast a long shadow over the city's musical scene in the next couple of decades, despite the valiant and wonderful efforts of Sinéad O'Connor to bask in her own sunlight and the singular genius of My Bloody Valentine, who were the true pioneers of the shoe-gazer alt-rock movement of the late 1980s (1991's *Loveless* is one of Dublin's greatest musical moments). But who was going to be the next U2? The answer was 'nobody', or, if you were boy-group impresario Louis Walsh, Boyzone and Westlife, his two most successful creations of the '90s obsession with anodyne pop.

Infinitely more memorable was the emergence of the dance music scene, a five-year party fuelled by ecstasy, bottled water and the pounding beat of techno as played by a host of top-class local DJs and a constant stream of (overpaid) international superstars.

The Contemporary Scene

The demise of the dance floor saw the return of the live gig as the preferred form of musical entertainment. The current scene is perhaps

Dublin Songs

I Don't Like Mondays (1979) Boomtown Rats

Lay Me Down (2001) The Frames

One (1991) U2

Raglan Road (1972) Luke Kelly & The Dubliners

Still in Love with You (1978) Thin Lizzy

DUBLIN ALBUMS

Five albums by Dublin artists to provide a decent soundtrack for your city visit:

➡ *Boy* (U2) Best debut album of all time? We think so.

➡ *I Do Not Want What I Haven't Got* (Sinéad O'Connor) Try listening to the Prince-penned 'Nothing Compares 2 U' and not feel her pain – or your own!

➡ *In a Perfect World* (Kodaline) Alt-rock quartet Kodaline released their full-length debut in 2013; we think it's the first of many.

➡ *Loveless* (My Bloody Valentine) Utterly intoxicating indie classic that just piles on the layers of sound and melody.

➡ *Becoming a Jackal* (Villagers) A superb debut by musical maestro Conor O'Brien.

Need proof that Bono can still belt them out? Just listen to the live version of *Miss Sarajevo,* recorded in Milan in 2005 and available on the *All Because of You* single. Luciano Pavarotti wasn't around to sing his bit as he did on the studio version (on U2 and Brian Eno's *Passengers* soundtrack album from 1995), so Bono does the honours – in Italian, and with a power and intensity that has reduced us to tears. *Grazie, maestro.*

more rich and varied than ever, as every new band and performer looks to negotiate the vicissitudes of the new-look music industry: lucrative record deals are as rare as hen's teeth, which leaves most acts reliant on gigging, word-of-mouth and online media to spread their respective musical gospels.

There are far more bands on the scene than we have room to mention here, but the good news is that there are gigs on all the time. Some names to look out for include alt-rockers Kodaline, whose two EPs garnered huge critical acclaim (including a nomination for the BBC's Sound of 2013 poll) ahead of the release of their debut album, *In a Perfect World,* in June 2013. With more than faint echoes of Bon Iver and Ray LaMontagne is James Vincent McMorrow from the northern suburb of Malahide, who released *Early in the Morning* in 2012. One of the most anticipated releases of 2013 was *Absolute Zero*, the debut album of Little Green Cars, a rock band with incredibly catchy melodies. Wexford-born folk singer Wallis Bird released her third album, *Wallis Bird*, in 2012; on it you'll hear exactly why she's labelled the Irish Fiona Apple or (if you like), a young Janis Joplin (and that's ignoring the fact that she's older than Joplin was when she died). Fusing electronica with alt rock is Richie Egan, whose band Jape released *Oceans of Frequency* in 2011 and picked up their second Choice Music prize, Ireland's highest rock accolade.

But easily the most critically acclaimed new act around are Villagers, an indie folk group fronted by Conor O'Brien, who writes all the songs and plays most of the instruments. His particular brilliance is reflected in *Becoming a Jackal* (2010) and *Awayland* (2013), both of which have been given lots of airplay in Britain and the US.

Architecture

Dublin's skyline is a clue to its age, with visible peaks of its architectural history dating back to the Middle Ages. Of course, Dublin is older still, but there's no traces left of its Viking origins and you'll have to begin your architectural exploration in the 12th century, with the construction of the city's castle and two cathedrals. Its finest buildings, however, date from much later – built during the golden century that came to be known as the Georgian period.

Medieval Dublin

Viking Dublin was largely built of not-so-durable wood, of which there's virtually no trace left. The Norman footprint is a little deeper, but even its most impressive structures have been heavily reconstructed. The imposing Dublin Castle – or the complex of buildings that are known as Dublin Castle – bears little resemblance to the fortress that was erected by the Anglo-Normans at the beginning of the 13th century and owes more to the neoclassical style of the 17th century. However, there are some fascinating glimpses of the lower reaches of the original, which you can visit on a tour.

Although the 12th-century cathedrals of Christ Church and St Patrick's were heavily rebuilt in Victorian times, there are some original features, including the crypt in Christ Church, which has a 12th-century Romanesque door. The older of the two St Audoen's Churches dates from 1190 and it too has a few Norman odds and ends, including a late-12th-century doorway.

Archéire (www.irish-architecture.com) is a comprehensive website covering all things to do with Irish architecture and design. If you want something in book form, look no further than Christine Casey's superb *The Buildings of Ireland: Dublin* (2005; Yale University Press), which goes through the city literally street by street.

Anglo-Dutch Period

After the restoration of Charles II in 1660, Dublin embarked upon almost a century and a half of unparalleled growth as the city raced to become the second most important in the British empire. The most impressive examples of the style are the Royal Hospital Kilmainham (1680), designed by William Robinson and now home to the Irish Museum of Modern Art; and the Royal Barracks (Collins Barracks; 1701) built by Thomas Burgh and now home to a branch of the National Museum of Ireland.

Georgian Dublin

Dublin's architectural apogee can roughly be placed in the period spanning the rule of the four English Georges, between the accession of George I in 1714 and the death of George IV in 1830. The greatest influence on the shape of modern Dublin throughout this period was the Wide Street Commissioners, appointed in 1757 and responsible for designing civic spaces and the framework of the modern city. Their efforts were complemented by Dublin's Anglo-Irish Protestant gentry who, flush with unprecedented wealth, dedicated themselves wholeheartedly towards improving their city.

Their inspiration was the work of the Italian architect Andrea Palladio (1508–80), who revived the symmetry and harmony of classical architecture. When the Palladian style reached these shores in the 1720s, the architects of the time tweaked it and introduced a number of, let's call them,

GEORGIAN PLASTERERS

The handsome exteriors of Dublin's finest Georgian houses are often matched by superbly crafted plasterwork within. The fine work of Michael Stapleton (1770–1803) can be seen in Trinity College (p52), Ely House near St Stephen's Green, and Belvedere House in north Dublin. The LaFranchini brothers, Paolo (1695–1776) and Filippo (1702–79), are responsible for the outstanding decoration in Newman House (p62) on St Stephen's Green. But perhaps Dublin's most famous plastered surfaces are in the chapel at the heart of the Rotunda Hospital (p133). Although hospitals are never the most pleasant places to visit, it's worth it for the German stuccodore, Bartholomew Cramillion's fantastic rococo plasterwork.

'refinements'. Most obvious were the elegant brick exteriors and decorative touches, such as coloured doors, fanlights and ironwork, which broke the sometimes austere uniformity of the fashion. Consequently, Dublin came to be known for its 'Georgian style'.

Sir Edward Lovett Pearce

The architect credited with the introduction of this style to Dublin's cityscape was Sir Edward Lovett Pearce (1699–1733), who first arrived in Dublin in 1725 and turned heads with the building of Parliament House (Bank of Ireland; 1728–39). It was the first two-chamber debating house in the world and the main chamber, the House of Commons, is topped by a massive pantheon-style dome.

Pearce also created the blueprint for the city's Georgian townhouses, the most distinguishing architectural feature of Dublin. The local version typically consists of four storeys, including the basement, with symmetrically arranged windows and an imposing, often brightly painted front door. Granite steps lead up to the door, which is usually further embellished with a delicate leaded fanlight. The most celebrated examples are on the south side of the city, particularly around Merrion and Fitzwilliam Sqs, but the north side also has some magnificent streets, including North Great George's and Henrietta Sts. The latter features two of Pearce's originals (at Nos 9 and 10) and is still Dublin's most unified Georgian street. Mountjoy Sq, the most elegant address in 18th-century Dublin, is currently being renewed after a century of neglect.

Richard Cassels

German architect Richard Cassels (Richard Castle; 1690–1751) hit town in 1728. While his most impressive country houses are outside Dublin, he did design Nos 85 and 86 St Stephen's Green (1738), which were combined in the 19th century and renamed Newman House, and No 80 (1736), which was later joined with No 81 to create Iveagh House, now the Department of Foreign Affairs; you can visit the peaceful gardens there still. The Rotunda Hospital (1748), which closes off the top of O'Connell St, is also one of Cassels' works. As splendid as these buildings are, it seems he was only warming up for Leinster House (1745–48), the magnificent country residence built on what was then the countryside, but is now the centre of government.

Sir William Chambers

Dublin's boom attracted such notable architects as the Swedish-born Sir William Chambers (1723–96), who designed some of Dublin's most impressive buildings, though he never actually bothered to visit the city.

TRINITY COLLEGE

Sir William Chambers designed the Examination Hall (1779–91) and the Chapel (1798), that flank the elegant 18th-century quadrangle of Trinity College, known as Parliament Sq. However, Trinity College's most magnificent feature, the Old Library Building, with its breathtaking Long Room (1712), were designed by Thomas Burgh.

It was the north side of the Liffey that benefited most from Chambers' genius: the chaste and elegant Charlemont House (Hugh Lane Gallery; 1763) lords over Parnell Sq, while the Casino at Marino (1755–79) is his most stunning and bewitching work.

James Gandon

It was towards the end of the 18th century that Dublin's developers really kicked into gear, when the power and confidence of the Anglo-Irish Ascendancy seemed boundless. Of several great architects of the time, James Gandon (1743–1823) stands out. He built two of Dublin's most enduring and elegant neoclassical landmarks, Custom House (1781–91) and the Four Courts (1786–1802). They were both built on the quays to afford plenty of space in which to admire them.

Regency & Victorian

The Act of Union (1801) turned Dublin from glorious capital to empire backwater, which resulted in precious little construction for much of the 19th century. Exceptions include the General Post Office (GPO; 1814), designed by Francis Johnston, and the stunning series of curvilinear glasshouses in the National Botanic Gardens, which were created mid-century by the Dublin iron-master Richard Turner (1798–1881).

After Catholic Emancipation in 1829, there was a wave of church building, and later the two great Protestant cathedrals of Christ Church and St Patrick's were reconstructed. One especially beautiful example is the splendidly ornate and incongruous Newman University Church (1856), built in a Byzantine style by John Hungerford Pollen (1820–1902) because Cardinal Newman was none too keen on the Gothic style that was all the rage at the time.

The Contemporary Landscape

Dublin has a somewhat troubled relationship with modern architecture. The big projects of the post-war years, such as Busáras (1953) and Liberty Hall (1965), have divided critics, who expressed a more favourable opinion of Paul Koralek's bold and brazen Berkeley Library (1967) in the grounds of Trinity College.

It wasn't until the explosive growth of the 1990s that the city's modern landscape really began to improve, even if some of the early constructions – such as the Irish Financial Services Centre (IFSC; 1987) and the Waterways Visitor Centre (1994) – don't seem as impressive now as they did when they first opened.

The most impressive makeover has occurred in the Docklands, which has been transformed from quasi-wasteland to a fine example of contemporary urban design. Old buildings have been refurbished, but it's the new buildings that really catch the eye. Three of these opened in 2010 to great applause: the impressive, tube-shaped National Convention Centre on the quays; the Grand Canal Quay's stunning Bord Gáis Energy Theatre, designed by Daniel Libeskind; and, just to the south, the new 50,000 capacity Aviva Stadium, easily visible thanks to its eye-catching curvilinear-shaped stand.

ARCHITECTURE REGENCY & VICTORIAN

THOMAS COOLEY

James Gandon's greatest rival was Thomas Cooley (1740–84), who died too young to reach his full potential. His greatest building, the Royal Exchange (City Hall; 1779), was butchered to provide office space in the mid-19th century, but returned to its breathtaking splendour in a stunning 2000 restoration.

Survival Guide

Transport

Ireland's capital and biggest city is the most important point of entry and departure for the country – the overwhelming majority of airlines fly in and out of Dublin Airport. The city has two ferry ports: the Dun Laoghaire ferry terminal and the Dublin Port terminal. Ferries from France arrive in the southern port of Rosslare. Dublin is also the nation's primary rail hub. Flights, cars and tours can be booked online at lonelyplanet.com.

ARRIVING IN DUBLIN

Dublin Airport

Dublin's international **airport** (☎01-814 1111; www.dublinair port.com) is located 13km north of the city centre. It has two terminals: most international flights (including all US flights) use the new Terminal 2; Ryanair and select others use Terminal 1. Both terminals have the usual selection of pubs, restaurants, shops, ATMs and car-hire desks.

There are direct flights to Dublin from all major European centres (including a dizzying array of options from the UK) and from Atlanta, Boston, Charlotte, Chicago, New York, Orlando, Philadelphia and Washington, DC in the USA. Flights from further afield (Australasia or Africa) are usually routed through another European hub such as London.

Most airlines have walk-up counters at Dublin airport; those that don't, have their ticketing handled by other airlines.

There is no train service from the airport to the city centre.

Bus

It takes about 45 minutes to get into the city by bus.

Aircoach (www.aircoach. ie; one-way/return €7/12) Private coach service with two routes from the airport to 18 destinations throughout the city, including the main streets of the city centre. Coaches run every 10 to 15 minutes between 6am and midnight, then hourly from midnight until 6am.

Airlink Express Coach (☎01-873 4222; www.dublinbus. ie; adult/child €6/3) Bus 747 runs every 10 to 20 minutes from 5.45am to 11.30pm between the airport, central bus station (Busáras) and Dublin Bus office on Upper O'Connell St. Bus 748 runs every 15 to 30 minutes from 6.50am to 10.05pm between the airport, and Heuston and Connolly Stations.

Dublin Bus (Map p248; ☎01-873 4222; www.dublinbus. ie; 59 Upper O'Connell St; ⊙9am-5.30pm Mon-Fri, 9am-2pm Sat) A number of buses serve the airport from various points in Dublin, including buses

16A (Rathfarnham), 746 (Dun Laoghaire) and 230 (Portmarnock); all cross the city centre on their way to the airport.

Taxi

There is a taxi rank directly outside the arrivals concourse. It should take about 45 minutes to get into the city centre by taxi and cost about €25, including a supplementary charge of €3 (not applied when going to the airport). Make sure the meter is switched on.

Dun Laoghaire Ferry Terminal

The **Dun Laoghaire ferry terminal** (☎01-280 1905; Dun Laoghaire), 13km southeast of the city, receives **Stena Line** (☎01-204 7777; www. stenaline.com; Ferry Terminal,

ONLINE BOOKING AGENCIES

→ www.bestfares.com
→ www.cheapflights. com
→ www.ebookers.com
→ www.expedia.com
→ www.flycheap.com
→ www.opodo.com
→ www.priceline.com
→ www.statravel.com
→ www.travelocity.com

CLIMATE CHANGE & TRAVEL

Every form of transport that relies on carbon-based fuel generates CO2, the main cause of human-induced climate change. Modern travel is dependent on aeroplanes, which might use less fuel per kilometre per person than most cars but travel much greater distances. The altitude at which aircraft emit gases (including CO2) and particles also contributes to their climate change impact. Many websites offer 'carbon calculators' that allow people to estimate the carbon emissions generated by their journey and, for those who wish to do so, to offset the impact of the greenhouse gases emitted with contributions to portfolios of climate-friendly initiatives throughout the world. Lonely Planet offsets the carbon footprint of all staff and author travel.

Dun Laoghaire) ferries to/ from Holyhead in Wales. The crossing takes just over three hours and costs around €25 for foot passengers or €95 for a medium-size car with two passengers. The fast-boat service from Holyhead to Dun Laoghaire takes a little over 1½ hours and costs €25 or €130 for the same.

Train

To travel between Dun Laoghaire ferry terminal and Dublin, take the DART to Pearse Station (for south Dublin) or Connolly Station (for north Dublin). Trains from Dublin to Dun Laoghaire take about 15 to 20 minutes. A one-way DART ticket costs €2.80.

Bus

To get into Dublin by bus, take bus 46A to St Stephen's Green, or bus 7, 7A or 8 to Burgh Quay.

Dublin Port Terminal

The **Dublin Port terminal** (☑01-855 2222; Alexandra Rd) is 3km northeast of the city centre. **Irish Ferries** (☑0818 300 400; www.irishferries.com; Ferryport, Terminal Rd South) serves Holyhead in Wales (three hours, €25 for foot passengers, €95 for a car with two passengers). **P&O Irish Sea** (☑01-407 3434; www.poferries.com; Terminal 3) and **Isle of Man Steam Packet Company/Sea Cat**

(☑01-836 4019; www.steam-packet.com; Maritime House, North Wall) have services to/ from Liverpool in England. Between Liverpool and Dublin the ferry service takes 8½ hours and costs €25 (foot passenger) or €180 (car with two passengers). Cabins on overnight sailings cost more. The fast-boat service takes four hours and costs up to €40 or €240 respectively.

Bus

Buses from Busáras are timed to coincide with arrivals and departures from the Dublin Port terminal. For the 9.45am ferry departure from Dublin, buses leave Busáras at 8.30am; for the 1am sailing to Liverpool, the bus departs from Busáras at 11.45pm. All buses cost adult/child €2.50/1.25.

Busáras Terminal

Busáras (Map p248; ☑01-836 6111; www.buseireann.ie; Store St) is just north of the river behind Custom House; it has different-sized lockers costing €6 to €10 per day.

It's possible to combine bus and ferry tickets from major UK centres to Dublin on the bus network. The journey between London and Dublin takes about 12 hours and costs around €34 return. For details in London, contact **Eurolines** (☑0870 514 3219; www.eurolines.com).

From here, Bus Eireann buses serve the whole national network, including

buses to town and cities in Northern Ireland.

Heuston & Connolly Train Stations

Dublin has two main train stations: **Heuston Station** (☑01-836 5421), on the western side of town near the Liffey; and **Connolly Station** (☑01-836 3333), a short walk northeast of Busáras, behind the Custom House. Heuston Station has left-luggage lockers of three sizes, costing €6 to €10 for 24 hours. At Connolly Station the facility costs €6.

Connolly Station is a stop on the DART line into town; the Luas Red Line serves both Connolly and Heuston stations.

GETTING AROUND DUBLIN

Bus

The **Dublin Bus Office** (☑01-872 0000; www.dublinbus.ie; 59 Upper O'Connell St; ◎9am-5.30pm Mon-Fri, 9am-2pm Sat) has free single-route timetables for all its services. Buses run from around 6am (some start at 5.30am) to about 11.30pm.

Bus Fares

Fares are calculated according to stages:

GREENER ARRIVALS

Although the vast majority of visitors will enter and exit Dublin via the airport, you can do your bit for the environment and arrive by boat – and have a bit of an adventure along the way. From Britain it's a cinch: you can buy a combined train-and-ferry ticket (known as Sail & Rail) for about €46 (see www.irishrail.ie for travel from Ireland or www.thetrainline.co.uk for travel from the UK) or, if you're really on a budget, get a bus-and-ferry ticket – from London it won't cost you more than the price of a meal.

You can also arrive at another Irish port. Rosslare in County Wexford has ferry services from France and southwestern Britain, while Larne, a short hop outside Belfast, is served from Stranraer in Scotland. Not only will you get to Dublin easily enough, but you can do some exploring on the way.

➡ one to three stages: €1.65
➡ four to seven stages: €2.15
➡ eight to 13 stages: €2.40
➡ 14 to 23 stages: €2.80
➡ More than 23 stages: €2.80 (inside Citizone; outer suburban journeys cost €4.40)

If you're travelling within the designated bus corridor zone (roughly between Parnell Sq to the north and St Stephen's Green to the south) you can use the €0.65 special City Centre fare. You must tender exact change when boarding; anything more and you will be given a receipt for reimbursement, only possible at the Dublin Bus main office. Avoid this by getting a **Leap Card** (www.leapcard.ie), a plastic smart card available in most newsagents. Once you register it online, you can top it up with whatever amount you need. When you board a bus, Luas or suburban train, just swipe your card and the fare – usually 20% less than a cash fare – is automatically deducted.

Fare-Saver Passes

Fare saver passes:

Freedom Ticket (adult/child €28/12) Three-day unlimited travel on all bus services, including Airlink and Dublin Bus Hop-On, Hop-Off tours.

Adult (Bus & Rail) Short Hop (one/three days €12/24.50) Valid for unlimited travel on Dublin Bus, DART and suburban rail, but not Nitelink or Airlink.

Bus/Luas Pass (one/seven days €8.10/32.80) Unlimited travel on both bus and Luas.

Family One-Day Short Hop (€17.70) Valid for travel for one day for a family of two adults and two children aged under 16 on all bus and rail services except Nitelink, Airlink, ferry services and tours.

Rambler Pass (one/three/five days €6.90/15/25) Valid for unlimited travel on all Dublin Bus and Airlink services, except Nitelink.

10 Journey Travel 90 (adult/child €25) Valid for 10 90-minute journeys on all Dublin Bus and Airlink services, except Nitelink.

Nitelink

Nitelink late-night buses run from the College, Westmoreland and D'Olier Sts triangle. On Fridays and Saturdays, departures are at 12.30am, then every 20 minutes until 4.30am on the more popular routes, and until 3.30am on the less frequented ones; there are no services Sunday to Thursday. Fares are €5.

See www.dublinbus.ie for route details.

Train

The **Dublin Area Rapid Transport** (DART; ☎01-836 6222; www.irishrail.ie) provides quick train access to the coast as far north as Howth (about 30 minutes) and as far south as Greystones in County Wicklow. Pearse Station is convenient for central Dublin south of the Liffey, and Connolly Station for north of the Liffey. There are services every 10 to 20 minutes, sometimes even more frequently, from around 6.30am to midnight Monday to Saturday. Services are less frequent on Sunday. A one-way DART ticket from Dublin to Dun Laoghaire or Howth costs €2.80; to Bray it's €3.30.

There are also suburban rail services north as far as Dundalk, inland to Mullingar and south past Bray to Arklow.

Train Passes

DART passes include the following:

Adult (Bus & Rail) Short Hop (one/three days €12/24.50) Valid for unlimited travel on Dublin Bus, DART and suburban rail travel, but not Nitelink or Airlink.

Family One-Day Short Hop (€17.70) Valid for travel for one day for a family of two adults and two children aged under 16 on all bus and rail services except for Nitelink, Airlink, ferry services and tours.

Tram

The **Luas** (www.luas.ie) light-rail system has two lines: the green line (running every five to 15 minutes) connects St Stephen's Green with Sandyford in south Dublin via Ranelagh and Dundrum; the red line (every 20 minutes) runs from Lower Abbey St to Tallaght via the north quays and Heuston Station. There are ticket machines at every stop or you can buy a ticket from newsagents in the city centre; a typical short-hop fare (around four stops) is €2. Services run from 5.30am to 12.30am Monday to Friday, from 6.30am to 12.30am Saturday and from 7am to 11.30pm Sunday.

Bicycle

Despite the intermittent presence of rust-red cycle lanes throughout the city centre, getting around by bike can be something of an obstacle course as cyclists have to share roads with buses and indifferent motorists. Bike theft is a major problem, so be sure to park on busier streets, preferably at one of the myriad U-shaped parking bars, and lock it securely. Never leave your bike on the street overnight or it may just be gone in the morning. **Dublin City Cycling** (www.dublincitycycling.ie) is an excellent online resource.

Bikes are only allowed on suburban trains (not the DART), either stowed in the guard's van or in a special compartment at the opposite end of the train from the engine. There's a flat €4 charge for transporting a bicycle up to 56km.

Dublinbikes

One of the most popular ways to get around the city is with the blue bikes of **Dublinbikes** (www.dublinbikes.ie), a pay-as-you-go service similar to the Parisian Vélib system: cyclists purchase a €10 Smart Card (as well as pay a credit-card deposit of €150) – either online or at any of the 40 stations throughout the city centre – before 'freeing' a bike for use, which is then free of charge for the first 30 minutes and €0.50 for each half-hour thereafter.

Hire, Purchase & Repair

Bike rental has become tougher due to the Dublinbikes scheme. Typical rental for a hybrid or touring bike is around €20 a day or €120 per week. Raleigh Rent-a-Bike agencies can be found through **Eurotrek** (☏01-456 8847; www.raleigh.ie).

Cycleways (www.cycleways.com; 185-186 Parnell St) An excellent bike shop that rents hybrids and touring bikes during the summer months (May to September).

Eurocycles & Eurobaby (57 South William St; ⊙10am-6pm Mon, Tue & Sat, to 8pm Wed-Fri, noon-6pm Sun) New bikes, all the gear you could possibly need and a decent repair service; but be sure to book an appointment as they are generally quite busy.

MacDonald Cycles (☏01-475 2586; www.macdonaldcycles.ie; 38 Wexford St) Does repairs, and will have your bike back to you within a day or so (barring serious damage).

Car & Motorcycle

Driving

Traffic in Dublin is a nightmare and parking is an expensive headache. There are no free spots to park anywhere in the city centre during business hours (7am to 7pm Monday to Saturday), but there are plenty of parking meters, 'pay and display' spots (€2.50 to €5 per hour) and over a dozen sheltered and supervised car parks (around €5 per hour).

Clamping of illegally parked cars is thoroughly enforced, and there is an €80 charge for removal. Parking is free after 7pm Monday to Saturday, and all day Sunday, in most metered spots and on single yellow lines.

Car theft and break-ins are a problem, and the police advise visitors to park in a supervised car park. Cars with foreign number plates are prime targets; never leave your valuables behind. When you're booking accommodation, check on parking facilities.

The **Automobile Association of Ireland** (AA; ☏01-617 9999, breakdown 1800 667 788; www.aaireland.ie; 56 Drury St) is located in the city centre.

Hire

Car rental in Dublin is expensive, so you're often better off making arrangements in your home country with some sort of package deal. In July and August it's wise

---

ROAD SAFETY RULES IN DUBLIN

➡ Drive on the left, overtake to the right.

➡ Safety belts must be worn by the driver and all passengers.

➡ Children aged under 12 are not allowed to sit on front seats.

➡ Motorcyclists and their passengers must wear helmets.

➡ When entering a roundabout, give way to the right.

➡ Speed limits are 50km/h or as signposted in the city, 100km/h on all roads outside city limits and 120km/h on motorways (marked in blue).

➡ The legal alcohol limit is 50mg of alcohol per 100mL of blood, or 22mg on the breath (roughly one unit of alcohol for a man and less than that for a woman).

to book well ahead. Most cars are manual; automatic cars are available but they're more expensive to hire. Motorbikes and mopeds are not available for rent. People aged under 21 are not allowed to hire a car; for the majority of rental companies you have to be at least 23 and have had a valid driving licence for a minimum of one year. Many rental agencies will not rent to people over 70 or 75.

Nova Car Hire (www. novacarhire.com) acts as an agent for Alamo, Budget, European and National, and offers greatly discounted rates. Typical weekly high-season rental rates are around €150 for a small car, €185 for a medium car and €320 for a five-seater people carrier.

The main rental agencies, which also have offices at the airport (open from 6am to 11pm), include the following:

Avis Rent-a-Car (☑01-605 7500; www.avis.ie; 35 Old Kilmainham Rd)

Budget Rent-a-Car (☑01-837 9611, airport 01-844 5150; www.budget.ie; 151 Lower Drumcondra Rd)

Europcar (☑01-648 5900, airport 01-844 4179; www. europcar.com; 1 Mark St)

Hertz Rent-a-Car (☑01-709 3060, airport 01-844 5466; www.hertz.com; 151 South Circular Rd)

Thrifty (☑01-844 1944, airport 01-840 0800; www.thrifty. ie; 26 Lombard St East)

Taxi

All taxi fares begin with a flag-fall fare of €4.10 (€4.45 from 10pm to 8am), followed by €1.03 per kilometre thereafter from 8am to 10pm (€1.35 from 10pm to 8am). In addition to these there are a number of extra charges – €1 for each extra passenger and €2 for telephone bookings. There is no charge for luggage.

Taxis can be hailed on the street and found at taxi ranks around the city, including on the corner of Abbey and O'Connell Sts; College Green, in front of Trinity College; and St Stephen's Green at the end of Grafton St.

Phone the **Garda Carriage Office** (☑01-475 5888) if you have any complaints about taxis or queries regarding lost property.

Numerous taxi companies dispatch taxis by radio.

City Cabs (☑01-872 2688)

National Radio Cabs (☑01-677 2222; www.radio cabs.ie)

TOURS

Dublin isn't that big, so a straightforward sightseeing tour is only really necessary if you're looking to cram in the sights or avoid blistered feet. What is worth considering, however, is a specialised guided tour, especially for those of a musical, historical or literary bent.

Boat

Liffey River Cruises (☑01-473 4082; www.liffey rivercruises.com; Bachelor's Walk; adult/student/child €14/10/8; ☺9am-5.30pm Mar-Oct) Dublin's history as seen from the river, from the Viking raids to the recent dockland development.

Sea Safaris (Map p252; ☑01-668 9802; www. seasafari.ie; National Convention Centre; adult/child €20/12.50) Historical tour of the River Liffey and Dublin Port, departing from outside the Convention Centre.

Viking Splash Tours (Map p240; www.vikingsplash. com; adult/child €20/12) A 75-minute tour of the city in an amphibian vehicle, complete with Viking helmets and splash down in the Grand Canal Basin.

Bus

Dublin Bus Tours

Dublin Bus (Map p240; ☑01-872 0000; www.dublinbus.ie; adult/child €28/14; ☺11am), the city's bus company, runs a variety of tours, all of which can be booked at its office, or at the Bus Éireann counter at **Dublin Discover Ireland Centre** (Map p240; www.visit dublin.com; St Andrew's Church, 2 Suffolk St; ☺9am-5.30pm Mon-Sat, 10.30am-3pm Sun). Tours include the following:

Dublin Tour (adult/child/ student €18/8/16; ☺every 15min 9am-5pm) A 90-minute hop-on, hop-off tour you can join at any of the 24 designated stops covering the city centre's major attractions; admission to the sights isn't included.

Ghost Bus Tour (adult €28; ☺8pm Mon-Thu, 8pm & 8.30pm Fri, 7pm & 9.30pm Sat & Sun) Popular two-hour tour of graveyards and 'haunted' places (not suitable for under-14s).

North Coast & Castle (adult/child €24/12; ☺tours 10am & 2pm) Takes in the Botanic Gardens in Glasnevin, the Casino at Marino, Malahide Castle and Howth, all in about three hours.

South Coast & Gardens Tour (adult/child €24/12; ☺11am) A 4½-hour tour running along the stretch of coastline between Dun Laoghaire and Killiney before turning inland to Wicklow and on to Powerscourt Estate (admission included).

Other Bus Tours

City Sightseeing (Map p248; www.citysight seeingdublin.ie; 14 Upper O'Connell St; adult/child €18/ free; ☺every 8-15min 9am-6pm) A typical tour should last around 1½ hours and lead you up and down O'Connell St, past Trinity College and

St Stephen's Green, before heading up to the Guinness Storehouse and back around the north quays, via the main entrance to Phoenix Park.

1916 Easter Rising Coach Tour (Map p252; www.1916easterrisingcoachtour.ie; Custom House Quay; adult/child €15/10) A 90-minute tour of the sites that played a part in the 1916 Easter Rising. Buy your tickets online or at the Dublin Tourism office in St Andrew's Church, Suffolk St.

Carriage

Old-style horse-and-carriage tour operators congregate at the top of Grafton St by St Stephen's Green. Each carriage takes up to five people. Half-hour tours cost up to €60, but different length trips can be negotiated: fix a price *before* the driver says giddy-up.

Segway

Glide Tours (☑01-822 3388; www.glidetours.ie; €50) Two-hour guided tours of the Phoenix Park (10am, 12.30 and 3pm Saturday and Sunday) or the Docklands (10am Sunday) aboard a segway. The tours are designed by local historian Pat Liddy. Phoenix Park tours go from the visitor centre in the park; Docklands tours (Map p252) from by the Jeanie Johnston ship on Custom House Quay.

Walking

1916 Rebellion Walking Tour (Map p240;☑086 858 3847; www.1916rising.com; 23 Wicklow St; per person €12; ☺11.30am Mon-Sat, 1pm Sun Mar-Oct) Superb two-hour tour starting in the International Bar, Wicklow St. Lots of information, humour and irreverence to boot. The guides – all Trinity graduates – are uniformly excellent and will not say no to the offer of a pint back in the International at tour's end.

Dublin Literary Pub Crawl (Map p240;☑01-670 5602; www.dublinpubcrawl.com; 9 Duke St; adult/student €12/10; ☺7.30pm daily Apr-Oct, 7.30pm Thu-Sun Nov-Mar) A tour of pubs associated with famous Dublin writers is a sure-fire recipe for success, and this 2½-hour tour/performance by two actors – which includes them acting out the funny bits – is a riotous laugh. There's plenty of drink taken, which makes it all the more popular. It leaves from the Duke on Duke St; get there by 7pm to reserve a spot for the evening tour.

Dublin Musical Pub Crawl (Map p236;☑01-478 0193; www.discoverdublin.ie; Oliver St John Gogarty's, 58-59 Fleet St; adult/student €12/10; ☺7.30pm daily Apr-Oct, 7.30pm Thu-Sat Nov-Mar) The story of Irish traditional music and its influence on contemporary styles is explained and demonstrated by two expert musicians in a number of Temple Bar pubs over 2½ hours. Tours meet upstairs in the Oliver St John Gogarty pub and are highly recommended.

Pat Liddy Walking Tours (Map p240;☑01-831 1109; www.walkingtours.ie; Dublin Tourism Centre, St Andrew's Church, 2 Suffolk St; €10) Dublin's best-known tour guide is local historian Pat Liddy, who leads a varierty of guided walks including **Dublin Highlights & Hidden Corners** and **The Best of Dublin – The Complete Heritage Walking Tour**. He is also available for private guided walks. Check the website for timings. He also has a bunch of podcast walks available for download.

Directory A–Z

Customs Regulations

Ireland has a two-tier customs system: one for goods bought duty-free outside the European Union (EU); the other for goods bought in another EU country where tax and duty are paid. There is technically no limit to the amount of goods transportable within the EU, but customs will use certain guidelines to distinguish personal use from commercial purpose.

Duty Free

For duty-free goods from outside the EU, limits include 200 cigarettes, 1L of spirits or 2L of wine, 60ml of perfume and 250ml of *eau de toilette*.

Tax & Duty Paid

Amounts that officially constitute personal use include 3200 cigarettes (or 400 cigarillos, 200 cigars or 3kg of tobacco) and either 10L of spirits, 20L of fortified wine, 60L of sparkling wine, 90L of still wine or 110L of beer.

Discount Cards

Senior citizens are entitled to discounts on public transport and museum fees. Students and under-26s also get discounts with the appropriate student or youth card. Local discount passes:

Dublin Pass (www.dublinpass. ie; adult/child 1 day €35/19, 2 day €55/31, 3 day €65/39, 6 day €95/49) Not only do you get free entry into 30 attractions, but you can skip whatever queue there is by presenting your card. The card is available from any of the Dublin Tourism offices or online.

Heritage Card (☎01-647 2461; www.heritageireland.ie; adult/child & student €21/8) This card entitles you to free access to all OPW-managed sights in and around Dublin. You can buy it at OPW sites or Dublin Tourism offices.

Electricity

230V/50Hz

Emergency

For emergency assistance, phone ☎999 or ☎112. This call is free and the operator will connect you with the type of assistance you specify: fire, police *(gardaí)*, ambulance, boat or coastal rescue. There are *garda* stations at **Fitzgibbon St** (Fitzgibbon St), **Harcourt Tce** (☎01-676 3481; Harcourt Tce), **Pearse St** (☎01-677 8141; Pearse St) and **Store St** (Store St).

A full list of all emergency numbers can be found in the front pages of the telephone book.

Gay & Lesbian Travellers

Dublin's not a bad place to be gay. Most people wouldn't bat an eyelid at public displays of affection between same-sex couples, or cross-dressing in the city centre, but discretion is advised in the suburbs. If you do encounter any sort of trouble or harassment call the **Gay & Lesbian Garda Liaison Officer** (☎01-666 9000) or the **Sexual Assault Unit** (☎01-666 6000) at the Pearse St Garda station.

Resources include the following:

Gaire (www.gaire.com) Online message board and resource centre.

Gay Men's Health Project
(☑01-660 2189; www.hse.
ie) Practical advice on men's
health issues.

**National Lesbian & Gay
Federation** (NLGF; ☑01-671
9076; 2 Scarlet Row, Temple
Bar) Publishers of *Gay Community News*.

Outhouse (☑01-873 4932;
www.outhouse.ie; 105 Capel
St) Gay, lesbian and bisexual
resource centre.

Internet Access

Wi-fi and 3G networks are
making internet cafes largely
redundant (except to gam-
ers); the few that are left will
charge around €6 per hour.
Most accommodations have
wi-fi service, either free or
for a daily charge (up to €10
per day).

Legal Matters

The possession of small
quantities of marijuana attracts a fine or warning, but
harder drugs are treated
more seriously. Public
drunkenness is illegal but
commonplace – the police
will usually ignore it unless
you're causing trouble. If you
need legal assistance contact the **Legal Aid Board**
(☑1890 615 200).

Money
ATMs

Most banks have ATMs that
are linked to international
money systems such as
Cirrus, Maestro or Plus. Each
transaction incurs a currency
conversion fee and credit
cards can incur immediate
and exorbitant cash-advance
interest-rate charges. We
strongly recommend that
if you're staying in the city
centre, you get your money
out early on a Friday to avoid
the long queues that can
form after 8pm.

PRACTICALITIES

Currency
Euro (€)

Newspapers
Most popular local newspapers:
➡ *The Herald* (www.herald.ie, €1.30)
➡ *Irish Independent* (www.independent.ie, €1.90)
➡ *Irish Daily Mail* (www.dailymail.co.uk, €1)
➡ *Irish Times* (www.irishtimes.com, €2)
➡ *Irish Examiner* (www.examiner.ie, €1.90)

Credit Cards

Visa and MasterCard credit
and debit cards are widely
accepted in Dublin. Smaller
businesses prefer debit
cards (and will charge a fee
for credit cards). Nearly all
credit and debit cards use
the chip-and-PIN system
and an increasing number of
places will not accept your
card if you don't.

Tipping

You're not obliged to tip if
the service or food was unsatisfactory (even if it's been
automatically added to your
bill as a 'service charge').

Hotels Only for bellhops who
carry luggage, then €1 per bag.

Pubs Not expected unless table
service is provided, then €1 for
a round of drinks.

Restaurants 10% for decent
service, up to 15% in more
expensive places.

Taxis 10% or rounded up to
the nearest euro.

Toilet attendants €0.50.

Opening Hours

The standard opening hours
in relatively late-rising Dublin
are as follows:

Banks 10am to 4pm Monday to
Friday (to 5pm Thursday).

Offices 9am to 5pm Monday
to Friday.

Post offices 9am to 6pm
Monday to Friday, 9am to 1pm
Saturday.

Pubs 10.30am to 11.30pm
Monday to Thursday, 10.30am
to 12.30am Friday and Saturday, noon to 11pm Sunday
(30 minutes 'drinking up' time
allowed). Pubs with bar extensions open to 2.30am Thursday
to Saturday, pubs with theatre
licences open to 3.30am;
closed Christmas Day and
Good Friday.

Restaurants Noon to 10.30pm;
many close one day of the
week.

Shops 9.30am to 6pm Monday to Saturday (until 8pm
on Thursday and sometimes
Friday, to 9pm for the bigger
shopping centres and super-
markets), noon to 6pm Sunday.

Post

The Irish postal service, An
Post, is reliable, efficient and
usually on time. Post boxes
in Dublin are usually green
and have two slots: one for
'Dublin only', the other for
'All Other Places'. There
are a couple of post offices
in the city centre including
An Post (Map p240; ☑01-
705 8206; St Andrew's St;
⊗8.30am-5pm Mon-Fri) and
the **General Post Office**
(Map p248; ☑01-705 7000;
O'Connell St; ⊗8am-8pm
Mon-Sat).

Postal Codes

Postal codes in Dublin (presented as 'Dublin + number')
are fairly straightforward.

Their main feature is that all odd numbers refer to areas north of the Liffey and all even ones to areas south of the Liffey. They fan out numerically from the city centre, so the city centre to the north of the river is Dublin 1 and its southern equivalent is Dublin 2.

Public Holidays

The only public holidays that will impact on you are Good Friday and Christmas Day, the only two days in the year when all pubs close. Otherwise, the half-dozen or so bank holidays (all of which fall on a Monday) mean just that – the banks are closed, along with about half the shops. St Patrick's Day, May Day and St Stephen's Day holidays are taken on the following Monday should they fall on a weekend.

New Year's Day 1 January

St Patrick's Day 17 March

Easter (Good Friday to Easter Monday inclusive) March/April

May Holiday 1 May

June Holiday First Monday in June

August Holiday First Monday in August

October Holiday Last Monday in October

Christmas Day 25 December

St Stephen's Day 26 December

Safe Travel

Dublin is a safe city by any standards, except maybe those set by the Swiss. Basically, act as you would at home. However, certain parts of the city are pretty dodgy due to the presence of drug addicts and other questionable types, including north and northeast of Gardiner St and along parts of Dorset St, on the north side, and west along Thomas St, on the south side.

Telephone
Mobile Phones

➡ Dublin (like the rest of Ireland) uses the GSM 900/1800 cellular phone system, which is compatible with European and Australian, but not North American or Japanese, phones.

➡ SMS ('texting') is a national obsession – most people under 30 communic8 mostly by txt.

➡ Pay-as-you-go mobile phone packages with any of the main providers start at around €40 and usually include a basic handset and credit of around €10.

➡ SIM-only packages are also available, but make sure your phone is compatible with the local provider.

Phone Codes

When calling Dublin from abroad, dial your international access code, followed by 353 and 1 (dropping the 0 that precedes it). To make international calls from Dublin, first dial 00, then the country code, followed by the local area code and number.

Country Code ☑353

City Code ☑01

International Access Code ☑00

Directory Enquiries ☑11811 or ☑11850

International Directory Enquiries ☑11818

Phonecards

Virtually every newsagent sells a range of different phonecards, which can be used to make cut-rate international calls. Cards come in €7, €15 or €20 values and give you plenty of minutes to call abroad with.

Time

In winter, Dublin (and the rest of Ireland) is on GMT, also known as Universal Time

Coordinated (UTC), the same as Britain. In summer, the clock shifts to GMT plus one hour. When it's noon in Dublin in summer, it's 3am in Los Angeles and Vancouver, 7am in New York and Toronto, 1pm in Paris, 8pm in Singapore, and 10pm in Sydney.

Toilets

There are no on-street facilities in Dublin. All shopping centres have public toilets; if you're stranded, go into any bar or hotel.

Tourist Information

You'll find everything you need to kick-start your visit at the **Dublin Discover Ireland Centre**. Besides general visitor information on Dublin and Ireland, it also has a free accommodation booking service, a concert-booking agent, local and national bus information, rail information, and tour information and bookings.

The following tourism centre branches are walk-in centres only.

Dublin Discover Ireland Centre (Map p240; www.visitdublin.com; St Andrew's Church, 2 Suffolk St; ☉9am-5.30pm Mon-Sat, 10.30am-3pm Sun) The main branch of Dublin Tourism.

Dublin Tourism Centre (Arrivals Hall, Dublin Airport; ☉8am-10pm)

Internet Resources

Web-based tourist information on Dublin is available at the following sites:

Dublinks (www.dublinks.com) A catch-all website with info on things such as shopping, parking, hotels, restaurants and other necessary info.

DublinTourist.com (www.dublintourist.com) An excellent and thorough guide to virtually

TRACING YOUR ANCESTORS

Go on, you're dying to see if you've got a bit of Irish in you, and maybe tracking down your roots is the main reason for your visit. It will have made things much easier if you did some preliminary research in your home country – particularly finding out the precise date and point of entry of your ancestors – but you might still be able to plot your family tree even if you're acting on impulse.

The **Genealogy Advisory Service** at the **National Library** (Map p244; www.nli.ie; Kildare St; ⊗9.30am-9pm Mon-Wed, 10am-5pm Thu & Fri, 10am-1pm Sat; ⊟all city centre) [FREE] will advise you on how to trace your ancestry, which is a good way to begin your research if you have no other experience. For information on commercial agencies that will do the research for you, contact the **Association of Professional Genealogists in Ireland** (APGI; www.apgi.ie; c/o the Genealogy Advisory Service, Kildare St). The **Births, Deaths & Marriages Register** (☑01-671 1863; www.birthsdeathsmarriages.ie; Joyce House, East Lombard St; ⊗9.30am-12.30pm & 2.15-4.30pm Mon-Fri) and the files of the National Library and the **National Archives** (☑407 2300; www.nationalarchives.ie; Bishop St, Dublin 8; ⊗10am-5pm Mon-Fri) are all potential sources of genealogical information.

There are also lots of books on the subject, with *Irish Roots Guide,* by Tony McCarthy, serving as a useful introduction. Other publications include *Tracing Your Irish Roots* by Christine Kineally and *Tracing Your Irish Ancestors: A Comprehensive Guide* by John Grenham. All these, and other items of genealogical concern, can be obtained from the **Genealogy Bookshop** (Map p240; 3 Nassau St).

---

every aspect of the city, from booking a room to going for a drink.

Pigsback.com (www. pigsback.com) Offers all kinds of city-wide discounts, from cinema tickets to free lunches.

Telephone Resources

If you want tourist information over the phone, call the relevant number:

Within Ireland ☑1850 230 330
From the UK ☑0800 039 7000
From rest of the world ☑00 353 66 979 2083

Travellers with Disabilities

Despite the fact that many of the city's hotels, restaurants and sights are increasingly being adapted for people with disabilities, there's still a long way to go. Fáilte Ireland's annual accommodation guide, *Be Our Guest,* indicates which places are accessible by wheelchair. Public transport can be a nightmare,

although a limited number of buses are now equipped with electronic elevators for wheelchairs, and nearly all DART stations have ramps and/or elevators.

The **Citizens Information Board** (☑0761 07 7230; www.citizensinformationboard. ie; 13A Upper O'Connell St; ⊗10am-5pm Mon-Fri, to 1.30pm Wed) provides plenty of helpful information regarding Dublin's accessibility for wheelchairs.

Another useful organisation is the **Irish Wheelchair Association** (☑01-818 6400; www.iwa.ie; Áras Chúchulain, Blackheath Dr, Clontarf).

Visas

If you're a European Economic Area (EEA) national, you don't need a visa to visit (or work in) the Republic of Ireland. Citizens of Australia, Canada, New Zealand, South Africa and the US can visit Ireland for up to three months. They are not allowed to work unless sponsored by an employer. To stay longer in the Republic,

contact the local *garda* station, the **Garda National Immigration Bureau** (☑01-666 9100; www.garda. ie; 13-14 Burgh Quay) or the **Department of Foreign Affairs** (Map p238; ☑01-478 0822; www.dfa.ie; Iveagh House, 80 St Stephen's Green South).

Although you don't need an onward or return ticket to enter Ireland, it could help if there's any doubt that you have sufficient funds to support yourself while in Dublin.

Women Travellers

Dublin should pose no problems for women travellers. Finding contraception is not the problem it once was, although anyone on the pill should bring adequate supplies. The morning-after pill is available without a prescription from all pharmacies.

In the unlikely event of a sexual assault, get in touch with the police and the **Rape Crisis Centre** (☑01-661 4911, 1800 778 888; 70 Lower Leeson St).

Behind the Scenes

SEND US YOUR FEEDBACK

We love to hear from travellers – your comments keep us on our toes and help make our books better. Our well-travelled team reads every word on what you loved or loathed about this book. Although we cannot reply individually to postal submissions, we always guarantee that your feedback goes straight to the appropriate authors, in time for the next edition. Each person who sends us information is thanked in the next edition – the most useful submissions are rewarded with a selection of digital PDF chapters.

Visit **lonelyplanet.com/contact** to submit your updates and suggestions or to ask for help. Our award-winning website also features inspirational travel stories, news and discussions.

Note: We may edit, reproduce and incorporate your comments in Lonely Planet products such as guidebooks, websites and digital products, so let us know if you don't want your comments reproduced or your name acknowledged. For a copy of our privacy policy visit lonelyplanet.com/privacy.

OUR READERS

Many thanks to the travellers who used the last edition and wrote to us with helpful hints, useful advice and interesting anecdotes:
Andrea Bauer, Ruth Clendennen, Noreen Fitzgerald, Stefan Greiffenberger

AUTHOR THANKS
Fionn Davenport

Thanks to Cliff, Sasha and all the boffins at Lonely Planet who answered my every query – no matter what time of the day or night – in a timely and helpful fashion. Thanks to all those Dubliners – native-born and imported, friends and strangers alike – who offered suggestions and guided me in the right direction, recommending cafes, restaurants and things to do in this beloved city of ours. Without their enthusiasm and knowledge I would never have discovered half the things I found for this guide.

ACKNOWLEDGMENTS

Cover photograph: Library, Trinity College. Ingolf Pompe/Alamy.

Illustrations pp54-5, pp156-7 by Javier Zarracina; pp152-3 by Michael Weldon

DART Commuter Network Map © Iarnród Éireann. Dublin Transit Map © Irish Rail

THIS BOOK

This 9th edition of Lonely Planet's *Dublin* guidebook was researched and written by Fionn Davenport, who also worked on the previous editions. This guidebook was commissioned in Lonely Planet's London office, and produced by the following:
Commissioning Editor
Clifton Wilkinson
Coordinating Editors
Lauren Hunt, Ross Taylor

Cartographer Jeff Cameron
Coordinating Layout Designer Lauren Egan
Managing Editor Sasha Baskett
Senior Editor Karyn Noble
Senior Cartographer Anthony Phelan
Managing Layout Designer Chris Girdler
Assisting Editor Helen Koehne
Assisting Layout Designer Clara Monitto

Cover Research Naomi Parker
Internal Image Research Aude Vauconsant
Illustrators Michael Weldon, Javier Zarracina
Thanks to Anita Banh, Brendan Dempsey, Ryan Evans, Larissa Frost, Jane Hart, Genesys India, Jouve India, Trent Paton, Kerrianne Southway, Angela Tinson, Gerard Walker

See also separate subindexes for:

🍴 **EATING P222**

🍷 **DRINKING & NIGHTLIFE P223**

☆ **ENTERTAINMENT P223**

🛍 **SHOPPING P223**

🏃 **SPORTS & ACTIVITIES P224**

🛏 **SLEEPING P224**

Index

Sights 000

Map Pages **000**

Photo Pages **000**

EATING

🏃 SPORTS & ACTIVITIES

🛏 SLEEPING

Dublin Maps

Sights

- Beach
- Bird Sanctuary
- Buddhist
- Castle/Palace
- Christian
- Confucian
- Hindu
- Islamic
- Jain
- Jewish
- Monument
- Museum/Gallery/Historic Building
- Ruin
- Sento Hot Baths/Onsen
- Shinto
- Sikh
- Taoist
- Winery/Vineyard
- Zoo/Wildlife Sanctuary
- Other Sight

Activities, Courses & Tours

- Bodysurfing
- Diving/Snorkelling
- Canoeing/Kayaking
- Course/Tour
- Skiing
- Snorkelling
- Surfing
- Swimming/Pool
- Walking
- Windsurfing
- Other Activity

Sleeping

- Sleeping
- Camping

Eating

- Eating

Drinking & Nightlife

- Drinking & Nightlife
- Cafe

Entertainment

- Entertainment

Shopping

- Shopping

Information

- Bank
- Embassy/Consulate
- Hospital/Medical
- Internet
- Police
- Post Office
- Telephone
- Toilet
- Tourist Information
- Other Information

Geographic

- Beach
- Hut/Shelter
- Lighthouse
- Lookout
- Mountain/Volcano
- Oasis
- Park
- Pass
- Picnic Area
- Waterfall

Population

- Capital (National)
- Capital (State/Province)
- City/Large Town
- Town/Village

Transport

- Airport
- Border crossing
- Bus
- Cable car/Funicular
- Cycling
- Ferry
- Metro station
- Monorail
- Parking
- Petrol station
- Subway station
- Taxi
- Train station/Railway
- Tram
- Underground station
- Other Transport

Note: Not all symbols displayed above appear on the maps in this book

Routes

- Tollway
- Freeway
- Primary
- Secondary
- Tertiary
- Lane
- Unsealed road
- Road under construction
- Plaza/Mall
- Steps
- Tunnel
- Pedestrian overpass
- Walking Tour
- Walking Tour detour
- Path/Walking Trail

Boundaries

- International
- State/Province
- Disputed
- Regional/Suburb
- Marine Park
- Cliff
- Wall

Hydrography

- River, Creek
- Intermittent River
- Canal
- Water
- Dry/Salt/Intermittent Lake
- Reef

Areas

- Airport/Runway
- Beach/Desert
- Cemetery (Christian)
- Cemetery (Other)
- Glacier
- Mudflat
- Park/Forest
- Sight (Building)
- Sportsground
- Swamp/Mangrove

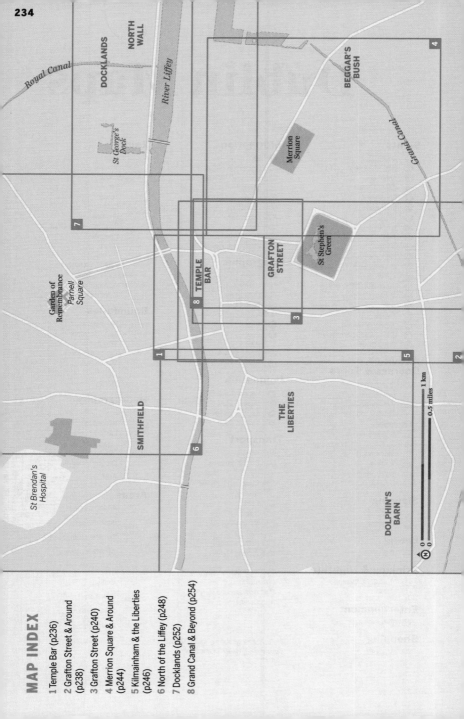

INDEX

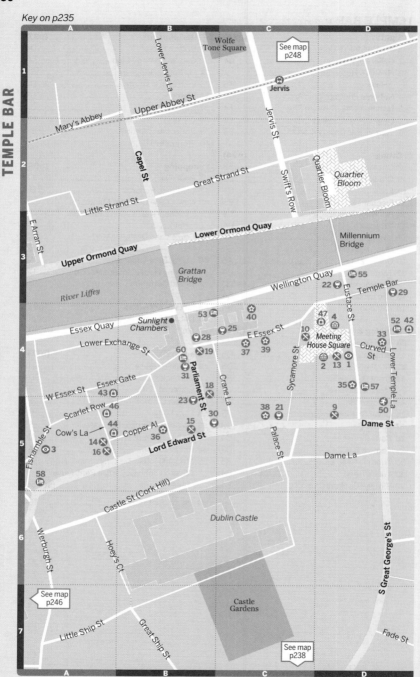

Key on p235

TEMPLE BAR

Wolfe Tone Square

See map p248

Jervis

Lower Jervis La

Upper Abbey St

Mary's Abbey

Jervis St

Capel St

Quartier Bloom

Quartier Bloom

Great Strand St

Swift's Row

Little Strand St

E Arran St

Lower Ormond Quay

Millennium Bridge

Upper Ormond Quay

Grattan Bridge

Wellington Quay

River Liffey

Temple Bar

55

22

Eustace St

29

Essex Quay

Sunlight Chambers

53

40

47
4

52 42

Lower Exchange St

28

25

E Essex St

10

Meeting House Square

33

Curved St

Lower Temple La

60

19

37

39

Sycamore St

2 13 1

W Essex St

31

Parliament St

18

Crane La

35

57

Essex Gate

43

23

30

38 21

9

50

Scarlet Row

46

Dame St

Fishamble St

44

Copper Al

15

Palace St

Cow's La

36

3

14

16

Lord Edward St

Dame La

58

Castle St (Cork Hill)

Dame La

Werburgh St

Hoey's Ct

Dublin Castle

S Great George's St

See map p246

Castle Gardens

Little Ship St

Great Ship St

Fade St

See map p238

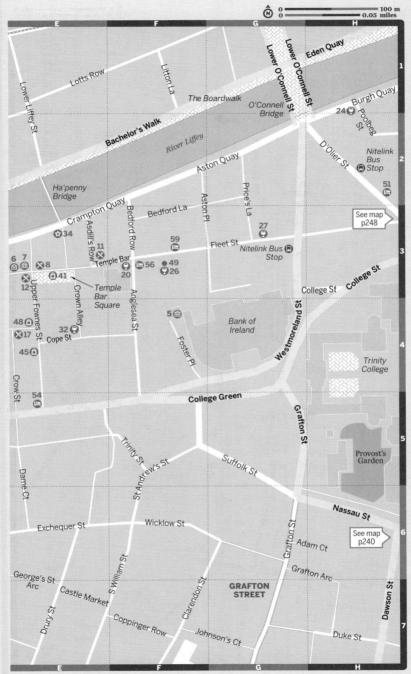

0 100 m
0 0.05 miles

Lotts Row

Litton La

Lower O'Connell St

Lower O'Connell St

Eden Quay

The Boardwalk

O'Connell Bridge

Burgh Quay

24

Poolbeg St

Lower Liffey St

Bachelor's Walk

River Liffey

Aston Quay

D'Olier St

Nitelink Bus Stop

51

Ha'penny Bridge

Crampton Quay

Asdill's Row

Bedford Row

Bedford La

Aston Pl

Price's La

Fleet St

27

34

11

Temple Bar

59

56

49

26

Nitelink Bus Stop

College St

College St

6 7

8

20

College St

12

41

Temple Bar Square

Upper Fownes St

Crown Alley

Anglesea St

5

Bank of Ireland

Westmoreland St

48

17

32

Cope St

Foster Pl

Trinity College

45

Crow St

54

College Green

Grafton St

Provost's Garden

Dame Ct

Trinity St

St Andrew's St

Suffolk St

Nassau St

Exchequer St

Wicklow St

See map p240

George's St Arc

Drury St

S William St

Castle Market

Grafton St

Adam Ct

Grafton Arc

Dawson St

Coppinger Row

Clarendon St

GRAFTON STREET

Johnson's Ct

Duke St

See map p248

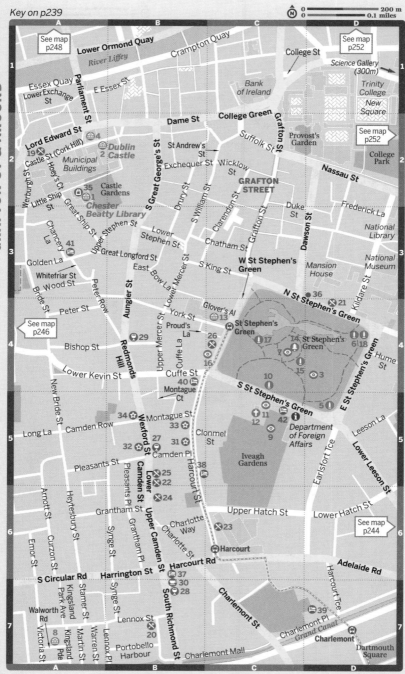

Key on p239

0 200 m
0 0.1 miles

See map p248

Lower Ormond Quay

River Liffey

Crampton Quay

College St

See map p252

Science Gallery (300m)

Trinity College

New Square

Essex Quay
Lower Exchange St

E Essex St

Parliament St

Bank of Ireland

College Green

Dame St

Grafton St

Provost's Garden

See map p252

College Park

Lord Edward St

19

Castle St (Cork Hill)

Hoey's Ct

4

Dublin Castle

Municipal Buildings

St Andrew's St

Suffolk St

Exchequer St

Wicklow St

GRAFTON STREET

Nassau St

Werburgh St

Little Ship St

Chancery La

35

1

Castle Gardens

Chester Beatty Library

S Great George's St

Drury St

S William St

Clarendon St

Grafton St

Duke St

Dawson St

Frederick La

National Library

National Museum

Golden La

41

Upper Stephen St

Lower Stephen St

Great Longford St

East

Chatham St

W St Stephen's Green

Mansion House

Kildare St

Whitefriar St

Wood St

Bow La

Lower Mercer St

S King St

N St Stephen's Green

36

21

Bride St

Peter St

Peter Row

Bishop St

Aungier St

Upper Mercer St

York St

Glover's Al

13

Proud's La

26

St Stephen's Green

17

14

St Stephen's Green

6 18

Hume St

See map p246

Redmonds Hill

Lower Kevin St

Cuffe La

16

Cuffe St

40

Montague Ct

10

7

15

3

Long La

Camden Row

34

Wexford St

Montague St

33

Clonmel St

S St Stephen's Green

5

E St Stephen's Green

29

11

12

42

Department of Foreign Affairs

Leeson La

Lower Leeson St

32

27

31

Camden Pl

Iveagh Gardens

Pleasants St

Lower Camden St

Pleasants Pl

Grantham Pl

38

Harcourt St

Upper Hatch St

Lower Hatch St

See map p244

Arnott St

Heytesbury St

Synge St

Grantham St

25

22

24

Charlotte Way

Charlotte St

23

Upper Camden St

Emor St

Curzon St

S Circular Rd

Harrington St

Harcourt Rd

Harcourt

37

30

28

Adelaide Rd

Charlemont St

Harcourt Tce

Harcourt Pl

Walworth Rd

Kingsland Park Ave

Stamer St

South Richmond St

Lennox St

8

20

Victoria St

Kingsland Pde

Martin St

Warren St

Lennox Pl

Portobello Harbour

Charlemont Mall

Charlemont

39

Charlemont Pl

Grand Canal

Dartmouth Square

GRAFTON STREET & AROUND *Map on p238*

See map p236

Temple Bar

See map p248

Wellington Quay

E Essex St

Meeting House Square

Eustace St

Temple Bar Square

Cope St

Upper Fownes St

Anglesea St

Foster Pl

College Green

5

Dame St

Dublin Discover Ireland Centre

26

Dame La

68

73

Dame Ct

75

Trinity St

46

St Andrew's St

106

113

St Andrew's Church

44

59

45

39

60

Dame Ct

St Andrew's La

74

50

29

103

19

79

34

Exchequer St

71

38

63

Wicklow St

52

S Great George's St

122

35

22

41

110

36

95

109

23

49

85

Castle Market

90

97

61

78

105

Clarendon St

58

125

Drury St

Coppinger Row

28

83

Johnson's Ct

27

104

81

82

30

65

62

66

Fade St

43

70

33

100

S William St

120

112

14

54

130

67

Harry St

Barre St

31

56

25

Chatham Row

48

96

Chatham St

69

Castle Gardens

Upper Stephen St

Lower Stephen St

Johnston Place

124

72

Great Longford St

Little Longford St

Diggers La

76

127

Lower Mercer St

East Bow La

S King St

24

Aungier St

51

See map p238

Glover's Al

108

123

W St Stephen's Green

18

119

See map p236
See map p248
See map p238

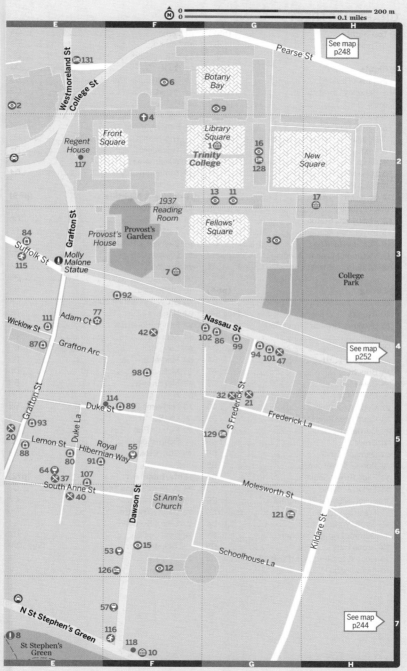

0 / 200 m
0 / 0.1 miles

See map p248
See map p252
See map p244

Pearse St

Westmoreland St
College St

131
6
Botany Bay
2
9
4
Front Square
Library Square
1
Trinity College
16
128
New Square
Regent House
117
13 11
17
Grafton St
1937 Reading Room
Fellows' Square
3
Provost's House
Provost's Garden
84
Suffolk St
115
Molly Malone Statue
7
College Park
92
Wicklow St
111
Adam Ct
77
42
Nassau St
102 86
99
94 101 47
87
Grafton Arc
98
32 21
S Frederick St
Frederick La
Grafton St
114
Duke St 89
129
20
93
Duke La
Molesworth St
88
Lemon St
80
Royal Hibernian Way
55
91
64
37
107
121
Kildare St
South Anne St
40
Dawson St
St Ann's Church
53
15
126
12
Schoolhouse La
57
N St Stephen's Green
116
8
St Stephen's Green
118
10

GRAFTON STREET *Map on p240*

GRAFTON STREET

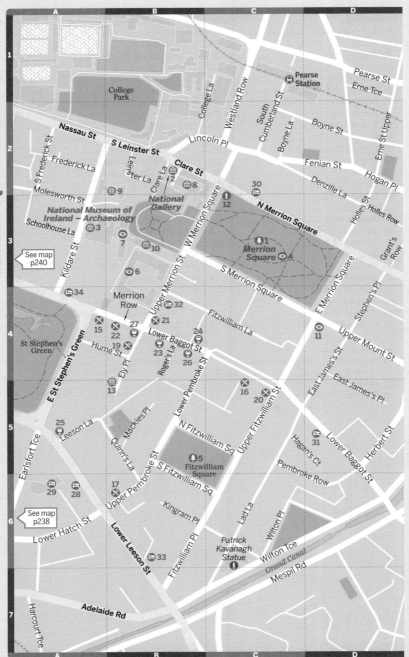

College Park

Pearse Station

Pearse St

Erne Tce

Erne St Upper

Nassau St

S Frederick St

S Leinster St

Frederick La

Leinster La

College La

Westland Row

South Cumberland St

Boyne La

Boyne St

Fenian St

Denzille La

Hogan Pl

Lincoln Pl

Molesworth St

9

Clare La

Clare St

2

8

National Gallery

30

12

Holles St

Holles Row

National Museum of Ireland – Archaeology

3

Schoolhouse La

See map p240

Kildare St

7

10

W Merrion Square

N Merrion Square

1

Merrion Square

4

E Merrion Square

Grant's Row

Stephen's Pl

6

S Merrion Square

34

Merrion Row

Upper Merrion St

32

Fitzwilliam La

11

Upper Mount St

15

22

27

21

19

Lower Baggot St

24

East James's St

East James's Pl

East James's La

St Stephen's Green

E St Stephen's Green

Hume St

23

Roger's La

26

Lower Pembroke St

16

20

Upper Fitzwilliam St

Hagan's Ct

31

Lower Baggot St

Herbert St

13

Ely Pl

25

Leeson La

Quinn's La

Mackies Pl

N Fitzwilliam Sq

S Fitzwilliam Sq

5

Fitzwilliam Square

Pembroke Row

Earlsfort Tce

29

28

17

Upper Pembroke St

Kingram Pl

Fitzwilliam Pl

Lad La

Wilton Pl

See map p238

Lower Hatch St

Lower Leeson St

33

Patrick Kavanagh Statue

Grand Canal

Wilton Tce

Mespil Rd

Harcourt Tce

Adelaide Rd

◉ **Top Sights** (p80)

1 Merrion Square C3
2 National Gallery B2
3 National Museum of Ireland –
   Archaeology A3

◎ **Sights** (p86)

4 Art Market...C3
5 Fitzwilliam Square B5
6 Government Buildings B3
7 Leinster House.................................B3
8 Millennium Wing National Gallery B2
9 National Library B2
10 Natural History Museum B3
11 No 29 Lower Fitzwilliam St...............D4
12 Oscar Wilde Statue..........................C3
13 Royal Hibernian Academy (RHA)
    Gallagher Gallery B5
14 St Stephen's 'Pepper Canister'
    Church...E5

🍴 **Eating** (p88)

15 Bang Café...A4
16 Chez Max C5
17 Dax...B6
18 Dobbins..E4
19 Ely B4
20 L'Ecrivain...C5
21 Restaurant Patrick Guilbaud............B4
22 Unicorn...B4

🍷 **Drinking & Nightlife** (p90)

23 Baggot Inn...B4
24 Doheny & Nesbitt's............................B4
25 Hartigan's...A5
26 James Toner's....................................B4
27 O'Donoghue's.....................................B4

🛏 **Sleeping** (p172)

28 Clarion Stephen's Hall............................A6
29 Conrad Dublin International....................A6
30 Davenport Hotel.....................................C2
31 Latchfords...D5
32 Merrion..B4
33 Number 31..B6
34 Shelbourne...A4

KILMAINHAM & THE LIBERTIES

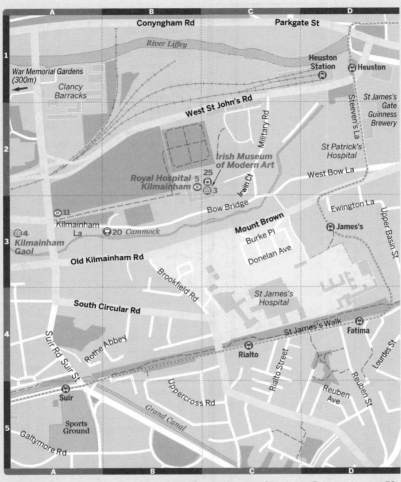

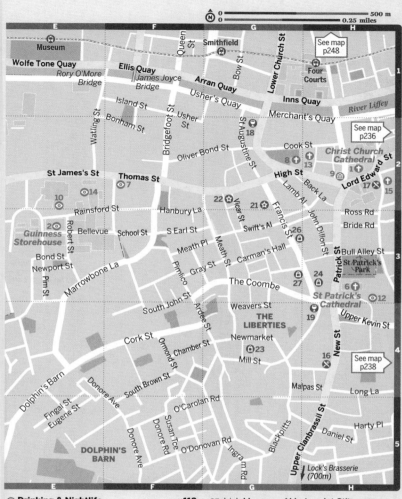

Key on p250

A   B   C   D

1

Great Western Square

Monck Pl

Norton's Ave

Sarsfield St

O'Connell Ave

Geraldine St

Berkeley St

Nelson St

Eccles St

St Joseph's Pde

2

Phibsboro Rd

Royal Canal Bank

City Basin

Primrose Ave

Upper Wellington St

Blessington Pl

Blessington St

Lower Wellington St

Auburn St

Fontenoy St

Mountjoy St

Paradise Pl

3

Western Way

Upper Dorset St

Frederick La

Dublin City Gallery – The Hugh Lane

Upper Dominick St

St Mary's Tce

34

4

Prebend St

Constitution Hill

16

Henrietta St

11

Bolton St

Dominick Pl

Lower Dominick St

Yarnhall St

Dominick La

King's Inns St

Morning Star Ave

Linenhall Tce

Henrietta Pl

Loftus La

5

Walshe's (200m); L Mulligan Grocer (300m); Arbour Hill Cemetery (700m)

N Brunswick St

Red Cow La

N King St

Halston St

Green St

Ryder's Row

46

Chapel La

47

SMITHFIELD

Friary Ave

Smithfield Tce

Bow St

Lower Church St

Beresford St

North Anne St

Little Britain St

Upper Jervis La

Lower Jervis La

Jervis St

Mary St

6

51

74

18

Cuckoo La

Georges Hill

Mary's La

Capel St

23

60

58

Wolfe Tone Square

17

Jervis

35

May La

25

St Michan's St

22

Jervis

Dice Bar (125m); Wuff (200m); National Museum of Ireland Decorative Arts & History (500m) Ryans (1km); Phoenix Park (1.2km)

Smithfield

Hammond La

Chancery St

Greek St

Four Courts

Ormond Sq

Mary's Abbey

Little Strand St

26

Upper Abbey St

Great Strand St

30

41

28

7

8

See map p246

Inns Quay

River Liffey

Chancery Pl

E Arran St

Upper Ormond Quay

39

32

31

75

37

Grattan Bridge

River Liffey

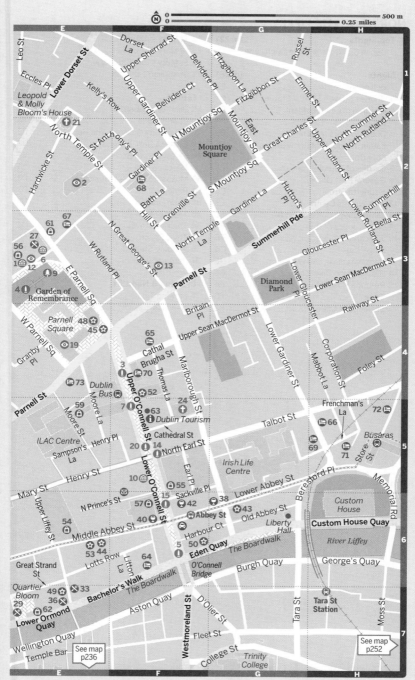

NORTH OF THE LIFFEY *Map on p248*

DOCKLANDS

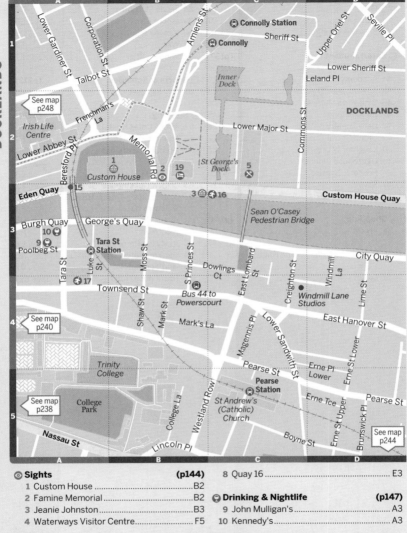

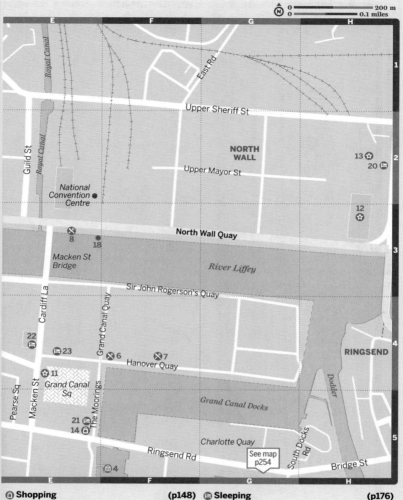

GRAND CANAL & BEYOND

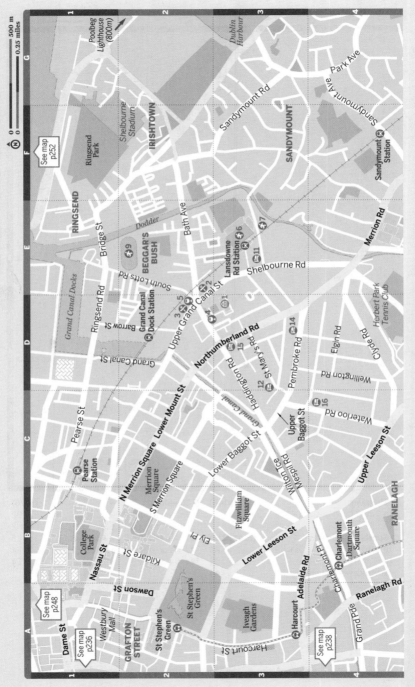

See map p252

See map p248

See map p236

See map p238

0   500 m
0   0.25 miles

N

Poolbeg Lighthouse (800m)

Dublin Harbour

Shelbourne Stadium

Ringsend Park

RINGSEND

IRISHTOWN

SANDYMOUNT

Sandymount Station

Park Ave

Sandymount Ave

Sandymount Rd

Grand Canal Docks

Ringsend Rd

Barrow St

Bridge St

Dodder

BEGGAR'S BUSH

South Lotts Rd

Bath Ave

9

Grand Canal Dock Station

5
3
2
1
4

Merrion Rd

Lansdowne Rd Station

6
7
11

Shelbourne Rd

Upper Grand Canal St

Grand Canal St

Northumberland Rd

15

14

Herbert Park Tennis Club

Elgin Rd

Clyde Rd

Pearse St

Pearse Station

N Merrion Square   Lower Mount St

Merrion Square

S Merrion Square

Kildare St

Ely Pl

Lower Baggot St

Harrington Rd

St Mary's Rd

12

Pembroke Rd

Wellington Rd

Upper Baggot St

Waterloo Rd

16

Fitzwilliam Square

Lower Leeson St

Mespil Rd

Wilton Tce

Upper Leeson St

College Park

Nassau St

Dawson St

GRAFTON STREET

St Stephen's Green

Iveagh Gardens

Harcourt St

Harcourt

Adelaide Rd

Charlemont Pl

Charlemont

Dartmouth Square

RANELAGH

Ranelagh Rd

Grand Pde

Westbury Mall

Dame St

Pearse Station

Grand Canal

Harding Canal

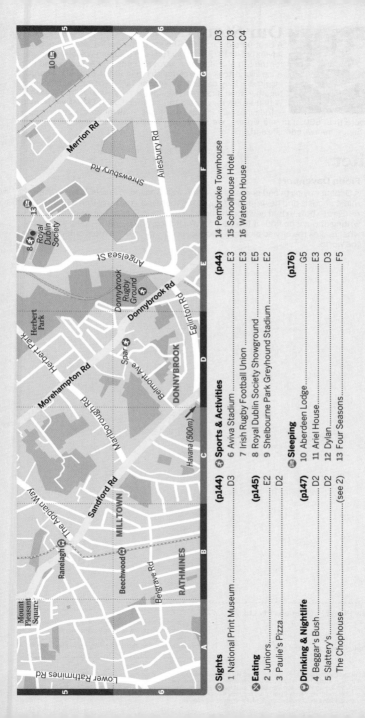

Our Story

A beat-up old car, a few dollars in the pocket and a sense of adventure. In 1972 that's all Tony and Maureen Wheeler needed for the trip of a lifetime – across Europe and Asia overland to Australia. It took several months, and at the end – broke but inspired – they sat at their kitchen table writing and stapling together their first travel guide, *Across Asia on the Cheap*. Within a week they'd sold 1500 copies. Lonely Planet was born.

Today, Lonely Planet has offices in Melbourne, London and Oakland, with more than 600 staff and writers. We share Tony's belief that 'a great guidebook should do three things: inform, educate and amuse'.

Our Writer

Fionn Davenport

A Dubliner by birth and persuasion, Fionn was amazed to find out that in the midst of crisis and never-ending bad news there is a great city that defiantly refuses to bow to bad news or the banks. He lives in Dublin, but when he's not writing about it he finds it too easy to take it for granted, and in doing so forgets what makes the city so bloody wonderful and its people the most entertaining in the world.

Published by Lonely Planet Publications Pty Ltd
ABN 36 005 607 983
9th edition – Nov 2013
ISBN 978 1 74220 204 4
© Lonely Planet 2013   Photographs © as indicated 2013
10 9 8 7 6 5 4 3 2 1
Printed in China